Fighting the Mau Mau

British Army counter-insurgency campaigns were supposedly waged within the bounds of international law, overcoming insurgents with the minimum force necessary. This revealing study questions what this meant for the civilian population during the Mau Mau rebellion in Kenya in the 1950s, one of Britain's most violent decolonisation wars. For the first time Huw Bennett examines the conduct of soldiers in detail, uncovering the uneasy relationship between notions of minimum force and the colonial tradition of exemplary force where harsh repression was frequently employed as a valid means of quickly crushing rebellion. Although a range of restrained policies such as special forces methods, restrictive rules of engagement and surrender schemes prevented the campaign from degenerating into genocide, the army simultaneously coerced the population to drop their support for the rebels, imposing collective fines, mass detentions and frequent interrogations, often tolerating rape, indiscriminate killing and torture to terrorise the population into submission.

HUW BENNETT is Lecturer in International Politics and Intelligence Studies, in the Department of International Politics, Aberystwyth University.

Cambridge Military Histories

Edited by:

Hew Strachan
*Chichele Professor of the History of War, University of Oxford and Fellow
of All Souls College, Oxford*

Geoffrey Wawro
*Professor of Military History, and Director of the Military History Center,
University of North Texas*

The aim of this series is to publish outstanding works of research on warfare
throughout the ages and throughout the world. Books in the series take a broad
approach to military history, examining war in all its military, strategic, political
and economic aspects. The series complements Studies in the Social and Cultural
History of Modern Warfare by focusing on the 'hard' military history of armies,
tactics, strategy and warfare. Books in the series consist mainly of single author
works – academically vigorous and groundbreaking – which are accessible to both
academics and the interested general reader.

A full list of titles in the series can be found at:
www.cambridge.org/militaryhistories

Fighting the Mau Mau

The British Army and Counter-Insurgency
in the Kenya Emergency

Huw Bennett

CAMBRIDGE
UNIVERSITY PRESS

CAMBRIDGE UNIVERSITY PRESS
Cambridge, New York, Melbourne, Madrid, Cape Town,
Singapore, São Paulo, Delhi, Mexico City

Cambridge University Press
The Edinburgh Building, Cambridge CB2 8RU, UK

Published in the United States of America by
Cambridge University Press, New York

www.cambridge.org
Information on this title: www.cambridge.org/9781107656246

First published 2013

Printed and bound in the United Kingdom by the MPG Books Group

A catalogue record for this publication is available from the British Library

Library of Congress Cataloging-in-Publication Data
Bennett, Huw C.
Fighting the Mau Mau : the British Army and counter-insurgency in
the Kenya Emergency / Huw Bennett.
     p.   cm. – (Cambridge military histories)
     Based on the author's thesis (doctoral)–University of Aberystwyth, 2006,
titled: British Army counterinsurgency and the use of force in Kenya, 1952–56.
Includes bibliographical references.
     ISBN 978-1-107-02970-5 (Hardback) – ISBN 978-1-107-65624-6 (Paperback.)
1. Kenya–History–Mau Mau Emergency, 1952–1960.   2. Kenya–History,
Military–20th century.   3. Counterinsurgency–Kenya–History–20th century.
4. Mau Mau–History.   5. Kikuyu (African people)–History.   6. Great
Britain–Armed Forces–Kenya–History–20th century.   7. Great Britain. Army.
I. Title.   II. Series: Cambridge military histories.
     DT433.577.B47 2012
     967.62′03–dc23
                                                                2012020245

ISBN 978-1-107-02970-5 Hardback
ISBN 978-1-107-65624-6 Paperback

Contents

List of maps	*page*	viii
List of abbreviations		ix
Acknowledgements		xi
Introduction		1
1	'A determined campaign against the terrorist bands'	8
2	'Harmonious relations': soldiers, civilians and committees	31
3	'Possibly restrictive to the operations': marginalising international law in colonial rebellions	60
4	'The degree of force necessary': British traditions in countering colonial rebellions	83
5	'Restraint backed by good discipline'	108
6	'A dead man cannot talk': the need for restraint	128
7	'A lot of indiscriminate shooting': military repression before Erskine's arrival	160
8	'Severe repressive measures': the army under Erskine	194
9	'An essential part of the campaign': civil-military alliances	229
Conclusion		264
Bibliography		270
Index		296

Maps

1 Kenya Colony *Page* 9
2 Administrative areas affected by the Emergency 10

Abbreviations

ADALS	Assistant Director of Army Legal Services
AG	Adjutant-General
BEM	British Empire Medal
CIGS	Chief of the Imperial General Staff
C-in-C	Commander-in-Chief
CO	Colonial Office
CO	Commanding Officer
CPEC	Central Province Emergency Committee
CPM	Colonial Police Medal
CSCCC	Chief Secretary's Complaints Co-ordinating Committee
CSM	Company Sergeant-Major
DALS	Director of Army Legal Services
DC	District Commissioner
DCM	Distinguished Conduct Medal
DDOps	Deputy Director of Operations
DEC	District Emergency Committee
DIS	Director of Intelligence and Security
DMIO	District Military Intelligence Officer
DO	District Officer
DOKG	District Officer Kikuyu Guard
FIA	Field Intelligence Assistant
FIO	Field Intelligence Officer
GM	George Medal
GOC	General Officer Commanding
G(Ops)	General Staff Operations Branch
GSO1 Ops (K)	General Staff Officer, Grade I, Operations, Kenya
HAA	heavy anti-aircraft artillery
ICRC	International Committee of the Red Cross
ICRGC	Inter-departmental Committee on the Revision of the Geneva Conventions

IMT	International Military Tribunal
IWMD	Imperial War Museum Department of Documents
IWMSA	Imperial War Museum Sound Archive
JAPOIT	joint army–police operational intelligence teams
JSCSC	Joint Services Command and Staff College
KAR	King's African Rifles
KCPIS	Kenya Colony political intelligence summary
KGCU	Kikuyu Guard Combat Unit
KIC	Kenya Intelligence Committee
KICFA	Kenya Intelligence Committee fortnightly appreciation
KISUM	Kenya intelligence summary
KNA	Kenya National Archives
KPR	Kenya Police Reserve
KRA	Kenya Regiment Archive
MELF	Middle East Land Forces
MIO	Military Intelligence Officer
MM	Military Medal
NAM	National Army Museum
OC	Officer Commanding
ODRP	Oxford Development Records Project, Rhodes House, Oxford
PA	prohibited area
PEC	Provincial Emergency Committee
PMIO	Provincial Military Intelligence Officer
QPMG	Queen's Police Medal for Gallantry
RIC	Royal Irish Constabulary
RMO	Regimental Medical Officer
RSM	Regimental Sergeant-Major
RUSI	Royal United Services Institute
SBFIS	Special Branch fortnightly intelligence summary
SFT	special force team
SIB	Special Investigations Branch
sitrep	situation report
TCT	tracker combat team
TNA	The National Archives, Kew
VCIGS	Vice-Chief of the Imperial General Staff
WOPC	Warrant Officer Platoon Commander

Acknowledgements

A large number of people have helped me in writing this book, which began life as a doctoral thesis. Colin McInnes and Martin Alexander offered advice and encouragement as supervisors, and continued to do so as the thesis morphed into a book. During eight years in Aberystwyth, I was fortunate to be taught by an outstanding group of historians, and would like to thank Susan Carruthers, Gerry Hughes, Peter Jackson and Len Scott. John Ferris very kindly hosted me as a visiting scholar to Calgary University; these months proved exceptionally productive. Kate Oen, Abigail and Nick Rangecroft, and Mark and Claire Wheildon supported me throughout. The Defence Studies Department at King's College London provided an excellent environment for deepening my understanding of British military history. Andrew Dorman, Stuart Griffin, Ashley Jackson, Greg Kennedy and Matt Uttley deserve special thanks for providing me with the time and resources to complete the project. Huw Davies, Geraint Hughes, Patrick Porter and Chris Tripodi attempted to ease the transition into life at a military college with good humour. Colleagues elsewhere deserving thanks include Ian Beckett, Daniel Branch, Paul Dixon, Mike Goodman, Karl Hack, George Kassimeris, John Lonsdale, Philip Murphy and Mike Rainsborough. Gordon Omenya and Justin Willis gave invaluable assistance in Nairobi. A number of veterans of the campaign in Kenya generously shared their experiences with me. Daniel Leader involved me in the Mau Mau court case, and he and David Roberts secured access to the Hanslope documents for me. David Anderson's advice has been essential to the completion of this book; his own research has been an inspiration. I offer profound thanks to David French for his sustained encouragement and advice. He read the manuscript and improved it in innumerable ways. Michael Watson, Chloe Howell and Hilary Scannell at Cambridge University Press have proved patient and helpful guides to the strange world of academic publication.

Historians rely upon the wisdom and kindness of archivists and librarians. The staff at the following institutions gave superb assistance: the

National Archives of the United Kingdom, the Kenya National Archives, the Imperial War Museum, the National Army Museum, the Bodleian Library of Commonwealth and African Studies, Cambridge University Library, the British Library, the Inniskillings Museum, the Joint Services Command and Staff College Library, the Military Intelligence Museum and Staffordshire Record Office. The research for this book was generously supported by a doctoral scholarship from the Economic and Social Research Council, and subsequently by King's College London and a Scouloudi Historical Award from the Institute of Historical Research, University of London. Thanks to the Foreign and Commonwealth Office for discovering the lost archives at Hanslope Park. We owe a great deal to an anonymous FCO official who resisted demands for this vast archive to be destroyed.

Earlier versions of some material in chapter 7 were published as: 'The British Army and Controlling Barbarization during the Kenya Emergency', in George Kassimeris (ed.), *The Warrior's Dishonour: Barbarity, Morality and Torture in Modern Warfare* (Aldershot: Ashgate, 2006), 59–80; and 'The Other Side of the COIN: Minimum and Exemplary Force in British Army Counter-insurgency in Kenya', *Small Wars and Insurgencies*, 18 (2007), 638–64. The following institutions and individuals have kindly given me permission to quote from material to which they own the copyright: the Library of the Joint Services Command and Staff College; the Royal Military Academy Sandhurst; the Bodleian Library of Commonwealth and African Studies, University of Oxford; the Imperial War Museum; the Military Intelligence Museum; Staffordshire Record Office; the National Army Museum; the Inniskillings Museum; Mr John Davis and the Kenya Regiment Trustees; P. Bristol; T. H. R. Cashmore; Ron Cassidy; John Chapman; Florence Edgar; General Sir Frank Kitson; John McFrederick; Richard Moore; Adrian Walker; Jennifer Windeatt. All reasonable effort has been made to contact the holders of copyright materials reproduced in this book. Any omissions will be rectified in future printings if notice is given to the publisher.

This book is dedicated to my family and to Claudia. They have helped me realise a childhood dream to write military history, and read and listened to my thoughts on this topic beyond any reasonable expectation. Most importantly, they reminded me that some things matter even more than military history.

Introduction

Recently home from a two-year stint commanding the security forces in Kenya, General Sir George Erskine went to Camberley to lecture on the 1955 Army Staff Course. After a few introductory remarks, General Erskine turned to a problem faced by every commander-in-chief dealing with a major rebellion. Would it be necessary to declare martial law? Since the 'unfortunate experiences' under Oliver Cromwell, British officers have regarded martial law tentatively. Concerned about legal constraints on the army, Erskine found to his relief that:

the Government of Kenya were determined to use the very considerable powers at their disposal to the fullest extent. They could and did pass Emergency regulations of severity and entirely appropriate to the military requirements.[1]

His former colleague and successor, Lieutenant-General Sir Gerald Lathbury, clashed with the Kenyan Attorney-General in November 1955. A roving police inspector discovered that the army were retaining prisoners for operational purposes beyond the time limits permitted. A senior staff officer in East Africa Command railed at these complaints, advocating a 'first class show-down on the grounds that it is not possible to fight a war within the concepts of British Common Law'.[2]

Whether in Surrey or Nairobi, British Army officers of the 1950s understood that the law was malleable to their definition of necessity. Since then the permissive nature of law in the decolonisation era has been largely forgotten. A triumphalist attitude grew in the 1960s into an orthodoxy within the military and academia. That orthodoxy discarded observations such as the two made above in 1955. It arose as a reaction to British decline, a need to feel that despite the Empire's demise, the British were in *control* of the process. The control was provided by

---

[1] Joint Services Command and Staff College (JSCSC) Library, 'The Mau Mau Rebellion', lecture given by General Erskine to the 1955 Course, Army Staff College, Camberley, 3–4.
[2] The National Archives, Kew (TNA), WO 276/430: Letter from [illegible], Lt.-Col. GSO1 Ops (K), to Chief of Staff, East Africa Command, 4 November 1955.

1

military professionalism, an expertise to be envied around the world. To enhance the myth's potency, French and American incompetence were loudly decried.[3] What came to dominate the orthodoxy was a conviction that British success in counter-insurgency derived from a determination to conduct operations within the law. Robert Thompson was a leading expert on counter-insurgency warfare who served in the Malaya Emergency and advised the American government in Vietnam.[4] He articulated the sentiment most influentially in 1966: 'the government must function in accordance with the law'.[5]

An organisational principle translated this abstract commitment into a practical rule. No more force should be used than the situation demands. Gradually the literature on British counter-insurgency, and the army itself, came to believe that this doctrinal precept represented reality. Apparently the principle of 'minimum force' resulted from both Victorian morality and the pragmatism of a small imperial army which could ill afford massive repression.[6] When countering revolt, the aim was always to contain rather than extirpate resistance through minimal rather than exemplary force.[7] From long experience the army had learnt that exemplary, excessive force provoked the population and was counterproductive to restoring the peace.[8] For some time, virtually all writers on the army since 1945 have identified minimum force as a key characteristic of British counter-insurgency.[9] The orthodoxy held that

[3] For a major reassessment of the French in Algeria, see M. Evans, *Algeria: France's Undeclared War* (Oxford University Press, 2012).

[4] For studies of his role in Vietnam, see I. F. W. Beckett, 'Robert Thompson and the British Advisory Mission to South Vietnam, 1961–1965', *Small Wars and Insurgencies*, 8 (1997), 41–63; P. Busch, 'Killing the "Vietcong": The British Advisory Mission and the Strategic Hamlet Programme', *Journal of Strategic Studies*, 25 (2002), 135–62.

[5] R. Thompson, *Defeating Communist Insurgency: Experiences from Malaya and Vietnam* (London: Chatto and Windus, 1966), 52.

[6] R. Thornton, 'The British Army and the Origins of its Minimum Force Philosophy', *Small Wars and Insurgencies*, 15 (2004), 83–106.

[7] C. Townshend, *Britain's Civil Wars: Counterinsurgency in the Twentieth Century* (London: Faber and Faber, 1986), 18.

[8] T. R. Mockaitis, *British Counterinsurgency, 1919–60* (New York: St Martin's Press, 1990), 17–62.

[9] D. A. Charters, 'From Palestine to Northern Ireland: British Adaptation to Low-Intensity Operations', in D. A. Charters and M. Tugwell (eds.), *Armies in Low-Intensity Conflict: A Comparative Analysis* (London: Brassey's, 1989), 194; K. Jeffery, 'Intelligence and Counter-Insurgency Operations: Some Reflections on the British Experience', *Intelligence and National Security*, 2 (1987), 119; A. J. Joes, *Resisting Rebellion: The History and Politics of Counterinsurgency* (Lexington, KY: University Press of Kentucky, 2004), 221; C. J. McInnes, *Hot War, Cold War: The British Army's Way in Warfare 1945–95* (London: Brassey's, 1996), 117; J. Pimlott, 'The British Army: The Dhofar Campaign, 1970–1975', in I. F. W. Beckett and J. Pimlott (eds.), *Armed Forces and Modern Counter-Insurgency* (London: Croom Helm, 1985), 23; R. Popplewell,

adherence to law could eliminate a dilemma in counter-insurgency warfare. Insurgents deliberately hide among the population. For the state, the core challenge is how to target insurgents without harming civilians. The debate on British counter-insurgency concluded that minimum force provided the answer. This is a seductive interpretation because it softens the loss of empire by elevating the British Army to a professional standard that all others failed to achieve.

Understanding violence in Britain's counter-insurgencies is impossible without recourse to the archives. Until recently these records have been neglected. In consequence, the doctrine-centric orthodoxy, elevating the importance of minimum force, has not been systematically challenged. In 2009 a group of Kenyans who alleged mistreatment at British hands during the Emergency began legal proceedings against the Foreign and Commonwealth Office. Two years later this led to the discovery of a hidden colonial archive at Hanslope Park, home to Her Majesty's Government Communications Centre. The papers contain records from thirty-seven British colonial territories, and consist of 8,800 separate files. They will all have been placed in the National Archives, file series FCO 141, by the end of 2013. The author of this book has acted as an expert witness in the Mau Mau case at the High Court in London, giving him privileged access to all of the files concerning Kenya. With the kind agreement of the Foreign and Commonwealth Office, a number of these archival records are presented in this book for the first time, in addition to a wider range of sources from archives in Britain and Kenya.

The literature on the Kenya Emergency's origins, conduct and consequences is rich and diverse.[10] This book is the first to take a detailed look at the British Army's role. But it is not a comprehensive, chronological military history. The focus is directly on the orthodoxy about British counter-insurgency. Two major questions drive the analysis. How important was the concept of minimum force in determining how the army used force? And how should the army's behaviour towards civilians best be understood? The argument is that in reality the army never succeeded in separating insurgents from civilians. The inherent dilemma about identification, violence and legitimacy has never been resolved. For this reason, the minimum force notion has merely aimed to paper over the cracks of a deep problem without any clear solution.

'"Lacking Intelligence": Some Reflections on Recent Approaches to British Counter-Insurgency, 1900–1960', *Intelligence and National Security*, 10 (1995), 337.

[10] For useful reviews, see S. L. Carruthers, 'Being Beastly to the Mau Mau', *Twentieth Century British History*, 16 (2005), 489–96; B. A. Ogot, 'Review Article: *Britain's Gulag*', *Journal of African History*, 46 (2005), 493–505.

Prompted by crises in Iraq and Afghanistan, writing on British counter-insurgency has taken a more critical turn.[11] Writers observed how the triumphalist orthodoxy failed to explain the difficulties encountered in Basra and Helmand. The British government's participation in human rights abuses, including those at Guantanamo Bay, attracted significant attention. At the same time as the debate on contemporary policy reignited, the historical literature underwent a revival. The interest in counter-insurgency dovetailed with the release of primary sources. A major comparative historical study by David French demonstrates just how often the harsh methods described in this book were employed to crush rebellions throughout the post-war British Empire.[12] Original historical work has been produced on conflicts such as Palestine, Malaya and Northern Ireland.[13] These studies show how the army used a greater degree of force than is normally acknowledged, at times leading to torture and illegal killing. Others have argued that the army's own

---

[11] D. Betz and A. Cormack, 'Iraq, Afghanistan and British Strategy', *Orbis*, 53 (2009), 319–36; D. Branch, 'Footprints in the Sand: British Colonial Counterinsurgency and the War in Iraq', *Politics & Society*, 38 (2010), 15–34; W. Chin, 'Why Did It All Go Wrong? Reassessing British Counterinsurgency in Iraq', *Strategic Studies Quarterly*, 2 (2008), 119–35; W. Chin, 'The United Kingdom and the War on Terror: The Breakdown of National and Military Strategy', *Contemporary Security Policy*, 30 (2009), 125–46; A. Danchev, 'The Reckoning: Official Inquiries and the Iraq War', *Intelligence and National Security*, 19 (2004), 436–66; A. Danchev, 'Accomplicity: Britain, Torture and Terror', *British Journal of Politics and International Relations*, 8 (2006), 587–601; R. Kerr, 'A Force for Good? War, Crime and Legitimacy: The British Army in Iraq', *Defense and Security Analysis*, 24 (2008), 401–19; R. Kerr, *The Military on Trial: The British Army in Iraq* (Nijmegen: Wolf Legal Publishers, 2008); G. Rangwala, 'Counter-Insurgency amid Fragmentation: The British in Southern Iraq', *Journal of Strategic Studies*, 32 (2009), 495–513; A. Roberts, 'Doctrine and Reality in Afghanistan', *Survival*, 51 (2009), 29–60.

[12] D. French, *The British Way in Counter-Insurgency, 1945–1967* (Oxford University Press, 2011).

[13] H. Bennett, 'Detention and Interrogation in Northern Ireland, 1969–75', in S. Scheipers (ed.), *Prisoners in War* (Oxford University Press, 2010), 187–205; K. Hack, 'Screwing Down the People: The Malayan Emergency, Decolonisation and Ethnicity', in H. Antlöv and S. Tonnesson (eds.), *Imperial Policy and Southeast Asian Nationalism* (London: Curzon, 1995), 83–109; K. Hack, '"Iron Claws on Malaya": The Historiography of the Malayan Emergency', *Journal of Southeast Asian Studies*, 30 (1999), 99–125; M. Hughes, 'The Banality of Brutality: British Armed Forces and the Repression of the Arab Revolt in Palestine, 1936–39', *English Historical Review*, 124 (2009), 313–54; S. Newbery, 'Intelligence and Controversial British Interrogation Techniques: The Northern Ireland Case, 1971–2', *Irish Studies in International Affairs*, 20 (2009), 103–19; J. Norris, 'Repression and Rebellion: Britain's Response to the Arab Revolt in Palestine of 1936–39', *Journal of Imperial and Commonwealth History*, 36 (2008), 25–45; N. Ó Dochartaigh, 'Bloody Sunday: Error or Design?', *Contemporary British History*, 24 (2010), 89–108. S. Shoul, 'Soldiers, Riot Control and Aid to the Civil Power in India, Egypt and Palestine, 1919–39', *Journal of the Society for Army Historical Research*, 346 (2008), 120–39.

doctrinal publications omitted any substantial reference to minimum force during the colonial era.[14]

To a certain degree, these writings repeat a point made forcefully in earlier scholarship. John Newsinger, in particular, has questioned the mythology surrounding British counter-insurgency since the 1980s.[15] But because archival records were unavailable to substantiate the critique, it failed to displace the orthodoxy. Therefore the account offered here is the first book-length examination of how the British Army treated civilians in one of its major post-war counter-insurgencies. The archival sources, including new material released under the Freedom of Information Act, allow for an understanding of how the army itself thought about and conducted the Emergency.

The argument is developed in nine chapters. Chapter 1 describes the evolution of the Kenya Emergency from the military perspective. The conflict is placed into four periods in order to set out the major events and operations. By doing so, the key continuities and innovations in the strategy for defeating the Mau Mau, and their relationship to wider events, is demonstrated. In chapter 2, the structure of civil-military relations is dissected, by looking at how the main political groups interacted with the army. The three most important groups were the provincial administration, the European settlers and the British political class. Each held multiple, contradictory views about the Emergency, and exerted an identifiable influence on the army, which is analysed in depth. Chapter 2 also examines the committee system which mediated civil-military relations, minimising frictions to promote a coordinated approach to defeating the Mau Mau.

Chapter 3 addresses a central claim in the orthodox interpretation of British counter-insurgency: that soldiers operated within a legal framework. The chapter dissects how the British government and armed forces understood the legal regime relevant to colonial rebellions after 1945. Widespread violence against civilians could occur in the colonies partly because such acts were considered within the bounds of international law.

---

[14] B. Reis, 'The Myth of British Minimum Force in Counterinsurgency Campaigns during Decolonisation (1945–70)', *Journal of Strategic Studies*, 34 (2011), 245–79.

[15] M. Curtis, *Web of Deceit: Britain's Real Role in the World* (London: Vintage, 2003); J. Newsinger, 'Revolt and Repression in Kenya: The "Mau Mau" Rebellion, 1952–1960', *Science and Society*, 45 (1981), 159–85; J. Newsinger, 'A Counter-insurgency Tale: Kitson in Kenya', *Race and Class*, 31 (1990), 61–72; J. Newsinger, 'Minimum Force, British Counter-Insurgency and the Mau Mau Rebellion', *Small Wars and Insurgencies*, 3 (1992), 47–57; J. Newsinger, *British Counterinsurgency: From Palestine to Northern Ireland* (Basingstoke: Palgrave, 2002).

The British government and army evidenced a conservative attitude, and awareness about even existing provisions was patchy. These attitudes reflected systematic weaknesses in the international legal regime itself. Arguably British conservatism was far from atypical. Three structural contradictions in international law undermined universal protections, and proved a problem for the British in practice. These were, first, the conflict between the military need for reflexive obedience and the legal requirement to refuse illegal orders; second, the conflict between military necessity and legal restraint; and third, the overly narrow codification which produced different rules for fighting non-Western opponents. Part of the reason why atrocities happened in the Empire was because they were not construed as international crimes. Government policy aimed to minimise the interference of international law in colonial emergencies. Knowledge within the armed forces about international law in general terms was poor, while the duty to obey all orders was paramount. As a result, soldiers sent to Kenya knew nothing about any formal obligations to prevent abuses committed against civilians.

Chapter 4 asks how far the army's internal doctrinal principles made up for this permissive attitude regarding international law. The chapter defines the concept of minimum force and outlines its development in official and semi-official documents. Without doubt the concept enjoyed wide circulation in military circles, and permeated doctrine throughout the twentieth century. But the idea must be appreciated on a rather more critical basis than is often the case, both in theoretical and practical terms. Arguably, the concept is only helpful in understanding actual behaviour when studied alongside the equally prominent idea of exemplary force. Exemplary force seeks to target whole populations in order to punish insurgents, and to warn others not to support the rebellion. It is by nature indiscriminate and terrorising. By tracing formative military experiences in the run up to the Kenya campaign, the chapter shows how minimum and exemplary force often co-existed.

In the fifth chapter attention returns to Kenya, to explore the impact of the minimum force ideal on military operations. Rather than deploying the full force of its military power in Kenya, the government calibrated violence at a level below the potential for all-out genocidal war. Minimum force mattered to how the army fought the campaign, and relied on tight discipline. Chapter 5 looks at how the army dealt with the inevitable offences committed by soldiers. A series of measures, involving orders, meetings and inquiries, succeeded in preventing soldiers from completely running amok. Chapter 6 argues that restrained conduct required more than military discipline. Operational policy also needed to distinguish between legitimate targets and innocent civilians.

Legally defined zones with distinct rules of engagement, developed prisoner policies, and special forces methods sought to control and limit the use of force.

Chapter 7 argues that despite avoiding the maximal possible violence, the army engaged in widespread violent coercion of the civilian population throughout the Emergency. This included forced population movement, beatings, rape, torture and shootings. These actions did not result from poor command and control, or a breakdown in military discipline. A determination to teach the Kikuyu a lesson drove a policy of punishment. The key policies in this respect are examined in broad terms, and at the micro level. Chapter 8 shows how these policies were connected to the structure of military discipline. General Erskine initially wanted to conduct a restrained campaign. Following resistance from the Governor, the settlers and some soldiers, he compromised. In effect, discipline in Kenya was negotiated between commanders and troops. Thus harsh measures against the Kikuyu population resulted from disciplinary compromise and strategic necessity.

Chapter 9 assesses how far civil-military relations influenced the implementation of policy. In most spheres the army prevailed, and in many areas strictly under civilian control soldiers exerted a strong influence. Soldiers and civilians broadly agreed on the need to crush the Mau Mau rebellion swiftly and harshly, before it undermined British rule and spread to other tribes.

1 'A determined campaign against the terrorist bands'

The Mau Mau movement wrought violence on Kenya for much of the 1950s (see map 1 for Kenya Colony). Confined mainly to the Kikuyu, Embu and Meru tribes of the central highlands, unrest had been gathering pace for several years before the government declared an official State of Emergency in October 1952. The rebellion was devolved and complex in organisation and motivation. A large number of grievances were involved, ranging from an anti-colonial desire to expel Europeans, to dissatisfaction with imposed agricultural techniques. Probably the most important single cause of the revolt was the belief that the Kikuyu had been cheated out of their rightful lands by European settlers. Despite the anti-colonial dimension, the conflict is normally now described as a civil war within the Kikuyu, as the squatters (temporary workers on European farms) fought against the landed establishment. Important alliances were forged between the rural dispossessed and urban activists in Nairobi.[1]

The rebellion was limited geographically, mainly to the Central and Rift Valley Provinces, and to Nairobi (see map 2). So in most of Kenya life carried on as normal during the Emergency. Out of a total African population of around 5 million, the 1.4 million Kikuyu were nearly all considered unreliable by the government. At this point the Asian community in Kenya stood at about 97,000, and the European settlers at 29,000. The settlers dominated local politics, and there was no democracy for the Asians or Africans in the country. The origins of the conflict can be seen in the Kikuyu's poor economic conditions, the lack of political representation, and a growing land hunger as the population

---

Chapter title from TNA, CO 822/378: Kenya Intelligence Committee fortnightly appreciation (KICFA) 7/53, 30 June 1953.

[1] R. Hyam, *Britain's Declining Empire: The Road to Decolonisation, 1918–1968* (Cambridge University Press, 2006), 188. John Lonsdale provides the following explanation for the meaning of the term 'Mau Mau': 'in Swahili *ka* is a diminutive prefix, *ma* an amplifying one, enhanced by repetition. *Mau* would thus connote something larger than *Kau* (the colloquial form of the Kenya African Union).' J. Lonsdale, 'Mau Maus of the Mind: Making Mau Mau and Remaking Kenya', *Journal of African History*, 31 (1990), 393–421.

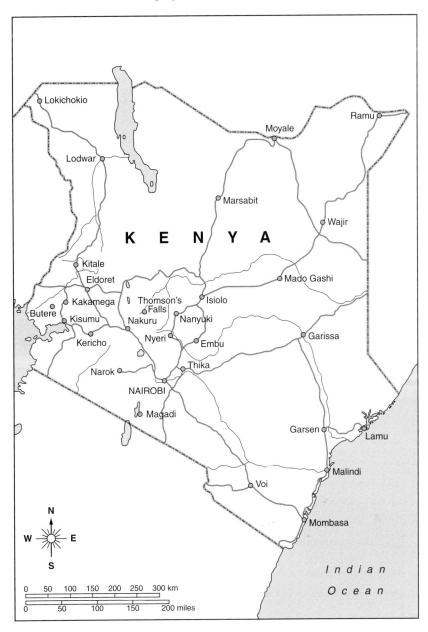

Map 1 Kenya Colony

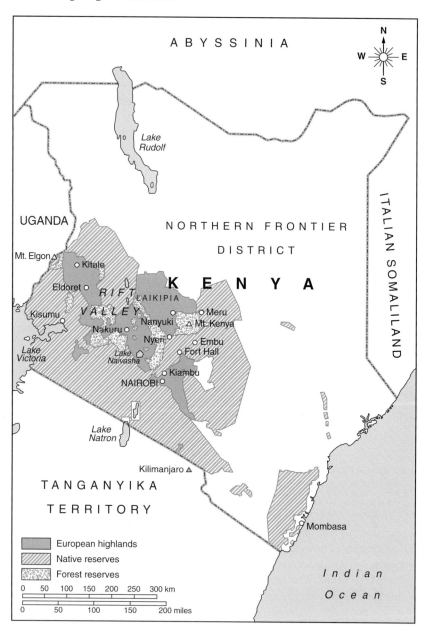

Map 2 Administrative areas affected by the Emergency

mushroomed. Perhaps the most convincing account of the brewing troubles argues that these causes prompted three political blocs to emerge by the 1950s. The conservative element in Kikuyu society comprised chiefs, headmen and senior Christian elders, who believed in supporting the colonial project. The moderate nationalists, such as Jomo Kenyatta and Koinage wa Mbiyu, were westernized, believing in social progress and political representation. These moderates formed such groups as the Kikuyu Central Association and later the Kenya African Union. The third group, the militant nationalists, first appeared in the 1930s. They gave shape to the Mau Mau in the 1950s and grew more influential as the failure of the moderates to achieve any meaningful progress became obvious. By 1952 Mau Mau attacks on settler property and on perceived collaborators were becoming widespread in Kikuyuland.[2]

Ten months into their campaign in Kenya, the army staff received a depressing progress report. It diagnosed a failure to disrupt the Mau Mau gangs, ineffective tactics, lack of discipline and efficiency in many military units, poor liaison with other security forces and incorrect intelligence methods. The author concluded that 'The military has, therefore, failed.'[3] Yet just over three years later, the military campaign against the Mau Mau was won, the gangs (as the authorities described them) were reduced to negligible proportions and the civil authorities were able to govern largely without military help. Compared with many other insurgency wars, the military phase lasted for a short period. The British Army performed a decisive role in crushing the rebellion relatively quickly. Drawing on experience, commanders knew how to coordinate their forces with the civil powers in overwhelming insurgency by force. Holding the population in place through the exercise of drastic restrictions on normal liberties, the army simultaneously sought to eliminate the armed rebels by killing or capturing them. The delicate balance required in targeting these two groups – the population as a whole and the armed gangs – shifted throughout the conflict. But the determination to coerce both at once remained a constant.

How the army tried to defeat the Mau Mau can best be understood in four distinctive, though in some senses overlapping, periods. From the declaration of the Emergency in October 1952, through to June 1953, the campaign lacked strategic leadership and sufficient forces to defeat the Mau Mau. The second period began when General Sir George Erskine arrived in June 1953. During his early military career Erskine

---

[2] D. M. Anderson, *Histories of the Hanged: Britain's Dirty War in Kenya and the End of Empire* (London: Weidenfeld and Nicolson, 2005), 9–53.
[3] TNA, WO 276/382: Memorandum by C. C. T. Aston on the Emergency Operations, 11 August 1953.

served in Ireland and India, and fought in Europe and the Middle East in the Second World War. For over a year he commanded the famous 7 Armoured Division, including in Normandy. From September 1944 he headed the Supreme Headquarters Allied Expeditionary Force's mission to Belgium, and in 1945 served as the deputy British military governor in Germany. After the war his most important post was in Egypt, where he commanded British troops from January 1949 until April 1952. During this period, widespread anti-British violence took place, and escalated to quite serious levels in Suez, Ismailia and Cairo.[4] These experiences, in colonial policing, major combat command, civil-military cooperation and suppressing rebellion, would prove highly relevant in Kenya. During his tenure of command Erskine attempted to introduce strategic direction and bring the various security forces under his control. The third period was the war's most decisive. It began with the massive security sweep through Nairobi, Operation Anvil in April 1954, and the taking control of the Kikuyu, Embu and Meru Reserves away from the Mau Mau. The fourth period witnessed the final surrender negotiations and large-scale, and then small special forces, operations in the forests to destroy the few remaining gangs, with the military finally handing over control to the civil power in the last areas in November 1956.

Opening moves, October 1952 to June 1953

When Governor Sir Evelyn Baring declared a State of Emergency on 20 October 1952, the military response to the Mau Mau began. But the police and administration had been countering growing violence throughout the year.[5] Arson attacks against European settler properties were common in 1952, with over sixty such crimes recorded from January to March around the town of Nyeri alone.[6] Settler farmers were not the only victims, with thirty-four Africans murdered between 1 August and 20 October.[7] From the year's start the settler community agitated for tough action, and the police responded, arresting 547 Kikuyu 'preventatively' in September.[8]

---

[4] Erskine, Sir George Watkin Eben James (1899–1965), by H. Bennett, *Oxford Dictionary of National Biography* (Oxford University Press, 2011), online edition, at www.oxforddnb.com/view/article/97289, accessed 1 June 2011.

[5] F. Furedi, *The Mau Mau War in Perspective* (London: James Currey, 1989), 3; D. A. Percox, 'British Counter-Insurgency in Kenya, 1952–56: Extension of Internal Security Policy or Prelude to Decolonisation?', *Small Wars and Insurgencies*, 9 (1998), 50–9.

[6] R. W. Heather, 'Counterinsurgency and Intelligence in Kenya: 1952–56' (doctoral thesis, Cambridge University, 1993), 20.

[7] D. Branch, 'Loyalism during the Mau Mau Rebellion in Kenya, 1952–60' (doctoral thesis, University of Oxford, 2005), 76–8.

[8] Furedi, *Mau Mau War*, 116, 119.

A major problem right from the outset was identifying exactly who in the Kikuyu population supported the Mau Mau. An intelligence drought severely hampered what operations could achieve, though many went ahead regardless.

Operation Jock Scott was conducted by the police and army in cooperation, setting a pattern for the future. Launched on 20 October, it aimed to decapitate the Mau Mau leadership; 150 members of the Kenya African Union, a legal organisation connected (erroneously) with the Mau Mau, were arrested. At the same time, the 1 Lancashire Fusiliers arrived from Egypt and immediately set about patrolling the settled areas in a bid to reassure the European inhabitants. In addition to the Fusiliers, the forces in Kenya comprised five King's African Rifles (KAR) battalions, a battalion of the territorial Kenya Regiment, the East Africa Armoured Car Squadron and the 156 (East African) Heavy Anti-Aircraft Artillery (HAA).[9] The KAR, the armoured car squadron and the artillery all consisted of African troops from Britain's colonial territories in East Africa, officered by British Army men on secondment, and were part of the regular chain of command. The Kenya Regiment was also officered by regulars on secondment, but the majority of the rank and file were European settlers, although a small number of Africans served with the unit during the Emergency. For administrative and financial purposes the Kenya Regiment came under the Kenya government, but for discipline and operations it followed the normal British Army chain of command.[10]

Military operations in the first months were quite seriously flawed. The initial arrests failed to halt the violence, but generated complacency in the government, which was subsequently sluggish in mounting offensive operations.[11] When these offensive sweeps eventually happened, in Kiambu and Nyeri, they achieved no tangible results.[12] The Kenya government came under criticism for lacking a clear strategy, reacting in a frantic and ad hoc manner to the Mau Mau.[13] Attacks on Europeans initially exerted a disproportionate influence on deployment decisions,

---

[9] *Ibid.*, 62.

[10] TNA, WO 276/542: Booklet 'The Story of the Kenya Regiment T.F. 1937–1959'. For a debate about how 'British' the Kenya Regiment and KAR were, see R. Thornton, '"Minimum Force": A Reply to Huw Bennett', *Small Wars and Insurgencies*, 20 (2009), 215–26; and H. Bennett, 'Minimum Force in British Counterinsurgency', *Small Wars and Insurgencies*, 21 (2010), 459–75.

[11] Heather, 'Counterinsurgency and Intelligence in Kenya', 32–3.

[12] Anderson, *Histories of the Hanged*, 69.

[13] B. Berman, *Control and Crisis in Colonial Kenya: The Dialectic of Domination* (London: James Currey, 1990), 347; W. Maloba, *Mau Mau and Kenya: An Analysis of a Peasant Revolt* (Bloomington: Indiana University Press, 1993), 81.

with small units scattered throughout the Rift Valley to protect the settlers.[14] As a result, some saw the opening months as nothing more than a 'phoney war', with confusion on both sides.[15]

Compared to the operations launched by three full brigades later on in the Emergency, the opening months certainly lacked large-scale military operations. However, the 'phoney war' tag, reflecting a eurocentric refusal to take African violence seriously, is deceptive. Such a characterisation masks the growing violence seen throughout this period. Both settler and government action accelerated the onset of the rebellion by radicalising a large proportion of undecided Kikuyu into supporting the Mau Mau cause either actively or passively through providing food and information.[16] Some even describe the period as one of 'pre-emptive repression' by the state.[17] Large numbers were expelled from their homes in the Rift Valley by settlers paranoid that each formerly loyal Kikuyu employee was waiting for nightfall to exert a bloodthirsty treachery with panga and spear.[18] The government viewed such (hugely disproportionate) retaliation as inevitable.[19] By doing nothing to stop the settlers, who often evicted their labour with illegal force, the government condoned their behaviour. While evicting all Kikuyu from areas where alleged Mau Mau crimes had occurred only became official policy on 15 December 1952, the authorities assisted with evictions before this date.[20] In the week following a violent attack on the Meiklejohn residence in Thomson's Falls in late October, resulting in Commander Meiklejohn's death and his wife's mutilation, the Lancashire Fusiliers removed 750 Kikuyu men and 2,200 children during a large sweep through the surrounding area.[21] In another case, after a European was killed in Leshau on 22 November, 4,324 Kikuyu were evicted.[22]

Several units mounted sweep operations throughout November. The 156 HAA Battery formed into sixteen motorised infantry patrols, each about ten men strong, and worked alongside various KAR units (and later independently).[23] By 12 November both police and army units were engaged in extensive and continuous sweeps through the Kikuyu

[14] Heather, 'Counterinsurgency and Intelligence in Kenya', 37.
[15] Berman, *Control and Crisis*, 348; Percox, 'Counter-Insurgency in Kenya', 62.
[16] Percox, 'Counter-Insurgency in Kenya', 67.   [17] Furedi, *Mau Mau War*, 8.
[18] Heather, 'Counterinsurgency and Intelligence in Kenya', 41. A panga is a heavy bladed tool, similar to a machete, used for agricultural work, but also lethal as a weapon.
[19] Percox, 'Counter-Insurgency in Kenya', 62.
[20] *Ibid.*, 68. The primary evidence does not fully clarify the distinction between autonomous settler removals and official government practice.
[21] Anderson, *Histories of the Hanged*, 90.   [22] Furedi, *Mau Mau War*, 119.
[23] Oxford Development Records Project (ODRP), Bodleian Library of Commonwealth and African Studies at Rhodes House, University of Oxford: P. E. Langford, MSS Afr. 1715.

Reserves.[24] These sweeps suffered from an intelligence deficiency and thus innocent persons were adversely affected. The police were in a poor position to provide accurate intelligence on which to base operations. There was hardly any substantial Kenya Police presence in the Reserves, the first posts having been built in these areas in 1943. At the Emergency's declaration, the police Special Branch, responsible for political policing, comprised only four officers and a handful of rank and file.[25] Another common type of operation was the screening of all persons in a given location, usually with the aid of loyalist chiefs, the administration and police. The exact meaning of 'screening' varied. The common denominator was the extraction of information from suspects. Soldiers wanted information to launch operations, policemen wanted information to secure criminal convictions, Special Branch and military intelligence men wanted information for building their intelligence networks, and the administration wanted information to punish and/or rehabilitate Mau Mau adherents. From early November 'A' Company of 23 KAR constantly took prisoners and searched property for signs of collusion with the Mau Mau. In a typical action on 28 January 1953 they helped screen 1,500 people at Limuru, resulting in 96 arrests.[26]

November also saw the extension of powers to magistrates for trying Mau Mau offences, alongside new regulations facilitating the seizure of property and increased penalties for certain crimes.[27] In December Governor Baring announced a new Emergency tax, levied against all Kikuyu, which proved extremely unpopular.[28] Similarly controversial with the African population, the trial of the popular and respected political leader Jomo Kenyatta began on 3 December, leading to his conviction for leading the Mau Mau.[29] On the military front Baring requested a director of operations in November and again in December, but the War Office instead appointed Colonel G. Rimbault as Personal Staff Officer, a position with limited authority.[30] His appointment reflected a wider failure on the part of the War Office to appreciate the seriousness of the situation. This was again evident when the reluctance to send more British battalions led to the overstretching of KAR units.[31]

---

[24] Percox, 'Counter-Insurgency in Kenya', 64.
[25] D. Throup (1992), 'Crime, Politics and the Police in Colonial Kenya, 1939–63', in D. M. Anderson and D. Killingray (eds.), *Policing and Decolonisation: Politics, Nationalism and the Police, 1917–65* (Manchester University Press, 1992), 129, 139.
[26] ODRP, H. N. Clemas, MSS Afr. 1715.
[27] Heather, 'Counterinsurgency and Intelligence in Kenya', 38.
[28] Percox, 'Counter-Insurgency in Kenya', 64.   [29] Anderson, *Histories of the Hanged*, 63.
[30] Heather, 'Counterinsurgency and Intelligence in Kenya', 49.
[31] Percox, 'Counter-Insurgency in Kenya', 62.

Perhaps given the worrying conflicts going on in Korea and Malaya, the refusal to prioritise Kenya in late 1952 to early 1953 should be considered reasonable.

In January 1953 substantial sweep operations pushed into the forests for the first time. After declaring the northern Aberdare Mountains area a prohibited area (PA) for all civilians, the army and police launched Operation Blitz on 6 January.[32] In PAs troops could open fire without warning. The PA policy received official sanction from Whitehall in late February on the condition that it was restricted to really dangerous areas, clearly defined, given adequate publicity, and that a reasonable amount of time elapsed between giving notice and starting operations.[33] The Blitz operations were confined to the forest fringes and thus the Mau Mau avoided the security forces fairly easily by moving deeper into the dense forests.[34] Still suffering from manpower shortages, the security forces were limited in their ability to launch offensives by the constant demands for static protection. Even when not on the offensive, the government found protecting all those vulnerable a difficult task.[35] But the pressure to do so mounted as attacks on settler farms increased in the first months of the year, creating a febrile atmosphere among the settlers.[36] The brutal murder of the Ruck family, including a young child, at Kinangop on 24 January radicalised the settlers more than any other incident so far in the Emergency.[37]

One solution to the manpower problem appeared to be creating Kikuyu, Embu and Meru Home Guard units, some of which existed in an unofficial capacity before the Emergency was declared. They were best organised in Nyeri, and by March 1953 there were 18,000 Home Guards in Central Province.[38] The nature of the Guard changed as the war did. Initially founded to protect chiefs and headmen, their role changed over 1953 as units began to patrol large areas and fight in combat. The abiding image of these units was of the increasingly ubiquitous fortified posts, surrounded by spike-filled moats, barbed wire and overlooked by watchtowers. Each post typically held ten rifles and shotguns allocated to the most trustworthy men, the rest carrying pangas, spears and other traditional weapons. When not manning the post, the Home Guard patrolled localities, guarded schools, escorted chiefs and headmen, acted as guides for the military and participated in

---

[32] Heather, 'Counterinsurgency and Intelligence in Kenya', 57.
[33] TNA, CO 822/442: Copy of draft reply, Secretary of State for the Colonies to Baring, in reply to his telegram of 24 February 1953, no date.
[34] Percox, 'Counter-Insurgency in Kenya', 71.
[35] Branch, 'Loyalism during the Mau Mau Rebellion', 96.
[36] Anderson, *Histories of the Hanged*, 91.   [37] *Ibid.*, 93.
[38] Branch, 'Loyalism during the Mau Mau Rebellion', 83–4.

screenings. They normally operated in the Reserves, leaving the forests to the police and army.[39]

Throughout February important changes were made to the command and control structure in Kenya. Major-General William Hinde arrived on the first of the month to take up the post of Chief Staff Officer to the Governor.[40] He spent a month touring the affected areas in order to draw up recommendations for combating the insurgency.[41] Aside from proposing social measures to win over the population, Hinde wanted the army to be active on offensive operations, and ended the unsuccessful 'grouse shoots' in favour of smaller-scale patrols.[42] In suggesting these approaches Hinde laid some of the groundwork for Erskine's fuller strategy developed several months later. He optimistically believed that the Mau Mau could be beaten with existing resources, reflecting the poor intelligence on the enemy at the time.[43] The Chief of the Imperial General Staff (CIGS), Field Marshal Sir John Harding, visited from 19 to 24 February. He took a less optimistic view and decided that further British battalions and air support were required, marking a growing prominence for the army in the conduct of the Emergency.[44] Harding recognised the need to curb the 'European hotheads', to develop an overall plan and to ensure that everybody worked to it effectively rather than pulling in different directions. As a result of his visit, the KAR battalions were brought up to strength, and 1 Devonshire Regiment, 1 Royal East Kent Regiment (The Buffs) and two brigade headquarters were earmarked for Kenya.[45]

Two events on a night in March 1953 escalated the conflict, pushing London into promoting Hinde to Director of Operations, and later sending General Erskine out to win an increasingly messy war.[46] On 26 March the Mau Mau attacked Lari village and Naivasha police station almost simultaneously. At Lari the Mau Mau massacred 120 civilians, while the raid at Naivasha, releasing prisoners and stealing arms and ammunition, greatly embarrassed the government. Lari represented the beginning of an assault on the Home Guard aimed at discouraging loyalism.[47] These events forced the authorities to realise that the Mau Mau was a serious, organised movement that would not go

---

[39] *Ibid.*, 22, 110, 112.   [40] Percox, 'Counter-Insurgency in Kenya', 71.

[41] Heather, 'Counterinsurgency and Intelligence in Kenya', 59.

[42] A. Clayton and D. Killingray, *Khaki and Blue: Military and Police in British Colonial Africa* (Athens, OH: Ohio University Center for International Studies, 1989), 256.

[43] Heather, 'Counterinsurgency and Intelligence in Kenya', 62.

[44] M. Carver, *Harding of Petherton* (London: Weidenfeld and Nicolson, 1978), 63.

[45] TNA, CO 822/442: Report by CIGS on his visit to Kenya, 27 February 1953.

[46] Percox, 'Counter-Insurgency in Kenya', 73.

[47] Branch, 'Loyalism during the Mau Mau Rebellion', 129.

away quickly.[48] A week later the government decided to systematically arm the Home Guard and appoint European officers to oversee them.[49] Judicial powers were enhanced and security force activities intensified.[50] In early April a major sweep took place around Kariokar in Nairobi, detaining or sending to the Reserves around 800 Kikuyu.[51] Intelligence reports noted how patrols by 23 KAR and the Home Guard 'met several groups of terrorists' in the Kiambu area near Lari. In one night the Home Guard claimed to have killed twenty-one, and 23 KAR another twenty-four (plus thirty-six wounded) 'in a running fight with a large simi-armed gang'. The report concluded, 'Most of those killed and wounded were thought to be involved in the LARI massacre.'[52] Who the others were is unclear. Following Lari, the security forces scarcely cared to pause and ponder such questions.

Having acclimatised and trained in Nyeri, The Buffs and the Devons were ready for operations by late April and fully deployed by 10 May. They formed part of the new 39 Brigade with responsibility for the Aberdares forest area, while 70 (East Africa) Infantry Brigade operated in the Reserve areas.[53] Meanwhile Hinde modified the colony's command system in a bid for greater coherence. He personally headed the Director of Operations Committee, below which were joint operations committees sitting from colony down to district level, with representatives from the military, police and administration.[54] They directed all operations by security forces and were distinct from the Emergency Committees, which focused specifically on policy matters.[55] In May the unwieldy Governor's Emergency Committee was replaced by the smaller Colony Emergency Committee, below which the existing provincial (PECs) and district Emergency Committees (DECs) were expanded in the Rift Valley and settled areas to include an unofficial European member. The authorities hoped that coopting the settlers would curtail their excessive behaviour.[56] This proved a little hopeful.

Other organisational reforms in May were of greater long-term importance. The military's operational intelligence capability received a boost with the creation of provincial and district military intelligence

---

[48] See Anderson, *Histories of the Hanged*, 119–80.
[49] Branch, 'Loyalism during the Mau Mau Rebellion', 107.
[50] Anderson, *Histories of the Hanged*, 133.
[51] Heather, 'Counterinsurgency and Intelligence in Kenya', 75.
[52] TNA, WO 276/379: Northern Brigade intelligence summary, 4 April 1953.
[53] Heather, 'Counterinsurgency and Intelligence in Kenya', 85.
[54] For further discussion of the command system, see chapter 2. The administration of the country was divided into the following levels: colony, province, district, location, sub-location.
[55] Heather, 'Counterinsurgency and Intelligence in Kenya', 82.   [56] *Ibid.*, 79.

officers (DMIOs), aided by field intelligence assistants (FIAs). These officers were specifically tasked with enhancing the intelligence network, and in particular giving new vigour to the army's relations with the Special Branch. The new system gradually improved intelligence collection, collation, analysis and dissemination.[57] On 29 May the War Office announced that East Africa, previously subordinate to Middle East Land Forces (MELF), would become an independent command, reporting directly to London and with Erskine as the commander-in-chief.[58] This marked a turning point in the professionalisation of the war's conduct. But it should not be interpreted as meaning that strategy prior to Erskine's arrival completely lacked coherence. As of 19 May, the security forces had managed to wound 343 Mau Mau and kill 619 of them. They had also, by 31 May, arrested 103,379 people, of whom 89,820 were screened.[59] An intelligence report from this time concluded that the government's failure to destroy the Mau Mau should be considered against broad success in preventing the insurgency spreading to other tribes and provinces, described as the 'Government's primary task'.[60] The need to demonstrate the state's commitment to crushing internal revolt to a wider audience than just the Kikuyu explains much about the use of force in the opening stages of the Emergency, and indeed beyond. Within Kikuyuland the insurgency had spread quickly, from Kiambu and Nairobi to Fort Hall, where it remained at its most fierce. By August 1953 it would spread to Embu, Meru and the Rift Valley areas adjacent to Central Province.[61] Rather than quelling the uprising, government action actually exacerbated the problem. This is especially true of the population movements taking place, with even Baring admitting that it 'has probably led to a further facilitation of gang recruitment and some diversion of effort on the part of the forces of law and order'.[62]

Erskine develops an operational plan, June 1953 to April 1954

General Erskine's arrival on 7 June 1953 came to mean both a decline in settler influence over the campaign and the beginning of the end for the

---

[57] *Ibid.*, 107.   [58] Percox, 'Counter-Insurgency in Kenya', 75.

[59] TNA, CO 822/373: Special Branch fortnightly intelligence summary (SBFIS) 5/53, Appendix A, 31 May 1953.

[60] TNA, CO 822/378: KICFA 4/53, 15 May 1953.

[61] Branch, 'Loyalism during the Mau Mau Rebellion', 129.

[62] TNA, CO 822/442: Savingram from Governor to Secretary of State for the Colonies, 24 February 1953.

Mau Mau.[63] While he transformed the Emergency, Erskine built on Hinde's decisions. Command and control reforms, offensive action, the PA policy, and the creation of a one-mile strip along the edges of the PAs were all instigated before Erskine's arrival.[64] The one-mile strip policy was intended to stem food supplies into the forest and allowed the security forces to monitor movement between the Reserves and the forests.[65] In September the government approved the burning down of property within the strip which owners had failed to destroy themselves.[66] But Erskine's first priority was to instil his troops with the correct ethos. His initial directive ordered 70 Brigade to be 'as aggressive and offensive as possible against the MAU MAU'.[67] Erskine assumed operational control over all the security forces and was thus able to direct a much more centralised campaign.[68] He supported the police force's expansion so that it could take control over areas cleared by the army, and expressed a clear desire for the army to avoid defensive policing tasks.[69] Keeping Hinde as his Deputy Director of Operations (DDOps) and General Cameron as deputy commander-in-chief for the rest of the East Africa theatre, Erskine concentrated his attention on quickly assuming the offensive.[70]

He deployed 39 Brigade and RAF aircraft in the Aberdares, Mobile Column A (of the armoured car unit) patrolling through the Reserves and around Mount Kenya, and 70 Brigade defensively in the Reserves and the settled areas. The army sustained almost continuous attacks throughout June and July, the first being Operation Buttercup around Fort Hall (23 June–8 July), then Operation Carnation I in South Nyeri (12–26 July), followed by Operation Grouse in Meru/Embu (10–15 July) and Operation Plover in the Rift (18 July–7 August).[71] Buttercup appeared to improve loyalist morale and civil-military cooperation alike.[72] As these operations took place, the two sides clashed in a series of brief but bloody skirmishes that had started after Lari and would continue until mid-1954.[73] Extensive search and screening operations

---

[63] Anderson, *Histories of the Hanged*, 180; Heather, 'Counterinsurgency and Intelligence in Kenya', 92.

[64] Percox, 'Counter-Insurgency in Kenya', 76.

[65] Heather, 'Counterinsurgency and Intelligence in Kenya', 94.

[66] ODRP, W. R. Hinde, MSS Afr.s.1580, Vol. IV: Director of Operations Committee minutes, 15 September 1953.

[67] TNA, WO 276/526: GHQ East Africa Operational Directive no. 1, 16 June 1953.

[68] Percox, 'Counter-Insurgency in Kenya', 75.

[69] TNA, CO 822/693: letter from Erskine to Harding (CIGS), 7 July 1953.

[70] Percox, 'Counter-Insurgency in Kenya', 76.

[71] Heather, 'Counterinsurgency and Intelligence in Kenya', 98–100.

[72] TNA, CO 822/378: KICFA 8/53, 15 July 1953.

[73] Branch, 'Loyalism during the Mau Mau Rebellion', 94.

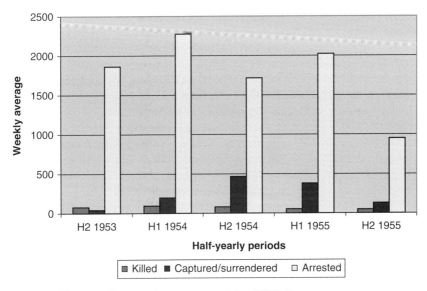

Figure 1 Counter-insurgency activity, 1953–5

were launched in Nairobi, the largest being Operation Rat Catcher (18–31 July), when 17,000 inhabitants were screened for their political allegiances. A second series of forest operations, Operation Carnation II (29 July–7 August), involved over 6,000 personnel and the RAF, but also failed in destroying gangs and diminishing the number of attacks.[74] Overall, major operations such as Buttercup succeeded in denying the Mau Mau a certain area, only for them to return once the operation concluded. Intelligence reports began to see a clear connection between a visible government presence and Mau Mau activity in an area.[75] For this reason, offensives against the armed gangs and population control measures in the Reserves relied on each other for success. Figure 1 shows the significance of arrest operations compared to the more limited number of fatalities inflicted on the Mau Mau.

From these intense actions Erskine decided to rest the Kenya Regiment, active without respite since October, and called for extra troops to escalate the offensive.[76] The pause allowed a new tactic to be developed. By 10 August, five tracks were constructed into the forest, with camps at the end, allowing for deep penetration into enemy-dominated

---

[74] Heather, 'Counterinsurgency and Intelligence in Kenya', 100–1.
[75] TNA, CO 822/373: SBFIS 10/53, 11 August 1953.
[76] TNA, CO 822/693: Letter from Erskine to Harding, 23 July 1953.

territory. Operation Primrose (10–27 August) in the Aberdares made use of the tracks for the first time. Subsequently Erskine ordered a further twenty tracks be constructed, and an element of 39 Corps Royal Engineers arrived in October to speed up their construction. After the large-scale forest operations from July and August, the army adopted a lower-profile role, using the tracks to launch small patrols, pursuing food denial measures and attempting to deny Mau Mau control of the Reserves while the police and administration strengthened their positions.[77]

The reinforcements arrived in September: 1 Black Watch replaced the Lancashire Fusiliers, 3 KAR arrived from Malaya and 49 Brigade, comprising 1 Royal Northumberland Fusiliers and 1 Royal Inniskilling Fusiliers, arrived from Britain.[78] Twelve battalions were now in Kenya, and by late October they were deployed in brigade areas where they stayed until the year's end: 39 Brigade operated in the east Aberdares, Fort Hall, South Nyeri and Thika; 49 Brigade in the western Aberdares and the Rift Valley; and 70 Brigade around Mount Kenya, Embu, Meru and Nanyuki.[79] During the late summer Erskine decided that the Mau Mau could not be beaten by military operations alone. In August he wrote to Harding that: 'Mau Mau is not like a town riot which can be brought under control by a show of force . . . Unless we deal with the fundamental causes which allowed Mau Mau to grow up and prosper we shall get further trouble in a different form.'[80] This thinking informed the decision to announce the first surrender offer on 24 August. The government publicised the offer via leaflets and word of mouth, with surrenderers instructed to carry green branches to identify themselves. It was hoped the scheme would boost the previously paltry surrender numbers, as up to this date only twenty-nine Mau Mau had given themselves up voluntarily.[81]

However, large-scale operations resumed in September, when the newly arrived and acclimatised units deployed. Some heavy losses were inflicted, but more significantly, the security forces managed to break the gangs down into smaller sizes, restricting their ability to launch attacks on loyalists and settlers. Despite this and improvements in the Reserves as the civil powers grew in strength, Nairobi remained lawless and the gangs were far from beaten.[82] Erskine decided that the eviction policy was in fact worsening matters, as it polluted the Reserves with 'bad chaps'.[83] Accordingly the practice was abandoned at the end of

---

[77] Heather, 'Counterinsurgency and Intelligence in Kenya', 105, 120.   [78] Ibid., 103.
[79] Percox, 'Counter-Insurgency in Kenya', 79.
[80] TNA, CO 822/442: letter from Erskine to Harding, 15 August 1953.
[81] Heather, 'Counterinsurgency and Intelligence in Kenya', 114–16.   [82] Ibid., 94.
[83] TNA, CO 822/693: Letter from Erskine to Harding, 29 September 1953.

September, except in exceptional circumstances, in order to stem the
flow of new recruits to Mau Mau.[84]

Operations continued in October, with the Inniskillings assisting the
Nairobi police on sweeps in African areas, resulting in notable intelligence improvements. By early November the emphasis of army operations shifted to the Mount Kenya region, with 49 Independent Infantry
Brigade in the west and 70 Brigade in the south.[85] These forest operations proved counterproductive, as they pushed many Mau Mau
fighters into the Reserves.[86] Perhaps the conduct of the campaign during
this period was also somewhat impaired by Erskine's need to focus on
discipline within the security forces. The parliamentary delegation in
Kenya from 8 to 26 January 1954 advised further developing the Home
Guard, despite their notorious reputation for abuses of power.[87]

The government enjoyed a major propaganda victory, and a turning
point in the intelligence war, when the important leader General China
fell into captivity on 15 January. His interrogation, conducted by Ian
Henderson of the Special Branch, provided invaluable insights into the
structure, deployments and *modus operandi* of the movement. Up to now
the 'Green Branch' surrender plan had been disappointing, with only
159 surrenders by 10 February. China's capture presented an opportunity for reviving the plan. However, the government was determined that
the new surrender offer should not appear as a sign of weakness, and
thus operations continued. Operation Columbus (26 March – 2 April)
involved large-scale sweeps through the Aberdares and the Fort Hall
district. The China plan involved similar conditions to the earlier 'Green
Branch' terms, with the significant difference that the government suspended the death penalty for prior offences. Unfortunately, talks mediated by China and the Special Branch with the Mau Mau were scuttled
by an accidental engagement between a KAR unit and Gatamuki's gang
at Gathuini on 7 April, as they met to discuss surrendering. This inad-
vertent episode led the Mau Mau leadership to believe the security
forces had set a deliberate trap, and so the China negotiations came to
an end.

At the political level, the Secretary of State for the Colonies, Oliver
Lyttelton, visited Kenya in March. He proposed a multiracial constitution, set up a Council of Ministers and established a small War

[84] TNA, CO 822/505: Telegram from Baring to Secretary of State for the Colonies, 28
September 1953.
[85] Heather, 'Counterinsurgency and Intelligence in Kenya', 129, 122.
[86] Branch, 'Loyalism during the Mau Mau Rebellion', 130.
[87] TNA, PREM 11/696: Report to the Secretary of State for the Colonies by the
Parliamentary Delegation to Kenya, January 1954, Cmd 9081.

Council to replace the inefficient Colony Emergency Committee. The new system increased the decision-making efficiency of the political leadership and gave Erskine greater power at the top table.[88] These reforms were vital for the next stage in the offensive, which demanded effective cooperation.

Dominating the population: Operation Anvil and villagisation, April to December 1954

These enhanced powers allowed Erskine to launch the most important military action of the Emergency, Operation Anvil. But before this the authorities cashed in on the information gleaned from China, arresting over 1,200 Mau Mau in the Reserves during Operation Overdraft (11–15 April).[89] On 16 April secret deployment for Anvil began. Erskine was determined to achieve surprise.[90] The Home Guard had been expanded in time to help patrol areas vacated by the army for Anvil, with Kikuyu Guard combat units fulfilling roles formerly taken only by the military.[91] By 4.30 am on 24 April, when the security forces sealed every road, track and path in and out of Nairobi, the government was prepared to put the 'Mau Mau's beating heart' into coronary arrest. No Africans were allowed to pass the checkpoints, and the city was a closed district for the next month, with five British battalions, one KAR battalion, 300 police, hundreds of Home Guards and numerous Kenya Police Reserve (KPR) officers systematically searching every area. Screening teams enjoyed absolute power; they detained around 24,000 people.[92] The government knew that not all of these people could be Mau Mau members, but thought the incarceration of innocents inevitable.[93] In fact the military planned to detain half the Kikuyu, Embu and Meru inhabitants before the operation began.[94] So the screening teams worked to a quota rather than making informed decisions about a person's subversive attributes. Those chosen for detention were sent away to camps, where many would remain for years without criminal charges being brought against them.

Operation Anvil marked a major turning point in the war. Mau Mau supplies, command and control and recruitment were severely disrupted,

---

[88] Heather, 'Counterinsurgency and Intelligence in Kenya', 145, 119, 157–9, 151, 160–7.
[89] *Ibid.*, 168.
[90] TNA, CO 822/774: telegram from C-in-C GHQ East Africa to VCIGS, 12 April 1954.
[91] Branch, 'Loyalism during the Mau Mau Rebellion', 131.
[92] Anderson, *Histories of the Hanged*, 200–1, 204.   [93] Maloba, *Mau Mau and Kenya*, 87.
[94] TNA, WO 276/473: Accommodation in detention camps. Note by Commander-in-Chief, 17 April 1954.

never to fully recover.[95] Other successes during the same month, such as 70 Brigade's operations in South Nyeri, northern Fort Hall and western Embu, resulting in 400 killed, were significant.[96] Although gang activity in Nairobi dramatically declined, large numbers of Mau Mau still roamed the forests with virtual impunity. Support for Mau Mau actually surged in Embu and Meru after large numbers of people were returned to the districts as part of Anvil.[97] Smaller searches were required in Nairobi afterwards, to maintain the gains made during Anvil. Operation Broom, ending on 9 August, led to 217 arrests.[98]

Anvil's impact in the city cannot be separated from what happened in the Reserves. The villagisation policy rapidly accelerated after the operation.[99] Traditionally, the Kikuyu, Embu and Meru peoples lived in small scattered settlements, which were difficult for the security forces to control. Villagisation was thus a considerable disruption to normal life, forcing people into larger villages surrounded by barbed wire, and under Home Guard protection. How far these new villages improved the standard of living and sense of security is contested. Throughout 1954 the administration villagised Central Province, with Embu and all three Kikuyu districts completed by August.[100] Although unpopular and often coercive, the policy proved highly successful from the military's perspective, allowing the authorities tight control over the population.[101] Kiambu district, in the Central Province, proved harder to villagise and the results there were less fruitful than elsewhere, as heavy gang activity continued in August and September.[102] This activity may have represented a renewed Mau Mau offensive around Nairobi, largely against the police and loyalists.[103] The attacks were futile, for two principal reasons. First, Anvil and villagisation changed the character of loyalism in Kenya. As the security of loyalists improved throughout the year, condemnations of Mau Mau from ordinary Kikuyu became more frequent. This coincided with the introduction of material benefits for loyalism in the second half of the year,

---

[95] Anderson, *Histories of the Hanged*, 244.
[96] Heather, 'Counterinsurgency and Intelligence in Kenya', 176.
[97] Branch, 'Loyalism during the Mau Mau Rebellion', 128.
[98] TNA, WO 276/42: Telegram from 49 Bde to Force Nairobi, 10 August 1954.
[99] Percox, 'Counter-Insurgency in Kenya', 85; Imperial War Museum, Sound Archive (IWMSA): R. Z. Stockwell, 10065/2.
[100] Branch, 'Loyalism during the Mau Mau Rebellion', 153.
[101] J. Newsinger, 'Revolt and Repression in Kenya: The "Mau Mau" Rebellion, 1952–1960', *Science and Society*, 45 (1981), 176.
[102] Heather, 'Counterinsurgency and Intelligence in Kenya', 202.
[103] D. M. Anderson, 'The Battle of Dandora Swamp: Reconstructing the Mau Mau Land Freedom Army October 1954', in E. S. Atieno Odhiambo and J. Lonsdale (eds.), *Mau Mau and Nationhood: Arms, Authority and Narration* (Oxford: James Currey, 2003), 162.

such as the preferential issuing of trading licences or government employ-ment.[104] Secondly, villagisation occurred alongside offensive military operations which gradually wore down the gangs.[105] By November, intel-ligence reports showed that villagisation was working in making contact between armed insurgents and their 'passive wing' supporters harder. Because their material support from the population was deteriorating, armed gangs spent longer on securing their own supplies and less time attacking people. Where gangs continued to rely on local supporters, their routes and habits became predictable, allowing the security forces to ambush them with a higher success rate than before. Screening operations in the villages were easier now the population were fixed compared to the high amount of transience earlier in the Emergency. The only perceived disadvantage was that villagisation made it more difficult for informers to circulate without people becoming suspicious.[106]

With Nairobi maintained as a secure base, post-Anvil operations developed in three phases. Phase 1 started with the districts closest to the city – Kiambu, Fort Hall and Thika, for example, with five battalions on Operation Pugilist in the Reserves in these areas. Phase 2, from August to November 1954, focused on Nyeri and Embu, with phase 3 in Meru and the settled areas next to Mount Kenya and the Aberdares. The security situation improved in all of these areas by the end of the year, with the post-Anvil operations considered militarily successful.[107] To increase the security of settler properties in the Rift Valley, the number of Farm Guards, similar to the Home Guard, was expanded by 50 per cent.[108] In addition, British soldiers on leave sometimes spent a weekend or a couple of weeks at settler farms in case of attack.[109]

By the end of 1954 the combination of military operations and villagisa-tion had largely driven the Mau Mau out of the Reserves, inflicted heavy casualties and prevented access to logistical and manpower reinforce-ments. The rebels found themselves mainly confined to the forests of the Aberdares and Mount Kenya. Not only did the security forces manage to inflict losses of over 600 per month on the Mau Mau between October and December, but the operational intelligence situation greatly improved. Havoc was wreaked on the Mau Mau by the elimination of fourteen gang leaders during 1954 and the establishment of a forest

[104] Branch, 'Loyalism during the Mau Mau Rebellion', 173, 44.
[105] Heather, 'Counterinsurgency and Intelligence in Kenya', 179.
[106] TNA, WO 276/408: Kenya intelligence summary (KISUM) 25/54, Appendix B, 1 November 1954.
[107] Heather, 'Counterinsurgency and Intelligence in Kenya', 177, 201, 203–4.
[108] Branch, 'Loyalism during the Mau Mau Rebellion', 153.
[109] IWMSA: T. L. Hewitson, 26853/12; R. J. Carriage, 18267/3.

warfare school at Nyeri.[110] These developments assumed significance in the final military stage of the Emergency, as small patrols proliferated and the hunt for key leaders such as Dedan Kimathi became an obsession.

Eliminating the forest gangs, January 1955 to November 1956

Two major forest operations took place before the shift to smaller-scale tactics. The first of these was Operation Hammer, from mid-December 1954 until 11 February 1955, in the areas immediately adjoining the Aberdares.[111] The second was Operation First Flute (22 February – 7 April) in the Mount Kenya area.[112] General Erskine was pleased with First Flute's results: 189 killed, 43 captured and 45 surrendered.[113] He set up a small number of tracker combat teams (TCTs) in July to try out smaller-scale, deep-penetration tactics.[114]

Meanwhile, several political developments took place. On 12 February the army handed over primary responsibility for law and order to the police and administration in Thika and Fort Hall districts of Central Province, and on 10 March all of Southern Province except Narok district, and all of the Rift Valley Province except for Laikipia and Naivasha districts. None the less, serious Mau Mau activity continued in Kiambu and Nyeri districts.[115] The War Council had decided in January to renew efforts to secure a mass surrender. The surrendered Major Chui played a key role with Special Branch, attempting to reach an agreement with the two senior Mau Mau leaders in the forests, Dedan Kimathi and Stanley Mathenge.[116] The final agreement benefited both Mau Mau surrenderers and the security forces. At the time, police CID investigations into serious Home Guard malpractices were thought to be undermining morale, to the point where a mutiny or widespread desertions might be provoked.[117] Therefore, on 18 January the government announced a 'double amnesty' whereby Mau Mau surrenderers would be immune from prosecution, as would all security force members for crimes committed before the amnesty. The authorities sought to partially rein in the Home Guards by disbanding them in January and absorbing them instead into the tribal police and local 'Watch and Ward' groups.[118]

---

[110] Heather, 'Counterinsurgency and Intelligence in Kenya', 173, 226, 206, 209, 233.
[111] *Ibid.*, 234. [112] *Ibid.*, 236.
[113] TNA, WO 276/450: Special Order of the Day, General Erskine to all units in Kenya, 11 April 1955.
[114] Heather, 'Counterinsurgency and Intelligence in Kenya', 237–8.
[115] *Ibid.*, 241. [116] *Ibid.*, 246.
[117] *Ibid.*, 229. [118] Branch, 'Loyalism during the Mau Mau Rebellion', 158.

Several months of difficult negotiations ensued, made more problematic by a split in the Mau Mau leadership between Kimathi and Mathenge. Security force operations continued throughout, which probably made it harder for the insurgent factions to meet and agree a common position. For example, Operation Hungerstrike took place in mid-April around Nanyuki, resulting in a decline in stock thefts in the area.[119] On 2 May 1955 Lieutenant-General Sir Gerald Lathbury arrived in Kenya and took over command from Erskine.[120] He had military experience in the Gold Coast before the Second World War, and North Africa and Europe during the war, most famously commanding a brigade at Arnhem in 1944. Just before going to Kenya he had been Commandant of the Staff College, and then the Vice-Adjutant-General.[121] Lathbury initially stuck to Erskine's approach. After negotiations broke down on 20 May when Mau Mau leaders came to a meeting without the token surrenderers they had promised, the campaign changed direction. The double amnesty, although unsuccessful in prompting a complete capitulation, achieved notable results. It yielded 979 surrenders, compared with the 857 surrenders for the entire Emergency up until January 1955.[122]

Operation Gimlet started soon afterwards, lasting until 30 June, and aimed at killing Mau Mau and splitting up the gangs in the central Aberdares.[123] This large operation involved elements of all three brigades and applied pressure leading to the withdrawal of the surrender offer on 10 July, which was widely publicised in an effort to draw more surrenders beforehand. The security situation continued to improve, with the civil powers taking control of Embu and Meru in June; Kiambu, South Nyeri, Naivasha, Laikipia and Nairobi in July; and Nanyuki in August, by which time the Royal Northumberland Fusiliers and part of the RAF could leave Kenya without replacement.[124] In these areas the government tightened its grip in the new villages by intensifying food control measures to stop people passing supplies to the Mau Mau.[125] An innovative tactic developed was the mass sweeping of Reserve locations with thousands of civilians assisting the security forces to ensure both wider coverage and loyalty on the part of the inhabitants.[126]

[119] Heather, 'Counterinsurgency and Intelligence in Kenya', 247, 240.
[120] TNA, WO 236/20: General Lathbury's final dispatch, 1.
[121] Lathbury, Sir Gerald William (1906–1978), by J. Hassan, rev. *Oxford Dictionary of National Biography* (Oxford University Press, 2004), online edition, at www.oxforddnb.com/view/article/31335, accessed 1 June 2011.
[122] Heather, 'Counterinsurgency and Intelligence in Kenya', 258, 260.
[123] TNA, WO 236/20: General Lathbury's final dispatch, 6–7.
[124] Heather, 'Counterinsurgency and Intelligence in Kenya', 259, 263.   [125] *Ibid.*, 239.
[126] Branch, 'Loyalism during the Mau Mau Rebellion', 152.

On 15 July Lathbury launched the final large-scale offensives of the Emergency. Operation Dante in the Central and Southern Aberdares, and Operation Beatrice around Mount Kenya, employed nearly every security force member in the colony. They used similar tactics to First Flute, sweeping through the forests to drive insurgents into manned stop lines on the forest edge. The objective was to break the gangs up, and in this they succeeded. From now on Lathbury would use only small, special-forces-style operations to destroy the few remaining Mau Mau.[127] These Special Methods Teams built upon the methods developed by Frank Kitson's pseudo-gangs and similar units run by the Kenya Regiment since 1953. By early 1956 the special methods teams were running most operations, sometimes using ex-Mau Mau in deep penetration, long-duration patrols into the forest to destroy the last gangs.[128] During this last phase many of the loyalist members of the labour force displaced from the Rift Valley were moved back to their former places of employment.[129] Although the Emergency continued until 12 January 1960, the military phase effectively concluded with the capture of Dedan Kimathi on 21 October 1956. British Army units were finally withdrawn from forest operations against the Mau Mau on 17 November.[130]

Countering the gangs, controlling the population

After the handling of the Emergency got off to a bad start, with poor intelligence leading to the misapplication of armed force, the conflict was gradually conducted with increasing expertise. This should come as no surprise, because initial failure followed by gradual strategic refinement is common in insurgency wars. That the security forces would hit out at the innocent was unavoidable in the beginning, given the limited information available about who the enemy were. The only alternative was for the state to wait until sophisticated knowledge concerning the erupting violence arrived. Paranoia from the settler community, and a real sense of weakness within the government, demanded offensive action.

General Hinde set in place some crucial reforms to the command system and introduced influential new policies, but the first major turning point in the conduct of operations came with Erskine's arrival

---

[127] TNA, WO 236/20: General Lathbury's final dispatch, 11–12.
[128] Heather, 'Counterinsurgency and Intelligence in Kenya', 261.
[129] Branch, 'Loyalism during the Mau Mau Rebellion', 171.
[130] For the internal security situation in Kenya between the end of military operations and independence, see D. A. Percox, 'Internal Security and Decolonization in Kenya, 1956–63', *Journal of Imperial and Commonwealth History*, 29 (2001), 92–116.

in June 1953. After a series of generally unsuccessful large-scale operations in the forests and Reserves, Erskine embarked upon the crucial
clearing of Nairobi, which along with the consolidation of government
control brought about by villagisation, would ultimately ensure the
defeat of the Mau Mau. Attempts at securing a mass surrender failed
but did prevent the war from becoming utterly indiscriminate, as did
policies such as the PAs. Recruitment of former Mau Mau members not
only provided vital intelligence, such as in the case of General China, but
also facilitated the work of pseudo-gangs and other special operations
forces. General Lathbury exploited these methods in successfully bringing the Emergency to an end. However far Hinde, Erskine and Lathbury
managed to professionalise the campaign in Kenya, they were both
unwilling and unable to halt its fundamental brutality. Tighter rules of
engagement came into force, but the strategic plan to coerce the entire
Kikuyu, Embu and Meru tribes remained a dominant theme from
October 1952 until the end. In Kenya in the 1950s, people from these
tribes were deemed guilty until proven innocent. Often proving one's
innocence was impossible whatever the evidence.

2   'Harmonious relations': soldiers, civilians and committees

The army's relations with outsiders are far from mysterious when it comes to the leading personalities in the Emergency. The opinions voiced by General Erskine, Governor Baring, settler leader Michael Blundell and Colonial Secretary Lyttelton were diligently recorded.[1] There is little doubt about the impact of personal rapport between key figures in the campaign against the Mau Mau. Such a perspective on the conflict coincides with an appreciation in studies on civil–military relations, which places the soldier–statesman dialogue at the very centre of strategy formation.[2] How should civil–military relations in Kenya be understood? This chapter analyses the relationship between soldiers and civilians in relation to the self-interest of major actors, and the institutional structures which mediated their interactions.

Writings on civil–military relations often address collaborative policy-making at the highest level in the state apparatus.[3] Many accept Samuel Huntington's idea that because war is a political phenomenon, soldiers follow directions from their political masters. The central concept is civilian control, where an autonomous military profession devises means to achieve policy ends enunciated by politicians.[4] This institutional approach examines political interaction, asking whether soldiers have obeyed, and why – or why not? Soldiers 'work or shirk', depending upon whether their masters monitor them effectively, and on a system of rewards and

---

[1] M. Blundell, *So Rough a Wind* (London: Weidenfeld and Nicolson, 1964); C. Douglas-Home, *Evelyn Baring: The Last Proconsul* (London: Collins, 1978); O. Lyttelton, *The Memoirs of Lord Chandos* (London: Bodley Head, 1962); F. Majdalany, *State of Emergency: The Full Story of Mau Mau* (Boston: Houghton Mifflin, 1963).

[2] E. A. Cohen, *Supreme Command: Soldiers, Statesmen and Leadership in Wartime* (London: Simon and Schuster, 2003), xii.

[3] Such as P. Smith (ed.), *Government and the Armed Forces in Britain 1856–1990* (London: Hambledon Press, 1996).

[4] S. P. Huntington, *The Soldier and the State: The Theory and Politics of Civil-Military Relations* (London: Belknap Press of Harvard University Press, 1985), 57, 72.

punishments.[5] Quite unlike the American experience, which informs most political theories on the subject, the British case has received scant attention. Because the British Army owes allegiance to the monarch, normally abstains from playing party politics and avoids launching *coups*, it tends to be considered almost totally apolitical.[6] Rather than the control model, the British tradition might better fit the principles of integration and mutual understanding proposed by Morris Janowitz.[7] By aligning the military's internal values and beliefs with those of civilian society, Janowitz thought they could be brought under 'subjective control'.[8] In assessing whether such convergence exists, scholars examined the close social and ideological proximity between the British military and political elites.[9] But they failed to explain how social composition affected behaviour in wartime. In this sense, the sociological approach offers few insights into British counter-insurgency.[10]

However, considering integration as well as hierarchical control is important. Effective strategy requires a dialogue between soldiers and statesmen.[11] The committee system applied in Britain's small wars promoted integration, because even tactical military action could have political ramifications.[12] Committees were suited to the political conditions present in the Kenya Emergency. The British colonial state lacked the manpower and knowledge to combat the insurgency independently, so it needed to make alliances at the local level.[13] The committees served as the vital bridge connecting government policy to variable

[5] P. D. Feaver, *Armed Servants: Agency, Oversight, and Civil-Military Relations* (London: Harvard University Press, 2003), 10, 2–3.

[6] A. Roberts, 'The British Armed Forces and Politics: A Historical Perspective', *Armed Forces and Society*, 3 (1977), 542.

[7] R. Egnell, 'Explaining US and British Performance in Complex Expeditionary Operations: The Civil-Military Dimension', *Journal of Strategic Studies*, 29 (2006), 1054.

[8] M. Janowitz, *The Professional Soldier: A Social and Political Portrait* (London: Collier-Macmillan, 1960).

[9] M. A. Garnier, 'Changing Recruitment Patterns and Organizational Ideology: The Case of a British Military Academy', *Administrative Science Quarterly*, 17 (1972), 499–507; C. B. Otley, 'The Social Origins of British Army Officers', *Sociological Review*, 18 (1970), 213–39; C. B. Otley, 'The Educational Background of British Army Officers', *Sociology*, 7 (1973), 191–209; C. B. Otley, 'Militarism and Militarization in the Public Schools, 1900–1972', *British Journal of Sociology*, 29 (1978), 321–39; P. E. Razzell, 'Social Origins of Officers in the Indian and British Home Army: 1758–1962', *British Journal of Sociology*, 14 (1963), 248–60.

[10] H. Strachan, *The Politics of the British Army* (Oxford: Clarendon Press, 1997), 11.

[11] H. Strachan, 'Making Strategy: Civil-Military Relations after Iraq', *Survival*, 48 (2006), 75, 67.

[12] Strachan, *The Politics of the British Army*, 163, 171.

[13] D. Branch, *Defeating Mau Mau, Creating Kenya: Counterinsurgency, Civil War, and Decolonization* (Cambridge University Press, 2009), 15, 26.

circumstances, and a forum for negotiating how official responses should be formulated in each specific location.

The army pursued a political association with three major actors: the provincial administration, the European settler community and the British political firmament.[14] Each group possessed considerable internal divisions and contradictions – including the army itself.[15] Thus caution must be exercised when studying these groups, because the dominant ideological fault lines in interpreting the conflict passed straight through them. As John Lonsdale argues, apart from agreeing on the need to defeat Mau Mau savagery, people belonging to the same organisational and social groups often held diametrically opposed conservative and liberal views. The conservative view thought Mau Mau a reversion to base African savagery, which could only be eradicated by punishment. By contrast, the liberal view held that modernisation had disrupted traditional ways of life, and those who followed the Mau Mau needed to be educated and reformed to understand the true benefits that modernity offered. Lonsdale states that the army held a separate conception: Mau Mau to the soldiers was a rational movement with political aims and a military strategy.[16] While certain soldiers, such as General Erskine, thought along these lines, the evidence suggests that military thought accepted elements of both the conservative and liberal interpretations simultaneously.[17] The point is that each group – the British political establishment, the settlers, the administration – held multiple, often contradictory beliefs about the Emergency. These competing views merged in policy formation and execution.[18] Each group exerted an identifiable influence on the army.

Within the British political establishment, serious influence derived mainly from the Cabinet, and in particular the Colonial Secretary, Oliver Lyttelton. The rest of the Cabinet were generally uninterested in Kenya, and Parliament and the press had limited sway. Despite short-lived press criticism and protracted pressure from a small group of backbench Labour MPs, the government ignored these critics on most questions, and they had little impact on the military. British political interference was circumscribed by the imperial principle of colonial

---

[14] These were arguably the most powerful actors. Further studies are required on the army's relationships with the police and other components of the Kenya government, international organisations and the missionary movements.

[15] R. G. L. von Zugbach, *Power and Prestige in the British Army* (Aldershot: Avebury, 1988).

[16] Lonsdale, 'Mau Maus of the Mind', 395, 405, 414.

[17] D. Kennedy, 'Constructing the Colonial Myth of Mau Mau', *International Journal of African Historical Studies*, 25 (1992), 245.

[18] Lonsdale, 'Mau Maus of the Mind', 410.

autonomy. The administration in Kenya is often seen to have exploited the opportunities provided by the Emergency to expand and re-assert its diminishing authority.[19] In doing so, provincial and district administrators resisted military influence and tried to play a leading role in directing the Emergency.[20] This chapter argues that while the administration may have wished to enhance its power, rather than seeing the army as a threat to this goal, most officers in the organisation realised that the army would help them achieve it. The administration was willing to suspend its status as the supreme authority in the African areas in exchange for the army's help in destroying the main threat to its position – African political activism. The settlers occupied a powerful position in dictating initial counter-insurgency policy. However, their influence is often exaggerated; it was successfully resisted before and after the arrival of General Erskine in June 1953.

The civil-military dialogue was institutionalised in the committee structure. The committees effectively advanced cooperation and reduced misunderstandings by providing a forum for regular debate. The military command structure could potentially have conflicted with the committees, but the dual role played by senior military commanders in aligning committees and command reduced these pitfalls to manageable proportions. There were instances when the committees exerted pressure on the military command hierarchy, and vice versa, yet in all cases the option to refer disputes upwards made resolution the likely outcome. A final threat to the cooperative attitude fostered by the committees arose from mistrust about the reliability of elements of the security forces. The Home Guard, army and police all experienced troubles with reliability which could have weakened the resolve of others to work with them; again, these were largely overcome.

Who were the civilians?

The administration

Bruce Berman argues that the provincial and district administration in Kenya must take centre stage when explaining the Emergency.[21] Under the Emergency Regulations, district officers (DOs) in the African

---

[19] Berman, *Control and Crisis*, 3, 347.
[20] Branch, *Defeating Mau Mau, Creating Kenya*, 71.
[21] B. Berman, 'Bureaucracy and Incumbent Violence. Colonial Administration and the Origins of the "Mau Mau" Emergency', in B. Berman and J. Lonsdale, *Unhappy Valley: Conflict in Kenya and Africa. Book 2: Violence and Ethnicity* (Oxford: James Currey, 1992), 230.

locations enjoyed huge discretion in how they chose to deal with the unrest.[22] New rules expanded the already considerable autonomy granted by central government to the man on the spot, who was entitled to treat higher policy as guidance open to challenge and adaptation. Discretion on such a scale prompted resistance to change, but by staffing the administration with men from a common social background the government sought to ensure broad ideological homogeneity.[23] Any disputes within the organisation tended to concern methods rather than first principles. The administration's self-interest and paternalism drove a rejection of outside interference, and an urge to crush the growing African political consciousness which threatened to undermine state power.[24]

This analysis has prompted Caroline Elkins to believe that the administration essentially ran the Emergency by late 1954, implying that the military were seen as either a threat or irrelevant in major policy fields.[25] Such an interpretation is mistaken. However much disagreement arose over methods for crushing the insurgency, the army fundamentally supported the administration's goals. As an external force, the British Army made no claim on the administration's power in Kenya, and believed tighter bureaucratic control to be the best long-term solution to the violence. Anecdotal evidence suggests that the common social background of most DOs, district commissioners (DCs) and provincial commissioners was similar to that of the British Army's officer class.[26] One British Army subaltern described the DOs he had known in Kenya as 'excellent young men on the whole; they were very brave'.[27] The shared social attitudes generated trust between officers in the army and administration, minimising friction and disagreement. When he arrived in June 1953, General Erskine was empowered by the Cabinet to assume operational command over all the security forces, and to declare martial law if he thought the situation serious enough.[28] These powers gave Erskine a strong hand, but the threat to impose martial law was never enacted, because the civil administration never completely broke down.[29]

[22] Berman, *Control and Crisis*, 363.
[23] Berman, 'Bureaucracy and Incumbent Violence', 232–4.   [24] *Ibid.*, 237, 253.
[25] C. Elkins, 'Detention and Rehabilitation during the Mau Mau Emergency: The Crisis of Late-colonial Kenya' (doctoral thesis, Harvard University, 2000), 5.
[26] Interview with General Sir Frank Kitson, Devon, 5 July 2010. See also the sources cited above in fn. 9.
[27] Interview with J. Chapman, J. McFrederick and R. Moore, formerly Royal Inniskilling Fusiliers, Windsor, 27 February 2010.
[28] Percox, 'British Counter-Insurgency in Kenya', 75.
[29] Kenya National Archives (hereafter KNA), WC/CM/1/1: Letter from General Erskine to Acting Chief Secretary, 16 February 1955.

Also within the army's power was the discretion to decide when to hand districts back to the administration and police. In February 1955 the army turned primary responsibility over to the administration and police in Thika and Fort Hall districts, and then also Southern Province (except Narok District) and Rift Valley Province (except Laikipia and Naivasha Districts) on 10 March. The administration and police took control of Embu and Meru districts in June 1955, Kiambu, South Nyeri, Naivasha, Laikipia and Nairobi in July and Nanyuki in August.[30] By deciding when control could safely be transferred, substantial authority rested with the army. In practice the army were eager to hand over control quickly, in order to concentrate on fighting the Mau Mau in the forests without restriction, as these were free-fire PAs.[31] General Erskine took the initiative in suggesting to the Minister for African Affairs and the Commissioner of Police that the first handover should happen in February 1955.[32] After the handover in a district the civil authorities could still call for military assistance, through the provincial joint operations committees.[33] Military representatives stopped attending district committees, and as such ceased to have any influence over local policy in these areas.[34] The administration's temporary suspension of its supreme authority in the African areas thus paid off once a handover had taken place.

The European settlers

According to many accounts, the European settlers in Kenya played a decisive part in shaping the reaction to Mau Mau, pushing the government to crush the revolt harshly and swiftly.[35] The Kenya government's susceptibility to settler demands was a long-standing problem in the colony.[36] Authors credit settler influence with moves such as expanding the number of capital offences,[37] arresting Jomo Kenyatta and other African political leaders,[38] and government participation in the mass

---

[30] Heather, 'Counterinsurgency and Intelligence in Kenya', 241, 263.

[31] TNA, WO 276/450: GHQ Operation Instruction no. 34, 16 August 1955, directed all battalions to place three companies in forest operations, with one company training.

[32] KNA, WC/CM/1/1: Operational Command in Fort Hall and Thika. Note by the Commander-in-Chief, 19 January 1955.

[33] TNA, WO 276/174: CPEC minutes of a meeting held on 11 February 1955.

[34] KNA, RN/4/113: Nairobi Extra-Provincial DEC minutes of a meeting held on 2 November 1955.

[35] F. Brockway, *African Journeys* (London: Victor Gollancz, 1955), 131; Newsinger, *British Counterinsurgency*, 60.

[36] J. Lonsdale, 'Kenya: Home County and African Frontier', in R. Bickers (ed.), *Settlers and Expatriates: Britons over the Seas* (Oxford University Press, 2010), 74.

[37] *Ibid.*, 106; Berman, *Control and Crisis*, 358.

[38] Douglas-Home, *Evelyn Baring*, 228; Anderson, *Histories of the Hanged*, 63.

eviction of Kikuyu squatter labour from the Rift Valley in early 1953.[39] Pressure on the government increased following violence against Europeans. In the most dramatic demonstration, large numbers marched on Government House on 25 January 1953, after the Ruck family were hacked to death the day before.[40] Or, as a Treasury Department civil servant more placidly regarded the event on hearing about it in his Nairobi clubhouse, 'the deputation of over 1000 Europeans who tried to see the Governor'.[41] The government could hardly afford to ignore settlers entirely, as their numbers grew from around 42,000 in 1953 to about 54,000 in 1956.[42]

But their political power must be accurately assessed. Europeans were divided on a range of issues, along town and country as much as conservative-liberal lines.[43] At times settlers condemned excessive violence; in November 1953 R. E. V. Denning complained about screening teams in Naivasha beating up his employees. The authorities deemed his allegations to be a 'frame-up', concocted by a man with 'a rather unsavoury past'.[44] The harsh measures often attributed to settler influence had, in the preceding few years alone, been implemented by the British Army and colonial governments in Malaya and Palestine, where settlers played a less prominent political role.[45] Just because the settlers called for a harsh reaction to the revolt, this does not mean that the colonial state would otherwise have abstained from repression. Berman argues their influence was reduced by bringing them into the state apparatus.[46] If anything, the government's intention here was to enhance the state's repressive power by increasing manpower resources and local knowledge rather than aiming to moderate extreme behaviour. The White Highland farmers who tended to join the KPR and Kenya

---

[39] R. B. Edgerton, *Mau Mau: An African Crucible* (London: Collier Macmillan, 1989), 76; Heather, 'Counterinsurgency and Intelligence in Kenya', 41.

[40] Anderson, *Histories of the Hanged*, 95.

[41] British Library, A. Hume, MSS Eur D724/84, diary entry 26 January 1953.

[42] Anderson, *Histories of the Hanged*, 84.

[43] Lonsdale, 'Kenya: Home County and African Frontier', 79; Lonsdale, 'Mau Maus of the Mind', 394.

[44] Witness statement number three of Huw Bennett, in the case of *Ndiku Mutua and others v. Foreign and Commonwealth Office*, Queen's Bench Division in the High Court of Justice, 25 May 2012 (hereafter Bennett witness statement 3), citing Hanslope document INT 10/4/2/2/9A: Naivasha district intelligence committee summary, 27 November 1953.

[45] H. Bennett, '"A very salutary effect": The Counter-Terror Strategy in the Early Malayan Emergency, June 1948 to December 1949', *Journal of Strategic Studies*, 32 (2009), 415–44; D. A. Charters, *The British Army and Jewish Insurgency in Palestine, 1945–47* (Basingstoke: Macmillan, 1989).

[46] Berman, *Control and Crisis*, 352.

Regiment continued practising brutality on the Kikuyu population once in uniform, a pattern which continued to the Emergency's end.[47]

Socialising brought intimacy between settlers and soldiers, especially in a shared enthusiasm for sporting pursuits.[48] A special scheme sought to assuage settler fears about the Mau Mau by giving soldiers weekend leave on farms. The side effect was better mutual understanding.[49] Personal connections changed relations between soldiers and settlers quite noticeably at times. Captain Richard Unett, with the King's Own Yorkshire Light Infantry in Kenya in August 1955, was relieved when his company commander went home on leave, as 'He didn't "get on" with the settlers.' His replacement did, and consequently life was easier.[50] At a senior level, Major-General Hinde's personal reputation for sympathising with the settlers attracted condemnation from some in government, and plaudits from those who noticed the benefits in areas where the security forces needed settler assistance, such as in food denial.[51]

Apparently the harmony produced a willingness in the army to disperse military units in small packets in the settled areas to protect farmers from attack in the first few months of the Emergency.[52] This should come as no surprise – disagreements over whether troops should be used defensively or offensively were common in Britain's small wars.[53] Platoons were widely spread out in many places.[54] Commanders needed to protect vital positions, such as the command ammunition depot at Gilgil, from potential Mau Mau assault.[55] But the army did conduct active offensive patrols throughout the early phase. Far from caving in to settler demands, small patrols operated because they allowed frequent activity throughout the Emergency districts with the limited manpower available. An intelligence report in February 1953 noted 'a very sharp rise in MAU MAU casualties, many of which have been inflicted by the Security Forces in offensive as opposed to defensive operations'.[56] However, a report from the end of March recognised

---

[47] Kennedy, 'Constructing the Colonial Myth of Mau Mau', 246; Anderson, 'The Battle of Dandora Swamp', 165.
[48] Clayton and Killingray, *Khaki and Blue*, 217.
[49] Edgerton, *Mau Mau: An African Crucible*, 165.
[50] Staffordshire Record Office, R. Unett, D3610/21/7/1–30: Letter from Captain R. Unett, King's Own Yorkshire Light Infantry, Kenya, to 'Mum and Dad', 31 August 1955.
[51] Anderson, *Histories of the Hanged*, 179.
[52] Heather, 'Counterinsurgency and Intelligence in Kenya', 37.
[53] Townshend, *Britain's Civil Wars*, 31.
[54] TNA, WO 305/261: Historical record of 7 KAR, 1 April 1953 to 31 March 1954.
[55] TNA, WO 305/265: War diary of 'A' Company, 26 KAR, 5 February 1953 to 23 November 1953.
[56] TNA, WO 276/378: Jock Scott intelligence summary, 27 February 1953.

military deployments in the settled areas to protect European farms.[57] Wherever possible, the army sought to pass responsibility to the civil authorities for static defensive tasks, such as guarding detention camps.[58]

Under General Erskine's auspices, the army's relationship with the settlers became rather hostile. His arrival ushered in the end of settler influence.[59] Erskine explicitly refused to waste troops on defensive tasks in the Rift Valley settler areas. John Lonsdale argues British troops were sent by London to stop the settlers taking control.[60] Building upon this idea, Randall Heather asserts that Erskine threatened martial law in order to quell the settlers.[61] Rather than displacing the settlers, though, the arriving British troops drew them closely into the security infrastructure as policemen, administrators, soldiers and intelligence agents. Erskine could hardly employ martial rule as a threat against the settlers when many of them urgently wished for its application. Philip Murphy asserts that General Erskine left Kenya because the settlers demanded his removal.[62] Apart from disregarding the fact that settler calls for Erskine's removal began almost immediately after he arrived, the claim is contradicted by archival evidence. The Cabinet Secretary's notebook records the Secretary of State for War, Antony Head, as saying that Erskine's agreed two-year appointment had finished, and Erskine himself wished to leave Kenya.[63] According to Frank Kitson, Erskine was the personal choice of Winston Churchill, which put him in a very strong position and ensured that his views carried great weight in all matters connected with the conduct of the Emergency.[64]

The historiography overemphasises settler influence on the army and downplays the military's ability to institutionalise European Kenyans in the chain of command and the counter-insurgency strategy. Through the committee system the army embraced the settlers, monitoring them, restricting their freedom of action, listening to them intently – and ignoring them. In September 1953 Group Captain Briggs, the European member on the CPEC, expressed concern about possible attacks in the settled areas. The Commander of 39 Brigade promised that a task force

[57] TNA, CO 822/378: KICFA no. 1/53, 31 March 1953.
[58] TNA, WO 276/475: 'Security of detention camps. Note by the Commander-in-Chief', c. July 1954.
[59] Anderson, *Histories of the Hanged*, 180.
[60] Lonsdale, 'Mau Maus of the Mind', 408.
[61] R. W. Heather, 'Of Men and Plans: The Kenya Campaign as Part of the British Counterinsurgency Experience', *Conflict Quarterly*, 13 (1993), 19.
[62] P. Murphy, *Alan Lennox-Boyd: A Biography* (London: I. B. Tauris, 1999), 154.
[63] TNA, CAB 195/13: Record of the Cabinet meeting held on 13 January 1955.
[64] Interview with General Sir Frank Kitson.

would assault any definite gang positions, hardly the defensive reassurance Briggs hoped for.[65] From September 1954 the CPEC endeavoured to calm settler concerns by providing them with operational briefings, in Nyeri and Nanyuki, every two months. By December the Commander of 70 Brigade was complaining of a very poor attendance at these meetings.[66] The settlers were thus on some occasions apathetic about trying to influence the army. A final corrective concerning settler influence is the comparison of aspiration with achievement. Many settlers wanted harsher repression. Writing in April 1954, settler leader Michael Blundell condemned General Erskine's policy in the following terms:

It appears to me that at the present time the great majority of the Kikuyu people are in the position of having their cake and eating it. That is to say, they can encourage and assist the Terrorist Movement in the Reserves with a view to overthrowing the Government and at the same time receive benefits from the Government in the form of social services and economic life. I am sure that we should treat the whole Kikuyu people as one. Tell them that unless the support of the gangs and the Mau Mau Movement ceases at one [sic], economic sanctions will be placed on the whole tribe with the exception of the Resistance Groups who are cooperating with Government ... It seems to me at the present time we alternatively [sic] kick the kid in the pants and then give it an ice cream.[67]

Blundell advocated a policy based solely on harsh repression. Although the military strategy contained elements of repression, it also included elements of restraint, as this book will show. The army's ability to ignore the settlers' demand to resort to the stick and abandon the carrot says a great deal about their limited influence.

Settler soldiers: the Kenya Regiment

The Kenya Regiment was supposedly created to control settler political aspirations.[68] During the Emergency, approximately 1,800 men served in the regiment, which posted about 300 soldiers to the KAR.[69] The army high command only partially managed to impose discipline on the Kenya Regiment, and relied upon them for local knowledge. Arguably the regiment received decorations for its services wholly disproportionate

---

[65] TNA, WO 276/170: CPEC minutes, 18 September 1953.
[66] TNA, WO 276/438: CPEC minutes, 3 September 1954 and 17 December 1954.
[67] TNA, WO 276/473: Notes on Commander-in-Chief's memorandum on Emergency Administrative Policy, WAR/C.15, signed M. Blundell, 1 April 1954.
[68] Clayton and Killingray, *Khaki and Blue*, 213.
[69] I. Parker, *The Last Colonial Regiment: The History of the Kenya Regiment (T.F.)* (Kinloss: Librario Publishing, 2009), 206–7, 261.

to its size.[70] It was honoured with one OBE, nine MBEs, five MCs, one DCM, five GMs, six MMs, ten BEMs, one QPMG, two CPMs, thirty Mentions in Despatches and fifteen C-in-C's Commendations.[71]

Brigadier Donald Cornah, in charge of Northern Brigade from 18 January 1953, recalled that his command had to turn 'the Nelson blind eye' to Kenya Regiment behaviour from time to time.[72] General Sir Frank Kitson was then a captain working as the MIO for Kiambu and Thika districts to which over time were added Nairobi and Narok. He also had some responsibilities in relation to Fort Hall district. In this capacity he directed the activities of the Kenya Regiment personnel operating as DMIOs and FIAs in these districts. He recalled that although these men needed much latitude to devise their own solutions in diverse field conditions, they none the less followed his instructions in the same way as any other British army soldier would do.[73] There is no doubt that the regiment contained individuals with hard-line views about the Emergency, and about Africans in general. But these views were not neatly confined; a war diary from mid-Emergency hoped for 3 KAR's lengthier placement in an area, in order to 'strike terror into the hearts of the civil population'.[74] Similarly, the Kenya Regiment's commanding officer (CO), Lieutenant-Colonel Guy Campbell, noted in 1955 his belief that 'The Kikuyu must be taught a lesson that will be remembered for generations and which will act as a warning to other tribes'.[75]

So views on the conflict cannot be neatly demarcated simply with reference to regiment. British regular officers serving with the Kenya Regiment, including the CO Guy Campbell, all came from one of two English regiments, namely the King's Royal Rifle Corps or the Rifle Brigade. They therefore shared a common regimental background with a number of the other British officers in the colony at the time, including General Erskine. This may have made it easier for the Kenya Regiment to work with British units.[76] In September 1953 the Governor met the Kenya Regiment's officers, who pressed him to propose a clear political plan for the colony's future. Baring resisted these calls, asserting this was an inappropriately political question for soldiers to raise, and told the

---

[70] L. Weaver, 'The Kenya Regiment', in M. Page, *A History of the King's African Rifles and East African Forces* (London: Leo Cooper, 1998), 249.

[71] TNA, WO 276/542: Booklet, 'The Story of the Kenya Regiment T.F. 1937–1959', 22–4.

[72] Kenya Regiment Archive (hereafter KRA), Vol. VI: Notes on the Mau Mau affair, from Brigadier Donald Cornah to Guy Campbell, no date; War Office, *The Army List, April 1953* (London: War Office, 1953), 99.

[73] Interview with General Sir Frank Kitson.

[74] TNA, WO 276/492: 3 KAR historical record, April 1954 to March 1955.

[75] KRA, Vol. VIa: Typed papers, marked 'Narok 1955'.

[76] Interview with General Sir Frank Kitson.

officers to concentrate on defeating the Mau Mau.[77] Events such as this suggest that the regiment, and the settler community from which it was recruited, was less uniformly conservative than some believed. It did have political power. When East Africa Command attempted to break up the regiment in 1955, its commander argued that settler opinion demanded that the unit retain an independent operational capacity.[78] Campbell railed against merging into British units because his soldiers held a 'conception of discipline ... influenced by an independent Colonial outlook ... The best is brought out of the Kenya youth by a wide application of discipline and I do NOT see this working harmoniously should the Kenya Regiment be completely "married" to a British Regiment.'[79] GHQ dropped the plan to attach complete platoons to British battalions and the Kenya Regiment retained an operational company.

Commanders knew that the settlers possessed the potential to cause unwelcome difficulties. Wishing to avoid trouble, and hungry for local knowledge and manpower, the army chose to harness the settlers to the campaign, expanding the colonial state, the Kenya Regiment and including settlers in the committees at every level. Settlers in uniform could overstep the line of acceptable behaviour, earning them reprimands from the high command, but those same commanders needed the settlers and, in many senses, agreed with them on the requirement to crush the Mau Mau violently.

British politics

The Cabinet

Writings on the British Army and government head in two opposing directions. One approach thinks that the military are less likely to achieve political goals without supervision from statesmen.[80] Politicians and the press certainly maintained a close interest in events in Kenya.[81] Alternatively, the nature of British politics and the imperial system is thought to have militated against tight civilian control. Because society was broadly sympathetic to the military and deemed soldiers highly professional, politicians seldom felt compelled to interfere.[82] Parliament failed to

---

[77] KNA, AH/5/2: Record of the meeting of H.E. the Governor with officers of the Kenya Regiment, 26 September 1953.

[78] TNA, WO 276/91: Letter from Major-General Heyman to Secretary, Emergency Joint Staff, 28 September 1955.

[79] TNA, WO 276/91: Letter from Guy Campbell to unknown recipient, 30 September 1955.

[80] Feaver, *Armed Servants*, 112; Cohen, *Supreme Command*, 5, 16.

[81] A. Clayton, *Counter-Insurgency in Kenya: A Study of Military Operations against Mau Mau* (Nairobi: Transafrica Publishers, 1976), 37, 40.

[82] Huntington, *The Soldier and the State*, 97.

compensate for the resulting complacency, as cross-party agreement existed on most defence issues, in an era when politics was highly consensual.[83] During operations within the Empire, the principle of indirect rule limited Whitehall's powers. Colonial rule relied upon local consent and collaboration, and due to extended lines of communication, deferred much decision-making to the 'man on the spot'.[84] In the Cabinet, only the Colonial Secretary sustained an energetic involvement, backing the army against the settlers and shielding East Africa Command from a spirited parliamentary lobby. Foreshadowing practice in Kenya, the Cabinet sustained its power to monitor faraway events by asking the various arms of government to report on each other's progress. So the lack of persistent Cabinet interference in military affairs might reasonably be adjudged the product of successful surveillance and soldiers and statesmen finding themselves in almost permanent consonance.

Within the Cabinet responsibility for the army in Kenya was split. The Prime Minister had supreme responsibility for defence.[85] From 1946 a Minister of Defence sat in Cabinet, a post held by Earl Alexander from March 1952 until he was succeeded by Harold Macmillan in October 1954, Selwyn Lloyd from April to December 1955 and Walter Monckton until October 1956. Winston Churchill behaved as though he held the office, and left the official ministers practically redundant. Even under Anthony Eden's premiership the Minister of Defence made no noticeable mark on events in Kenya.[86] Already eighty-one on the declaration of a State of Emergency, Churchill's deteriorating health

[83] P. Hennessy, *Having It So Good: Britain in the Fifties* (London: Allen Lane, 2006), 236.

[84] P. Murphy, *Party Politics and Decolonization: The Conservative Party and British Colonial Policy in Tropical Africa, 1951–1964* (Oxford: Clarendon Press, 1995), 14.

[85] N. Singh, *The Defence Mechanism of the Modern State: A Study of the Politico-Military Set-up of National and International Organisations with Special Reference to the Chiefs of Staff Committee* (New York: Asia Publishing House, 1964), 14.

[86] F. A. Johnson, *Defence by Committee: The British Committee of Imperial Defence 1885–1959* (Oxford University Press, 1960), 338; Alexander, Harold Rupert Leofric George, first Earl Alexander of Tunis (1891–1969), by D. Hunt, rev. *Oxford Dictionary of National Biography* (Oxford University Press, 2008), online edition, at www.oxforddnb.com/view/article/30371, accessed 7 July 2010; Lloyd, (John) Selwyn Brooke, Baron Selwyn-Lloyd (1904–1978), by D. R. Thorpe, *Oxford Dictionary of National Biography* (Oxford University Press, 2009), online edition, at www.oxforddnb.com/view/article/31371, accessed 7 July 2010; Macmillan, (Maurice) Harold, first earl of Stockton (1894–1986), by H. C. G. Matthew, *Oxford Dictionary of National Biography* (Oxford University Press, 2009), online edition, at www.oxforddnb.com/view/article/40185, accessed 7 July 2010; 'Monckton, Walter Turner, first Viscount Monckton of Brenchley (1891–1965)', by M. Pugh, *Oxford Dictionary of National Biography* (Oxford University Press, 2008), online edition, at www.oxforddnb.com/view/article/35061, accessed 7 July 2010.

probably limited his ability to monitor and intervene in events in Kenya. Roy Jenkins and Peter Hennessy consider him to have been unfit for office in the 1950s, often failing to read documents.[87] Despite these problems, in March 1953 Churchill asked in the Cabinet Defence Committee whether helicopters could be used in Kenya; and in May he advised in Cabinet against mass executions being allowed.[88] These interventions show that his military and political judgements remained sound, but after his stroke in June, his ability to supervise diminished severely.[89]

The other two ministers directly concerned were the Secretaries of State for War and the Colonies. Antony Head served at the War Office throughout the military phase of the Emergency.[90] From the archival record, he seems to have taken hardly any interest in the conflict. For a generation of soldiers and politicians exposed to the Second World War, Kenya was a minor sideshow, a distraction from the potential for nuclear combat against the Soviet Union.[91] In contrast the Colonial Secretary observed events carefully and intervened when necessary. Oliver Lyttelton, in post from October 1951 until July 1954, played an active part in proceedings. He wanted the rebellion to be crushed first, with political reform coming afterwards.[92] Lyttelton visited Kenya in late October 1952 to assess the situation for himself. The Secretary of State met settler politicians in two separate sessions. At the first meeting, Michael Blundell argued that only drastic action could succeed in quelling the trouble. Ideally this meant 'shooting and a considerable number of deaths . . . it would clearly establish that force lay with Government'. In addition, collective fines would help matters along. Lyttelton rejected both notions.[93] At the second meeting another settler, Mr Edye, pressed for harder methods against the Mau Mau, saying:

This question of shooting people. I feel that until some real sign of force is shown, to show that you mean business – I am not advocating wholesale shooting, I am wondering how far the police have been restricted in their use of fire arms – if there is any restriction.

---

[87] R. Jenkins, *Churchill* (London: Macmillan, 2001), 845–6; Hennessy, *Having It So Good*, 179.

[88] M. Gilbert, *Never Despair: Winston S. Churchill 1945–1965* (London: Heinemann, 1988), 803, 834.

[89] P. Hennessy, *The Prime Minister: The Office and its Holders since 1945* (London: Allen Lane, 2000), 181, 187–8.

[90] Head, Antony Henry, first Viscount Head (1906–1983), by J. Colville, rev. *Oxford Dictionary of National Biography* (Oxford University Press, 2008) online edition, at www.oxforddnb.com/view/article/31214, accessed 7 July 2010.

[91] Interview with General Sir Frank Kitson.

[92] Lyttelton, *Memoirs of Lord Chandos*, 397.

[93] TNA, CO 822/460: 'Verbatim report. Meeting of Secretary of State and European Elected Members, held at Government House on Thursday, 30 October 1952 at 12.00 pm.

In his response, Lyttelton strongly resisted the implied suggestion, show-ing that the Cabinet offered a bulwark against settler demands for totally indiscriminate and widespread repression:

You are entering, naturally, as everybody will agree, an extremely dangerous area of Government action ... I mean, to go to the extreme case, where you gave police officers everywhere unlimited power to act as they thought fit, at the very best you could expect out of that would be widely different action, according to a man's temperament, or how he felt in the afternoon, which is the first way of bringing all forms of Government into disrepute, the tough guy attitude. One has to be frightfully careful. I would quite agree in these circumstances you do not want to put unnecessary restrictions on them, but there must be a very large measure of restriction, otherwise – I am not suggestion [*sic*] that is the point you are making – once you have said to the police 'Act as you think fit' you are in fact abrogating the principal function of Government.[94]

Thus the Cabinet rejected the proposal to permit the police to shoot anyone they chose. This restriction applied equally to the army.

Later chapters will fully assess how far the restrictions were adhered to in practice. In the back of Lyttelton's mind during the meeting with settlers were the words of Mr Mathu, the African politician who had spoken to him barely an hour or so earlier. Mathu complained how, despite protestations to the Governor and his senior officers, large numbers of innocent Africans continued to be mistreated.[95] Speaking to Kenya in a radio broadcast on 4 November, Lyttelton asserted that it was only 'by these qualities of decision and restraint and not in the spirit of reprisal that we must seek to restore and maintain the Queen's peace'.[96] Back in London, the Colonial Secretary updated the Cabinet on 14 and 21 October about Baring's plans, including the arrest operations, the need for emergency powers and the reinforcement by 1 Lancashire Fusiliers.

Churchill's proposal of a demonstration parachute drop to frighten the rebels was judged impractical by Earl Alexander and quickly forgot-ten.[97] In 1953 Lyttelton's parliamentary private secretary, Hugh Fraser,

---

[94] TNA, CO 822/460: Verbatim report. Meeting of Secretary of State and Nominated Official Members, held at Government House on Thursday, 30th October, 1952 at 5.30 pm.

[95] TNA, CO 822/460: Verbatim report. Meeting of Secretary of State and African Representative Elected Members, held at Government House on Thursday, 30th October, 1952 at 3.45 pm.

[96] TNA, CO 822/459: Transcript of speech broadcast by Oliver Lyttelton on 4 November 1952 from Nairobi.

[97] TNA, CAB 195/10: Cabinet Secretary's record of Cabinet meetings on 14 October 1952 and 21 October 1952.

visited the country for the government.[98] Fraser noted that troop numbers were insufficient for widespread and constant offensive action.[99] By May Lyttelton confidently reported to the Cabinet that intelligence on the Mau Mau was very full and the atmosphere much improved. All that was needed was 'more punch and a few more troops to bring it off'.[100] The Secretaries of State for War and the Colonies agreed in late May 1953 on the need to inject greater urgency into the campaign by appointing General Erskine.[101] When the new Commander-in-Chief asked for reinforcements in August, Head and Lyttelton backed him in Cabinet and quickly acquired Churchill's approval.[102] Hugh Fraser returned to Kenya in September in order to observe the new arrangements. He found that:

Possibly the Kenya top combination is a good one. Erskine tends to be too decisive and H.E. not decisive enough. At lower levels relations seem in general to be harmonious. Generally I have only one main criticism which I have expressed to Sir George Erskine in more delicate language: 'Couldn't he get on faster, and couldn't his planning be a trifle less rigid?' Nevertheless, if a trifle elephantine, Erskine is being a success.[103]

Despite the convention of trusting the man on the spot, matters in Kenya were considered sufficiently serious for the Colonial Secretary and his envoys to monitor progress through visits and direct interventions. In February 1954, the Cabinet discussed the on-going surrender negotiations which attracted such opposition from the settlers. Churchill thought Mau Mau General China should be spared execution in reward for his efforts to bring about further surrenders, whereas Lyttelton preferred to leave the decision to Baring. Ultimately China was spared the noose.[104] When Lyttelton met provincial commissioners in Nairobi in March, the Commissioner for Central Province congratulated the army for 'establishing good relations in the Reserve, particularly with the Kikuyu Guard'.[105] Asking one arm of the state to comment on the

[98]   Fraser, Sir Hugh Charles Patrick Joseph (1918–1984), by J. Biggs-Davison, rev. *Oxford Dictionary of National Biography* (Oxford University Press, 2004), online edition, at www.oxforddnb.com/view/article/31122, accessed 7 July 2010.

[99]   TNA, CO 822/479: Paper attached to report by Hugh Fraser MP, 'Instruments of policy against the Mau Mau', 14 April 1953.

[100] TNA, CAB 195/11: Cabinet Secretary's record of meeting held on 21 May 1953.

[101] TNA, CO 822/457: Letter to Minister of Defence from A. H. Head, 27 May 1953.

[102] TNA, CAB 195/11: Cabinet Secretary's record of meeting held on 18 August 1953.

[103] TNA, CO 822/479: Report of visit to Kenya 17th Sept. – 5th October by the Hon. H. C. P. J. Fraser, MBE, MP.

[104] TNA, CAB 195/11: Cabinet Secretary's record of meetings held on 10 February 1954 and 17 February 1954.

[105] TNA, CO 822/822: Minutes of a meeting between the Secretary of State for the Colonies and Provincial Commissioners held at Government House, Nairobi, on the 1st March 1954.

performance of another proved an efficient monitoring method for a Cabinet far removed from the action.

Alan Lennox-Boyd succeeded Lyttelton as Colonial Secretary in July 1954. He believed in using force to retain Britain's colonial possessions, making him sympathetic to the army. Like his predecessors, he upheld the notion of deferring to the man on the spot. When it came to complaints in Parliament and the press about brutality in Kenya, he sought to rebuff the allegations rather than change government policy.[106] Although Lennox-Boyd played a less prominent part in the Emergency than Lyttelton, this was due to the contours of the campaign having already been decided prior to his appointment, rather than his lack of interest. On visiting Kenya in September 1954 Lennox-Boyd discovered the settlers dissatisfied with cooperation between the army and the police, which they claimed hindered operations. He heard criticism about military tactics, especially large patrols and aerial bombing. Lennox-Boyd ignored the settlers, and both practices continued. Governor Baring thought General Erskine should be retained until the next year. Baring further expressed his confidence in senior officers such as Chief of Staff Major-General Heyman and Brigadier Thurlow.[107]

The Colonial Secretary backed General Erskine's push for a renewed surrender scheme in January 1955, arguing in Cabinet that 'This is [the] moment for [an] imaginative move'.[108] Whether under Lyttelton or Lennox-Boyd at the Colonial Office, or Churchill or Eden in the premiership, the Cabinet consistently prioritised defeating the Mau Mau militarily before moving on to political, social and economic reforms in Kenya.[109] The Cabinet took important steps to support General Erskine in his efforts to improve discipline in the army through the Griffiths courts-martial and the McLean Court of Inquiry, discussed in chapter 5. But here, as with the reinforcements granted by London, the initiative came from GHQ in Nairobi, with London acting to monitor events and approve suggestions. Lyttelton's early visits to the country placed clear limitations on what the government would accept from the settler community and reinforced the argument made here for reassessing the impact of these Europeans on military policy. The Cabinet generally trusted the army to conduct operations with the minimum of supervision from London.

---

[106] Murphy, *Alan Lennox-Boyd*, 102, 104, 151.
[107] TNA, 822/823: Notes on visit to Kenya, 10 September 1954.
[108] TNA, CAB 195/13: Cabinet Secretary's record of a meeting held on 13 January 1955.
[109] Percox, 'British Counter-Insurgency in Kenya', 65.

Parliament and press

Despite formal legal subordination, since 1945 the British Army has avoided rigorous parliamentary scrutiny.[110] Party discipline has kept a firm grasp on MPs, permitting little intra-party dissent on defence matters.[111] In opposition, Labour largely agreed with Churchill's policies on defence, except on nuclear weapons. The defence debate remained an area of high politics, largely removed from parliamentary and public influence.[112] There were exceptions to this – such as the popular calls for withdrawal from Palestine in 1948 following the high-profile murders of British servicemen – but nothing of the sort roused popular interest in the army in Kenya.[113] A similar situation prevailed regarding colonial affairs. Though formally also the imperial Parliament, Westminster was in reality a minor player in the colonial political system.[114] Few clashes over the colonies arose within the Conservative party during the Emergency. Most important ministerial decisions on Africa were never debated in Parliament.[115] The Colonial Office tried to avoid parliamentary scrutiny, a desire which was aided by the broad cross-party consensus on colonial matters.[116] In late July 1955 the Kenyan authorities provided information to the Colonial Office in response to a parliamentary question from Anthony Wedgwood Benn MP about offences committed by Europeans against Africans. Nairobi listed seven cases since October 1952, all connected to the Emergency.[117] As we shall see in chapters 7 and 8, the list seriously misrepresented the situation, contradicting much information sent to London since the Emergency's start.

---

[110] Strachan, *The Politics of the British Army*, 265.

[111] P. Norton (ed.), *Dissension in the House of Commons: Intra-Party Dissent in the House of Commons' Division Lobbies 1945–1974* (London: Macmillan, 1975).

[112] W. P. Snyder, *The Politics of British Defense Policy, 1945–1962* (Columbus, OH: Ohio State University Press, 1964), 47–8, 66, 77.

[113] P. Dixon, 'Britain's "Vietnam syndrome"? Public Opinion and British Military Intervention from Palestine to Yugoslavia', *Review of International Studies*, 26 (2000), 99–121.

[114] V. Bogdanor (ed.), *The British Constitution in the Twentieth Century* (Oxford University Press for the British Academy, 2003), 19; Murphy, *Party Politics and Decolonization*, 12.

[115] Murphy, *Party Politics and Decolonization*, 2, 23.

[116] R. Holland, 'Britain, Commonwealth and the End of Empire', in V. Bogdanor (ed.), *The British Constitution in the Twentieth Century* (Oxford University Press for the British Academy, 2003), 656; J. Lewis and P. Murphy, 'The Old Pals' Protection Society? The Colonial Office and the British Press on the Eve of Decolonisation', in C. Kaul (ed.), *Media and the British Empire* (Basingstoke: Palgrave Macmillan, 2006), 55.

[117] Bennett witness statement 3, citing Hanslope document CAB 19/4 Vol. I: Savingram from the Officer Administering the Government of Kenya to the Secretary of State for the Colonies, Parliamentary Question, 28 July 1955.

At the outset, the opposition pledged to support the government's desire to crush the Mau Mau rebellion.[118] Official Labour support for the government was challenged by a group of committed, persistent critics.[119] A parliamentary motion in December 1952 condemned the way the Emergency was being handled.[120] Fenner Brockway MP and the Congress of Peoples Against Imperialism voiced concerns about settler racism and its imprint on British policy, while urging greater concentration on remedying the conflict's economic causes.[121] By aiming first to crush the rebellion, with economic reforms coming later, the government rejected Brockway's appeals. When Brockway and fellow MP Leslie Hale visited Kenya in 1953 they were obstructed from talking to Africans on several occasions; so Parliament's ability to monitor government action, let alone criticise it, faced severe limitations.[122] When Barbara Castle MP visited the colony in 1955 her movements were closely monitored by the intelligence services, who thought her to be 'endeavouring to obtain information on atrocities committed by Security Forces in Kenya'.[123] Although there is anecdotal evidence that soldiers knew about the opinions espoused by Brockway and others, there is no evidence showing that this knowledge changed military behaviour.[124] After Labour MPs queried the utility of area bombing in the PAs, General Erskine produced arguments and statistics to prove the tactic's value, and continued using it as before.[125] The most heated parliamentary debates on Kenya, at their height in the autumn of 1955, concerned detention policy rather than the army. Even here Lennox-Boyd preferred to ignore his critics instead of changing course.[126] According to one source, MPs asked thirty-one questions on the Mau Mau from 1952 to late 1955, twenty-five of which concerned detention.[127]

---

[118] D. Goldsworthy, *Colonial Issues in British Politics 1945–1961: From 'Colonial Development' to 'Wind of Change'* (Oxford: Clarendon Press, 1971), 212.

[119] On the Labour Party's attitudes towards decolonisation, see also K. O. Morgan, 'Imperialists at Bay: British Labour and Decolonization', *Journal of Imperial and Commonwealth History*, 27 (1999), 233–54.

[120] Percox, 'British Counter-Insurgency in Kenya', 64.

[121] S. Howe, *Anticolonialism in British Politics: The Left and the End of Empire, 1918–1964* (Oxford: Clarendon Press, 1993), 204.

[122] Brockway, *African Journeys*, 140–2.

[123] Bennett witness statement 3, citing Hanslope document INT 10/4/2/4/8A: Central Province South – provincial intelligence committee summary, 24 November 1955.

[124] F. Kitson, *Gangs and Counter-gangs* (London: Barrie and Rockliff, 1960), 6.

[125] S. L. Carruthers, *Winning Hearts and Minds. British Governments, the Media and Colonial Counter-Insurgency 1944–1960* (London: Leicester University Press, 1995), 172–3.

[126] C. Elkins, *Britain's Gulag: The Brutal End of Empire in Kenya* (London: Jonathan Cape, 2005), 275.

[127] D. R. Peterson, 'The Intellectual Lives of Mau Mau Detainees', *Journal of African History*, 49 (2008), 85.

Press coverage of the Mau Mau was sensationalist and short lived. When the Emergency broke out, British newspapers gave extensive coverage, mainly stressing the horrific African barbarism seen in the murders and cattle hamstringing.[128] From the end of the month to December 1955, the *Daily Mirror* criticised state repression and settler behaviour, and demanded that the government redress economic inequality in the colony. Concerning the Griffiths court-martial, the *Daily Mail* supported the army, whereas the *Daily Mirror* adopted a critical line, calling for an inquiry.[129] On the whole, the press gave coverage to government policy at several junctures throughout the Emergency, but there is little evidence to prove a decisive effect on policy-making.[130]

The evidence suggests only marginal concern in military quarters with external oversight. The Royal Inniskillings complained in their war diary in January 1955 that 'fear of House of Commons comment' prevented them taking collective action against the Kikuyu.[131] A soldier serving with 3 KAR in Nanyuki moaned about the 'constant flow of MPs, War Ministers & Generals to my HQ, which upsets the equilibrium a bit'.[132] A police officer recounted discontent with the 'outraged cry of condemnation' coming from naïve humanitarians in England, without changing his behaviour.[133] Several witnesses at the McLean Inquiry made bitter remarks about press coverage.[134] Setting these relatively trivial remarks aside, neither the fourth estate nor the Commons managed to convert public condemnation into policy shifts, suggesting that defence and colonial affairs preserved their elite status during the 1950s, susceptible only to the direction of Cabinet ministers.

Command and control or war by committee?

Elitism and indirect rule therefore dictated that the civil-military dialogue would primarily take place in Kenya itself. The major interest

---

[128] J. Lewis, '"Daddy Wouldn't Buy Me a Mau Mau": The British Popular Press and the Demoralization of Empire', in E. S. Atieno Odhiambo and J. Lonsdale (eds.), *Mau Mau and Nationhood: Arms, Authority and Narration* (Oxford: James Currey, 2003), 231–3.

[129] *Ibid.*, 235, 240–2.   [130] Carruthers, *Winning Hearts and Minds*, 170–7.

[131] Inniskillings Museum: Regimental Diary of the Royal Inniskilling Fusiliers, Vol. VII: March 1952 to January 1962, entry for January 1955.

[132] National Army Museum, Department of Archives, Photographs, Film and Sound (NAM): NAM.2001–10–124–2, Letter from 'Neil' to Mr and Mrs W. Cannell, 11 January 1954.

[133] P. Hewitt, *Kenya Cowboy: A Police Officer's Account of the Mau Mau Emergency* (Weltevredenpark, South Africa: Covos Day Books, 2001), 12.

[134] TNA, WO 32/21720: Proceedings of the McLean Court of Inquiry (hereafter McLean proceedings), 35 (2nd Lt. R. E. Campbell, 6 KAR); 299 (Capt. S. E. Franklin, Kenya Regiment); 452 (Rev. F. T. Squire, Royal Army Chaplains' Department attached Devons).

groups exerted their influence on the army through two vitally important, and connected, structures: the chain of command and the committee system.[135] An agreed upon *modus vivendi* regulated relations between command and committees. The position was formalised in June 1953. The committees helped to ensure cooperation and coordination. Officers, whether in the army, the police or the administration, were commanded by their own responsible officers.[136] As General Erskine put it, 'Planning by Committees is essential but command by Committees is fatal.'[137]

The evolving committee system

The command and control structure, devised in 1950, placed the Colony Emergency Committee at the pinnacle, with the Governor in charge and the Attorney-General coordinating security policy. The Governor also chaired the Sitrep (Situation Report) Committee, overseeing operations.[138] The military worked through East Africa Command, at first subordinate to MELF, and then an independent command. East Africa Command included, at the Emergency's outset, Northern Area headquarters. In January 1953 the headquarters in Kenya were reformed into Northern Brigade and Kenya Garrison.[139] The remit of the Governor's Emergency Committee was clarified in March 1953 as to:

formulate and approve policy governing all measures necessary to re-establish law and order. In pursuance of this function the Committee will (a) issue policy instructions for the conduct of operations to the Chief Staff Officer to the Governor. (b) issue policy instructions to Government Departments on matters designed to further the restoration of law and order. (c) co-ordinate the decisions of the Committee for social and economic improvement ('second-prong' Committee) with the measures necessary to re-establish law and order.[140]

The Chief Staff Officer directed the conduct of operations by the police and the military. He suggested policy changes to the Governor's Committee for approval, and issued the orders necessary to see that the Committee's decisions were implemented. The Chief Staff Officer was

---

[135] M. Howard, 'Civil-Military Relations in Great Britain and the United States, 1945–1958', *Political Science Quarterly*, 75 (1960), 38.
[136] TNA, WO 276/526: Emergency Directive no. 7, 19 June 1953.
[137] JSCSC Library, 'The Mau Mau Rebellion', 5.
[138] Percox, 'British Counter-Insurgency in Kenya', 54, 69.
[139] TNA, WO 276/177: Signal from Force Nairobi to Troopers, no date, ref. signal of 24 June 1953.
[140] KNA, CS/2/8/198: Functions of Emergency Committees etc, forwarded from J. M. Kisch, Secretary to the Governor's Emergency Committee, to the Chief Secretary, Cabinet members, Provincial Commissioners *et al.*, 19 March 1953.

empowered to 'frame and issue operational plans for the guidance of Provincial Committees'. In doing so, he chaired the Operations Committee, which advised him on how best to exercise his powers. The PECs directed operations in their area under the chairmanship of the Provincial Commissioner. They carried out instructions from the Chief Staff Officer and issued their own orders to security forces in their area. During joint operations, the PEC would nominate one officer to command. They were authorised to instruct the district committees, and ensure cooperation between all government departments in re-establishing law and order. The district committees exactly replicated their structure and function at the lower administrative level.[141]

Baring announced these new arrangements to the press on 10 April 1953, citing the Malayan model as his inspiration. At the same time he declared that Major-General Hinde would be the Director of Operations. The other members on the Governor's Committee apart from Baring and Hinde were the Chief Secretary (H. S. Potter), the Member for Finance (E. A. Vasey), the Member for Agriculture (F. W. Cavendish Bentick), the General Officer Commanding (GOC) East Africa (Lieutenant-General Cameron) and settler leader Michael Blundell. Baring highlighted that each PEC and DEC would comprise administration, police and army representatives, and an unofficial European settler member. The DECs were to have an executive officer, who would chair the district operations committee, which was to meet daily to coordinate operations, through a district operations room.[142] In practice the administration representative normally chaired the committees, while settlers often acted as the executive officers for the operations committees.[143]

Hinde possessed an efficient personal staff comprising an army, a police and an administration officer.[144] He liked paying unannounced flying visits to the security forces in the field, which proved surprisingly popular.[145] General Erskine arrived on 7 June, finding Baring indecisive and weak, but managed to work around these flaws with the new Deputy Governor, Frederick Crawford.[146] Erskine possessed an able Chief of Staff in Major-General Heyman.[147] Field Marshal Lord Carver, who

[141] *Ibid.*

[142] TNA, CO 822/486: Telegram from Baring to Colonial Secretary, 10 April 1953.

[143] C. C. Trench, *Men who Ruled Kenya: The Kenya Administration, 1892–1963* (London: Radcliffe Press, 1993), 239, 240, 254.

[144] *Ibid.*, 239.

[145] D. Franklin, *A Pied Cloak: Memoirs of a Colonial Police Officer (Special Branch)* (London: Janus, 1996), 55; Kitson, *Gangs and Counter-gangs*, 48.

[146] Douglas-Home, *Evelyn Baring*, 243–5.

[147] KRA, Vol. Via: Guy Campbell papers: Views on Commanders, no date.

served for a time as Deputy Chief of Staff, thought that the division of responsibility between Erskine as GOC and Hinde as DDOps created confusion.[148] His view was confirmed in an illuminating letter to the Colonial Office from August 1953:

The soldiers tend to work in a watertight compartment, and being an unimaginative lot, have difficulty in understanding political stresses and implications. (One senior officer who has been dealing with the emergency for more than six months asked the other day what a 'squatter' was) . . . It is true that General Hinde, who in my opinion is first class, attends the Emergency Committee as the link between the Commander in Chief and the administration; but he is in a difficult position and does not always know all that is going on at G.H.Q.[149]

In February 1954, following Erskine's advice, Lyttelton and Harding pushed through reforms to the committee system. They dissolved the Governor's Emergency Committee, replacing it with the War Council, and abolished what had become the DDOps committee (originally the Operations Committee).[150] The smaller War Council met twice a week, and drew Erskine deeper into the committee system.[151] Only the Governor, the Commander-in-Chief, the Deputy Governor, and an unofficial member (Blundell) sat on the Council, which heard intelligence reports from GHQ and the Commissioner of Police once a fortnight.[152] The War Council devised long-term plans for the Emergency, as evident in War Council Directive no. 1, which set out the scheme for operations after Anvil. The plan advocated denying the Mau Mau arms and ammunition, stopping the Kikuyu in the Reserves from assisting the insurgents, building up loyalist elements and destroying gangs in the forests and Reserves. Interestingly on the attitude towards the Kikuyu, the plan stated 'There is little prospect of succeeding by enticement.'[153]

Directive no. 1 required the army to operate mainly in the forest, the police to develop the capability to operate without army support, and the administration to control the population more closely. Commander 39 Brigade was given the lead in planning operations after Anvil in the Thika–Fort Hall–Kiambu areas. Importantly, the directive was signed by

---

[148] M. Carver, *Out of Step: Memoirs of a Field Marshal* (London: Hutchinson, 1989), 260.
[149] TNA, CO 822/697: Letter from John Moreton, Government House Kenya, to Henry [Hall], Colonial Office, 14 August 1953.
[150] Percox, 'British Counter-Insurgency in Kenya', 81.
[151] Heather, 'Counterinsurgency and Intelligence in Kenya', 157.
[152] TNA, WO 276/473: Emergency Organisation. War Council, WAR/C.6, 26 March 1954.
[153] TNA, WO 276/90: Appendix A to War Council Directive no. 1. Appreciation on action to be taken after Anvil, 23 April 1954.

Erskine, Blundell and Acting Governor Crawford.[154] In June 1954 the War Council created an Emergency Joint Staff to study issues in detail as directed by the Council and on their own initiative. The Staff, chaired by a man from the Ministry for Internal Security and Defence, also included members from the Ministry of African Affairs, the Treasury and GHQ.[155] Periodically the War Council gave reports to the Council of Ministers; but the latter failed to influence military affairs.[156] Instead, despite its unofficial position in the Kenyan Constitution, the War Council appears to have issued directives to the (constitutional) Council of Ministers. Erskine complained about 'certain Ministers resent[ing] being invited to do something by a certain date'. The Attorney-General condemned the War Council as 'Unconstitutional and Unprincipled'. Erskine resolutely refused to subordinate the War Council to the Council of Ministers.[157]

Intelligence committees

Alongside the committee system sat a parallel intelligence structure. For the first few months, the police, administration and army maintained separate intelligence systems. Visiting the colony in February 1953 Sir Percy Sillitoe, the Director-General of MI5, advised a reorganisation. At the pinnacle would sit the KIC, under which existed provincial and district intelligence committees, meeting at least once a fortnight.[158] The Intelligence Adviser chaired the KIC, with the Assistant Chief Secretary, the Assistant Commissioner for Special Branch, the Security Liaison Officer (from MI5) and representatives of the Chief Native Commissioner and the GOC attending. It reported to the Governor and the Operations Committee. The provincial and district committees included administration, police, Special Branch and the army, in order to provide an agreed view on the situation. The Special Branch officer would carry out most of the work as he employed the appropriate staff. These provincial and district intelligence committees reported sideways to the DECs and PECs, in addition to the KIC.[159]

[154] TNA, WO 276/90: War Council Directive no. 1, Emergency Policy, 23 April 1954.
[155] KNA, WC/CM/1/1: Establishment of an Emergency Joint Staff, note by the War Council Secretariat, 2 June 1954.
[156] TNA, WO 276/419: Monthly reports for the Council of Ministers, December 1955 to December 1956.
[157] TNA, WO 276/524: Letter from Erskine to Harding, 20 December 1954.
[158] KNA, DC/NKI/3/1/14: Letter from Potter, Chief Secretary, to all Provincial Commissioners, Commissioner of Police, and Heads of Departments, 4 March 1953.
[159] KNA, DC/NKI/3/1/14: Memorandum on the reorganisation of intelligence in Kenya Colony, 4 March 1953.

In May 1953 the KIC disbanded the extant joint army–police operational intelligence teams (JAPOITs), and replaced them with a more integrated organisation. Instead, soldiers now served as Provincial and District Military Intelligence Officers (PMIOs and DMIOs), aided by FIAs (normally Kenya Regiment sergeants). They directly briefed the intelligence and the emergency committees and coordinated all intelligence activity in their areas.[160] The system, called the 'Operational Intelligence Organisation', aimed to obtain information of tactical value. It worked closely with Special Branch, which was a separate organisation until the Branch assumed responsibility for collecting operational intelligence in July 1955.[161] A Mau Mau investigation centre, also referred to more descriptively as the Mau Mau interrogation centre, opened in September 1954 near Nairobi, with a branch office opening in Mombasa in October. Special Branch ran the centre, the declared aim being 'the checking of any attempt at a Mau Mau revival and the identification of terrorists filtering back to the city, the interrogation of suspects sent in from outside districts, screening of convicts suspected of Mau Mau offences, and the arrest of petty criminals'.[162] By September 1956 there were two military FIOs assisting their Special Branch colleagues at the centre.[163]

Although subordinate to the Colony MIO who worked in Special Branch headquarters, Frank Kitson spent most of his time touring his area to keep in touch with his subordinates and also the DECs for whom they worked.[164] Away from the committee rooms, the police and army cooperated at every level on a daily basis.[165] By the end of January 1955 the army employed fifty-two FIOs – and planned to increase the number to seventy-three.[166] According to a report by the Intelligence Adviser, the police and army enjoyed good relations:

During the present Emergency, co-operation between the Special Branch and Military Intelligence has been very close. Apart from the valuable assistance

---

[160] Heather, 'Counterinsurgency and Intelligence in Kenya', 107.

[161] Bennett witness statement 3, citing Hanslope documents Chief Secretary, Vol. III: 40A, War Council minutes, 1 February 1955, WAR/C/MIN.81; Chief Secretary, Vol. VIII: 40B, 'Long term requirements of District Officers (Kikuyu Guard) and Field Intelligence Officers. Report by the Emergency Joint Staff', 9 July 1955.

[162] Bennett witness statement 3, citing Hanslope document CAB/MM/7/7: 'Mau Mau and the Kamba', by R. D. F. Ryland, April 1959.

[163] Bennett witness statement 3, citing Hanslope document AA 45/79/7A Box 148: Summary of CPEC (South) Plan in response to War Council Directive no. 10, 10 September 1956.

[164] Interview with General Sir Frank Kitson.

[165] Kitson, *Gangs and Counter-gangs*, 23.

[166] KNA, WC/CM/1/1: The Operational Intelligence Organisation. Memorandum by the KIC, 28 January 1955.

given by the Army in furnishing officers to fill the posts of P.M.I.O., D.M.I.O. and, in some cases, F.I.A.S, senior military officers are represented on intelligence committees at all levels. The Intelligence Adviser maintains frequent contact with the Commander-in-Chief and the P.A. to the Intelligence Adviser daily visits G.H.Q., East Africa, to ensure close liaison with army staff officers planning future operations. G.II(I), East Africa, is in almost daily contact with S.B.H.Q. and an officer of similar rank is now attached to S.B.H.Q. for dealing with operational intelligence.[167]

The DECs and PECs occasionally intervened in intelligence matters when there were operational implications. For example, in the Central Province, the Commander of 39 Brigade complained that intelligence was not being properly disseminated to all commanders, and called for an investigation. The following week, the PEC directed the intelligence officers to issue summaries down to company commanders.[168] Other evidence suggests that the challenge was inculcating the right habits, rather than profound civil-military discord. Touring around his units, 70 Brigade's commander often came across 'useful bits of info which has [sic] not been passed up either to the PMIO to DMIOs, or Bde HQ'. He urged battalion intelligence officers to assiduously debrief troops returning from patrol and incorporate the relevant information into twice-weekly summaries, and to liaise closely with the PMIO and DMIOs.[169]

Averting disagreements

Although these emergency and intelligence committee systems were complementary, they provided the government with two sources of information on the implementation of policy. There were two potential threats to the smooth functioning of the system. The first was that the military command might clash with the committees, and the second that distrust might destroy cooperation between the various organisations. On the first point Anthony Clayton argues the military command and the committees clashed, in particular over the detention policy.[170] By contrast Frank Kitson believes many army officers were familiar with civil-military committes from past service in places like India or Malaya. Furthermore many of those on the Emergency committees would have recently served in the

---

[167] Bennett witness statement 2, citing Hanslope document DO 3/2: Reorganisation of Intelligence in Kenya Colony. Progress Report August 1953 Part I, by the Intelligence Adviser, 7–8.

[168] TNA, WO 276/170: CPEC minutes, 23 October 1953 and 29 October 1953.

[169] Military Intelligence Museum: Letter from Bde Cmd, HQ 70 (EA) Inf Bde, to OCs [officers commanding] 3 KAR, 5 KAR, 7 KAR and 23 KAR, 3 November 1953.

[170] Clayton, Counter-insurgency in Kenya, 9.

armed forces in the Second World War and thus understood each other. Few clashes arose because GHQ only issued orders for large-scale operations and the broad outlines of policy. Otherwise it was the DECs that directed all day-to-day activity – and both committees and security force commanders understood and applied this distinction.[171]

Commanders occasionally asked committees to do things; the DECs in Central Province (South) were required to send a weekly progress report on operations to the Provincial Commissioner and Commander of 39 Brigade at the army's behest.[172] On the other hand, committees sometimes asked commanders to launch operations, or extend existing operations, such as Operation Hungerstrike in May 1955.[173] As stipulated in policy, committees arranged joint operations under a nominated commander, such as the operation in Konyu location in October 1953, headed by the CO of 23 KAR and involving police and Home Guard forces.[174] Problems arose from time to time, as when FIAs started to conduct operations in the Central Province without informing their DECs.[175] But on the whole the relationship between the military command and the committees was widely understood and caused little friction.

The second potential source of trouble was over the reliability of the security forces. If soldiers distrusted their counterparts in the police, administration or Home Guard, how could they work effectively together? The Home Guard especially had a reputation for leaking information, prompting officers to withhold plans until the last minute.[176] Sometime between March and June 1954 twenty Home Guards deserted in two incidents, causing GHQ to warn that their 'loyalty should not be taken for granted', and to recommend better material conditions and European leadership.[177] Interrogations of Mau Mau prisoners revealed that the Home Guard gave them information on their own camps.[178] The administration suffered information leakages in Nairobi and at provincial headquarters, forcing the Chief Secretary to demand tighter control in all government departments, and the appointment of security officers.[179] Five months

---

[171] Interview with General Sir Frank Kitson.
[172] TNA, WO 276/171: CPEC (South) minutes of meeting held on 1 June 1954.
[173] KNA, VP/2/23: CPEC minutes, 13 May 1955.
[174] KNA, VP/2/22: Minutes of a meeting of the Nyeri DEC held on 2 October 1953.
[175] TNA, WO 276/439: CPEC, minutes, 11 November 1955.
[176] Clayton and Killingray, *Khaki and Blue*, 256.
[177] TNA, WO 276/7: Ground operations, 20 Mar–27 Jun 54, no date.
[178] TNA, WO 276/383: Report on Mau Mau tactics, Sergeant J. Dykes, Kenya Regiment attached to Special Branch, 19 August 1953.
[179] KNA, DC/LAMU/2/21/4: Letter from H. S. Potter, Chief Secretary, to All Heads of Departments and All Provincial Commissioners, 15 April 1953.

later, an inquiry discovered details of the surrender negotiations were leaked to the press in August 1953, directly contravening instructions.[180]

The police also faced questions about their own reliability. A report by military intelligence on Kiambu district in December 1952 unveiled cases where the police accepted bribes to ignore curfew breakers.[181] However, the military were not immune to questions concerning their reliability. Soldiers from 26 KAR were accused of indulging in looting in the Fort Hall district.[182] A Lieutenant Davies found himself ignominiously sent back to the Kenya Regiment by the Nyeri Emergency Committee for breaching arms security.[183] KAR soldiers in 70 Brigade fell under such serious suspicion of selling arms and ammunition to the enemy that their commanders prohibited them from taking these items on leave, and only let them out until 6 pm.[184] East Africa Command noted that between October 1953 and June 1955 the military police investigated 125 cases of supplying ammunition to the enemy, leading to 62 discharges from the army and 33 soldiers being placed in detention.[185] The Commander of 70 Brigade distrusted his civilian African employees sufficiently to request that they all be screened in July 1955.[186]

These few examples highlight how questions could be raised about the reliability of all three elements of the security triumvirate in Kenya. Had only one been suspect, then the distrust could have destroyed civil-military cooperation. Because administration, police and army alike suffered lapses in security, the problems could be forgotten rather than held as a matter for recrimination. Command and committees managed a harmonious co-existence because the rules governing their respective powers were clear, both systems employed efficient functionaries, and acrimony surrounding trustworthiness was dissipated by inadequacies on everyone's part.

Civil-military relations in Kenya

Civil-military relations are frequently assessed in terms of civilian control and military compliance. For the British Army in Kenya, these concerns mattered only to a minor extent and on few occasions. The

[180] KNA: DC/LAMU/2/21/4: Letter from Potter to All Heads of Departments, all Provincial Commissioners, all District Commissioners, all Provincial and District Emergency Committees, Deputy Director of Operations, Director of Intelligence and Security, and the Director of Information, 19 September 1953.
[181] TNA, WO 276/378: Report on visit by GII (Int) to Kiambu District on 18 Dec 52.
[182] *Ibid.*   [183] KNA, VP/2/22: Nyeri DEC minutes, 15 August 1953.
[184] KNA, VP/2/22: Nyeri DEC minutes, 21 January 1954.
[185] KNA, WC/CM/1/4: Subversive activities in East African Forces. Memorandum by the Chief of Staff, 13 June 1955.
[186] TNA, WO 276/439: CPEC minutes, 22 July 1955.

Cabinet trusted the army to handle what was deemed, understandably given recent history, a sideshow. Cabinet ministers intervened to strengthen the army's hand and provide additional resources, not to restrain it or offer opinions on how best to fight the campaign. Parliament and the press took fleeting interest in the revolt, and the attention they did lavish on events tended to focus on Mau Mau beastliness or detention camp abuses. East Africa Command, and indeed fairly junior ranking officers in the field, as a consequence held substantial political power.

There were certainly differences of opinion between soldiers and their civilian counterparts in Kenya. One can easily find in the historical record numerous examples of soldiers and civilians disagreeing on a daily basis. But these disputes tended to be about trivial, tactical matters. On the strategic issues, the settlers, administration, police and army all agreed. The Mau Mau had to be crushed, as soon as possible, by collective measures against all members of the Kikuyu, Embu and Meru tribes. Rather than it being considered an opponent, settlers and administration knew that the army was in Kenya to protect and enhance their interests. The command arrangements allowed the army to maintain independence, yet to draw the other branches of government into its campaign plan. The committees proved an essential tool for keeping good relations alive. As we shall see in chapter 9, they also permitted the army to intervene in a range of policy areas strictly speaking outside their domain. Civil-military relations are normally concerned with civilians controlling soldiers. In the Kenya Emergency, the army operated largely free from civilian control.

3 'Possibly restrictive to the operations': marginalising international law in colonial rebellions

British counter-insurgency is often claimed to be special because it operates within a legal framework. Yet in Kenya the security forces perpetrated remarkably intense violence. Their actions have been condemned for violating the 1951 European Convention on Human Rights, the 1948 Universal Declaration of Human Rights, the 1930 Forced Labour Convention and the 1949 Geneva Conventions.[1] How can these antithetical ideas be reconciled? This chapter steps back from events in Kenya to show how the British approach to international and military law shaped the reaction to colonial rebellions. Besides the unique characteristics of the Kenya Emergency, we must understand the wider conditioning official mentality which shaped policy on the ground. Widespread mistreatment of the civilian population was legitimated via a complex legal regime. The British created a permissive legal environment conducive to atrocity behaviour which none the less contained elements of restraint strong enough to forestall genocidal practices. Law was indeed central to British counter-insurgency, but not in the way normally understood.

This chapter explains how the United Kingdom approached international law after the Second World War. The structure of that part of international law concerned with war changed dramatically. Because the *Zeitgeist* on these issues is so different today from in the 1950s there is a compelling reason to establish how far the British government and British Army adapted to these changes. In the 1940s and 1950s new ideas in international law about obedience to authority and extending protections into civil conflicts were not received sympathetically. The British government and British Army adopted a conservative attitude, and even awareness about existing provisions was patchy. These attitudes reflected systematic weaknesses in the international legal regime itself. Arguably British conservatism was far from atypical. Three

[1] Elkins, *Britain's Gulag*, 96–7, 117, 129–30, 135, 304, 315.

structural contradictions in international law undermined universal protections, and proved a problem for the British in practice. These were, first, the conflict between the military need for reflexive obedience and the legal requirement to refuse illegal orders; second, the conflict between military necessity and legal restraint; and third, the overly narrow codification which produced different rules for fighting non-Western opponents. Part of the reason why atrocities happened in the Empire was because they were not construed as crimes against international law.

In the years immediately following the Second World War, monumental changes occurred in the international system as the world was reordered. Where the laws of war were concerned, the two greatest developments took place with a trial in 1946 and a convention in 1949.[2] For the purposes of this book, the most important legacy of the International Military Tribunal (IMT) at Nuremberg came from the demand that soldiers receive no legal protection for committing atrocities under superior orders.[3] Common Article 3 of the 1949 Geneva Conventions promised a revolutionary change in extending basic protections to non-combatants in internal conflicts, who had been previously exempt from the law's orbit.[4] From reading the key texts in international law at the outbreak of the Emergency in 1952, one could have concluded that soldiers knowingly fought within legal restrictions, and were obliged to refuse any orders violating those restrictions. However, institutional changes after 1945 took time to ripple through into state thinking and behaviour.[5] In the period prior to the Kenya Emergency, when attitudes on what constituted correct behaviour were formed, the two major changes in international law made little impact on the British people, government and army.

These concerns were pondered by those making decisions during the Emergency. After leaving Kenya in 1955, General Erskine stated: 'there were no Prisoners of War since we were not at war and did not give the Mau Mau the rights of a belligerent'.[6] Denying combatant rights removed many basic protections.

---

[2] For a historical overview of developments from 1945 to 1950, see G. Best, *War and Law since 1945* (Oxford: Clarendon Press, 1994), 67–231.

[3] H. McCoubrey, 'From Nuremberg to Rome: Restoring the Defence of Superior Orders', *International and Comparative Law Quarterly*, 50 (2001), 386.

[4] L. C. Green, *The Contemporary Law of Armed Conflict*, 2nd edn (Manchester University Press, 2000), 44.

[5] R. Falk, 'Telford Taylor and the Legacy of Nuremberg', *Columbia Journal of Transnational Law*, 37 (1999), 693–4.

[6] JSCSC Library, 'The Mau Mau Rebellion', 4.

Nuremberg and the duty to refuse illegal orders

Following expert advice from Cambridge's Professor Hersch Lauterpacht, the British and Americans changed their official manuals of military law in 1944, anticipating the post-war trials.[7] The British *Manual* now stated:

> The fact that a rule of warfare has been violated in pursuance of an order of the belligerent Government or of an individual belligerent commander does not deprive the act in question of its character as a war crime; neither does it, in principle, confer upon the perpetrator immunity from punishment by the injured belligerent.[8]

According to the King's Regulations, soldiers of all ranks were held personally responsible for acquainting themselves with published orders, such as the 1944 amendment.[9] There is clear evidence showing that civilian international lawyers accepted the Nuremberg Principle.[10] Whether soldiers found time to study all the published material sent to them by the War Office is open to question. Both the initial officer training facility, the Royal Military Academy Sandhurst, and the Staff College taught international affairs and military law during the period 1945–52. Many of the junior officers who served in Kenya were National Servicemen, who received a shorter, sixteen-week, officer training course. Given the time limitations, it is unlikely they were given much training in international law. The syllabuses for these institutions lack sufficient detail to assess whether the duty to refuse illegal orders was taught. Military traditionalists argue that expecting an army to teach and think about disobeying orders is fanciful as it undermines the basis of the organisation's existence.[11]

In the British context, however, awareness about the Nuremberg changes is evident in several articles published in the early 1950s in the

---

[7] Best, *War and Law since 1945*, 190; G. Best, *Humanity in Warfare: The Modern History of the International Law of Armed Conflicts* (London: Weidenfeld and Nicolson, 1980), 293; L. C. Green, 'Superior Orders and Command Responsibility', *Military Law Review*, 175 (2003), 327.

[8] War Office, *Manual of Military Law, 1929, Amendments No. 34*, Notified in Army Orders for April 1944 (London: HMSO, 1944), 1.

[9] War Office, *The King's Regulations for the Army and the Royal Army Reserve, 1940* reprint incorporating amendments nos. 1–44 (London: HMSO, 1945), 208.

[10] See, for example, G. Brand, 'The War Crimes Trials and the Laws of War', *British Year Book of International Law* (1949), 414–27; L. Oppenheim, *International Law: A Treatise. Disputes, War and Neutrality*, 7th edn, rev. and ed. Vol. II: H. Lauterpacht (London: Longmans, Green and Co., 1952), 568.

[11] M. J. Osiel, 'Obeying Orders: Atrocity, Military Discipline, and the Law of War', *California Law Review*, 86 (1998), 4.

Journal of the Royal United Services Institute (*RUSI Journal*). The RUSI is a thinktank closely linked to government, and its publicly available journal enjoys a considerable readership in the armed forces. Serving officers frequently expressed their views in its pages. The first articles on the Nuremberg Principle appeared in 1951, some five years after the trial concluded, coinciding with Britain's first conventional engagement since 1945, in Korea. By 1951 'the fighting man ... is told that he must concern himself not only with the law of his own Country, he must also take into account the International Law of war'.[12] Soldiers found themselves bound only by legal orders, and readers were treated to a quotation from the *Manual*'s 1944 amendment in case they had missed the original.[13] In practice an officer would face few problems in discerning which orders were contrary to international law. The principles occupied not only the strange world of treaties, but also the familiar Army Act, the foundational document in army discipline, known to all officers. Courts would treat pleas of obedience sympathetically only if a superior officer exercised 'a degree of coercion [so] as to deprive him of the will or capacity to resist the execution of the order'.[14]

Officers may have assimilated knowledge on these points from participating in or observing the trials of the 1,783 Axis individuals convened by the British authorities up to 1949. These trials upheld Nuremberg's refusal to accept superior orders as a valid defence, although they were taken into account in sentencing in certain cases.[15] Despite the awareness of the Principle shown in the journal debate, the overall sense of uninterest and complacency is inescapable. Along with the other victorious armed forces, the post-war army basked in a sense of its own moral rectitude.[16] It had little incentive to take any great heed of Nuremberg, believing that Britain had followed the laws of war and already possessed a tradition inimical to automatic obedience, unlike the Germans.[17] The crimes committed by the Axis powers were seen as 'perhaps least of all likely to arise in the British Armed Forces with [their] traditions of self-respect and initiative'.[18]

---

[12] H. A. Smith, 'The Defence of Superior Orders', *RUSI Journal*, 96 (1951), 617.

[13] Anon., 'Obedience to Lawful Commands', *RUSI Journal*, 96 (1951), 71; The Earl of Cork and Orrery, 'Obedience to Lawful Command', *RUSI Journal*, 96 (1951), 258.

[14] N. C. H. Dunbar, 'The Responsibility of Junior Officers to the Laws of War', *RUSI Journal*, 97 (1952), 171.

[15] D. A. L. Wade, 'A Survey of the Trials of War Criminals', *RUSI Journal*, 96 (1951), 67.

[16] P. Fussell, *Wartime: Understanding and Behaviour in the Second World War* (Oxford University Press, 1989), 229; M. Howard, *War and the Liberal Conscience* (London: Temple Smith, 1978), 115.

[17] Wade, 'A Survey', 68.   [18] Anon., 'Obedience to Lawful Commands', 72.

Military perspectives on the Nuremberg Principle reflected the government's hostility and the public's apathy towards the IMT and the subsequent 'lesser' trials. The Americans, especially under President Truman's leadership, pushed for establishing the tribunal. Prime Minister Churchill personally favoured shooting the entire Nazi leadership summarily, and accepted the American initiative only with great reluctance.[19] For the Allied leadership, the primary purpose of holding the Nuremberg and Tokyo trials was to vindicate their own war aims and punish the aggressors. Establishing the individual duty to refuse illegal orders was hardly a priority, and the British prosecutors focused mainly on the offence of 'crimes against peace'.[20] Debates about the legal ramifications were deemed a minor concern.[21] Lasting nearly a year, the proceedings soon lost the interest of a war-weary public, bored by the complicated technical arguments.[22] Even after prolonged exposure to wartime propaganda about Nazi misdeeds, the true enormity of the mass killings in Europe only gradually sank in.[23] The IMT had limited impact on the national consciousness, and thus on the men who filled the British Army's ranks in Kenya.

Greater attention fell upon certain other trials taking place at the same time.[24] Public opinion demanded prosecutions in cases where British servicemen were the victims, such as the Stalag Luft III murders popularised in the film *The Great Escape*.[25] By 1949, 496 Japanese and over a thousand Germans and their European collaborators had been tried. Despite the high number, it is questionable whether the trials had an impact on the public or the army. The government's attitude towards the trials was unenthusiastic, under both Conservative and Labour administrations. The War Office and the British Army of the Rhine, the command responsible for holding the trials, complained about insufficient

---

[19] R. Overy, 'The Nuremberg Trials: International Law in the Making', in P. Sands (ed.), *From Nuremberg to The Hague: The Future of International Criminal Justice* (Cambridge University Press, 2003), 4–6. The literature on Nuremberg is extensive. Two particularly interesting books are R. Overy, *Interrogations: Inside the Minds of the Nazi Elite* (London: Penguin, 2002) and A. Tusa and J. Tusa, *Nuremberg Trial* (London: BBC Books, 1995).

[20] D. Bloxham, 'British War Crimes Trial Policy in Germany, 1945–1957: Implementation and Collapse', *Journal of British Studies*, 42 (2003), 97.

[21] J. Rabkin, 'Nuremberg Misremembered', *SAIS Review*, 19 (1999), 81–96.

[22] Overy, 'The Nuremberg Trials', 24.

[23] D. Stone, 'The Domestication of Violence: Forging a Collective Memory of the Holocaust in Britain, 1945–6', *Patterns of Prejudice*, 33 (1999), 13.

[24] D. Bloxham, '"The Trial That Never Was": Why there was no Second International Trial of Major War Criminals at Nuremberg', *History*, 87 (2002), 41.

[25] P. D. Jones, 'Nazi Atrocities against Allied Airmen: Stalag Luft III and the End of British War Crimes Trials', *The Historical Journal*, 41 (1998), 543–65.

financial and manpower resources.[26] The Foreign Office first opposed the post-war trials, and then prevented a second major trial through 'honourable' stalling, rather than denouncing the American suggestion outright.[27] Foreign Office opinion solidified around pragmatically favouring German reintegration into the international community as the Cold War began.[28]

The reluctant attitude to innovation in international law was further seen in the government's preference for holding the subsequent trials under the Royal Prerogative-derived Warrant of 14 June 1945, rather than through the Control Council Acts.[29] The Royal Warrant excluded 'crimes against humanity'.[30] Furthermore, the interpretations by the lesser trials of the duty to refuse illegal orders were generally more sympathetic towards the military desire for obedience.[31] The dominant impression in Britain at the time was that the German military were largely innocent of involvement in Nazi atrocities.[32] The myth of the apolitical, honourable soldier reflected not only impressions about the Germans, but also the British soldiery. Those few whose passions were aroused by the trials felt them unfair and the noted legal conservatism, emerging Cold War agenda and staff shortages dictated that the 'lesser' trials would leave no stronger impression than their grander forebears in Nuremberg and Tokyo. By the time the Kenya Emergency began in October 1952 there were few reasons to suppose that an ordinary soldier would know about his duty to refuse illegal orders, including the victim-isation of civilians.

Attitudes to Geneva's Common Article 3

Common Article 3 of the 1949 Geneva Conventions promised to revolu-tionise the legal restraints on the conduct of counter-insurgency warfare. The provision extended basic protections to non-combatants in internal wars for the first time. If soldiers knew that they were supposed to act with restraint they might moderate their behaviour. Ignorance might lead soldiers to believe that they could treat the civilian population in any way they or their commanders chose, because international law was

---

[26] *Ibid.*, 550.   [27] Bloxham, '"The Trial That Never Was"', 49–50, 60.
[28] Jones, 'Nazi Atrocities against Allied Airmen', 543–4.
[29] A. P. V. Rogers, 'War Crimes Trials under the Royal Warrant: British Practice 1945–1949', *International and Comparative Law Quarterly*, 39 (1990), 780–800; Bloxham, '"The Trial That Never Was"', 54.
[30] Bloxham, 'British War Crimes Trial Policy', 96.
[31] McCoubrey, 'From Nuremberg to Rome', 391; Osiel, 'Obeying Orders', 4.
[32] Bloxham, 'British War Crimes Trial Policy', 112.

deemed irrelevant. The British government participated in the negotiations leading to the conventions with reticence, displayed open hostility towards Common Article 3 and delayed ratification until 1957. As a result, soldiers knew virtually nothing about the potential legal constraints on their actions. Although ignorance is not a legally admissible excuse for committing a crime, historically it helps in understanding the mentalities which created an atmosphere where atrocities could happen.

While praising the International Committee of the Red Cross (ICRC) for its role in the Second World War, the government distrusted any interference in national security, fearing that sovereignty would be undermined.[33] The Foreign Office contemplated attending the preparatory conference mainly for the benefit of other countries:

> The fact is that the horrors of the war in Europe showed that much needs to be done to uphold decent and humane standards and as the Power with far and away the best record of all the belligerents I think we ought to be ready to speak at all these meetings.[34]

These noble intentions vanished when the government failed to send anyone to the preparatory meetings in Stockholm. Representatives eventually arrived in Geneva after a last-minute decision to send them.[35] Under the chief negotiator, Sir Robert Craigie, the delegation constantly proposed amendments and quickly acquired pariah status for an 'obsessive and niggling' attitude.[36] These problems partly resulted from the absence from the preparatory discussions. To a larger extent, though, they stemmed from misgivings about the consequences for internal security and counter-insurgency in the colonies. Even two years prior to signing, the government anticipated the impact that a civil war clause might have on operations such as the campaign then underway in Palestine.[37] The government attempted to minimise the extent to which Common Article 3 would apply in the colonies by delegitimising their opponents. A report for the Army Staff College course of 1947 described the 'campaign of violence, terror, sabotage and murder' waged by 'illegal armed organisations' in Palestine.[38] The Security

---

[33] G. Best, 'Making the Geneva Conventions of 1949: The View from Whitehall', in C. Swinarski (ed.), *Studies and Essays on International Humanitarian Law and Red Cross Principles in Honour of Jean Pictet* (Geneva/The Hague: ICRC/Martinus Nijhoff, 1984), 6, 8–10.

[34] Foreign Office minute, 3 July 1946, cited in Best, 'Making the Conventions', 8.

[35] Best, *War and Law*, 81, 170.   [36] *Ibid.*, 89, 100.

[37] TNA, WO 32/12524: Army Council Secretariat Confidential Paper no. CRGC/P(47)7, Memo by Chairman of the Interdepartmental Committee on the Revision of the Geneva Conventions (ICRGC), 24 September 1947, 2.

[38] JSCSC, Army Staff College syllabus, 1947.

Service was 'concerned to ensure that we were not handicapped in dealing with such a situation as existed in Palestine'.[39] The insurgency in Palestine was viewed as 'terrorists campaigning against law and order'.[40] Such reasoning rendered international law inapplicable in the colonies before the negotiations at Geneva were completed.

While Palestine dominated thinking beforehand, events in Malaya loomed large during the negotiations themselves. Common Article 3 provoked lengthy, and at times acerbic, discussion.[41] Craigie reported in May 1949 that 'the desirability of applying the Conventions to civil war is accepted by all countries except the United Kingdom'.[42] After much obstruction and counter-argument, for example, that the (unbinding) Universal Declaration of Human Rights and the (unenforceable) Genocide Convention sufficed, constructive engagement ensued.[43] The Cabinet authorised the delegation to accept the civil war clause, provided the sovereign power could decide whether the clause applied to a conflict.[44] Despite the absence of a specific formula on these lines from the final convention, Craigie predicted that in practice the sovereign power would have the last word.[45] This interpretation precluded any encouragement which 'subversive movements' might glean from the article, while mitigating the horrors inherent in these savage wars.[46] The Home Office took a less positive view than the Foreign Office on the clause:

in colonial territories in particular [it] might successfully be used as a propaganda document to instruct the native that he owed no allegiance towards lawfully constituted authority.

According to the Home Office, the clause struck 'at the root of national sovereignty and endangers national security'.[47] Several months after the signing ceremony, the Army Council also expressed concerns:

---

[39] TNA, WO 32/12526: Extract from the minutes of the second meeting of the ICRGC, 17 September 1947, 3.

[40] TNA, WO 32/12526: Extract from the minutes of the second meeting of the ICRGC, 17 September 1947, 2.

[41] Best, *War and Law*, 96; TNA, LO 2/674: Extracts from Sir Robert Craigie's Report related to points raised in the Cabinet, 1949, para. 41.

[42] TNA, LO 2/674: Secret letter from Sir Robert Craigie, UK delegation in Geneva, to H. A. Caccia, Foreign Office, 9 May 1949.

[43] Best, *War and Law*, 171–4.

[44] TNA, LO 2/674: Secret letter from Sir Robert Craigie to H. A. Caccia, 9 May 1949, Enclosure 1.

[45] TNA, CAB 130/46: Letter from Craigie to Caccia, 9 May 1949.

[46] TNA, LO 2/674: Extracts from Sir Robert Craigie's Report related to points raised in the Cabinet, 1949, para. 43.

[47] TNA, LCO 2/4309: Brief prepared by the Home Office working party on the Civilian Convention, no date, 4–5.

we may come under pressure to apply Article 3 of the Conventions in Malaya and would find the application of the Article in full extremely objectionable and possibly restrictive to the operations.[48]

This feared eventuality never transpired as the Foreign Secretary's inter-pretation dictated that 'the Article was not meant to apply in the case of ephemeral revolts or disturbances of the bandit type'.[49] Thus the gov-ernment easily dismissed the post-war counter-insurgency campaigns from international law's restrictions on the use of force. Instead, under national law, an insurrection '[d]iffers from a riot in having an object of a general and public nature, and is really a species of treason known technically as "levying war against the King"'.[50]

The government ensured the irrelevance of Common Article 3 by postponing ratification until 1957. To be sure, there were other reasons for the delay. Clauses on a prohibition on applying the death penalty, extending leniency in trials of foreign nationals and incorporating penal sanctions against grave breaches into domestic law proved trouble-some issues.[51] Lengthy inter-departmental deliberations began when-ever another country ratified with reservations.[52] The War Office, the Foreign Office and the Lord Chancellor's Department all blamed the Home Office, responsible for completing the ratification, for the delay.[53] The Home Office encountered immense difficulties in incorporating an international treaty into domestic law.[54] The War Office sympathised, stating:

The United Kingdom cannot undertake to incorporate anything in its national law since all legislation must be approved by the legislature. In addition, the difficulties of incorporating the Convention which is not drafted in legal language into legislation and to provide appropriate penalties for offences would be well

---

[48] TNA, WO 32/13616: Army Council Secretariat brief for Secretary of State for War, 1 December 1949, in preparation for Cabinet meeting of 2 December.
[49] TNA, CAB 130/46: Memo from Foreign Secretary to the Cabinet, 25 November 1949, 11.
[50] JSCSC, Army Staff College syllabus, 1947.
[51] TNA, LCO 2/4312: Concluding notes of meeting of the ICRGC, 28 September 1950; Minutes of ICRCG meeting of 24 May 1951; Records of ICRGC for 1948–49 available in TNA, TS 46/103.
[52] See the correspondence between departments in: TNA: LCO 2/4313.
[53] TNA, LCO 2/4312: Concluding notes of 28 September 1950 for inter-departmental disagreement over the need for legislation; TNA, PREM 11/2205: Letter of 12 March 1957, Lord Woolton to Marquess of Salisbury for blaming the Home Office; TNA, WO 32/18511: Detailed material from 1957 relating to the Bill's preparation.
[54] In addition to the issues mentioned above, the Home Secretary had problems with the provisions on extraditing civilians, see TNA, WO 32/18511: Army Council Secretariat extract from the conclusions of the 56th (51) meeting of the Cabinet, 30 July 1951.

nigh insuperable. Furthermore, it would be undesirable, if not impracticable, to prosecute every act contrary to the Convention.[55]

According to Best, the requirement to incorporate the conventions into domestic law was only understood late in the day.[56] However, the evidence shows that technical problems were expected. An inter-departmental committee met several times prior to the signing, and a draft Bill emerged in 1952.[57] Best also points out that the legislative timetable was packed and the Geneva Conventions Bill was a low priority, especially given the vast reconstruction required after the war.[58] In 1952, for example, the Housing Bill was a more pressing concern.[59] Although Best provides a valid explanation, he underestimates the extent to which delaying ratification allayed concerns about the ramifications for national security. This is not to imply that nobody in government called for ratification. The Lord Chancellor wished to overcome the technical obstacles.[60] The Foreign Office advocated ratification for 'humanitarian reasons' and to maintain Britain's reputation abroad.[61] The War Office wanted the conventions' protection in inter-state wars, and thought that ratifying would set the USSR an example.[62] Yet the concern about inter-state wars is informative for what it leaves out: the counter-insurgencies engaged in throughout the post-war period were seldom considered within the orbit of international law. Indeed, the government recognised that bringing these campaigns within such limitations would hinder operations. The next section will demonstrate how the international legal system itself permitted such an interpretation.

The permissive international legal framework

Several scholars have argued that the British followed a particularly brutal trajectory in violating international law. According to this analysis,

---

[55] TNA, LCO 2/4309. Undated commentary.
[56] Best, 'Making the Geneva Conventions', 11, 15.
[57] For the details see TNA, WO 163/329; Draft Bill contained in: TNA, HO 45/25944.
[58] Best, 'Making the Geneva Conventions', 5.
[59] This sense of the conventions being a low priority permeates the records in TNA, LCO 2/4313 for 1956–57; see also TNA, WO 32/18511: Army Council Secretariat extract from the conclusions of the 17th (52) meeting of the Cabinet, 14 February 1952.
[60] TNA, WO 32/18511: Army Council Secretariat extract from the conclusions of the 56th (51) meeting of the Cabinet, 30 July 1951.
[61] TNA, LCO 2/4312: Letter from C. G. Kemball, Foreign Office, to D. W. Dobson, Lord Chancellor's Office, 26 February 1952; TNA, WO 32/18511: Letter from C. G. Kemball, Foreign Office, to S. S. J. Evans, War Office, 29 October 1953.
[62] See the series of minutes from the ICRGC in TNA, LCO 2/4312; TNA, WO 32/18511: Letter from S. S. J. Evans to C. G. Kemball, 11 December 1953.

brutality in colonial wars was the product of something uniquely British.[63] However, structural flaws within international law itself allowed this violation, in three ways. First, the Nuremberg Principle called for a utopian standard which armies would always consider unrealisable because it fatally undermined discipline and cohesion. Second, the humanitarian orientation towards restraint in the laws of war conflicted with the military requirement to kill people and destroy things. In the dispute between limitation and necessary violence, the legal regime permitted such a broad definition of 'necessity' that almost anything became justifiable. Third, the move towards human rights exemplified in agreements such as Common Article 3 of the Geneva Conventions and the European Convention on Human Rights clashed with the demands of state sovereignty. With a few minor exceptions, sovereignty triumphed and this meant that the international legal regime provided few protections for those subject to British methods in Kenya.

The Nuremberg tribunal is renowned for confirming the principle that soldiers have a duty to refuse illegal orders which have atrocities as their aim. However, debates about superior orders and command responsibility for atrocities date back at least five hundred and fifty years. The principle applies whether a conflict is a recognised war or not, an important point given British government efforts to conduct its counter-insurgencies within an emergency framework and away from international law. For example, English common law deemed killing a prisoner obviously illegal.[64] The *Manual of Military Law* closely mirrored the wording devised by the Nuremberg tribunal and from 1944 onwards expected soldiers to question or even refuse 'obviously illegal' orders. When a soldier struggled to decide whether an order was illegal he was to obey it and make a formal complaint afterwards.[65] The 1951 *Manual* stated that when an order was 'manifestly illegal, [a soldier] is under a legal duty to refuse to carry out the order and if he does carry it out he will be criminally responsible for what he does in doing so'.[66] So when the Emergency erupted in 1952 neither civilian nor military law permitted obedience to superior orders as a defence for

---

[63] T. Parsons, 'Book Review: David Anderson, *Histories of the Hanged: The Dirty War in Kenya and the End of Empire*; Caroline Elkins, *Imperial Reckoning: The Untold Story of Britain's Gulag in Kenya*', *American Historical Review*, 110 (2005), 1295–7; M. Curtis, 'Britain's Real Foreign Policy and the Failure of British Academia', *International Relations*, 18 (2004), 276. See also M. Curtis, *The Ambiguities of Power: British Foreign Policy since 1945* (London: Zed Books, 1995); Curtis, *Web of Deceit*.

[64] Green, 'Superior Orders and Command Responsibility', 310, 361, 329.

[65] The element on making a complaint afterwards was removed in 1956: McCoubrey, 'From Nuremberg to Rome', 391.

[66] Cited in Green, 'Superior Orders and Command Responsibility', 334.

committing atrocities. Both systems employed a common-sense test based on the idea of 'manifest illegality'.[67]

A judgment by Justice Soloman during the Boer War in 1900 set the tone for the rest of the century:

[I]t is monstrous to suppose that a soldier would be protected where the order is grossly illegal ... I think it is a safe rule to lay down that if a soldier honestly believes he is doing his duty in obeying ... and the orders are not so manifestly illegal that he ... ought to have known they were unlawful, [he] will be protected by the orders.[68]

War is not a black and white business, and problems arise in the grey areas.[69] Much depended upon the conditions experienced, such as the recent behaviour of the enemy, and would be informed by the unit's subculture. As Osiel observes, manifest illegality rests upon social foundations, and when these break down, the concept provides little preventative power. As a concept it presumes that an ordinary person can easily decide what is legitimate behaviour.[70] When illegal acts are widespread, or the acts no longer appear to be illegal under local law, as happened in Kenya with the use of torture for perceived instrumental purposes, the notion of manifest illegality becomes less meaningful to those making decisions about how to act.

The traditionalist attitude supports absolute obedience. The argument normally proceeds along two lines. The first posits the soldier's incapacity for complex moral reasoning.[71] Authors ridicule images of 'the private soldier ... march[ing] to war with his knapsack stuffed with tomes by eminent international jurists';[72] and 'stopping in the midst of some desperate engagement to ponder what Aristotle would do in such a circumstance'.[73] The patronising assumptions aside, there is psychiatric evidence that in combat conditions soldiers cannot make complicated decisions.[74] Second, the approach advocates complete obedience because it is thought inherent and absolutely necessary for the military to fight effectively.[75] Discipline is seen to increase military effectiveness and offers a means of coping with the intense confusion present in war.[76] Obedience is the foundation of military cohesion, and therefore the

[67] *Ibid.*, 314.   [68] Cited in *ibid.*, 321.

[69] J. Blackett, 'Superior Orders – the Military Dilemma', *RUSI Journal*, 139 (1994), 15.

[70] Osiel, 'Obeying Orders', 3, 39.   [71] Blackett, 'Superior Orders', 14.

[72] R. Grenfell, 'This Question of Superior Orders', *RUSI Journal*, 96 (1951), 266.

[73] W. M. Hudson, 'Book Reviews. "Obeying Orders: Atrocity, Military Discipline and the Law of War"', *Military Law Review*, 161 (1999), 234.

[74] Osiel, 'Obeying Orders', 9.   [75] McCoubrey, 'From Nuremberg to Rome', 391.

[76] M. van Creveld, 'The Clausewitzian Universe and the Law of War', *Journal of Contemporary History*, 26 (1991), 422.

conflict between a duty to disobey illegal orders and the need for obedience in combat is probably irresolvable.[77] In reality, however, the so-called 'soldier's dilemma' between being hung by a judge or shot by a court-martial is only a dilemma on paper because few dare question orders and suffer the social consequences. In addition, from basic training onwards soldiers are taught to obey orders immediately, so that obeying a superior becomes a reflex reaction.[78] While these views surface in armed forces across the world, the British Army preached them too. A War Office study from 1947 saw a core function of discipline as:

producing a habit of obedience to those in authority which should have most of the automatic nature of a conditioned reflex, and whose inculcation will presumably obey most of the laws known to apply to such reflexes.[79]

An article in the *British Army Review*, an in-house magazine, suggested maintaining the standards of discipline found during the First World War, where orders were obeyed 'without hesitation, with energy and cheerfulness'.[80] A contributor in the *RUSI Journal* worried about the Nuremberg Principle, speculating that 'it must give rise to questioning of all orders, which, in itself, is inimical to military discipline'.[81] Another writer thought unquestioning obedience essential to successful military operations, and Nuremberg a challenge to the army's ancient ethos.[82] Indeed, some viewed the only sound policy as 'to place no limits to obedience and to enforce discipline in the army irrespective of any ethical considerations'.[83] A War Office study circulated to commanders in 1952 approvingly quoted the American military theorist, S. L. A. Marshall:[84]

Words repeated out loud down to the last man will be obeyed. But an order only half heard becomes a convenient excuse for non-compliance. Warmth in the giving of an order is better than studied self-containment. At the lower levels men do not fight calmly, and are not reassured by commanders with the manner of an undertaker or a poker-player.[85]

---

[77] Osiel, 'Obeying Orders', 15.   [78] Blackett, 'Superior Orders', 12, 16.
[79] TNA, WO 291/1306: The Training of the National Service Man: A Preliminary Survey, Military Operational Research Unit, July 1947.
[80] 'A Senior Officer to Young Officers', 'The Duties of an Officer', *British Army Review*, 3 (1950), 46.
[81] Cork and Orrery, 'Obedience to Lawful Command', 261.
[82] Grenfell, 'This Question of Superior Orders', 266.
[83] D. Pal, 'Limits to Obedience', *Army Quarterly*, 72 (1956), 81.
[84] His most famous work is S. L. A. Marshall, *Men against Fire: The Problem of Battle Command* (Norman, OK: University of Oklahoma Press, 2000).
[85] TNA, WO 291/1537: Selected Quotations from '*MEN against FIRE*' by Colonel S. L. A. Marshall, Army Operational Research Group Occasional Note no. 1, June 1952.

In any case, although identifying serious atrocities should not have required any specialist knowledge, the lack of legal training in the army reduced the likelihood that a soldier would disobey orders. The capacity to question orders is closely intertwined with the extent of knowledge.[86] On these lines, the eminent lawyer and expert on military law Gerald Draper considered education as a preventative measure more effective than penal measures for stopping atrocity behaviour.[87] While the army altered the *Manual of Military Law* in 1944, changing the law in the books is only the start of organisational change. Training and education are also essential.[88] The available evidence on army education in this period, while far from comprehensive, plainly indicates the low priority accorded to current affairs and legal education.[89]

Several articles from the period do mention the teaching of military law. It was recognised that officers needed to study the subject, and that ignorance had been common in the past. Experience of court-martial proceedings was thought especially desirable.[90] Military law was taught at initial officer training and later on.[91] The records for Sandhurst from 1950 show military law being routinely taught.[92] Even so, this was not necessarily the same as international law, and much time in the classroom would be spent on barrack-room matters.[93] Subjects covered under military law at Sandhurst included rules of evidence, arrest, summary and minor punishments, and discipline. There is no mention of the laws of war until 1961, when one hour was devoted to the Geneva Conventions. Students at the Staff College discussed the *Manual of Military Law* and the King's Regulations, the former including the laws of war – yet typically only an hour and a half was dedicated to these issues.[94] At both the Academy and the College international affairs were

---

[86] McCoubrey, 'From Nuremberg to Rome', 392.

[87] G. I. A. D. Draper, 'The Ethical and Juridical Status of Constraints in War', *Military Law Review*, 55 (1972), 185.

[88] Hudson, 'Obeying Orders', 227.

[89] For studies of army education see J. Beach, 'Soldier Education in the British Army, 1920–2007', *History of Education*, 37 (2008), 679–99; J. Crang, *The British Army and the People's War 1939–1945* (Manchester University Press, 2000); S. P. MacKenzie, *Politics and Military Morale: Current-affairs and Citizenship Education in the British Army, 1914–1950* (Oxford: Clarendon Press, 1992).

[90] M. J. P. M. Corbally, 'The Education and Employment of Senior Subalterns', *Army Quarterly*, 52 (1946), 223–6.

[91] F. Warhurst, 'Training Army Officers', *Army Quarterly*, 52 (1946), 252–61; C. N. Barclay, 'The Training of National Armies in War', *Army Quarterly*, 58 (1949), 98–108.

[92] The Sandhurst Collection, Royal Military Academy Sandhurst. The syllabuses for the years 1945–9 are unavailable.

[93] W. K. B. Crawford, 'Training the National Service Army Officer at Eaton Hall', *RUSI Journal*, 96 (1951), 134–8.

[94] For example, JSCSC, Army Staff College syllabus, 1947.

taught, as was internal security, and these may have included elements on the laws of war; unfortunately the syllabuses are too vague to be sure.

A brief content analysis of the three major military journals places the importance attributed to international law in context. Over the 1945–68 period the *RUSI Journal* contained 1,894 articles. Of these only nine dealt explicitly with the laws of war and four included some minor reference. In an ideal situation, an officer who read every article of each edition of the journal for twenty-three years would have spent 0.69 per cent of his readings on the laws of war. The *Army Quarterly* exhibited slightly greater awareness of legal matters: out of 1,178 articles, 9 embodied a detailed discussion, while 6 mentioned it in passing. Although an improvement at 1.27 per cent, this could hardly be called a substantive focus. In his foreward to the first edition of the *British Army Review*, CIGS Field Marshal Sir William Slim said: 'I want every officer and NCO to read the British Army Journal and I want a lot of you to contribute to it.'[95] It was to be distributed like any other General Staff training publication, namely one per company in the regular army and territorials, and one per contingent or battalion in the cadet forces. Over the period, 731 articles were published, 7 directly concerning the laws of war and 9 indirectly. This amounted to a total coverage of 2.19 per cent, still a minuscule proportion.

Although there is no conclusive proof showing that the army failed to teach international law to ordinary soldiers, there are strong grounds for considering the eventuality extremely likely. From 1945 to 1948 military education was preoccupied with retraining soldiers for civilian life as mass demobilisation took place. After 1948 most activity focused upon vocational training as the majority of soldiers lacked the educational experience necessary for anything more sophisticated.[96] Many soldiers struggled with basic literacy, and thus coping with the laws of war would have been considered too demanding. The Nuremberg tribunal proceedings coincided with a decline in the teaching of current affairs.[97]

---

[95] The *British Army Review* remained in intermittent publication from its inception in 1863. The title was *British Army Journal* until July 1954, when it changed temporarily to *British Army Annual*. In September 1955 the *Review* title was adopted. For the sake of convenience it is referred to as *British Army Review* throughout.

[96] On the National Service policies and experience see T. Hickman, *The Call-Up: A History of National Service* (London: Headline, 2004); T. Royle, *National Service: The Best Years of Their Lives* (London: André Deutsch, 2002); L. V. Scott, *Conscription and the Attlee Governments: The Politics and Policy of National Service 1945–1951* (Oxford: Clarendon Press, 1993).

[97] V. C. White, *The Story of Army Education 1643–1963* (London: George G. Harrap & Co. Ltd, 1963), 157, 181–9.

Writing in 1966, Gerald Draper considered lack of training in the laws of war throughout one's military career a major deficiency. Under the Geneva and Hague Conventions, states were required to give instruction during both peace and war, including disseminating the original treaty texts. Even in 1966 it was still apparent that instruction on the Geneva Conventions was not being provided at the staff colleges, Imperial Defence College or any other 'key Service institutions and units'. The Directorate of Army Legal Services failed to provide instruction and, even worse, itself needed instruction in the conventions.[98]

Devising a military legal system capable of reconciling conceptions of civilian justice and military discipline can never be an easy task.[99] Despite changing the *Manual* in 1944, the army maintained traditional attitudes towards obedience and neglected to disseminate to either officers or men the duty to refuse illegal orders. This arose from an institutional dislike for abstract thinking, the belief that the army would never issue illegal orders of the kind seen in the Second World War anyway, and a determination to uphold absolute discipline. The international legal system favoured a military interpretation of what constituted legitimate force, reducing the likelihood that the Nuremberg Principle would be invoked at all.

What *isn't* necessary?

Military necessity is one of the oldest and most firmly entrenched principles of the laws of armed conflict.[100] It allows all acts required for achieving victory, so long as they adhere to the laws of war.[101] Defenders of the idea emphasise its pragmatism in recognising the need for violence in war while imposing workable limits. Critics see the doctrine as dangerous because what is necessary is ultimately decided subjectively by the commander on the spot, thus giving an excuse for almost every conceivable action.[102] In a sense, then, the military engages in 'manufacturing necessity' after the event.[103] Regardless of how atrocious

---

[98] G. I. A. D. Draper, 'The Place of the Laws of War in Military Instruction', *RUSI Journal*, 111 (1966), 189–98.

[99] D. P. O'Connell, 'The Nature of British Military Law', *Military Law Review*, 19 (1963), 155.

[100] W. V. O'Brien, 'The Rule of Law in Small Wars', *Annals of the American Academy of Political and Social Sciences*, 541 (1995), 42.

[101] A. P. V. Rogers, *Law on the Battlefield*, 2nd edn (Manchester University Press, 2004), 5.

[102] I. Detter, *The Law of War*, 2nd edn (Cambridge University Press, 2000), 394; Rogers, *Law on the Battlefield*, 3.

[103] The phrase is R. W. Gordon's, cited in M. D. A. Freeman, *Lloyd's Introduction to Jurisprudence*, 7th edn (London: Sweet and Maxwell, 2001), 1065.

a course of action may seem to the outside observer, the military can always argue that the commander only pursued the action demanded by the situation. As Jochnick and Normand contend: 'By endorsing military necessity without substantive limitations, the laws of war ask only that belligerents act in accord with military self-interest.'[104] By adopting legal language, acts become validated simply by being legal, ignoring the surrounding politics and morality. Rather than supporting or deterring actions, then, the law actively internalises entire belief systems and legitimises them.[105] This is a helpful notion for understanding how perpetrators came to see atrocities as strictly necessary; for example, torture in the Kenya case.

The concept of *Kriegsraison*, generally ascribed to the German strategic style, dictates that military necessity should always outweigh international law, and holds that a ruthless war is quicker and therefore more humane overall. Arguably international law institutionalises the idea, although most would see the laws of war and *Kriegsraison* as intrinsically incompatible.[106] Whatever the relationship between the two concepts, when adopting a quick, ruthless approach to the use of force a commander or army rapidly 'creates an atmosphere permissive of atrocities',[107] even when atrocities are not directly ordered.

These conceptual points from international law were connected to British practice. The orthodox perspective sees British counter-insurgency as conducted firmly within a legal framework which demanded that only minimum force be used. However, as McInnes first intimated, the precise phrase in British legal and military doctrine is *minimum necessary force*. The national concern with the degree of force therefore reflects international law's conception of military necessity. As most writers on international law avoid criticising its fundamental ability to limit violence, so writers on British counter-insurgency assume that what McInnes calls 'the constraints of civil law' effectively control armed force.[108] But because both international and national systems depend upon a highly permissive definition of necessity, an impression has emerged of impregnably solid standards when in practice fluid pragmatism benefiting the powerful prevailed. As chapter 4 shows, the British colonial experience provides ample instances of exemplary force, designed to 'nip rebellion in the bud'. The permissive nature of international law, and the British interpretation thereof, allowed repression to be considered legal by those who applied it.

---

[104] C. A. Jochnick and R. Normand, 'The Legitimation of Violence: A Critical History of the Laws of War', *Harvard International Law Journal*, 35 (1994), 58.
[105] *Ibid.*, 57.   [106] *Ibid.*, 64.
[107] *Ibid.*, 65.   [108] McInnes, *Hot War, Cold War*, 115.

Besides the Nuremberg Principle and the Geneva Conventions, there are grounds for suspecting that other aspects of international law may have affected military operations in Kenya. Systematically surveying human rights during British decolonisation, legal scholar Brian Simpson found the Universal Declaration of Human Rights to be not in the least bit binding upon states. Rather, the Declaration was seen as a general statement of intent, lacking the power of a mandatory treaty.[109] The British government was aware of the potential breach of the Forced Labour Convention, but circumvented it (legally) by engaging detainees only on works related to bringing the Emergency to an end.[110] The agreements which deserve fuller discussion are the Geneva Conventions and the European Convention on Human Rights.

Before Common Article 3 to the 1949 Geneva Conventions the laws of war simply did not apply to internal conflicts. In classical international law, internal conflict exists in three escalating categories: rebellion, insurgency and belligerency. Only when belligerency is reached do the laws of war apply.[111] Crucially, the condition must be formally recognised by either a third state or the official government.[112] This situation, so obviously detrimental to insurgents, resulted from the close relationship between the emergence of modern international law and the rise of the state.[113] Although expert commentators and bodies such as the ICRC had long viewed the distinction between internal and international conflicts as unjustifiable, they had failed to change the system.[114] States could counter revolts in any manner they thought effective, without legal constraints on the severity of the measures adopted. In practice recognition of belligerent status was seldom accorded, last happening in 1902.[115]

When the 1949 conventions were drafted many states, besides Britain, expressed concern over the ramifications that Common Article 3 would

---

[109] A. W. B. Simpson, *Human Rights and the End of Empire: Britain and the Genesis of the European Convention* (Oxford University Press, 2001), 11.

[110] See the documents in TNA, LAB 13/2714 and TNA, CAB 128/27 on the applicability of the convention to Kenya during the Emergency. Elkins disagrees with this interpretation, viewing the efforts to circumvent the convention as illegitimate: *Britain's Gulag*, 304.

[111] L. Moir, *The Law of Internal Armed Conflict* (Cambridge University Press, 2002), 4.

[112] A. Cullen, 'Key Developments Affecting the Scope of Internal Armed Conflict in International Humanitarian Law', *Military Law Review*, 183 (2005), 66. Cullen views 'internal armed conflict' as synonymous with 'non-international armed conflict'.

[113] Van Creveld, 'The Clausewitzian Universe', 412.

[114] J. G. Stewart, 'Towards a Single Definition of Armed Conflict in International Humanitarian Law: A Critique of Internationalized Armed Conflict', *International Review of the Red Cross*, 85 (2003), 313.

[115] Moir, *Law of Internal Armed Conflict*, 13, 19.

have for sovereignty.[116] As a consequence the delegates devised the compromise term 'non-international armed conflicts'. Unfortunately it was not clearly set out what this term meant, and indeed no official definition emerged until an International Criminal Tribunal for the Former Yugoslavia ruling in 1997.[117] In addition to the sovereignty issue, delegates disagreed on the precise level of violence necessary to trigger the article, although they agreed that the insurgents should possess a degree of organisation, including a coherent command structure, and be able to adhere to the article themselves.[118] Even the article's supporters admit that it is easily avoided by states.[119] As Cullen argues, this is because '[t]he absence of a definition has ... undermined the implementation of the international humanitarian law, allowing states latitude to deny the existence of armed conflict'.[120]

Even when applied, Common Article 3 is severely limited in scope.[121] For example, captured persons do not enjoy prisoner of war status and are liable to be tried for treason, which in effect happened in Kenya under the Emergency legislation.[122] Government criminalisation of the insurgents can lead to a breakdown in reciprocity, and thus contribute towards atrocities happening.[123] A common argument made about low-intensity conflicts is that symmetry is less likely, and consequently reciprocity breaks down.[124] But the utilitarian logic present in the laws of war actually encourages deterioration by refusing to extend a symmetrical system of legal protections.[125] Another important weakness concerns reprisals, especially relevant here because collective punishment could be deemed a form of reprisal. In general the 1949 conventions prohibit reprisals against protected persons only, and Common Article 3 provides only very limited protections.[126] On the other hand Draper argues that the conventions outlaw reprisals as an enforcement mechanism, which is precisely

[116] L. Lopez, 'Uncivil Wars: The Challenge of Applying International Humanitarian Law to Internal Armed Conflicts', *New York University Law Review*, 69 (1994), 930.

[117] Moir, *Law of Internal Armed Conflict*, 25, 31, 34, 42.

[118] S. R. Ratner and J. S. Abrams, *Accountability for Human Rights Atrocities in International Law: Beyond the Nuremberg Legacy* (Oxford University Press, 2001), 96; Moir, *Law of Internal Armed Conflict*, 36.

[119] J. B. Kelly, 'Legal Aspects of Military Operations in Counterinsurgency', *Military Law Review*, 21 (1963), 100; Detter, *The Law of War*, 201.

[120] Cullen, 'Key Developments', 82.

[121] Lopez, 'Uncivil Wars', 918.

[122] Green, *The Contemporary Law of Armed Conflict*, 45, 318.

[123] Kelly, 'Legal Aspects of Military Operations', 106–9.

[124] K. W. Abbott, 'International Relations Theory, International Law, and the Regime Governing Atrocities in Internal Conflicts', *American Journal of International Law*, 93 (1999), 370.

[125] Osiel, 'Obeying Orders', 27.   [126] Detter, *The Law of War*, 300.

what collective punishment aims at.[127] Therefore there was no unambiguous position on the legality of collective punishment in internal conflicts under international treaty law by 1952. Not until the 1977 additional protocols were reprisals against civilians entirely criminalised.[128] At a deeper level, the article is flawed through the absence of enforcement or implementation mechanisms.[129]

Much expert legal opinion suggests that Common Article 3 was inapplicable during the Kenya Emergency, and even if it had been applicable, the article would have afforded limited and ineffective protections. Britain signed the conventions in 1949 and ratified them in 1957, updating the *Manual of Military Law* in 1958.[130] Therefore international law failed to constrain military operations in Kenya. Or could Geneva have been applicable via customary international law instead? Writing in 1958, Draper declared the conventions in force from October 1950.[131] On treaty law Roberts and Guelff state that:

By its *signature*, a state indicates its intent to be bound by a treaty . . . In general, a signatory state must subsequently ratify a treaty if it is to be bound. A state which has signed but not ratified a treaty is obliged to refrain from acts which would defeat the object and purpose of the treaty.[132]

Therefore the British Army need only have acted in accordance with the spirit of the 1949 conventions; although as shown above, this was interpreted to exclude Common Article 3. This is also noticeable in the War Office's behaviour in relation to conventional conflicts. For example, on 3 December 1952, British Command Japan informed the War Office that the UN Commander-in-Chief in Korea had instructed all forces to treat prisoners of war in accordance with the 1949 convention, and that its humanitarian principles in general were in force.[133] Furthermore, in December 1953 the War Office observed that:

we have not been hindered by non-ratification since we have proceeded on the assumption that the enabling legislation will have been passed before there is a war or that there would then be a declaration by the Government that the 1949 Conventions would be applied.[134]

---

[127] Draper, 'The Ethical and Juridical Status of Constraints in War', 182.
[128] Osiel, 'Obeying Orders', 21.   [129] Lopez, 'Uncivil Wars', 925.
[130] War Office, *The Law of War on Land, being Part III of the Manual of Military Law* (London: HMSO, 1958).
[131] G. I. A. D. Draper, *The Red Cross Conventions* (London: Stevens & Sons, 1958), 1.
[132] A. Roberts and R. Guelff (eds.), *Documents on the Laws of War*, 3rd edn (Oxford University Press, 2000), 17. Emphasis in original.
[133] TNA, WO 32/19272: Confidential cipher telegram, Britcom Japan to War Office, received 3 December 1952.
[134] TNA, WO 32/18511: Letter from Evans to Kemball, 11 December 1953.

However, several writers argue that Common Article 3 only became part of customary international law from around the mid-1970s to the late 1980s.[135] A rule of customary international law develops when most states behave in a certain way.[136] Britain was certainly not alone in ignoring Article 3 in its colonies in the 1950s, so in both theoretical and practical terms the article exerted little restraint on the armed forces. The customary rules relating to internal conflicts were extremely limited, and states cannot become subject to legal obligations without their consent.[137] The evidence clearly demonstrates the British government's refusal to restrict itself under Common Article 3.

In one last sense, however, international law confined the state's actions. In March 1951 Britain ratified the European Convention on Human Rights. The convention came into effect in Kenya on 23 October 1953, just over a year into the Emergency. Simpson depicts an enthusiastic Foreign Office, responsible for signing the convention, at odds with a suspicious Colonial Office. The Colonial Office and other detractors saw the convention as unnecessary when Britain was the true mother of liberty, who had protected her people's freedoms perfectly well without foreign agreements.[138] The convention attracted hardly any attention in Britain in the early years. There is no mention of it in the East Africa Command files and the likelihood of the average officer, let alone soldier, having been aware of its restrictions during the Emergency is virtually nil.

As only inter-state complaints were allowed until 1966, nobody in Kenya could have invoked the convention in order to change government policy. As the other European powers found themselves in similar messy counter-insurgencies during this period as well, they would hardly have raised complaints with Britain at the intergovernmental level (and in fact did not).[139] Derogations were allowed during emergencies, and the government lodged a rather late 'laconic' derogation on 24 May 1954. Certain things were still inviolable, such as the right to life, freedom from torture and slavery.[140] Therefore from 23 October 1953 until 24 May 1954 the army was restrained by the European Convention,

---

[135] Ratner and Abrams, *Accountability for Human Rights Atrocities*, 99, 106; M. Schmoeckel, 'Review of Best, *War and Law since 1945* and Andreopolous, *The Laws of War*', *Journal of Modern History*, 69 (1997), 572; Cullen, 'Key Developments', 67.

[136] M. Byers, *Custom, Power and the Power of Rules: International Relations and Customary International Law* (Cambridge University Press, 1999), 157; Peter Malanczuk, *Akehurst's Modern Introduction to International Law*, 7th rev. edn (London: Routledge, 1997), 39.

[137] Rogers, *Law on the Battlefield*, xxi; Byers, *Custom, Power and the Power of Rules*, 14.

[138] Simpson, *Human Rights*, 2–6, 808, 838, 17, 22.

[139] *Ibid.*, 4, 809, 824.   [140] *Ibid.*, 874–81.

and to a lesser extent afterwards. However, the army cannot be said to have been constrained in any conscious sense. And what is more, the worst excesses arose between October 1952 and June 1953, when none of the legal protections applied. In short, international law created a permissive environment for atrocities in Kenya.

Keeping law weak in colonial rebellions

Although directives explicitly ordering atrocities in Kenya were never issued, a permissive legal environment allowed atrocity behaviour to take place. The reasons for this stemmed from international law itself and the British interpretation of it. As a reaction to the Second World War, there were two major changes relevant to atrocities in internal wars: the rules on obedience and the extension of the laws of war to these conflicts. The government's formal position on obedience changed in line with the Nuremberg Principle, but in practice very few people within the army knew about it. After the war, military education and training concentrated on other priorities than instilling an understanding about Nuremberg. The country as a whole was apathetic about war crimes trials and focused on rebuilding and renewal. For most British soldiers, as for most of British society, the notion that the British Army needed to take heed of a legal reform designed to stop state-sanctioned brutality was absurd. Systematic abuse of civilians was something the Germans did, not something British soldiers could ever be capable of. The army as an institution resisted the Nuremberg Principle because reflex obedience would have been undermined by implementing the notion in training regimes. Compounding matters, the army's regimental structure promoted subcultures which may have compromised a soldier's ability to decide whether an action was 'manifestly illegal', a concept reliant upon universal reasoning. The consequence for the Kenya Emergency was that soldiers lacked the knowledge and training to discern illegal abuse and to stop it happening. As we shall see, the Emergency Regulations in Kenya permitted a great deal of force, and the ordinary soldier was poorly informed about his duty to challenge the widespread brutality he encountered. The soldier's intellectual impotence to halt abuses condoned by the state resulted from the deliberate government decision to exclude Nuremberg from military training and education.

The British government faced further incursions by international law into how the security forces countered colonial rebellions. The government adopted a plainly hostile line to Common Article 3 of the 1949 Geneva Conventions. Resenting the encroachment into sovereignty, above all else the government resisted the article for its potential effect on operations in Palestine, Malaya and elsewhere. The British government's ability to sideline law in counter-insurgencies actually derived from international law itself, and not solely from national politics. As British policy on obedience reflected a transnational concern for maintaining military effectiveness within professional armies, so the reluctance to be bound by expanding rules on internal conflict reflected how international law traditionally elevated the state above all other entities. Military necessity privileged commanders in using whatever force they required. Extending Common Article 3, or for that matter other limitations such as the European Convention, to the colonies would have undermined state authority and prevented the use of repression as a method. This book will show how committed the government remained to using repression in Kenya. The British stance succeeded because international law on internal conflicts was weak in the 1950s, and most countries agreed with the position. The decolonisation wars which wracked the world through the decades following the Geneva negotiations ultimately proved the need for stronger protections. For the Kikuyu, Embu and Meru in Kenya, and many elsewhere, the ability of a colonial power to declare its policies outside international law had terrible consequences.

4 'The degree of force necessary': British traditions in countering colonial rebellions

International law bestowed few protections on those caught up in the British Empire's decolonisation wars. Yet some vestiges of restraint remained, an achievement normally attributed to the British 'minimum force' principle. After exploring what minimum force was and what it was supposed to achieve, this chapter presents a sustained critique. The concept is far from unique to Britain, and while an irresolvable debate about which came first is avoided, we should at least recognise co-existence with international law. The notion of minimum force stemming from national characteristics is rejected on the grounds that such claims constitute little more than romantic self-delusion.

Minimum force is better perceived as an organisational norm, but one perhaps less central or benign than sometimes thought. In conceptual terms, minimum force is less constraining to soldiers than advocates believe, as it replicates the international norm of *Kriegsraison* in granting virtually any action *ex post facto* legitimation. Instead of dominating how British military behaviour in small wars is studied, minimum force should be given equal prominence with the phenomenon of exemplary force. Because the army disliked abstract thought and soldiers derived their conceptual understanding from actual practice, we must examine practice as much as doctrine. For this reason, the chapter provides a concise overview of military operations from the beginning of the twentieth century to 1952.[1] It examines how thinking about the use of force developed, and how in practice the notion of exemplary force often proved important. These years constituted the organisation's immediate tradition, from which lessons about the legally permissible application of force in counter-insurgency situations were derived.

---

[1] B. Holden Reid, 'Introduction: Is There a British Military "Philosophy"?', in J. J. G. Mackenzie and B. Holden Reid (eds.), *Central Region vs. Out-of-area: Future Commitments* (London: Tri-Service, 1990), 1; C. J. McInnes, 'The British Army's New Way in Warfare: A Doctrinal Misstep?', *Defense and Security Analysis*, 23 (2007), 127–41.

Filling the gap? Minimum force in British military thinking

Despite international law's structural failure to prescribe sufficient restraint on the employment of force, moderating influences may also exist within a national strategic culture.[2] In the British case, the main influence resided in the British Army's organisational culture. Minimum force is deeply ingrained in international law in the principles of proportionality and discrimination.[3] Still, the British Army developed a distinctive view on the concept that is worthy of investigation.

The origins and nature of the concept

The minimum force concept originated in the English common law tradition which allowed the executive the right to restore the peace with no more force than absolutely necessary.[4] At first limited to civil unrest in Britain alone, the concept evolved to incorporate all forms of unrest, from riots to full-scale revolution.[5] The common law obliged every citizen, including soldiers who were technically nothing more than citizens in uniform, to assist the civil power in enforcing law and order when required.[6] During civil disturbances it was a commander's duty to open fire if he could not otherwise stop the violence before him. The commander who does nothing 'certainly will be wrong'. By extension, he legally had to use enough force to be effective.[7] During insurrections, the duty to stop violence with violence applied most strongly, which meant troops had to 'be prepared to live and fight hard'.[8] Thornton moves beyond Townshend's and Mockaitis's emphasis on the common law in arguing that the concept derived from the national culture. In his view two sources were paramount: pragmatism and 'Victorian values'.[9] These values were translated 'via a quartet of socializing media: the ideal of empire, the class and public school

[2] Van Creveld, 'The Clausewitzian Universe', 424; C. S. Gray, *Modern Strategy* (Oxford University Press, 1999), 68.
[3] I. Clark, *Waging War: A Philosophical Introduction* (Oxford: Clarendon Press, 1988), 35, 43.
[4] Townshend, *Civil Wars*, 19; Mockaitis, *British Counterinsurgency*, 18.
[5] Mockaitis, *British Counterinsurgency*, 13.
[6] JSCSC, Army Staff College syllabus, 1947.   [7] *Ibid.*; Townshend, *Civil Wars*, 19.
[8] JSCSC, Army Staff College syllabus, 1945.
[9] R. Thornton, 'Understanding the Cultural Bias of a Military Organization and its Effect on the Process of Change: A Comparative Analysis of the Reaction of the British and United States Armies to the Demands of Post-Cold War Peace Support Operations in the Period, 1989–1999' (doctoral thesis, University of Birmingham, 2001), 128.

systems, and popular culture'.[10] Furthermore, the British national character emphasised free will and individuality, leading to pragmatism within organisations. The army avoided developing a complicated counter-insurgency doctrine, preferring to extol individual decision-making, with minimum force as a simple guideline to be followed in all situations.[11]

The concept apparently produced positive practical results. Large-scale casualties alienated the population, and avoiding civilian deaths helped win the population's support.[12] Although reprisals were occasionally effective in the short term, in the long run they produced hate, fear and mistrust. The Army Staff College course presented them as 'patently unjust and uncivilised'.[13] Instead of employing maximum fire-power in a bid to kill as many people as possible, taking prisoners provided intelligence, helpful for defeating elusive opponents.[14] When suspects were interrogated, the need for trustworthy intelligence ruled out torture, thought to provide unreliable information.[15] 'Respect ... is necessary: respect is achieved by law and order applied fairly and promptly'; keeping to this policy meant that the 'inhabitants will gradually drift apart from guerrillas'.[16] The Staff College course recognised the difficulty in assessing the degree of force to use:

Generally speaking, success in battle depends upon the use of overwhelming force at the correct time and place. For internal security operations the reverse applies, since the most important single principle is that of minimum force.[17]

The position is reflected in the key 1949 booklet *Imperial Policing and Duties in Aid of the Civil Power*:

There is ... one principle that must be observed in all types of action taken by the troops: no more force shall be applied than the situation demands.[18]

At the Staff College the principle was oft repeated, for example in 1947: 'To enforce law and order no one is allowed to use more force than is necessary'.[19] British soldiers naturally grasped the idea, by their 'friendly

---

[10] *Ibid.*, 74, 83, 89.   [11] *Ibid.*, 75.
[12] Charters, 'From Palestine to Northern Ireland', 223.
[13] JSCSC, Army Staff College syllabus, 1947.
[14] Charters, 'From Palestine to Northern Ireland', 172.
[15] Mockaitis, *British Counterinsurgency*, 25–7, 54–7.
[16] JSCSC, Army Staff College syllabus, 1945.
[17] JSCSC, Army Staff College syllabus, 1948.
[18] TNA, WO 279/391. Booklet, *Imperial Policing and Duties in Aid of the Civil Power*. War Office Code no. 8439, issued by the Army Council 13 June 1949, superseding *Notes on Imperial Policing*, 1934, and *Duties in Aid of the Civil Power*, 1937 (and 1945 amendment), 5.
[19] JSCSC, Army Staff College syllabus, 1947, and also for 1948.

attitude' and 'instinctive kindness and decency'.[20] A January 1949 article in the *British Army Review* encouraged 'discipline and behaviour [that was] absolutely correct', 'fair play', not doing 'any avoidable damage', and 'the minimum force necessary to achieve your object' during internal security operations.[21] Another article a year later emphasised the importance of restraint in low-intensity operations.[22] In one view, reprisals against a community for acts committed by its inhabitants who could not be identified were sometimes justified. Incarceration, fines and the seizure or destruction of property were options at the commander's disposal. None the less, they remained measures only to be resorted to in extreme circumstances, expert opinion deeming them generally illegal.[23] In riots the use of firepower was the last resort, for example, in self-defence. When used, a specified number of single shots were to be directed at individual ring-leaders and intended to wound instead of kill.[24] The Staff College course enjoined 'rigid discipline' when conducting searches, with 'civility'.[25]

The doctrine, professional journal articles and Staff College syllabuses clearly show that the concept was specifically laid down, taught and discussed. An added incentive came from the official position actively criminalising excessive force:

> a soldier is guilty of an offence if he uses that excess, even under the direction of the civil authority, provided he has no such excuse as that he is bound in the particular circumstances of the case to take the facts, as distinguished from the law, from the civil authority.[26]

Enforcement came through the ordinary courts, which could scrutinise the legality of the use of force after the event.[27] This legal situation was taught at the Staff College, where it was stressed that self-discipline and the soldier's 'high code' safeguarded him from prosecution.[28] Raghavan argues that supervision by the civil power and fear of punishment ensured that the concept became a practical reality.[29]

[20] JSCSC, Army Staff College syllabus, 1945.

[21] No Author, 'Hints on Internal Security', *British Army Review*, 1 (1949), 54–61.

[22] C. J. Gittings, 'The Bertrand Stewart Prize Essay, 1949', *Army Quarterly*, 59 (1950), 161–77.

[23] Wade, 'War Crimes Trials'.   [24] JSCSC, Army Staff College syllabus, 1948.

[25] JSCSC, Army Staff College syllabus, 1947.

[26] War Office, *Manual of Military Law*, 1929 edition, 246. The 1958 edition altered the wording of this paragraph only for clarification's sake. War Office, *Manual of Military Law, Part II*, 8th edn (London: HMSO, 1958), Section V, 1.

[27] Townshend, *Civil Wars*, 19.   [28] JSCSC, Army Staff College syllabus, 1947.

[29] S. Raghavan, 'Protecting the Raj: The Army in India and Internal Security, c. 1919–39', *Small Wars and Insurgencies*, 16 (2005), 259–60.

In his prominent study on British counter-insurgency, Mockaitis asserts that minimum force gradually expanded in doctrine and practice. Initially the *Manual of Military Law* distinguished between riots, where the concept applied, and insurrections, where it did not. Over time the distinction became blurred.[30] Moreman concurs by pointing out how 'colonial warfare' transformed into 'imperial policing' after the First World War.[31] Raghavan places the change in the revised 1929 *Manual*.[32] However, in Mockaitis's view a more substantial change arose in the 1934 publication *Notes on Imperial Policing*. The War Office pamphlet stipulated that when fighting rebels away from civilian areas the principle did not come into effect. But when dealing with a riot or other situations where the innocent were mixed in with the guilty, minimum force applied.[33] Arguably the final consolidation between riots and insurrections occurred in 1949 with the publication of *Imperial Policing and Duties in Aid of the Civil Power*. The pamphlet dictated that: no more force shall be applied than the situation demands.'[34] The impetus for the evolving extension came from changing attitudes in Britain towards violence, evidenced in the public reactions to the Boer War, the Irish War of Independence and the Amritsar massacre.[35] As a result the army largely avoided retaliatory measures and the indiscriminate use of force.[36]

Conceptual weaknesses

There is no denying the common law tradition from which minimum force emerged. However, as Simpson notes, in counter-insurgency situations it came into operation alongside emergency laws, which originated in Ireland in the nineteenth century. These generally suspended incompatible laws, including basic liberties such as *habeas corpus*, so the notion that minimum force worked within a liberal framework is certainly mistaken.[37] Carruthers describes the rule of law under Emergency legislation in Kenya as 'sham legalism', and in this respect Kenya was identical to Britain's other colonial campaigns.[38]

---

[30] Mockaitis, *British Counterinsurgency*, 18, 24.
[31] T. R. Moreman, *The Army in India and the Development of Frontier Warfare, 1849–1947* (Basingstoke: Macmillan, 1998), xvii.
[32] Raghavan, 'Protecting the Raj', 260.   [33] Mockaitis, *British Counterinsurgency*, 24.
[34] Cited in *ibid.*, 25.   [35] *Ibid.*, 18.   [36] *Ibid.*, 27.
[37] Simpson, *Human Rights*, 78, 84.
[38] Carruthers, 'Being Beastly to the Mau Mau', 494.

From the military perspective, the concept bears a striking resemblance to the principle of economy of force, and as such is less than entirely ethical-legal in origin.[39] Similarly, 'Victorian values' should be treated with scepticism. As Ellis insists:

the widespread use of automatic weapons against adversaries armed only with clubs and spears could not by any stretch of the imagination be regarded as fair play. To a large extent, consciences could be calmed by the knowledge that Africans were not quite human, and therefore beyond the pale of Imperialist morality.[40]

Arguments about national characteristics rely heavily on syrupy anecdotal evidence. The assertion that national characteristics remain consistent over centuries ignores alterations to social norms driven by technological developments, immigration and numerous other factors.[41] The Empire and British society were both highly pluralistic, bringing into question the notion of a monolithic 'imperial culture'.[42] If there was no single imperial culture, condensing national characteristics into two categories (such as pragmatism and Victorian values) is problematic.

The case made by Mockaitis for the ubiquity of the concept, supported by the Staff College syllabus, cannot be entirely refuted. However, he does exaggerate the extent to which minimum force applied in all situations. Official thinking supported much greater latitude in the use of force in dealing with insurrections than riots, and this matters because insurgencies were considered to be insurrections and not riots. For example, even by 1958 the *Manual* stated that: 'The existence of an armed insurrection would justify the use of any degree of force necessary effectually to meet and cope with the insurrection.'[43] Official doctrine and practice allowed a far greater degree of force to be used in the colonies than in the United Kingdom. Importantly, the key 1949 publication noted how: 'The degree of force necessary and the methods of applying it will obviously differ very greatly as between the United Kingdom and places overseas.'[44] As Mockaitis admits, two standard textbooks taught at Sandhurst and the Staff College advocated harsh early action to nip trouble in the bud, in contrast to the minimum force concept.[45] In addition the Colonial Office admitted that the concept clashed with British practices in the colonies:

---

[39] Jochnick and Normand, 'The Legitimation of Violence', 4.

[40] J. Ellis, *The Social History of the Machine Gun* (London: Pimlico, 1993), 106.

[41] Thornton, 'Understanding the Cultural Bias of a Military', 74.

[42] A. Thompson, *The Empire Strikes Back? The Impact of Imperialism on Britain from the Mid-Nineteenth Century* (Harlow: Pearson Education, 2005), xiv.

[43] War Office, *Manual of Military Law*, Part II, 1958 edn, section V, 10.

[44] War Office, *Imperial Policing*, 5.   [45] Mockaitis, *British Counterinsurgency*, 26.

a number of Colonies (notably in Africa) have on their Statute Book collective punishment Ordinances which provide that this form of punishment may be used to deal with offences such as cattle stealing and the like ... There are, however, the more difficult cases of the present disturbances in Malaya, and (to quote the most obvious example) the use of punitive bombing in the Aden Protectorate ... what might be described as 'collective punishment' *has* been used [in Malaya] – e.g., the burning of villages, and so on – and may well be used again.[46]

The 1949 pamphlet recognised that collective punishment contravened minimum force and also the Hague Convention, but regarded the consequent hardships as 'inevitable' and 'a necessity'.[47]

Another weakness with the concept reflected the problem with military necessity in international law. The concept was always limited by the question of who decided exactly what the term meant: the military commander present at the time. As only a soldier was in a position to know the power of his weapons, and the commander was present at the critical moment, he alone could decide how much force to use.[48] What minimum force meant was uncertain, and therefore arbitrary. This was partially inevitable as the circumstances of each particular case obviously varied.[49] In addition, although advocates claim that soldiers remained answerable to the civil courts, in practice commanders and soldiers were hardly ever called to account after putting down insurrections.[50] The 1947 Staff College course taught its students that so long as commanders believed their actions to be right, they should not fear an inquiry into their conduct.[51] In order to protect soldiers who had used force, the government usually passed an Act of Indemnity.[52] This was 'a statute intended to make transactions legal which were illegal when they took place, and to free the individuals concerned from legal liability'.[53] Therefore the idea that the military were subject to rigorous civilian oversight and dreaded prosecution is misleading.

The organisational concept of minimum force partially compensated for the lack of interest in international law within the British Army. The concept derived from common law, was adopted for ethical and pragmatic reasons, found clear doctrinal and educational expression and was

---

[46] TNA, LCO 2/4309: Letter from Trafford Smith, Colonial Office, to C. G. Kemball, Foreign Office, 25 June 1949. Emphasis in original.
[47] War Office, *Imperial Policing*, 35.
[48] JSCSC, Army Staff College syllabus, 1947. 'Commander' denotes anyone in command of other soldiers, potentially anyone from a field marshal to a lance-corporal.
[49] JSCSC, Army Staff College syllabus, 1947.   [50] Simpson, *Human Rights*, 61.
[51] JSCSC, Army Staff College syllabus, 1947.
[52] The double amnesty of January 1955 was effectively an Act of Indemnity for the security forces.
[53] JSCSC, Army Staff College syllabus, 1949.

bounded by civilian oversight. However, the concept is generally over-emphasised in accounts of British counter-insurgency. Emergency laws were widely permissive, the concept's ethical origins cannot be taken seriously, and it did not apply fully in insurrections or in the colonies. Widespread practices such as collective punishment were contradictory, and the commander could use almost any degree of force with impunity.

Exemplary force in British military thought and practice

A major argument in this book is that the role of minimum force has been exaggerated, at the expense of the equally important notion of exemplary, punitive force, characterised by a rapid, and harsh, response to rebellion which punished the general population and aimed at dissuading others from revolting. How exemplary force played a role in British responses to colonial rebellions is explored in two ways. First, by examining two key (though strictly speaking unofficial) doctrinal publications, showing the relationship between the use of force and the need to 'nip trouble in the bud'. Second, by re-examining three examples espoused by minimum force advocates: the Boer War, India (especially the Amritsar massacre) and the Irish War of Independence. Following this, similar examples from elsewhere in the Empire are provided to show that the practices found in these cases were commonplace. Finally, the chapter looks at some events in Kenyan history, establishing several trends which re-emerged in the Mau Mau Emergency. Regiments seldom received training in colonial warfare before going overseas, and lessons learnt were seldom recorded for the benefit of future generations.[54] Therefore the conflicts examined here constituted a traditional way of countering rebellion. They were the army's living memory about how to crush revolts in the Empire, engrained in regimental and personal recollections, ready to be drawn on anew when troops deployed to Kenya in 1952.

Exemplary force in theory

Charles Callwell was the British Army's most influential, and systematic, thinker on 'Small Wars'. His 1896 treatise, *Small Wars: Their Principles and Practice*, received official endorsement from the CIGS.[55] Callwell

---

[54] T. R. Moreman, '"Small Wars" and "Imperial Policing": The British Army and the Theory and Practice of Colonial Warfare in the British Empire, 1919–1939', *Journal of Strategic Studies*, 19 (1996), 108; Moreman, *Army in India*, xix.

[55] Callwell, Sir Charles Edward (1859–1928), by T. R. Moreman, *Oxford Dictionary of National Biography* (Oxford University Press, 2008), online edition, at www.oxforddnb.com/view/article/32251, accessed 31 May 2011.

studied conflicts where regular troops fought irregular fighters, or 'savages' who came from 'semi-civilised races'.[56] Unlike in conventional war, where the object was to destroy the enemy's centre of gravity – his armed forces – small wars affected the entire population. This often involved confiscating cattle and burning villages, which Callwell recognised might 'shock the humanitarian'.[57] These 'punitive measures' would force the opponent either to fight in the open, and thus be destroyed in battle, or submit to British rule.[58] Callwell thought that severe actions at the outset to 'crush the enemy' eventually proved more humane, because they prevented a long and troublesome campaign from developing.[59] In any case, the 'lower races' only understood the language of force, and 'attribute[d] leniency to timidity'.[60]

Charles Gwynn was another highly influential writer on countering rebellion in the colonies, who served as Commandant of the Army Staff College from 1926 to 1931.[61] He differed from Callwell in advocating minimum force for practical and moral reasons. Excessive severity might foster lasting antagonism, and soldiers should always remember that rebels were fellow citizens in the Empire.[62] However, Gwynn believed that 'the power and resolution of the Government forces must be displayed'.[63] During rebellions, government forces typically encountered difficulties in fixing individual responsibility for acts such as sabotage, and it was frequently 'necessary to deal with them by collective punishments'.[64] If reprisals were undertaken, they should be officially authorised.[65] Gwynn agreed with Callwell in recommending prompt offensive action to restore order at the beginning of a revolt.[66] Otherwise, enemy leaders gained in confidence and were able to attract more followers to their cause.[67] Gwynn suggested balancing exemplary, punitive action with minimum force:

Allied with the principle of the minimum use of force is that of firm and timely action. Delay in the use of force, and hesitation to accept responsibility for its employment when the situation clearly demands it, will always be interpreted as

---

[56] C. E. Callwell, *Small Wars: Their Principles and Practice*, 3rd edn (London: University of Nebraska Press, 1996), 21.
[57] *Ibid.*, 40.   [58] *Ibid.*, 145.   [59] *Ibid.*, 74.   [60] *Ibid.*, 72, 148.
[61] Gwynn, Sir Charles William (1870–1963), by G. Sinclair, *Oxford Dictionary of National Biography* (Oxford University Press, 2010), online edition, at www.oxforddnb.com/view/article/98221, accessed 31 May 2011.
[62] C. W. Gwynn, *Imperial Policing*, 2nd edn (London: Macmillan, 1939), 5, 14.
[63] *Ibid.*, 5.   [64] *Ibid.*, 23.   [65] *Ibid.*, 24.   [66] *Ibid.*, 383.   [67] *Ibid.*, 385.

weakness, encourage further disorder and eventually necessitate measures more severe than those which would suffice in the first instance.[68]

As noted earlier, this type of argument mirrored the logic inherent in *Kriegsraison* at the international level.[69] The British normally described the idea as 'nipping trouble in the bud'.[70] A foremost advocate who killed Africans as though on an enjoyable country shoot at the beginning of the century, Richard Meinertzhagen, outlined the rationale behind the idea:

In the long run, inflicting heavy casualties on an enemy will shorten the duration of a conflict, it will teach a lesson and will result in a more enduring peace than less violent measures.[71]

Callwell advocated awing the population with force in such a fashion.[72] Because the Empire lacked enough men to police every area, British power rested not only on prestige and credibility, but ultimately on fear.[73] There were two elements to the punitive use of force early in a revolt. First, advocates such as Callwell and Meinertzhagen thought that awing the population with overwhelming (and indiscriminate) force was the most effective means of avoiding protracted conflict. Second, this was desirable because the Empire was too vast for extended fighting commitments in many areas simultaneously; thus a quick, sharp shock prevented manpower problems from arising. The collapse of Ottoman Turkey and the resulting expansion of the British Empire exacerbated the problem.[74] Even by the end of the 1940s, when approximately 300,000 personnel were involved in extra-European defence commitments, military overstretch caused headaches for strategic planners. Employing force punitively at an early stage prevented Britain from

---

[68] *Ibid.*, 15.

[69] Hew Strachan suggests there was a relationship between the nature of colonial violence and the emergence of total war in the twentieth century: H. Strachan, 'Total War in the Twentieth Century', in A. Marwick, C. Emsley and W. Simpson (eds.), *Total War and Historical Change: Europe 1914–1955* (Buckingham: Open University Press, 2001), 264–5. The literature on total war is large, and growing. For a review, see W. Mulligan, 'Review Article: Total War', *War in History*, 15 (2008), 211–21.

[70] Simpson, *Human Rights*, 53.

[71] R. Meinertzhagen, *Kenya Diary 1902–1906* (London: Welbeck Street, 1957), vi.

[72] N. Collett, *The Butcher of Amritsar: General Reginald Dyer* (London: Hambledon and London, 2005), 436.

[73] D. Reynolds, *Britannia Overruled: British Foreign Policy and World Power in the Twentieth Century* (London: Longman, 1991), 29.

[74] D. Omissi, 'Britain, the Assyrians and the Iraq Levies, 1919–1932', *Journal of Imperial and Commonwealth History*, 17 (1989), 301; see also D. French, 'Big Wars and Small Wars between the Wars, 1919–39', in H. Strachan (ed.), *Big Wars and Small Wars: The British Army and the Lessons of War in the Twentieth Century* (London: Routledge, 2006), 36–53.

'losing face', providing a lesson for those elsewhere in the Empire who might consider challenging British rule.[75]

The relationship between limiting manpower and financial commitments and punitive force is clearest when considering air power. After the First World War, several large garrisons were slowly replaced by the new system of 'air control'.[76] As David Killingray argues, air control operations against 'uncivilized' opponents, such as Kurds, Afridis, Somalis and Sudanese, permitted the indiscriminate use of machine-guns and aerial bombardment that was politically unacceptable against 'civilized' opponents, such as the Irish in 1919–21.[77] Air control adherents employed euphemisms such as 'salutary moral effect', and officials removed references to civilian casualties to obfuscate the indiscriminate, destructive reality.[78] In effect, air control relied upon exemplary, terrorising violence.[79]

At the beginning of the twentieth century punitive expeditions were the tool most often taken up to nip trouble in the bud. During these operations the security forces marched through the miscreant area burning villages and crops, confiscating cattle and sheep and fighting with the inhabitants. Those spared an immediate death risked starvation resulting from the destruction of their livelihoods.[80] Even by 1957 General Lathbury, Erskine's successor in Kenya, expressed his support for the idea: 'It is often kinder to take strong measures in the beginning and so avoid subsequent loss of life.'[81] The logic behind 'nipping trouble in the bud' advanced punishing a recalcitrant population and taking revenge on them for misdeeds (*Notes on Imperial Policing* advised this).[82] Destroying property and people warned others what to expect if they stepped out of line. In general terms, mass killing is more likely when policing resources are overstretched, the territory is regarded as a vital

---

[75] S. Croft, A. Dorman, W. Rees and M. Uttley, *Britain and Defence 1945–2000: A Policy Re-evaluation* (Harlow: Pearson Education, 2001), 31–2.

[76] Omissi, 'Britain, the Assyrians and the Iraq Levies', 301. See also D. Omissi, 'Technology and Repression: Air Control in Palestine 1922–36', *Journal of Strategic Studies*, 13 (1990), 41–63.

[77] D. Killingray, '"A Swift Agent of Government": Air Power in British Colonial Africa, 1916–1939', *Journal of African History*, 25 (1984), 432.

[78] A. Clayton, *The British Empire as a Superpower, 1919–39* (London: Macmillan, 1986), 80.

[79] P. Satia, 'The Defense of Inhumanity: Air Control and the British Idea of Arabia', *American Historical Review*, 111 (2006), 16–51.

[80] D. Killingray, 'The Maintenance of Law and Order in British Colonial Africa', *African Affairs*, 85 (1986), 434.

[81] Lieutenant-General Sir Gerald Lathbury, Foreword in Meinertzhagen, *Kenya Diary*, vii.

[82] Simpson, *Human Rights*, 63; K. Jeffery, 'Colonial Warfare 1900–39', in C. J. McInnes and G. Sheffield (eds.), *Warfare in the Twentieth Century: Theory and Practice* (London: Unwin Hyman, 1988), 37.

interest, the victims cannot retaliate effectively and there is little chance of outside intervention.[83] Many of these conditions existed in the twentieth century, as Britain decolonised reluctantly and often only after a bitter fight.[84] They certainly prevailed in Kenya, which was regarded as a vital strategic base, with Mombasa commanding the Indian Ocean.[85]

There is a weight of evidence illustrating how the British lacked sufficient manpower to police the Empire according to the minimum force concept. There were frequently critical deficiencies in resourcing defence policy in the post-war period.[86] In the short term before the Kenya Emergency the Conservative government cut defence spending, because the level of expenditure was damaging the economy and hindering post-war recovery.[87] However, the manpower problem was a long-term headache for all British governments, with the army suffering manpower shortages throughout the eighteenth and nineteenth centuries.[88] The shortfall arose from maintaining an over-extended empire without the concomitant commitment of resources.[89] The lack of resources argument can, however, be pushed too far. In 1950 Britain initiated, with American support, a massive rearmament programme, while maintaining a large conscript army.[90] In addition by 1952 arms production exceeded that of all Britain's European NATO allies combined, so the cuts started from a very high level of production.[91] At least in the 1950s Britain could hardly have devoted any more resources to the military without ruining the country's finances. The Empire demanded manpower, and the government used several techniques to stretch resources. These included adopting the latest high-technology equipment as a force multiplier, pursuing burden-sharing with allies, seeking arms limitation agreements, appeasing potential enemies and adopting

[83] B. A. Valentino, *Final Solutions: Mass Killing and Genocide in the Twentieth Century* (London: Cornell University Press, 2004), 89–90.

[84] F. Furedi, *Colonial Wars and the Politics of Third World Nationalism* (London: I. B. Tauris, 1994), 9.

[85] Reynolds, *Britannia Overruled*, 189.

[86] J. Baylis, *British Defence Policy: Striking the Right Balance* (Basingstoke: Macmillan, 1989), xi.

[87] R. N. Rosecrance, *Defense of the Realm: British Strategy in the Nuclear Epoch* (London: Columbia University Press, 1968), 156; J. Baylis and A. Macmillan, 'The British Global Strategy Paper of 1952', *Journal of Strategic Studies*, 16 (1993), 200.

[88] D. French, 'Have the Options Really Changed? British Defence Policy in the Twentieth Century', *Journal of Strategic Studies*, 15 (1992), 54. For a rigorous reassessment of British military policy after the Second World War, see D. French, *Army, Empire, and Cold War: The British Army and Military Policy, 1945–1971* (Oxford University Press, 2012).

[89] M. Dockrill, *British Defence since 1945* (Oxford: Basil Blackwell, 1988), 11.

[90] Rosecrance, *Defense of the Realm*, 152.

[91] C. J. Bartlett, 'The Military Instrument in British Foreign Policy', in J. Baylis (ed.), *British Defence Policy in a Changing World* (London: Croom Helm, 1977), 30–6.

deterrence strategies.[92] Employing local security forces also proved cheaper than sending British soldiers abroad. In colonial counter-insurgencies the machine gun 'offered the most economical solution to the problem of keeping down the whole population of a continent with small bodies of police and soldiers'.[93] In this sense, exemplary force resulted from the perennial British refusal to match commitments to resources.

Exemplary force in practice – the Boer War

The twentieth century opened with the British Army accused of practising scorched earth policies, rape, looting, summary execution and operating deadly concentration camps in South Africa.[94] Selecting the Boer War as a case supporting the importance of minimum force is quite odd. Huge forces were sent on large-scale operations, deploying superior firepower and waging war against non-combatants. Liberal leader Sir Henry Campbell-Bannerman's urge to denounce the 'methods of barbarism' had virtually no impact upon the war's conduct.[95] These methods prompted introspection amongst some army officers, who doubted their morality, without being moved to resistance.[96] While some claims against the army, such as raping Boer women during the guerrilla phase, cannot be fully substantiated, there is little question that there were such incidents.[97] Similarly, the precise cost in lives exacted by the official policy of summarily executing irregulars in British uniforms is unknown.[98] The military police experienced trouble in restraining the troops from looting and drunkenness.[99] These problems may have arisen partly from weak discipline, but were hardly out of place when policy demanded war against civilians on the veldt. The farm-burning policy,

---

[92] French, 'Have the Options Really Changed?', 51.

[93] Ellis, *Social History of the Machine Gun*, 92.

[94] K. Surridge, 'Rebellion, Martial Law and British Civil-Military Relations: The War in Cape Colony 1899–1902', *Small Wars and Insurgencies*, 8 (1997), 35–60. Helpful works on the Boer War include M. M. Evans, *Encyclopedia of the Boer War, 1899–1902* (Oxford: ABC-Clio, 2000); D. Lowry (ed.) *The South African War Reappraised* (Manchester University Press, 2000); B. Nasson, 'Waging Total War in South Africa: Some Centenary Writings on the Anglo-Boer War', *Journal of Military History*, 66 (2002), 813–28.

[95] D. Judd and K. Surridge, *The Boer War* (London: John Murray, 2003), 4.

[96] K. Surridge, '"All you soldiers are what we call pro-Boer": The Military Critique of the South African War, 1899–1902', *History*, 82 (1997), 591–3.

[97] Judd and Surridge, *The Boer War*, 11.

[98] B. Vandervort, *Wars of Imperial Conquest in Africa, 1830–1914* (London: UCL Press, 1998), 188. It should be noted that combatants wearing enemy uniforms in battle are not normally protected by international law.

[99] E. M. Spiers, *The Late Victorian Army 1868–1902* (Manchester University Press, 1992), 323.

started in June 1900, produced over 600 burnt homesteads by November in the Orange Free State region alone. The policy came directly from the punitive mentality, aimed at punishing the families of rebels.[100] Eventually around 30,000 farms were partly or completely destroyed, along with about forty towns.[101]

In early March 1900 the troops began systematic drives through the countryside, trying to catch guerrillas while simultaneously taking everything that might support them, from horses, cattle and sheep to women and children. Whether the scorched earth and population movement policies worked will long stay open to dispute; nevertheless they were officially sanctioned.[102] Women and children picked up from the veldt, the families of prisoners of war or those made homeless by the burning campaign found themselves in concentration camps. Established in the summer of 1900 they contained around 160,000 people at their peak.[103] These camps came under the army chain of command. From the outset they were deliberately constructed and run on the cheap. Lord Kitchener, the Commander-in-Chief in South Africa, hoped that the tough living conditions endured by the inmates would encourage guerrillas to surrender. Accordingly, the families of those who surrendered received improved rations.[104] For many, however, these improvements came too late. Overcrowding, insanitary conditions, a poor diet and bad planning left the women and children highly susceptible to numerous lethal diseases. Measles, typhoid, jaundice, bronchitis, malaria and pneumonia swept the camps. In the month of October 1901, 3,156 people died as a result.[105] Despite the efforts of campaigners such as Emily Hobhouse and Millicent Fawcett, the military failed to act quickly enough. Approximately 28,000 Boers and at least 17,000 black Africans died in the camps.[106] Kitchener did not halt incoming inmates until mid-December 1901, and although apologists argue that he never aimed at genocide, his actions were grossly negligent.[107] Stephen Miller's research on the army in South Africa reveals that soldiers regularly refused Boer irregulars quarter, shooting those attempting to surrender.[108]

---

[100] Judd and Surridge, *The Boer War*, 191.
[101] A. Wessels, 'Afrikaners at War', in J. Gooch (ed.), *The Boer War: Direction, Experience and Image* (London: Frank Cass, 2000), 101.
[102] T. Pakenham, *The Boer War* (London: Abacus, 2003), 493, xvii.
[103] Judd and Surridge, *The Boer War*, 194.   [104] Pakenham, *The Boer War*, 494–5.
[105] Judd and Surridge, *The Boer War*, 194.   [106] Wessels, 'Afrikaners at War', 102.
[107] Pakenham, *The Boer War*, 494–5, 548.
[108] S. M. Miller, 'Duty or Crime? Defining Acceptable Behaviour in the British Army in South Africa, 1899–1902', *Journal of British Studies*, 49 (2010), 311–31.

Exemplary force in practice – British India

The second case mentioned by Mockaitis concerning minimum force is the 1919 massacre at the Jallianwallah Bagh in Amritsar, considered here alongside operations in India in general.[109] Since the massive repression seen in the 1857 Indian Mutiny, the British had regularly responded with severity, such as in the punitive operations against the Kuki tribes on the North-East Frontier from November 1917 to March 1919.[110] Dominant attitudes among the British ruling class in India regarded the country as outside European laws of morality, and by 1919 restraint was viewed as an obstacle to the enforcement of military power.[111] The Mutiny's shadow loomed large, and exemplary force warned the population against wide-scale rebellion.[112] The massacre at the Jallianwallah Bagh in 1919, when 379 peaceful protesters were killed and hundreds of wounded were left untended, was not a singular event but part of a longer tradition of repression.[113] Even in the immediate circumstances this one act did not stand alone. In the following days and weeks systematic repression was applied in large areas of the Punjab. Collective punishments, public floggings without trial and the notorious 'crawling order' prevailed.[114] These and other measures served to facilitate punishment and set an example rather than control disorder, which had already largely stopped.[115]

Minimum force advocates have seen Amritsar as an aberration, but also as a major catalyst in solidifying the concept's dominance within British doctrine and practice.[116] Mockaitis attributes this change to the public reaction against the massacre. However, this perspective is flawed. Although martial law was subsequently declared less often, the emergency powers system that took its place allowed the military equal, if not greater, freedom of action.[117] Even assuming that the army learnt lessons from the massacre, the impact may have been localised and remained with the

---

[109] Mockaitis, *British Counterinsurgency*, 21–5.

[110] Moreman, '"Small Wars" and "Imperial Policing"', 120.

[111] S. Narain, *The Historiography of the Jallianwalla Bagh Massacre* (South Godstone: Spantech and Lancer, 1998), 51; Collett, *The Butcher of Amritsar*, 435.

[112] Narain, *Historiography*, 22; D. Sayer, 'British Reaction to the Amritsar Massacre 1919–1920', *Past and Present*, 131 (1991), 131.

[113] Sayer, 'British Reaction to the Amritsar Massacre', 132, 134.   [114] *Ibid.*, 141.

[115] *Ibid.*, 143. For a reinterpretation which views the use of force as reasonable in the circumstances, see N. Lloyd, *The Amritsar Massacre: The Untold Story of One Fateful Day* (London: I. B. Tauris, 2011).

[116] Thornton, 'Understanding the Cultural Bias of a Military', 120–1. Here he draws on McInnes, *Hot War, Cold War*; Strachan, *The Politics of the British Army* and Mockaitis, *British Counterinsurgency*.

[117] Simpson, *Human Rights*, 70.

army in India.[118] Research by Simeon Shoul indicates that after Amritsar the approach to riot control remained 'inadequate, lacking in necessary self-analysis, over-rigid in its methodology, inconsistently trained for, and tragically resistant to change'.[119] The caution following the massacre was real but very short-lived.[120] The killing of forty-seven people during the 1935 Karachi riots shows that the impact of Amritsar faded with time.[121] As the Indian government pursued its own imperial policy, so the army existed as an almost entirely separate organisation.[122] Training and doctrine in India followed a distinctive pattern, and lessons adopted there were not systematically circulated throughout the rest of the empire.[123]

The Hunter Committee, which investigated Brigadier-General Dyer's actions, censured him for using excessive force in a riot situation. Doctrine still permitted 'any degree of force necessary' for dealing with insurrections. Although the Hunter Committee and the Indian government reprimanded Dyer, their views were in the minority. Dyer argued that his actions were intended to act as a deterrent because he thought that the entire Punjab was in a state of open rebellion.[124] While the Cabinet called for his resignation, neither Dyer nor the Governor of the Punjab, O'Dwyer, faced any punishment.[125] The CIGS, along with many other officers, supported Dyer, as did most Europeans in India and large portions of the British public. The *Morning Post* raised a substantial sum from its readers for Dyer's benefit. Indeed, the public and parliamentary outrage in Britain after the massacre concerned the perceived injustices done to Dyer.[126] This continued for some time; in 1924 O'Dwyer won a libel action which concluded that Dyer had acted properly under the circumstances.[127] The punitive and exemplary nature of the massacre could be seen in later events. Punitive operations were conducted in Waziristan during the winter of 1919–20.[128]

---

[118] Raghavan, 'Protecting the Raj', 253.

[119] S. Shoul, 'In Aid of the Civil Power: The British Army's Riot Control Operations in India, Egypt, and Palestine, 1919–1939', paper presented at the 'Britons at War: New Perspectives' conference, University of Northampton, 21 April 2006. See also S. Shoul, 'Soldiers, Riots, and Aid to the Civil Power, in India, Egypt and Palestine, 1919–1939' (doctoral thesis, University College London, 2006).

[120] Omissi, *Sepoy and the Raj*, 219.   [121] Shoul, 'In Aid of the Civil Power'.

[122] P. Darby, *British Defence Policy East of Suez 1947–1968* (Oxford University Press, 1973), 2; Moreman, *Army in India*, xx. For further on defence policy in the Middle East, see D. R. Devereux, *The Formulation of British Defence Policy towards the Middle East, 1948–56* (London: Macmillan, 1990).

[123] Moreman, '"Small Wars" and "Imperial Policing"', 112, 125, 127.

[124] Raghavan, 'Protecting the Raj', 257–8.   [125] Collett, *The Butcher of Amritsar*, ix.

[126] Sayer, 'British Reaction to the Amritsar Massacre', 150–1, 157, 159.

[127] Narain, *Historiography*, 50.

[128] Moreman, '"Small Wars" and "Imperial Policing"', 113.

During another campaign in Waziristan, in 1936–7, villages suspected of supporting insurgents were destroyed.[129] The authorities thought that the Indian people would interpret hesitation as a sign of weakness; force was the only language the masses could understand. Coercion remained at the heart of British rule in India, including after the fateful events of 1919.[130]

Exemplary force in practice – the Irish War of Independence

The army's practices deviated from minimum force in the Irish War of Independence, from 1919–1921, coming only three years after the 'savage repression' applied during the 1916 Easter Rising.[131] As ever, the army complained about having insufficient troops. Police numbers dropped to dangerously low levels, leading to the evacuation of police stations in troubled areas, with negative consequences for intelligence-gathering. In Ireland the British government adopted a coercive approach and escalated the conflict through pursuing a 'police war' where the division of responsibility between police and army, and the legal framework, remained confused throughout.[132] Abuses were commonplace, including torture to gain information on the rebels.[133] Criticisms concerning the campaign normally focus upon two areas: the conduct of paramilitary forces and the reprisal measures taken.[134]

There were two types of auxiliary forces operating in Ireland. The first were called the 'Black and Tans' because of the unusual uniforms they wore, and fell under the Royal Irish Constabulary (RIC) chain of command. These troops were raised quickly, had little training and no disciplinary code imposed upon them. Their size increased rapidly in 1920 and dramatically changed the war's nature. The second unit, the Auxiliary Division, though technically also part of the RIC, fell under direct War Office command.[135] Paramilitary excesses were widespread; a

---

[129] Moreman, *Army in India*, 160. See also Clayton, *British Empire as a Superpower*, 386–415; G. Kudaisya, '"In Aid of Civil Power": The Colonial Army in Northern India, c.1919–42', *Journal of Imperial and Commonwealth History*, 32 (2004), 41–68.

[130] Omissi, *Sepoy and the Raj*, xviii, 194, 218.

[131] D. Fitzpatrick, 'Militarism in Ireland, 1900–1922', in T. Bartlett and K. Jeffery (eds.), *A Military History of Ireland* (Cambridge University Press, 1996), 396.

[132] M. Hopkinson, *The Irish War of Independence* (Dublin: Gill and Macmillan, 2002), 51, 49, xix, 53.

[133] Clayton, *British Empire as a Superpower*, 87.

[134] For an important reappraisal, which stresses British military success at the local level, see W. Sheehan, *A Hard Local War: The British Army and the Guerrilla War in Cork, 1919–1921* (Stroud: History Press, 2011).

[135] Clayton, *British Empire as a Superpower*, 28, 49. For a detailed study, see D. M. Leeson, *The Black and Tans: British Police and Auxiliaries in the Irish War of Independence* (Oxford University Press, 2011).

few examples illustrate their nature. On 20 September 1920 the RIC burned four public houses, forty-nine houses and a factory in Balbriggan, and killed two suspects. The next day in Clare they killed four people and burned twenty-six buildings in Ennistymon, Lahinch and Milltown Malbay. On 11 December 1920 the Auxiliaries set fire to a section of Cork City in reprisal for an attack on their barracks earlier in the day. On 9 February 1921 the Auxiliaries looted and burned property in Trim, County Meath. The same night in Dublin two prisoners were summarily shot in a field in the suburb of Drumcondra. Major-General Hugh Tudor, the police commander in Ireland, refused to impose effective discipline on his men, fearing the impact this might have on morale.[136] A similar concern would later arise in Kenya. Eventually Brigadier-General Frank Crozier, the Auxiliary commander, and Lieutenant-Colonel J. H. M. Kirkwood, one of his senior officers, resigned in disgust at the protection and encouragement given by their superiors to security force personnel who terrorised the population.[137] As would happen in Kenya, reluctance to restrain excesses amounted to official endorsement.

Reprisals in Ireland started out as unauthorised occurrences but soon became official policy. The military blamed the police for these actions, with General Sir Nevil Macready asserting that the army only carried out four reprisals during the whole conflict – certainly an understatement.[138] Reprisals were normally against the whole community and were perceived to be effective, at least in the short term.[139] High-level discussions about making reprisals official began in September 1920. In early October the Cabinet ordered that burnings stop, but Prime Minister David Lloyd George made clear to Macready that he still favoured the shooting of suspects.[140] The failure to take serious steps to discipline offenders further heightened suspicions that the Cabinet unofficially endorsed the emerging reprisal policy.[141] In other words, British forces carried out a counter-murder campaign against Sinn Fein suspects from 1920–1.[142] The army also conducted reprisal tactics, as Bond argues:

In November 1920 the military authorities made the remarkable admission, in an attempt to gain official approval for reprisals, that 'the troops are getting out of

---

[136] C. Townshend, *The British Campaign in Ireland 1919–1921: The Development of Political and Military Policies* (Oxford University Press, 1975), 115, 138, 163–6, 95.

[137] A. D. Harvey, 'Who were the Auxiliaries?', *The Historical Journal*, 35 (1992), 667.

[138] Townshend, *British Campaign in Ireland*, 96.

[139] Hopkinson, *Irish War of Independence*, 84.

[140] Townshend, *British Campaign in Ireland*, 119–21.

[141] Clayton, *British Empire as a Superpower*, 88.

[142] K. Jeffery, *The British Army and the Crisis of Empire 1918–22* (Manchester University Press, 1984), 85.

control, taking the law into their own hands, and that besides clumsy and indiscriminate destruction, actual thieving and looting as well as drunkenness and gross disorder are occurring'.[143]

To what extent these practices were condoned at a high level naturally remains disputed.[144] In December the government finally authorised the practice which had been taking place with tacit approval for months.[145] The reprisal policy stayed in place for six months and during this time about 150 official reprisals were enacted, according to conservative estimates.[146] Others arrive at a larger figure, with 6 Division alone destroying 191 houses; the total number was probably much higher.[147] The army killed suspects in retaliation as well as destroying buildings, with four separate shootings in Limerick, Fermoy, Tuam and Tipperary in the first half of 1920.[148] Another reprisal was carried out by the 17 Lancers on 29 September 1920 after the IRA attacked their barracks at Mallow in County Cork.[149] On 20 February 1921 a combined Hampshire Regiment and Black and Tans force executed twelve IRA suspects.[150] Certain regiments, such as the East Lancashires, adopted a shoot-to-kill policy. One soldier recalled how when an intelligence officer led them to target a specific person, if he could not be located, the soldiers would take anyone, let him escape and then shoot him running away.[151] The Manchester Regiment also shot suspects 'escaping'.[152] The army's penchant for shooting people running away resurfaced in Kenya.

As with all Britain's counter-insurgencies, such tactics operated within a wider repressive legal framework, primarily under martial law and the Restoration of Order in Ireland Act. In December 1920 the government introduced new provisions subjecting anyone carrying arms or ammunition to the death penalty. Separate proclamations sanctioned the use of civilian hostages in military convoys to deter ambushes.[153] By January 1921 reprisals against property were authorised, again after several months of unofficial practice. As Hart succinctly puts it: 'Sometimes

---

[143] B. Bond, *British Military Policy between the Two World Wars* (Oxford: Clarendon Press, 1980), 19. On questions of policy, see also J. R. Ferris, *The Evolution of British Strategic Policy, 1919–26* (London: Macmillan, 1989).

[144] For a forensic examination of reprisals in Cork, see Sheehan, *A Hard Local War*, 24–47.

[145] Hopkinson, *Irish War of Independence*, 82.

[146] Townshend, *British Campaign in Ireland*, 149.

[147] Hopkinson, *Irish War of Independence*, 93.

[148] Townshend, *British Campaign in Ireland*, 96.   [149] *Ibid.*, 117.

[150] P. Hart, *The I.R.A. and Its Enemies: Violence and Community in Cork, 1916–1923* (Oxford: Clarendon Press, 1999), 98. See also P. Hart, *The I.R.A. at War 1916–1923* (Oxford University Press, 2003).

[151] Hart, *I.R.A. and Its Enemies*, 95.   [152] *Ibid.*, 96.

[153] Hopkinson, *Irish War of Independence*, 93.

the houses and shops destroyed belonged to republican families. More often they did not.'[154] The army played a central role in suppressing rebellion by punishing the general population for IRA activities.[155]

Exemplary force in the wider British Empire

The presence of exemplary force in the British military strategy towards rebellions in South Africa, India and Ireland is therefore evident. The approach extended more widely throughout the Empire. In Asia, the British participated in the combined colonial response to the 1900 Boxer Rebellion in China with punitive raids and the execution of all prisoners.[156] In 1904, during a punitive expedition in Tibet, the 1 Norfolk Regiment suffered only a handful of casualties while inflicting between six and seven hundred deaths on the Tibetans.[157] When the Moplahs rebelled in India in 1919, the state inflicted at least four thousand casualties, and the army was accused of 'extraordinarily cruel' methods, such as shutting prisoners up in railway vans, where they died of suffocation.[158]

In the Middle East, the methods for handling the Egyptian uprising in 1919 included flogging, summary execution, house burning and the destruction of crops and livestock.[159] Fifty-seven people were executed by the military.[160] Gwynn argued that these measures were necessary because otherwise the enraged troops would have taken the law into their own hands.[161] Whether such drastic measures had official sanction probably mattered very little to those on the receiving end. In 1920 a major revolt erupted in Iraq, requiring fifty-one British infantry battalions, twenty-one artillery batteries, six cavalry regiments and three RAF squadrons for its suppression. British forces put down the rebellion with the punitive use of machine guns, artillery and air strikes. Crops were burnt, fines imposed and at least 63,000 cattle confiscated.[162] The commander during the revolt, General Sir Aylmer Haldane, vigorously implemented Callwell's ideas on punitive columns.[163]

---

[154] Hart, *I.R.A. and Its Enemies*, 100.   [155] *Ibid.*, 102.

[156] V. G. Kiernan, *Colonial Empires and Armies 1815–1960* (Stroud: Sutton Publishing, 1998), 121.

[157] Ellis, *Social History of the Machine Gun*, 98.

[158] Kiernan, *Colonial Empires and Armies*, 193.   [159] Simpson, *Human Rights*, 67.

[160] Clayton, *British Empire as a Superpower*, 114.

[161] Gwynn, *Imperial Policing*, 80. For evidence that troops took the law into their own hands, see Shoul, *Soldiers, Riots, and Aid to the Civil Power*.

[162] Clayton, *British Empire as a Superpower*, 117, 123, 124.

[163] M. Jacobsen, '"Only by the Sword": British Counter-Insurgency in Iraq, 1920', *Small Wars and Insurgencies*, 2 (1991), 358.

Similar methods reappeared in the response to the Arab revolt in Palestine from 1936 to 1939. Policy centred around using violence to intimidate the whole population into submission.[164] Military doctrine permitted collective punishments and reprisals, with property destruction becoming systematic and Arabs being shot at random.[165] Civilians were hauled before military courts, restrictions were placed on movement, collective fines, crop and property destruction and whippings were practised by the army.[166] In Palestine a special joint army–police unit was formed to target Arab rebels. The reputation of these 'Special Night Squad' paramilitaries for borderline (and occasionally outright) illegal behaviour, including indiscriminate killings, inflamed resentment of British rule. Security forces placed hostages in trains and in taxis in front of armoured cars to dissuade mine-laying saboteurs.[167] The Palestine police ran several torture centres for six months in 1938–9, one at Allenby barracks.[168] Basing their methods on Ireland and India, the army in Palestine sought 'to instil the view that resisting British authority would bring swift, harsh retribution'.[169]

In Africa indiscriminate force reared its head on many an occasion. Hubert Moyse-Bartlett's lengthy study of the KAR in the first half of the twentieth century remains the core reference on these operations. Although the author's personal service in the KAR leads him to largely avoid mentioning enemy casualties and to favour euphemisms such as 'pacification', and 'a sharp lesson', the notion of 'British prestige' being sustained by force is present throughout the work. The familiar policies of stock confiscation, property destruction and 'severe punishments' were repeated many times.[170] The century began with a rebellion in the Gold Coast, where military forces conducted punitive operations against villages in the Kumase area for several weeks in September 1900.[171] In September of the following year, British-officered forces

---

[164] Norris, 'Repression and Rebellion', 25–45.
[165] Hughes, 'The Banality of Brutality', 313–54.
[166] Clayton, *British Empire as a Superpower*, 497, 499.   [167] *Ibid.*, 506.
[168] M. Hughes, 'A History of Violence: The Shooting in Jerusalem of British Assistant Police Superintendent Alan Sigrist, 12 June 1936', *Journal of Contemporary History*, 45 (2010), 736.
[169] S. Anglim, 'Orde Wingate and the Special Night Squads: A Feasible Policy for Counter-terrorism?', *Contemporary Security Policy*, 28 (2007), 31.
[170] H. Moyse-Bartlett, *The King's African Rifles: A Study in the Military History of East and Central Africa, 1890–1945* (Aldershot: Gale and Polden, 1956). On policing in Kenya in the first half of the twentieth century, see D. M. Anderson, 'Policing the Settler State: Colonial Hegemony in Kenya, 1900–1952', in D. Engels and S. Marks (eds.), *Contesting Colonial Hegemony: State and Society in Africa and India* (London: British Academic Press, 1994), 248–64.
[171] Moyse-Bartlett, *King's African Rifles*, 38.

suppressed a revolt by the Suk and Turkana tribes in Uganda, confiscating hundreds of cattle and around 10,000 sheep and goats.[172] Campaigns were waged against the 'Mad Mullah of Somaliland' until 1904. The British inflicted 'severe punishment' on the Mullah and his supporters, burning villages and taking tens of thousands of sheep and cattle and about a quarter of a million sheep.[173]

In Kenya itself, the KAR crushed the Nandi uprising, lasting from 1895 to 1906, during which period over 100,000 were killed according to one estimate.[174] As Ogot argues, 'colonial rule in Kenya had always been brutal and dirty methods were always used to crush any rebellion'.[175] By 1902 tough measures ruled the day. Meinertzhagen, a KAR officer on the punitive expeditions, vividly described the events on 8 September:

I gave orders that every living thing except children should be killed without mercy ... Every soul was either shot or bayoneted ... We burned all the huts and razed the banana plantations to the ground.[176]

Two years later, on 17 March 1904 the population still needed strong measures:

To my mind the people of Embo have not been sufficiently hammered, and I should like to go back at once and have another go at them. During the first phase of the expedition against the Irryeni we killed about 796 niggers, and during the second phase against the Embo we killed about 250. We took from the Irryeni 782 cattle and 2150 sheep and goats, and from the Waembo 498 cattle and 1500 sheep and goats.[177]

In the 1905–6 campaign the Nandi lost 1,117 killed, while 16,213 head of cattle were captured besides 36,205 sheep and goats; 4,956 huts and grain stores were burned down.[178] The punitive expedition concerned, one of the largest ever assembled in East Africa, moved the Nandi 'by force' into a new Reserve area, completing the process by August 1906.[179] The KAR pursued punitive expeditions in the Kenya Highlands between 1902 and 1914, such as that against the Kikuyu in 1904, when capturing over 11,000 stock resulted in the 'submission of recalcitrant chiefs'.[180] In 1906 forces in Northern Nigeria shot around

---

[172] *Ibid.*, 93.   [173] *Ibid.*, 160–2, 170, 189.

[174] Ogot, 'Review Article: *Britain's Gulag*', 496. See also A. T. Matson, *Nandi Resistance to British Rule 1890–1906* (Nairobi: East African Publishing House, 1972).

[175] *Ibid.*, 495.   [176] Meinertzhagen, *Kenya Diary*, 51.   [177] *Ibid.*, 152.

[178] D. Ellis, 'The Nandi Protest of 1923 in the Context of African Resistance to Colonial Rule in Kenya', *Journal of African History*, 17 (1976), 558.

[179] Moyse-Bartlett, *King's African Rifles*, 201–3.   [180] *Ibid.*, 205, 206–9.

2,000 people, beheading the dead and placing the heads on spikes, and burning villages, as a warning to other tribes.[181] Punitive expeditions continued in Nigeria well into the 1920s with similar results.[182] Elsewhere, in East Africa, campaigns intended to 'punish' were waged against the Kisii and Turkana tribes before the First World War, and over 3,000 cattle were confiscated from the Masai at the end of 1918.[183] The KAR undertook frequent expeditions in Uganda, such as that in October 1904, aimed at teaching 'the troublesome Yobo people a lesson'. In this case the lesson was reinforced by a hundred deaths and around 2,500 stock confiscations.[184] Operations in the north of the country in 1911–12 resulted in hundreds more casualties, over 7,000 cattle taken and numerous huts and fields of crops destroyed.[185] Such activities continued during and, albeit on a smaller scale, after the First World War.[186]

Between minimum and exemplary force

A clear pattern of repression standing in direct contradiction to the minimum force concept can be observed in a wide variety of instances in the fifty years prior to the Mau Mau Emergency. Driven by insufficient manpower, the need to rule through fear and sometimes blatant racism, the armed forces employed exemplary force in an indiscriminate manner in order to cow the population into submission. Typical tactics included collective punishment, stock confiscations, summary executions, destruction of property and produce and forced population movement. Although minimum force clearly occupied a central role in British doctrine, the exemplary, punitive use of force received scant mention in official publications. How then can this be squared with its repeated employment in actual operations? A substantial flaw in the optimistic view of minimum force is the reliance upon doctrinal texts. The issue seldom explored in sufficient depth is whether practice conformed with written ideas about what should be done. This chapter has not attempted to totally disprove the existence of minimum force in a pragmatic sense, but instead to show that there was another equally powerful tendency in the British military tradition which co-existed with it.

In the constant interplay between minimum and exemplary force, the latter sometimes dominated, but this has not been properly accounted

---

[181] Vandervort, *Wars of Imperial Conquest*, 187.
[182] Killingray, 'The Maintenance of Law and Order in British Colonial Africa', 420.
[183] Moyse-Bartlett, *King's African Rifles*, 207, 210, 447.
[184] *Ibid.*, 231–2.   [185] *Ibid.*, 237–42, 246.   [186] *Ibid.*, 417, 436.

for in the counter-insurgency literature. While minimum force can be characterised as a doctrine which was often operationalised, punitive, exemplary force should be thought of as a practical tradition without full doctrinal expression. As Gwynn argues, tradition often became 'the only means of broadcasting experience', and produced 'remarkably satisfactory results'.[187] The army has historically been averse to doctrine, fearing that it might constrain decision-making.[188] Consequently, tradition may represent a more satisfactory explanatory device. Proving a precise causal connection from one conflict to another is problematic, given that creating an 'institutional memory' across the entire army was difficult as a result of the regimental system's counter-centralising influence.[189]

Possibly the best way to deal with this methodological issue would be to conduct a series of detailed cohort studies, following the careers of important officers and asking whether previous military experience influenced their behaviour in Kenya. Battalion and company commanders would form the appropriate group in the counter-insurgency context, given the low level at which operations were carried out. Until the relevant personnel data become available at the National Archives, such an endeavour is impossible. Investigations along these lines using information about the careers of battalion commanders from regimental museums produced only three results. Lieutenant-Colonel Robert Glanville commanded 6 KAR in Kenya from April 1953; he had previously served in East Africa in the 1930s.[190] Lieutenant-Colonel David Rose commanded 1 Black Watch in Kenya, having seen action in Palestine from 1937 to 1939.[191] Lieutenant-Colonel Basil J. Donlea commanded 7 KAR in Kenya during 1953 and 1954, having earlier fought in Waziristan and on the Indian North-West Frontier from 1938 to 1939.[192] These examples suggest that officers may have been influenced by experience in campaigns of a similar type earlier in their careers.

International law, through inherent flaws and a deliberate government policy, promised few protections to civilians in colonial wars. The British Army's organisational culture, especially as embodied in the concept of

---

[187] Gwynn, *Imperial Policing*, 6.

[188] H. Strachan, Introduction in H. Strachan (ed.), *Big Wars and Small Wars: The British Army and the Lessons of War in the Twentieth Century* (London: Routledge, 2006), 4.

[189] *Ibid.*, 8; Charters, *The British Army and Jewish Insurgency in Palestine*, 1.

[190] Obituary in the Duke of Cornwall's Light Infantry journal *The Silver Bugle*, summer 2006. Information kindly provided by Major T. W. Stipling, Regimental Secretary and curator of the Light Infantry museum.

[191] E-mail to the author from Thomas B. Smyth, Black Watch archivist, 4 October 2006.

[192] E-mail to the author from Captain J. Knox, curator of the Royal Ulster Rifles Museum, 12 October 2006.

minimum force, is supposed to have compensated for the vacuum. This chapter has shown how much thinking about the concept might generally be deemed too optimistic. Emergency laws were extremely permissive of state violence, claims about the ethical origins of the concept were suspect and minimum force did not apply in insurrections or in the colonies. Weak civilian oversight further rendered the concept a poor constraint on military behaviour. Doctrine alone is meaningless, and must be scrutinised by assessing actual practice.

Identifying the exact nature of the causal relationship between the suppression of revolts throughout the Empire in the years preceding the Emergency and activities in Kenya is impossible. But the conflicts analysed here strongly suggest a repeating pattern of behaviour involving stock confiscations, summary justice, collective fines, property destruction and exemplary force. These elements contradict the minimum force doctrine and should probably be considered an equally important countervailing tradition which informed behaviour in Kenya.

5   'Restraint backed by good discipline'

Given the tendency to meet colonial rebellions with exemplary force, and international law's silence on the matter, British policy could have resulted in genocide. It has been claimed that the strategy pursued in Kenya amounted to genocide.[1] But there is no evidence for either an intention to eliminate the Kikuyu or that efforts were made to destroy the entire group.[2] With its available forces, the army could have killed a far greater number of people. Massive retaliatory measures by artillery or aerial bombardment were avoided when forces were available for pursuing these options.[3] In all, the evidence is insufficient to entirely jettison minimum force in explaining army behaviour in Kenya.[4]

British military strategy in Kenya contained aspects of restraint from the beginning of the Emergency. The most significant restrained policies were the creation of legally defined zones with distinct engagement rules, initiatives to take prisoners, the fair treatment of prisoners and the use of special forces. These policies are assessed in chapter 6; here the aim is to show how they rested upon the army's ability to maintain internal discipline despite much provocation. Crime exists in all societies, including the armed forces, so the occurrence of some atrocities in the campaign against the Mau Mau should come as no surprise.[5] What is more important is how the army dealt with these offences, trying to maintain a well-behaved force. In the sections of this chapter, a detailed account is given of how the army in Kenya attempted to maintain restraint by exercising its traditional disciplinary functions. Through public announcements, orders, meetings,

---

[1] Elkins, *Britain's Gulag*, xiv.
[2] Weitz considers intentionality and physical efforts at destroying an entire group as critical criteria in any definition of genocide: E. D. Weitz, *A Century of Genocide: Utopias of Race and Nation* (Oxford: Princeton University Press, 2003), 9–10.
[3] Clayton, *Counter-Insurgency in Kenya*, 6.
[4] T. R. Mockaitis, 'Minimum Force, British Counter-Insurgency and the Mau Mau Rebellion: A Reply', *Small Wars and Insurgencies*, 3 (1992), 87.
[5] E. Durkheim, 'The Normal and the Pathological', reprinted in E. J. Clarke and D. H. Kelly (eds.), *Deviant Behaviour: A Text-Reader in the Sociology of Deviance*, 6th edn (New York: Worth, 2003), 80–4.

inquiries and courts-martial, GHQ managed to restrain soldiers from running amok. In short, the army in Kenya upheld a higher disciplinary standard than local forces such as the Home Guard and KPR.

Discipline in the army in Kenya

As we have seen, armies tend to view cohesion in wartime as dependent upon strict discipline. In the British Army, the 1945 King's Regulations dictated that:

An officer is at all times responsible for ensuring that good order and the rules and discipline of the service are maintained; he will afford the utmost aid and support to the C.O. It is his duty to notice, repress, and instantly report, any negligence or impropriety of conduct on the part of warrant officers, N.C.Os. and private soldiers, whether on or off duty, and whether the offenders do or do not belong to his own unit.[6]

From basic training onwards, the army aimed to cultivate in soldiers a highly disciplined attitude, accepting obedience to the hierarchical command structure.[7] A 1947 report on training National Servicemen noted how: 'The function of discipline [is] ... producing a habit of obedience to those in authority which should have most of the automatic nature of a conditioned reflex.'[8] After breaking down the individual's identity during basic training and subsequently re-forming it in the army's image, the organisation's continuing influence over a soldier's identity throughout his service ideally resulted in consistent obedience.[9] David French and Timothy Parsons have shown how both British and KAR battalions strengthened unit cohesion and discipline by isolating themselves from civil society.[10] Socialisation carried on within the regiment after formal training had finished.[11]

---

[6] War Office, *King's Regulations for the Army, 1940*, 208. This section went unchanged in the 1955 version.

[7] D. French, *Military Identities: The Regimental System, the British Army, and the British People, c. 1870–2000* (Oxford University Press, 2005), 62.

[8] TNA, WO 291/1306: Military Operational Research Unit, July 1947, 'The Training of the National Service Man: A Preliminary Survey', para. 24.

[9] On basic training see J. Bourke, *An Intimate History of Killing: Face-to-Face Killing in Twentieth Century Warfare* (London: Granta, 2000), 69–102; and D. Grossman, *On Killing: The Psychological Cost of Learning to Kill in War and Society* (London: Little, Brown and Company, 1996); on the relationship between training and cohesion see H. Strachan, 'Training, Morale and Modern War', *Journal of Contemporary History*, 41 (2006), 211–27.

[10] French, *Military Identities*, 143; T. H. Parsons, *The African Rank-and-file: Social Implications of Colonial Military Service in the King's African Rifles, 1902–1964* (Oxford: James Currey, 1999), 9, 55. However, the military legal system started to undergo a process of civilianisation from 1951; see G. R. Rubin, *Murder, Mutiny and the Military: British Court Martial Cases, 1940–1966* (London: Francis Boutle, 2005), 43.

[11] Thornton, 'Understanding the Cultural Bias', 110.

As in the United Kingdom, in Kenya the army was technically constrained by both civil and military law.[12] In practice, commanders normally dealt with their men under military justice. The 1881 Army Act, largely unchanged until 1955, fully codified military offences and the composition and rules of courts-martial.[13] The records for Kenya from October 1952 to January 1954 show that seventy-five courts-martial were held, for offences ranging from indecency to drunkenness, fraud, theft, insubordination and assault.[14] This is a relatively low number given that by the end of September 1953 three brigades were deployed in the country. Summary justice dealt out by the commanding officer is the quickest means of enforcing discipline, and is appropriate for less serious malefactions.[15] The records for these minor disciplinary hearings have not survived. The dearth of personal papers from soldiers serving in Britain's post-war counter-insurgencies is balanced by existing oral history recordings.[16] These reveal that soldiers were satisfied with discipline in their units. Charles Wallace, a company commander in 4 KAR, recalled how drunkenness was the only occasional cause of problems, and was easily dealt with by his African RSM and NCOs.[17] Donald Nott, also a 4 KAR officer, dealt severely with an early case of looting, dissuading other askaris from straying by threatening dismissal from the regiment, which would make them social pariahs.[18]

Major Anthony Gay commanded troops in 23 KAR from November 1952, finding them extremely well disciplined.[19] According to the CO of 26 KAR, the askaris were little different in their professionalism from the British soldiers.[20] Were National Service soldiers any more or less disciplined than regular troops? The question arises as by 1951 they comprised half the army's total manpower.[21] The matter cannot easily be answered by comparative analysis because conscripts served alongside regulars in the same units.[22] A regular officer in 1 Devonshire Regiment from 1953 to 1955 had a high opinion of National Servicemen, noting

---

[12] TNA, WO 32/15556: Personal and confidential letter, Erskine to CIGS, 9 July 1953.
[13] J. W. Rant, *Courts-Martial Handbook: Practice and Procedure* (Chichester: John Wiley and Sons, 1998), 5.
[14] TNA, WO 93/56: Courts-martial in Kenya, 1952–3. Precisely comparable figures for the 1954–6 period are not available.
[15] Rant, *Courts-Martial Handbook*, 2; Thornton, 'Understanding the Cultural Bias', 112.
[16] D. French, 'History and the British Army, 1870–1970: Where are We and where Might We go?' Keynote lecture given at the 'Britons at War: New Perspectives' conference, University of Northampton, 21 April 2006.
[17] ODRP: C. St.J. Wallis, MSS Afr. 1715.   [18] ODRP: D. H. Nott, MSS Afr. 1715.
[19] IWMSA, A. W. Gay, 10258/2.   [20] ODRP, P. Thompson, MSS Afr. 1715.
[21] Darby, *British Defence Policy*, 39.
[22] Only when the full personnel files for soldiers who served in the Emergency are released by the Ministry of Defence can this question be thoroughly researched.

how the presence of regular sergeants and company commanders with combat experience helped the new subalterns immensely.[23] A subaltern in the Devons, Captain Peter Burdick, admitted that his platoon sergeant in Kenya taught him more about soldiering than the instructors at Sandhurst.[24] Eric Burini, with 3 KAR from 1954 to 1957, found the National Service officers seconded to his unit enthusiastic and intelligent.[25] The evidence from these oral histories suggests that the conscript soldiers assumed the behaviour of the regulars.[26]

Throughout the conflict in Kenya disciplinary measures were taken to prevent atrocities by the army, although the period between 23 June 1953 and 11 March 1954 marked the most intensive period and receives the closest analysis here. On 11 February 1953 the first directive on discipline among the security forces was issued by Governor Evelyn Baring. It read:

If in the future there are good grounds to believe that inhuman methods have been used severe disciplinary action will be taken against those responsible. Success in the struggle against the Mau Mau movement cannot be finally attained unless the Kikuyu as a whole wish to remain peaceful and in security. This they will not do if we alienate those who are either inactive or definitely our friends. Inhuman methods are not only cruel but they are also in almost all cases ineffective and I am sure that in the future the admirable work done will not in any way be marred by recourse to such methods ... It is the duty of all officers to bring this directive to the notice of their subordinates and to ensure that its terms are carried out.[27]

On 17 April 1953 Baring issued a press release declaring that the government thoroughly condemned 'acts of indiscipline involving the unlawful causing of death or injury, the rough handling of members of the public, suspects, or prisoners'. The communiqué emphasised that the security forces had already received instructions to act with restraint. It stated that all complaints were investigated and that where sufficient evidence existed, prosecutions launched. Naturally these cases were insignificant in number.[28] After taking command in June 1953, General Erskine decided to impose his mark on the forces in East Africa.[29] On 23 June all officers received a stern message:

It must be most clearly understood that the Security Forces under my command are disciplined forces who know how to behave in circumstances which are most distasteful.

[23] IWMSA, J. P. Randle, 20457/34.   [24] IWMSA, P. Burdick, 11143/3.
[25] IWMSA, E. B. Burini, 19630/18.   [26] IWMSA, A. Cainey, 26864/14.
[27] TNA, CO 822/474: Kenya Government notice, 11 February 1953.
[28] TNA, WO 32/21721: McLean Court of Inquiry Exhibit 29: Press Office handout, dated 17 April 1953.
[29] Anderson, *Histories of the Hanged*, 261.

... I will not tolerate breaches of discipline leading to unfair treatment of anybody.

... I most strongly disapprove of 'beating up' the inhabitants of this country just because they are the inhabitants. I hope this has not happened in the past and will not happen in the future. Any indiscipline of this kind would do great damage to the reputation of the Security Forces and make our task of settling MAU MAU [*sic*] much more difficult. I therefore order that every officer in the Police and the Army should stamp on at once any conduct which he would be ashamed to see used against his own people.

... Any complaints against the Police or Army which come from outside sources will be referred to me immediately on receipt and will be investigated.[30]

Further measures were taken to ensure that everyone received and understood the new commander's views. All newly arrived troops were issued with the order.[31] The 23 June order was apparently obeyed by the army thanks to tradition, discipline, awareness of the practical benefits of good conduct and the knowledge that Parliament was keeping a close eye on the situation in Kenya.[32] Erskine and Baring were committed, at least rhetorically, to investigating allegations and prosecuting offenders.[33]

Investigating Major Griffiths and preventing wider abuses

The day before the directive went out an inquiry was held into the activities of 'B' Company, 5 KAR over the previous week. General Erskine ordered Brigadier Cornah, commanding 70 Brigade, to initiate a court of inquiry after receiving police reports that twenty-one men were taken prisoner and then shot by 5 KAR.[34] 7 KAR's CO, Lieutenant-Colonel R. G. T. Collins, presided and Major N. F. Rawkins from 23 KAR also participated.[35] After taking evidence from African civilians, askaris and British officers, Collins informed Roger Wilkinson, the local DC, that he would adjourn and reconvene later. Judging from the available testimonies, the court probably adjourned around 27 June.[36] Ten askaris were accused of shooting dead twenty African civilians near Chuka on

---

[30] TNA, WO 32/21721: Exhibit 5, Message to be distributed to all officers of the Army, Police and the Security Forces, GHQ Nairobi, 23 June 1953.
[31] Clayton, *Counter-Insurgency in Kenya*, 38.   [32] *Ibid.*, 40.
[33] Heather, 'Counterinsurgency and Intelligence in Kenya', 139.
[34] TNA, WO 276/177: Signal from Force Nairobi to 70 (EA) Infantry Brigade, no date, Personal for Brigadier Cornah from C-in-C.
[35] TNA, WO 32/21721: McLean Inquiry Exhibit 3, Order of Battle, 17 June 1953.
[36] TNA, WO 32/16103: Signed statement of Roger Aubone Wilkinson, DC, Embu, 20 September 1953; Signed statement of Sarastino M'Chabari s/o Mukapo, 27 July 1953; Signed statement of Major N. F. Rawkins, 23 KAR, 2 November 1953.

17–18 June, and placed under open arrest at Nairobi's Buller Camp pending further inquiries.[37]

Whereas the brigade court of inquiry sought to establish the sequence of events at Chuka, the enquiries now pursued by CSM Hateley of the Royal Military Police's Special Investigations Branch (SIB) constituted a full criminal investigation.[38] During these investigations the authorities discovered that 'B' Company's commander, Major Gerald S. Griffiths, had shot dead two additional civilians several days earlier, on 11 June. Unravelling events proved arduous as Griffiths and Second Lieutenant Howard, one of his platoon commanders, conspired to cover up both incidents. The SIB was strengthened over the second half of 1953 to cope with these difficulties.[39] 'B' Company's victims were known locally and it quickly transpired that some of them were Home Guard members. Perhaps for this reason, but also in response to accusations of ill-discipline, GHQ issued a directive on 15 July aimed at clarifying the military's relationship with the militia force. The order recognised that the Home Guard were the administration's responsibility, but asked soldiers in contact with them to control and report any 'lawless behaviour'.[40]

To guarantee that soldiers understood the practical imperative to maintain a disciplined stance when dealing with the Kikuyu in order to win the conflict, GHQ issued Operational Intelligence Instruction no. 4 on 1 July. The instruction stipulated the correct procedure for dealing with 'Mau Mau prisoners and surrendered personnel', which included both captured insurgents and, more frequently, suspected civilians. Prisoners were given an immediate tactical interrogation by whoever captured them along the lines of 'who are you?', 'where have you come from?', 'where is the gang?', to produce actionable intelligence. They were then handed over to the police as soon as possible, normally within twenty-four hours, and exceptionally within seventy-two hours if the informant could lead a patrol to a Mau Mau hideout. On interrogation methods, the instruction warned that 'violent methods seldom produce accurate information'.[41] Another order, from 70 Infantry Brigade on 24 September, directed commanders to check that their soldiers

---

[37] TNA, WO 32/16103: Signed statement of Cpl. Killis s/o Kiyundu, 'B' Company, 5 KAR, 13 August 1953; Statement of Cpl. Cheserch s/o Kipobo, 'B' Company, 5 KAR, 13 August 1953.

[38] TNA, WO 32/16103: Note by Lt.-Col. R.H. Cowell-Parker, Assistant Director of Army Legal Services (ADALS), East Africa Command, 23 December 1953.

[39] A. V. Lovell-Knight, *The Story of the Royal Military Police* (London: Leo Cooper, 1977), 288.

[40] TNA, CO 822/497: Emergency Directive no. 8, Role of and co-operation with the Kikuyu, Embu and Meru Guards, issued by GHQ East Africa Command, 15 July 1953.

[41] TNA, WO 32/21721: Exhibit 4, Operational Intelligence Instruction no. 4, dated 1 July 1953.

understood that violence was not to be offered to any Kikuyu in the Reserves, including prisoners.[42] Such was the instrumental justification used to support the moral appeal against 'beating up the inhabitants' issued by Erskine a few weeks previously. In practice, as we shall see when discussing strategies of restraint, treating prisoners well facilitated the surrender programmes which helped bring the Emergency to an end.

Erskine took steps to prevent overwrought troops from taking their frustrations out on the civilians. He told Harding that the Kenya Regiment needed a rest as they had been 'at it for nine months and some of the officers and men are getting into a "jittery" state. I am anxious to give them about two weeks training out of operations.'[43] Aside from resting his troops Erskine aimed to change behaviour by banning a hitherto commonplace practice, one also common in Malaya.[44] Erskine banned the security forces from chopping off the hands from dead bodies in order to fingerprint them and provide the intelligence system with information on who had been killed. GHQ's Training Instruction no. 7 of 1 August stipulated that 'Under NO circumstances will bodies be mutilated, even for identification.' Bodies were to be removed to the nearest police station where possible, and when the terrain proved impenetrable, full fingerprints were to be taken from the corpse.[45]

GHQ's general order in fact postdated a number of local directives, such as one put out to its six constituent battalions by 39 Infantry Brigade on 1 July, directing all enemy dead to be buried and specifically prohibiting the removal of limbs for identification.[46] The issue shows how quickly and thoroughly the army could respond to the new commander's imposition of a new set of military norms, banning a practice widespread when he arrived and considered a military necessity. It demonstrates the fluidity of 'military necessity' and the ease with which alternative, and to Erskine and British press sensibilities, less barbarous, practices could be implemented. Although his personal papers do not

---

[42] TNA, WO 32/21721: Exhibit 12, Discipline of Security Forces on Operations, 70 Infantry Brigade order to 3, 5, 7, 23 KAR and East Africa Armoured Car Squadron Mobile Column A, 24 September 1953.

[43] TNA, CO 822/693: Letter from Erskine to Harding, 23 July 1953.

[44] TNA, WO 32/21720: McLean proceedings, 376. A Major Morgan, formerly in Malaya, was reported as imparting the practice at the East Africa Battle School, according to Major R. K. Denniston, 1 Black Watch.

[45] TNA, WO 32/21721: Exhibit 8, Training Instruction no. 7, Operations against the Mau Mau, issued by GHQ, 1 August 1953.

[46] TNA, WO 32/21721: Exhibit 25, 39 Inf Bde Jock Scott Op Instr no. 7, 9 July 1953. The constituent battalions on this date were 1 Buffs, 1 Devons, 1 Lancashire Fusiliers, Kenya Regiment, 4 KAR, and 6 KAR (including a component seconded from 26 KAR).

reveal his thinking on the issue, Erskine possibly realised that mutilation of the dead comprised a war crime under the Hague and Geneva Conventions and in any case won the army few plaudits either at home, abroad or in Kenya itself.

Meanwhile GHQ came to comprehend Major Griffiths's role in the two atrocities in June, transferring him to the East Africa Training Centre on 25 August.[47] The ten askaris were placed under close arrest and separated from one another.[48] This was probably because they were colluding in their statements after Second Lieutenant Innes-Walker, another of Griffiths's subalterns, intimidated them into covering up the incidents.[49] 70 Brigade's commander was replaced in August, possibly because the first court of inquiry failed to fully disclose the crimes committed by Griffiths's company. As a positive sign for the army the Christian Missionary Society noted the 'improved attitude' of soldiers and policemen.[50] On 12 September the SIB held an identification parade at Langata for civilians who observed events at Chuka.[51] On 23 September a Nairobi pathologist confirmed that one of the victims' skulls contained several .303 calibre bullet holes, sufficient to cause death.[52]

By the beginning of October, Hugh Fraser, parliamentary private secretary to the Colonial Secretary, could boost army morale by reporting on the 'improved discipline and even courtesy of the military and police'.[53] But the Command remained determined to instil discipline by making an example of infractors, and decided to charge Griffiths for the first incident. As Erskine explained to the War Office, action 'against Griffiths indicates my intention to stop unjustifiable methods'.[54] Two accessories to the crime, Sergeant Llewellyn, the CSM, and a Royal Electrical and Mechanical Engineers officer, Captain Joy, were granted immunity for agreeing to testify against Griffiths at the court-martial.[55] Before the trial began, Erskine wrote to his wife describing

[47] TNA, WO 32/21722: War Office briefing note prior to parliamentary questions for Secretary of State, signed T. L. Binney, 4 December 1953.

[48] TNA, WO 32/21722: Telegram from GHQ East Africa to War Office, 30 November 1953.

[49] TNA, WO 32/16103: Note by Lt.-Col. R. H. Cowell-Parker, ADALS, 23 December 1953.

[50] Heather, 'Counterinsurgency in Kenya', 139.

[51] TNA, WO 32/16103: Signed statement of Daudi s/o Maringa, 14 September 1953.

[52] TNA, WO 32/16103: Pathology report by G. C. Dockeray, Medical Research Laboratory, Nairobi, 23 September 1953.

[53] TNA, PREM 11/472: Report by Hugh Fraser MP to the Colonial Secretary, 6 October 1953.

[54] TNA, WO 32/21722: Telegram from Erskine to Adjutant-General (AG), War Office, no date.

[55] TNA, WO 32/21722: Letter from DALS East Africa to DALS, War Office, 31 October 1953.

how he would shortly try the 'most revolting and unforgivable case', predicting in consequence 'a most violent outcry'.[56] The next day he wrote to the VCIGS in London, explaining his desire 'to face the music and uphold the discipline and standards of the army rather than permit such things to be smothered over'. He wished to base his strategy on a distinction between loyal Kikuyu and Mau Mau: 'Indiscriminate shooting of all Africans (which is loudly advocated by some people) would lead to a Black V White War and an extension of the campaign which would have almost no limits.'[57] So we can see how during his first months in command Erskine conceived of a clear connection between military discipline and military strategy.

The prediction that the trial would be a sensation was accurate. While participating in a sweep operation in June 1953, Major Gerald Griffiths pulled up to a 'stop' post manned by two askaris in the 7 KAR company which temporarily fell under his command. Finding three prisoners in their custody he asked the askaris why they had not killed these forestry workers, before promptly sending one of them on his way. The other two men were handed back their passes, told to proceed and then shot in the back at close range by Griffiths with a Bren light machine-gun. Returning to the scene about half an hour later to find one man alive, writhing on the road, Griffiths shot him dead at close range with his sidearm, after the recently arrived CSM Llewellyn refused an order to do so. At his trial the two askaris and Captain Joy, who was in Griffiths's jeep with him at the time, testified to seeing him shoot the men – who were not running away as the accused claimed. CSM Llewellyn additionally saw him kill the one man with a pistol, a charge Griffiths accepted without quibble.[58] In the end Griffiths was acquitted as the prosecution failed to prove the identity of the man executed with the pistol. As one of the Emergency's staunchest contemporary critics pointed out, the prosecution only pressed a charge for one murder, and through incompetence the murder of another person was proven. Arguably Griffiths should straight away have stood trial for murdering an unknown man.[59] Even the Deputy Governor attacked the acquittal due

[56] Imperial War Museum Department of Documents (IWMD), General Sir George Erskine, Accession no. 75/134/1; box 1, file 6: letter dated 27 October 1953.

[57] TNA, WO 276/524: Letter from Erskine to Lt.-Gen. Sir Harold Redman, 28 October 1953.

[58] TNA, WO 71/1218: Proceedings of the General Court-Martial of G. S. L. Griffiths, for murder, 25 November 1953 to 27 November 1953.

[59] P. Evans, Law and Disorder, or Scenes of Life in Kenya (London: Secker and Warburg, 1956), 262.

to the improper exclusion of evidence on the identity of the body and the admission of hearsay evidence in Griffiths's defence.[60]

General Erskine was astonished at the court-martial's outcome.[61] In consequence steps were taken to guard against any possible misreading of the acquittal, arising from parliamentary pressure on the Secretary of State for War and Erskine's own desire to see his vision safeguarded. On 30 November GHQ's June order on conduct was reissued with minor modifications, stressing the commander's determination to 'catch and punish' those who were 'taking the law into their own hands and acting outside my orders'.[62] Erskine posted letters to each formation commander requesting a personal assurance that abuses were non-existent. Affirmative replies arrived on his desk within the week.[63] Leader of the Opposition Clement Attlee led questions in the Commons asking the government whether they would call a court of inquiry into allegations stemming from the Griffiths trial, specifically the offering of monetary rewards for kills and competition for kills between units.[64] After discussing the various avenues open in the Griffiths case with the Attorney-General, Erskine decided against a retrial as the other events were still under investigation and might offer better chances of a conviction.[65] In relation to these events the role of 5 KAR's CO, Lieutenant-Colonel Evans, came under the spotlight, Erskine calling for a report on his conduct.[66] On 3 December the authorities reopened the ten askaris case by starting a summary of evidence preparatory to another court-martial. Erskine suspected that although these killings were undertaken by ordinary soldiers, Griffiths orchestrated the whole affair. At the same time, SIB investigated a beating and torture incident in 7 KAR. Erskine declared his intention to 'uncover everything and force into court even the most unpleasant crimes. I am sure you would much prefer a clean up than a cover up.'[67]

---

[60] TNA, WO 32/21722: Telegram from Governor's Deputy to Baring (in London), 1 December 1953.

[61] IWMD: Erskine papers, letter to his wife, dated 28 November 1953.

[62] TNA, WO 32/21721: Exhibit 6: Message to be distributed to all members of the Army, Police and the Security Forces, GHQ, 30 November 1953.

[63] TNA, WO 32/15834: Letter dated 30 November 1953 from Erskine to Brig. Tweedie (39 Infantry Brigade), Brig. Taylor (49 Infantry Brigade), Brig. Orr (70 Infantry Brigade), Major Huth (Armoured Car Squadron Mobile Column), Major Langford (156 East African HAA Battery) and Lt.-Col. Campbell (Kenya Regiment). The replies from each commander, all sent within a week, are also in this file.

[64] TNA, PREM 11/696: Hansard excerpt, 30 November 1953, 770.

[65] TNA, WO 32/21722: Telegram from Erskine to AG, War Office, 1 December 1953.

[66] TNA, WO 32/21722: Telegram from Erskine to Secretary of State for War, 2 December 1953.

[67] TNA, WO 32/21722: Telegram from Erskine to War Office, 3 December 1953.

Cleaning up, not covering up: the McLean Court of Inquiry

Two days later Erskine decided how to proceed in his push to bring the army completely under control. First, the SIB continued collecting all available evidence on offences committed by Griffiths, leading to another trial. Secondly, Erskine ordered a court of inquiry into army misconduct.[68] Shortly afterwards the Cabinet agreed to the inquiry, announcing it in Parliament on 10 December.[69] On 5 December the Commander-in-Chief assembled all officers of the rank of lieutenant-colonel and above, and their police equivalents, at a special meeting to ram home the issue. In short, the order was deadly serious, would be fully implemented by him and strictly interpreted by all commanders on the spot, as he could not predict 'every possible stupidity', such as kill scoreboards or 'other flippant or evil practices'. The officers were informed about the impending court of inquiry and instructed to cooperate with it.[70] The meeting's immediate impact may be seen in Lieutenant-Colonel Glanville's order two days later to his battalion, 6 KAR, commanding his officers to explain General Erskine's order to all British and African non-commissioned officers and other ranks. The strongly worded directive reflected the grave tone adopted by Erskine at the meeting, as Glanville not only passed on the gist but added his own desire to protect the battalion's reputation and 'anyone, be he British or African, who dirty's [sic] it will have no mercy from me'.[71]

70 Infantry Brigade, responsible at this point for 3, 5, 7 and 23 KAR, sent out a comparable order on 8 December. Also intending to disseminate the Commander-in-Chief's views to all ranks, Brigadier Orr reminded his soldiers how to deal with prisoners, to avoid killing competitions and not to shoot people out of hand. After all, it was 'a task for which we are all trained, and is not difficult'.[72] One further event happened before the court of inquiry which acted to support Erskine's desire to see his forces 'play to M.C.C. rules'.[73] There is little

---

[68] TNA, WO 32/21722: Letter from Erskine to General Sir Cameron Nicholson (AG), 5 December 1953.

[69] TNA, WO 32/21722: Telegram from Troopers (AG) to GHQ East Africa, no date.

[70] TNA, WO 32/21721: Exhibit 7: Record of an address made by C-in-C at GHQ East Africa at 1000 hrs Sat 5 Dec 1953.

[71] TNA, WO 32/21721: Exhibit 9: Conduct of Security Forces on Ops., issued by CO 6 KAR, 7 December 1953.

[72] TNA, WO 32/21721: Exhibit 13: Discipline, issued HQ 70 Infantry Brigade, 8 December 1953.

[73] The phrase comes from a letter to his wife: IWMD, Erskine papers, letter dated 30 September 1953.

information on the General Court-Martial of Sergeant Pearson and Private Taylor, two Kenya Regiment soldiers both convicted on 10 December for 'assaulting an African and maliciously burning a house and occasioning bodily harm', with Pearson also convicted for 'maliciously wounding an African'. Pearson's award for these offences was a year in prison, while Taylor received nine months' incarceration.[74] This outcome may be interpreted as a victory for the army's resolve to field disciplined forces subject to the rule of law.

Investigations into 5 and 7 KAR continued throughout December as preparations for the court of inquiry were made, tentatively under General Goodbody, then commanding 56 (London) Division of the Territorial Army.[75] All units in Kenya were informed about the inquiry on 12 December and asked to invite all ranks to appear voluntarily forty-eight hours before the court convened.[76] The inquiry, eventually headed by Lieutenant-General Sir Kenneth McLean from the War Office, would look into three areas: first, the offering to soldiers of money for Mau Mau killings; second, the keeping and exhibition of scoreboards recording official and unofficial kills and other activities in operations against Mau Mau; and third, the fostering of a competitive spirit among units with regard to kills in anti-Mau Mau operations.[77] After Fenner Brockway MP created a 'minor stink' over an article in the journal of the Devonshire Regiment, the terms were expanded slightly.[78] The article quoted the CO of 1 Battalion offering £5 for the unit's first kill in Kenya. According to one account, an attached subaltern recently cashiered from the regiment for incompetence sent the article to Brockway in revenge. In addition to Brockway's questions, the *Daily Herald* published a front-page article with the headline 'Is your son a murderer?'[79] The War Office wanted McLean to question the Devons on the point when he met them.[80]

---

[74] TNA, WO 32/21721: Exhibit 22: List of cases brought to the notice of GHQ East Africa in which members of the Military Forces have been charged before Civil Courts, or Courts Martial, or Summarily for offences against Africans, compiled by Assistant AG, GHQ.

[75] TNA, WO 32/21722: Telegram from Erskine to AG, War Office, 9 December 1953; 'Obituary: Gen. Sir Richard Goodbody, Former Adjutant-General to the Forces', *The Times*, 6 May 1981, 19.

[76] TNA, WO 32/21722: Order from GHQ East Africa to all units, 12 December 1953.

[77] TNA, PREM 11/691: Excerpt from Cabinet Conclusions, minute 2, 8 December 1953.

[78] TNA, WO 32/21722: Letter from Heyman (Chief of Staff East Africa) to McLean, 22 December 1953.

[79] IWMD: Lieutenant-Colonel J. K. Windeatt, Accession no.: 90/20/1; Mau Mau rebellion Kenya. 1st Bn. The Devonshire Regiment Record 1953–55, written 1962.

[80] TNA, WO 32/21722: Telegram from Troopers to East Africa, exclusive for Heyman from AG, no date.

In order to proceed impartially, the court was chaired by a lieutenant-general without previous involvement in Kenya, accompanied by Colonel G. Barratt, the Deputy Director of Army Legal Services (DALS) at the War Office, to guarantee compliance with the rules of procedure, and Colonel G. A. Rimbault, the Deputy Chief of Staff in East Africa Command who had been present from the start of the Emergency.[81] There are other reasons besides Lieutenant-General McLean's seniority and detachment, for supposing the court would proceed objectively in striving 'to clean up rather than to cover up', as the Secretary of State for War stated its purpose in the Commons.[82] First, witnesses gave evidence on oath.[83] Second, while they could face prosecution for perjury, evidence given by witnesses could not subsequently be used against them.[84] These measures clearly granted a freedom of expression which might have proved troublesome otherwise. Third, investigations were extensive, absorbing information from 147 witnesses over a twelve-day period, from every major unit and formation in theatre at the time. These included staff officers, twelve regiments (even necessitating travelling to Uganda to interview 4 KAR), a Roman Catholic bishop and regimental medical officers (RMOs).[85] McLean invited the Christian Council of Kenya to put forward any specific allegations against the army, but they had none.[86]

In terms of ranks, witnesses ranged from brigadier to private soldier; the most strongly represented category was in the crucial major to second-lieutenant group, the company and platoon commanders who exercised greatest influence in the conduct of this decentralised conflict.[87] Eleven National Servicemen took part, as did fourteen African warrant officers

---

[81] TNA, WO 32/15834: Telegram from Troopers to GHQ East Africa, 9 December 1953.

[82] TNA, WO 32/15834: Statement by Secretary of State for War Anthony Head to House of Commons, 10 December 1953.

[83] TNA, WO 32/15834: Telegram Erskine to AG, War Office, 12 December 1953.

[84] TNA, WO 32/21720: McLean proceedings, 6. This point was explained by Colonel Barratt to Brigadier Orr as embodied in Rule of Procedure 125A, para. G.

[85] The full list of units and formations represented is: GHQ staff officers, 70 Infantry Brigade, 49 Infantry Brigade, 39 Infantry Brigade, 3 KAR, 4 KAR, 5 KAR, 6 KAR, 7 KAR, 23 KAR, 26 KAR, 1 Royal Northumberland Fusiliers, 1 Royal Inniskilling Fusiliers, 1 Black Watch, 1 Devonshire Regiment, 1 The Buffs, Kenya Regiment, Medical Officer in Charge of the Civil Native Hospital, Nyeri, Nanyuki Church of England Garrison Chaplain, Roman Catholic Bishop of Nyeri, Head of Consolata Mission, Deputy Assistant Provost Marshal, Deputy ADALS.

[86] TNA, WO 32/21722: McLean Court of Inquiry report and findings.

[87] The complete breakdown is: three brigadiers, sixteen lieutenant-colonels, forty-five majors, twenty captains, five lieutenants, nine second lieutenants, two regimental sergeant-majors (RSMs), eleven company sergeant-majors, ten warrant officer platoon commanders (WOPCs), four warrant officers, seven sergeants, one lance-corporal, seven private soldiers.

from the KAR. Commanders were required to give their men forty-eight hours' warning and six other ranks volunteered to appear as a result.[88] The provision of interpreters, an encouraging attitude towards nervous officers and the willingness to pursue matters beyond the defined three-point remit indicated a court resolved to clear the army's name by thorough, honest examination of uncomfortable issues. Prominent among these of course was Major Griffiths, who himself gave evidence.[89] Reverend J. F. Landregan, padre to 49 Infantry Brigade, stated that everyone from the brigadier downwards was amazed by the revelations and 'we would not tolerate any atrocities of any description against prisoners'.[90] A fellow officer, from 4 KAR, thought Griffiths got off very lightly,[91] while the 1 Black Watch's RMO said that his unit viewed the case as exceptional.[92]

On the assigned terms of reference McLean, Barratt and Rimbault reached the following conclusions. First, they found one instance where two company commanders, with their CO's knowledge, offered 100 shillings to kill the Mau Mau leader Dedan Kimathi, in place of a similar police reward to which soldiers were not entitled. The court considered this mistake 'explicable in the circumstances'. The money offered by the Devonshire Regiment to the first sub-unit to kill a Mau Mau was deemed fair and permissible because it happened in a PA, where non-combatants were explicitly banned. Elsewhere officers rewarded their troops with a few beers for working hard on an operation – though the court deemed the practice unproblematic because the reward was not for killing. Finally in this category came Griffiths's own admission of offering cash rewards to his troops. Secondly, it transpired that Griffiths had exaggerated the existence of scoreboards. The scoreboards were defined as 'a visual record kept and displayed solely or mainly to foster unhealthy and irresponsible competition in killings between units and sub units'. Statistics were kept for situation reports and assessing military effectiveness, sometimes in restricted company or battalion situation rooms on charts consolidating official information. At the lower levels, officers either memorised the information or kept it in notebooks or files. The court found no evidence for 'unofficial kills'.

Third, the court considered the competitive spirit between units, where soldiers might become so eager to ratchet up higher kill scores that they began to disregard legal restrictions and indulge in wanton

---

[88] Six commanders recorded having issued the requisite information, although not every witness was asked whether they had or not.
[89] TNA, WO 32/21720: McLean proceedings, 223, 268.   [90] *Ibid.*, 197.
[91] *Ibid.*, 339 (Capt. I. Grahame of Duntrune, 4 KAR).
[92] *Ibid.*, 366 (Lt. L. G. Fallows, Black Watch RMO).

killing. The vast majority of those questioned had no idea how many Mau Mau their own or neighbouring units had recently killed; generally, only the adjutants and others participating in administration possessed the figures. Some officers knew how many fatalities their unit had inflicted because of continuous engagement in the same area or low, static numbers. Soldiers widely recognised the role played by chance in determining which unit killed enemy insurgents, especially when commanders impressed upon them the cooperative nature of many operations, where one unit might drive insurgents into another's path. Units also quantified success with reference to captured prisoners, arms and ammunition. Wide disbursement throughout the operational areas militated against competition between battalions who hardly ever saw each other. Often, even companies from the same battalion found themselves isolated for months on end. On the other hand, the court found some competitive spirit, but deemed it nothing 'beyond the natural rivalry to be found between sub units in all good regiments'.

The testimonies given at the McLean Court of Inquiry reveal new perspectives on the chopping off of hands and the replacement fingerprinting policy. It was the general practice to chop the hands off a dead body which could not be brought back, a 7 KAR officer describing it as 'a sort of order'.[93] Captain Russell, serving with the 7 KAR since the start of the Emergency, blamed the order on the police, who wanted the hands for identification purposes.[94] His explanation is plausible given that by the end of 1953 the police Criminal Records Office held fingerprint slips for 475,884 people, so there were records to check against.[95] Another six witnesses concurred on the prevalence of the practice in the early days.[96] Brigadier Tweedie, who banned the practice in his brigade three months after arriving, believed it was done 'not as bestiality but simply because they had no alternative'.[97] With Erskine's intervention a simple enough alternative appeared. At the inquiry in December, thirty-four witnesses expressed positively knowing the practice was banned.[98] Of these, twenty-four mentioned carrying the fingerprinting kits as prescribed by GHQ. This evidence suggests that the army command

[93] *Ibid.*, 102 (Major J. A. Robertson, 7 KAR).
[94] *Ibid.*, 276 (Capt. H. C. Russell, 7 KAR).
[95] D. Throup, 'Crime, Politics and the Police in Colonial Kenya, 1939–63', 146.
[96] TNA, WO 32/21720: McLean proceedings, 223 (Lt.-Col. L. W. B. Evans, 5 KAR); 227 (Major W. E. B. Atkins, 5 KAR); 331 (Major M. J. Harbage, 4 KAR); 393 (Brig. J. W. Tweedie, 39 Infantry Brigade); 399 (Major W. B. Thomas, 39 Infantry Brigade); 403 (Capt. J. W. Turnbull, Kenya Regiment).
[97] *Ibid.*, 393 (Brig. J. W. Tweedie, 39 Infantry Brigade).
[98] TNA, WO 32/21720: McLean proceedings. Not all witnesses were asked about it.

succeeded in imposing discipline even when it went against a procedure established for nine to ten months.

Therefore the McLean Inquiry concluded that the abnormalities mentioned were in the minority, and on the whole the army's conduct, 'under difficult and arduous circumstances, showed that measure of restraint backed by good discipline which this country has traditionally expected'.[99] While the court of inquiry seemed to overwhelmingly vindicate the army, equally significant from the disciplinary perspective was the instructional role it played. If any doubts remained after the various orders issued by Erskine about his views on how to conduct the campaign they were dispelled by the court's interaction with representatives from units participating in anti-Mau Mau operations. Soldiers who stood before the court took the experience back to share with others in their unit. The whole tone of the questioning and the comments made on evidence given consistently expressed a clear view on the parameters of acceptable behaviour. For example, the court repeatedly pressed 39 Infantry Brigade's brigade major on whether the new fingerprinting kits were adequately distributed to all units.[100] In another case, they pointed out to a Devons company commander the potential dangers in allowing rivalry between platoons patrolling in the Reserves.[101] Most notable, though, were the frequent references to the various orders restricting the use of force, shown especially to battalion and company commanders.

Discipline after McLean

At the beginning of January 1954 Richard Crossman, Labour MP for Coventry and author of critical newspaper articles on the Emergency, visited the country. Crossman toured the operational areas and observed the Devons on patrol. Later on, several soldiers confronted him about his accusations in the press, and on returning to Britain he wrote a corrective piece for the *Sunday Pictorial*.[102] Thus even critics thought that McLean had proved effective. At some point in late 1953 or early 1954 the Kenyan authorities set up a 'Watch Committee' to monitor allegations against the security forces. It was later given the more

---

[99] TNA, WO 32/15834: Summary of Report by the McLean Court of Inquiry into allegations made during the trial of Captain G. S. L. Griffiths, DLI, against conduct of the British Security Forces in Kenya, no date.

[100] TNA, WO 32/21720: McLean proceedings, 400 (Major W. B. Thomas, 39 Infantry Bde).

[101] *Ibid.*, 444 (Major J. Rogers, Devons).

[102] IWMD, Windeatt, Mau Mau rebellion Kenya. 1st Bn. The Devonshire Regiment Record 1953–55.

colourful title of the 'Chief Secretary's Complaints Co-ordinating Committee'. The surviving records are incomplete; the first 112 minutes of the committee's meetings are missing. What remains is revealing.[103] Beginning in late April 1954, the records show that the authorities paid attention to questions about discipline in the security forces and that the police, administration and army cooperated closely in deciding how to handle these cases. Most concerned the non-military security forces. Soldiers were accused of a range of crimes, including murder, rape and assault; they were tried in the civil courts only with GHQ East Africa's permission. Two men from the Rifle Brigade were to be tried in a civil court in June 1955 for allegedly murdering a farm labourer in Nanyuki a month earlier.[104] After a joint police–army investigation, a Royal Irish Fusilier was to be tried in the civil courts for allegedly committing murder at Naivasha in July.[105] A court acquitted Private Kiptano son of (hereafter 's/o') Kaptinge of manslaughter, but he was 'bound over in a bond of Sh.500/-' for assault causing actual bodily harm.[106] General Erskine gave permission for an RAF sergeant to be tried in the civil courts, which convicted him on three counts of assault, imposing a 300-shilling fine in July 1954.[107]

Soldiers were also convicted by court-martial. A Royal Northumberland Fusilier received eighty-four days' detention for manslaughter after he shot an African herdsman when 'playing with his rifle' in Nanyuki.[108] Sergeant Murray, from the Kenya Regiment, was sentenced to nine months' imprisonment for shooting an African during an interrogation session in February 1955.[109] A court-martial awarded Driver Yates six months' detention for shooting and wounding two farm labourers at Timau.[110] Several soldiers were punished for committing sexual crimes. Sappers Keohoe and Richardson, and Sergeant Cooke were each sentenced to six years' imprisonment for rape.[111] A Kenya Regiment soldier was acquitted by a court-martial hearing after a woman alleged ill treatment in October 1954.[112] Another court-martial convicted the Kenya Regiment's Sergeant Whyatt for an indecent assault committed at Meru, sentencing him to six months' detention and a discharge from

---

[103] Bennett witness statement 3, citing Hanslope document CO 968/266: Colonial political intelligence summary no. 12, December 1953.

[104] Bennett witness statement 3, citing Hanslope document CAB 19/4 Vol. I: Chief Secretary's Complaints Co-ordinating Committee (CSCCC) minutes, 8 August 1955.

[105] *Ibid.*, 11 July 1955, 8 August 1955.   [106] *Ibid.*, 28 June 1954.

[107] *Ibid.*, 31 May 1954, 14 June 1954, 12 July 1954.   [108] *Ibid.*, 7 February 1955.

[109] *Ibid.*, 7 March 1955, 6 June 1955.   [110] *Ibid.*, 7 March 1955, 2 May 1955.

[111] *Ibid.*, 6 September 1954, 15 November 1954, 6 December 1954.

[112] *Ibid.*, 4 October 1954, 15 November 1954, 6 December 1954.

the service with ignominy.[113] Those who decided to disregard orders on conduct could expect to face justice in at least some cases.

General Erskine achieved a major symbolic victory in his campaign aimed at imposing tight discipline on 11 March 1954, when his *bête noire* was convicted in a second court-martial. Writing to his son in February, Erskine bemoaned how 'This blasted man Griffiths is giving me more trouble'. New evidence on another event presented the chance to proceed with a murder charge.[114] This time, though, Erskine decided on the lesser counts of grievous bodily harm and disgraceful conduct of a cruel kind. In summary the incident concerned a series of related incidents over two days during a patrol led by Major Griffiths in June 1953. On 14 March, a 'B' Company, 5 KAR patrol collected two Kikuyu prisoners from Embu police station, who were to accompany them on a mission to find Mau Mau. That evening Griffiths handed his personal knife to Private Ali Segat, ordering him to threaten one of the prisoners with emasculation. Shortly afterwards Griffiths instructed the same soldier to cut off the prisoner's ear. Afterwards the accused failed to assist the wounded man and left him to suffer in agony. The next morning, Griffiths ordered Segat to pierce the other prisoner's ear with a bayonet and pass through it a long wire to lead the man like a dog on the patrol. Although it was not placed on the charge sheet, one prisoner subsequently died, with substantial evidence that he was murdered and not 'shot whilst trying to escape', as originally claimed.[115]

When the court handed down a guilty verdict on 11 March, General Erskine's authority and ethical operational concept were strongly reinforced. Newsinger has argued that this second trial was merely 'a public relations exercise following the public outcry over Griffiths's earlier acquittal'.[116] While East Africa Command and the War Office certainly responded to parliamentary and newspaper reactions to the first trial and the McLean Inquiry, the various letters written by Erskine to his family during this period emphasise his immense frustration with 'this blasted man', 'this damned man' whose behaviour was 'absolutely inexcusable and unnecessary' in this 'most revolting and unforgivable case'.[117] Erskine genuinely reviled everything Griffiths had done and

[113] *Ibid.*, 11 July 1955, 8 August 1955.
[114] IWMD: Erskine papers, Erskine in letter to Philip Erskine, 2 February 1954.
[115] TNA, WO 71/1221: Proceedings of the General Court Martial of Captain G. S. L. Griffiths, for cruelty.
[116] Newsinger, 'Revolt and Repression in Kenya', 179.
[117] IWMD, Erskine papers, Erskine in letter to Philip Erskine, 2 February 1953; Erskine in letter to Philip Erskine, 23 February 1953; Erskine in letter to Philip Erskine, 12 January 1954; Erskine in letter to his wife, 27 October 1953.

stood for, namely the supposition that the army's conduct depended upon the enemy against whom they were fighting and whether the enemy themselves observed the rules of war. As Mr John Hobson said in his summing up for the prosecution:

I hope this Court will not accept any such doctrine and will make it plain that so far as the British Army is concerned and its officers it expects its officers to conduct themselves properly and with propriety towards those who are in its custody and against whom they are fighting.[118]

The court duly found the accused guilty, and he was cashiered from the army and sent to Wormwood Scrubs prison for five years.[119] In finding Griffiths guilty the court accepted Hobson's opinion, showed that command orders on conduct would be implemented and converged with a broader centralising in the direction of the war effort seen, for example, with the creation of the four-man 'War Council' at the highest level.[120]

Conclusion

In many senses, then, British forces did pursue the minimum force approach. The discipline imposed not only satisfied ethical-legal concerns with regard to non-combatants, but equally importantly in the British tradition performed an instrumental role in achieving strategic objectives. Many soldiers realised that killing civilians was both wrong and militarily counterproductive. The army in Kenya attempted to impose tight discipline in the face of enemy provocation, and discriminate policies to ensure that the conduct of its soldiers was more restrained than might otherwise have been the case. A reading of his correspondence and reports shows the utter disgust of General Erskine with the misdeeds of those such as Major Griffiths palpably. Crimes in war – or counter-insurgency emergencies – are inevitable; the issue is rather whether anything is done about them when they do happen. In Kenya, Erskine and the other commanders took serious steps to not only issue orders, but to ensure that they were complied with. Thus the Griffiths courts-martial and the McLean Court of Inquiry, examined here to the fullest extent yet, should be considered as symbolic instructional disciplinary events. How far Erskine succeeded in achieving

---

[118] TNA, WO 71/1221: Second trial of Captain Griffiths, Proceedings, Second Day, 10: Prosecuting Counsel Mr J. Hobson.
[119] Rubin, *Murder, Mutiny and the Military*, 293.
[120] R. W. Heather, 'Intelligence and Counter-Insurgency in Kenya, 1952–56', *Intelligence and National Security*, 5 (1990), 60.

his early vision of a disciplined and moral army in Kenya is addressed again in later chapters, when we shall see the limits to the measures outlined above. The army's views on discipline were designed to guarantee the ability to pursue a logical military strategy which could contain elements of restraint and selective targeting. To these policies we turn next.

6 'A dead man cannot talk': the need for restraint

Having imposed tighter discipline on the army, General Erskine attempted to calibrate the use of force in his strategy to defeat the Mau Mau. Central to his plan was the desire to apply violence directly against the insurgents, yet with sufficient discrimination to spare loyalists. He knew that targeting the entire Kikuyu population, as practised before his arrival, eliminated all incentives for people to support the government. In fact, repression was counterproductive and mobilised the uprising. The military strategy needed to find a number of policies which would not only help discriminate between insurgents and the wider population, but also clearly communicate to the population the government's desire to do so. These policies were seen as militarily effective and help explain, alongside discipline, why the army refrained from a genocidal war.

This chapter analyses four major policy areas where the army aimed at increased restraint concerning the use of force. First, the foundational policy of dividing the colony into legally distinct zones with different rules of engagement is explored. Secondly, throughout the Emergency the authorities aimed to encourage surrenders, on an individual as well as a mass basis. This pursuit is notable bearing in mind that the army was not obliged under international law to take any prisoners at all. The policy proved highly successful and relied in turn upon good discipline. Third, the likelihood of army atrocities against prisoners was minimised because they were quickly handed to the police, thus reducing the chances of any 'heat of battle' massacres. None the less, the army issued comprehensive guidelines on dealing with the various categories of prisoner to promote good conduct. Finally, the army engaged in discriminate operations by developing the pseudo-gang and other special forces techniques. In these operations the risks of non-combatants being harmed, central to any definition of restraint, were minimised.

Creating different legal zones

The troops in Kenya operated in two different legal environments thanks to the area system created by the Emergency Regulations from 3 January 1953 onwards. In the Special Areas troops were formally guided by the minimum force principle. Soldiers opened fire only if an order to stop was disobeyed after two challenges. The Special Areas generally covered all of the Kikuyu, Embu and Meru Reserves, and any other areas subject to disorder. In this way, soldiers directed force selectively against the Mau Mau, trying to avoiding harming the general population.

In the PAs anybody present would be shot on sight: soldiers fought in these areas as though at war. The PAs were confined to the forest areas of the Aberdares, Mount Kenya and Eburru, which were normally uninhabited.[1] Operation Blitz, a combined army–police sweep conducted in the northern Aberdare mountain area on 6 January 1953, was the first operation in the new PAs.[2] Because these areas were uninhabited, the RAF and KPR air wing carried out bombing raids in them throughout the Emergency.[3] Erskine thought this 'absolutely fair because nobody is supposed to be in a prohibited area', while initially banning the offensive use of airpower in all other areas.[4] The policy changed in June 1954, allowing senior military officers to call for air attacks in the Reserves, 'with certain precautions'.[5] By July 1955 this special 'Mushroom' procedure had only been used nine times, apparently without harm to civilians.[6]

Instructions on the types of zones and any geographical changes on where they applied were gazetted and available to all units.[7] Modifications took place, for example with Nairobi being made a Special Area in April 1953, but these were minor changes after the first few months.[8]

[1] IWMD, Erskine papers, GHQ East Africa (1954) *The Kenya Picture*, 2nd edn, Nairobi, para. 41; IWMD, Erskine papers, Report to the Secretary of State for War, 'The Kenya Emergency', signed Erskine, 2 May 1955, paras. 14–16.

[2] Heather, 'Counterinsurgency in Kenya', 57.

[3] As this book focuses on the army, air operations are excluded. For a concise analysis, see S. Chappell, 'Air Power in the Mau Mau Conflict: The Government's Chief Weapon', *RUSI Journal*, 156 (2011), 64–70; see also P. Towle, *Pilots and Rebels: The Use of Aircraft in Unconventional Warfare 1918–1988* (London: Brassey's, 1989), 95–106; J. S. Corum and W. R. Johnson, *Airpower in Small Wars: Fighting Insurgents and Terrorists* (Lawrence, KS: University Press of Kansas, 2003); A. Mumford, 'Unnecessary or Unsung? The Utilisation of Airpower in Britain's Colonial Counterinsurgencies', *Small Wars and Insurgencies*, 20 (2009), 636–55.

[4] TNA, CO 822/693: Letter from Erskine to Harding, 7 July 1953.

[5] TNA, WO 276/171: Minutes of a meeting of CPEC, 4 June 1954.

[6] KNA, WC/CM/1/4: Use of aircraft outside the prohibited areas (the 'Mushroom procedure'), Memorandum by the Chief of Staff, 1 July 1955.

[7] TNA, WO 32/21720: McLean proceedings, 1–2 (Lt.-Col. A. D. B. Tree, GHQ).

[8] Heather, 'Counterinsurgency in Kenya', 77.

The administration held responsibility for informing the local populace about where the zones were. Commanders were obliged to know the exact boundaries in their areas, both on the map and on the ground.[9] On 30 April the army issued a detailed directive on opening fire without challenge in the PAs. Major-General Hinde warned that:

This power is an exceptional one calling for the exercise of great care and discretion by the security forces lest unnecessary casualties be inflicted on our own forces or on friendly Africans.

Apart from the security forces, nobody could enter the PAs without a proper permit. Soldiers operating in these areas had to be fully briefed on the whereabouts and appearance of other security forces, such as trackers, scouts and the Home Guard, to avoid friendly-fire accidents.[10] In June 1953 East Africa Command extended the zoning policy by introducing a 'one-mile strip' along the edge of the prohibited forest areas. Because Mau Mau guerrillas were acquiring supplies from dwellings next to the forests, the army decided to destroy the dwellings and make the strips PAs.[11] According to an officer serving with the Devons:

the Reserve edge of the Strip was marked by white-washed piles of stones, and the Strip itself was forbidden ground for any natives. The object of this forbidden zone was to make it more difficult for the forest gangs to obtain food from the Reserves.[12]

Alan Liddle, an officer with 23 KAR, observed that the mile-broad area was clearly discernible and visible.[13] As three former Inniskillings subalterns recalled, the advantage was that the rules were clear to soldier and African alike.[14]

An intelligence assessment in early 1953 summarised the benefits derived from the zoning policy:

the number of terrorists killed and captured has risen sharply. The armed bands of thugs are becoming increasingly bold, driven by hunger and their need for arms, but now that they are beginning to be forced more and more to take to the forests, the task of hunting them down and destroying them is beginning to assume the nature of a straightforward

---

[9] ODRP, W. R. Hinde, MSS Afr.s.1580, Vol. XI: Directives for the Use of the Director of Operations. Directive no. 4, Office of DDOps, 30 April 1953.
[10] *Ibid.*
[11] A. P. Castro and K. Ettenger, 'Counterinsurgency and Socioeconomic Change: The Mau Mau War in Kirinyaga, Kenya', *Research in Economic Anthropology*, 15 (1994), 80; L. Gill, *Military Musings* (Victoria, BC: Trafford Publishing, 2003), 36.
[12] IWMD, Windeatt Mau Mau rebellion Kenya. 1st Bn. The Devonshire Regiment Record 1953–55.
[13] IWMSA, A. L. K. Liddle, 10091/4.
[14] Interview with Chapman, McFrederick and Moore.

bandit-hunt without the fear of destroying loyal KIKUYU, which, hitherto has been a serious handicap in the Reserves.[15]

The Emergency committees agreed on new zones and discussed changes in the *modus operandi*. The army normally operated in the PAs, so exceptions like allowing the Home Guard to follow up stock thefts into the mile strip had to be notified at committee meetings.[16] The committees ensured that the mile strips were clearly marked, pushing the DO for Othaya, for example, to hurry up in placing marking cairns.[17] They also prompted the security forces to give local inhabitants due warning before activating new PAs.[18] The army zealously guarded the zoning policy's implementation, the commander of 39 Brigade reporting to the CPEC 'much movement of local inhabitants' through the mile strip in Fort Hall, and that the demarcation cairns had fallen into disrepair.[19]

In Embu district the government's efforts were impeded by squatters refusing to pull down huts in the mile strip, and the cairns being destroyed at night time – a practice discouraged by communal fines on nearby residents.[20] In several areas the administration, police and army launched combined operations to clear crops and destroy huts in places newly designated as prohibited.[21] For the military, having a cleared mile strip – bereft of undergrowth as well as habitation – offered a clear view of any Mau Mau leaving or entering the forests, and a clear firing line.[22] In a few instances soldiers broke the rules. On 7 January 1954 a patrol by the Royal Inniskillings found twenty suspects hiding in the mile strip; rather than shooting them, they handed them over to the Meru police.[23] The next month the battalion discovered an elderly man in the Fort Hall PA, turning him over to the Kangama police.[24] In North Tetu division, Nyeri district, the administration and army clashed over the zoning policy in November 1953. The army wanted a fully cleared mile strip in the division, against the DC's and DO's wishes. Since May, the security forces had effectively worked to a 'zones-of-operation' scheme, whereby the army, police and administration operated in exclusive zones. An increase in gang activity and personnel changes resulted in calls to end

[15] TNA, WO 276/378: Jock Scott intelligence summary, 6 February 1953.
[16] TNA, WO 276/170: CPEC minutes, 23 May 1953.
[17] KNA, VP/2/22: Nyeri DEC minutes, 24 May 1953 and 2 June 1953.
[18] TNA, WO 276/238: Record of the meeting of the DDOps Committee held at Government House on Tuesday, 7th July 1953.
[19] TNA, WO 276/170: CPEC minutes, 28 August 1953.
[20] TNA, WO 276/170: CPEC minutes, 4 September 1953.
[21] KNA, VP/2/22: Nyeri DEC minutes, 13 October 1953.
[22] TNA, WO 276/439: CPEC minutes, 19 August 1955.
[23] TNA, WO 276/294: HQ 49 Brigade situation report, 8 January 1954.
[24] TNA, WO 276/290: 39 Infantry Brigade operational sitrep, 9 February 1954.

the agreement. The Buffs' company commander doubted the Home Guard's ability to look after their allotted zone, and persuaded the divisional committee to end the agreement and initiate the mile strip.[25]

Commanders issued orders to see that all troops understood the regulations. Brigadier Orr instructed his men on 24 September 1953 only to fire in self-defence in the Reserves (Special Areas), unless a person failed to halt on challenge or evaded capture by running away.[26] A 3 KAR officer noted how working in the Reserve was much harder than the forests because soldiers were always very worried lest they shot the wrong person, but luckily this never happened.[27]

Brigadier Tweedie opted to pass on the message personally in April 1953 because when arriving he found that 'a lot of these orders were written in a very legal phraseology which you could not possibly expect a young platoon commander to understand, and this was an attempt to try to make them clear'.[28] At a subordinate level, Major Small taught his men in 'D' Company of the Devons where to shoot and where not, and how to call suspects to halt. He claimed to have personally passed this information on to each new draft coming into the company.[29] Three witnesses at the McLean Inquiry recounted incidents where men were shot for failing to halt when ordered in Special Areas.[30] Another three men expressed their willingness to fire on anyone they came across in the PAs.[31] East Africa Command's directives on limiting the conflict's destruction were understood and implemented by men in the field. The legal zoning policy enabled the army to apply force with a certain degree of discrimination.

Women participated in the Mau Mau rebellion, for example, in supplying food to active combat units. Despite this, a traditional prohibition against harming women persisted in some soldiers' minds. Most of the troops in Major Cooper's company of the Kenya Regiment refused to fire on women running away in the PAs.[32] Second Lieutenant Cooke's men, also in the Kenya Regiment, normally chased women down,

[25] KNA, VP/9/9: Minutes of divisional intelligence meeting held at the Show Ground, North Tetu, on 16 November 1953.

[26] TNA, WO 32/21720: McLean proceedings, 11 (Brig. J. R. H. Orr, 70 Infantry Brigade).

[27] IWMSA, R. Z. Stockwell, 10065/2.

[28] TNA, WO 32/21720: McLean proceedings, 394 (Brig. J. W. Tweedie, 39 Infantry Brigade). His order is in WO 32/21721, Exhibit 24, Sentries orders and orders to fire HQ 39 Brigade to 1 Buffs, 1 Devons, 1 Lancashire Fusiliers, 20 April 1953.

[29] TNA, WO 32/21720: McLean proceedings, 449 (Major G. W. Small, Devons).

[30] Ibid., 179 (Fusilier R. Williams, Royal Northumberland Fusiliers); 303 (2nd Lt. M. Cooke, Kenya Regiment); 389 (Private K. MacCash, Black Watch).

[31] Ibid., 275 (Capt. H. C. Russell, 7 KAR); 295 (Major N. M. C. Cooper, Kenya Regiment); 433 (Major D. N. Court, The Buffs).

[32] Ibid., 295 (Major N. M. C. Cooper, Kenya Regiment).

whereas they had no compunction about shooting at men.[33] Eventually 39 Brigade's commander, Brigadier Tweedie, felt compelled to:

talk to the men about it. I said that they must not be silly about it, these people were just as bad as the men. We hate shooting women even if they are doing wrong. The men were surprisingly upset because some of them are only just past being schoolboys.[34]

Encouraging surrenders

Throughout the Emergency the army actively sought to persuade Mau Mau members, individually and in large groups, to give up the armed struggle and surrender, despite vocal opposition from the European settlers.[35] Police Special Branch played the critical role in the major surrender schemes, especially in 1954 and 1955.[36] Although the government had accepted surrenders from the Emergency's inception, General Erskine instituted the first concerted drive to persuade insurgents to surrender in August 1953. This coincided with, and relied upon, the improved discipline seen in the army since his arrival. Before August surrendered insurgents were subject to the full power of the law, which proved a strong deterrent as the death penalty applied to many Mau Mau offences besides murder, such as consorting with terrorists or supplying them.

The 1953 'Green Branch' surrender scheme

Surrender schemes were first considered in June 1953 by the KIC. Those present at the meeting made comparisons with Malaya. They 'felt that there was more hope of breaking terrorism in Kenya by force than in Malaya'. Communists needed a more subtle psychological approach than the Mau Mau.[37] Plans were drawn up in July. The scheme would not protect surrendered terrorists from prosecution, nor apply to those forced into surrendering, who were designated 'captured' insurgents. People who gave themselves up voluntarily would not be prosecuted for the capital offences of

---

[33] *Ibid.*, 303 (2nd Lt. M. Cooke, Kenya Regiment).

[34] *Ibid.*, 394 (Brig. J. W. Tweedie, 39 Infantry Brigade).

[35] Anderson, *Histories of the Hanged*, 273; P. Catterall (ed.), *The Macmillan Diaries: The Cabinet Years, 1950–1957* (London: Macmillan, 2003), 382.

[36] Heather, 'Counterinsurgency in Kenya', 114.

[37] TNA, WO 276/62: Minutes of the 10th meeting of the KIC, 17 June 1953.

adhering to terrorism and carrying arms, but were liable to prosecution for murders and other atrocities.[38]

The exemption from prosecution for Mau Mau who had not committed crimes was based on a recognition that many Kikuyu were forced into the movement against their will.[39] Meanwhile, the government waited for the right moment to announce the terms, relying on intelligence guidance. An assessment on 11 August noted that administration officials in Naivasha were convinced a surrender campaign would pay off, but suggested 'further blows' in the Aberdares before opening the offer.[40] Building up to the announcement, General Erskine asked London to send out an expert in psychological warfare.[41] The time came when Mau Mau leader Dedan Kimathi communicated with Special Branch:

On 20th August, Special Branch received, within a few hours, two letters purporting to come from Dedan Kimathi, the most notorious of the gang leaders, claiming that he had ordered his terrorist forces to desist from attacks with effect from 1st August, and that he was anxious for the early restoration of peace. One of these letters was received through the post, while the other was found in a cleft bamboo planted in the middle of a trail leading from the Aberdares. Preliminary examination suggested that both letters were genuine, and this was rapidly confirmed by expert C.I.D. examination after comparison with specimens of handwriting known to be that of Dedan Kimathi ... It would be unwise to read too much into this development until further facts are available. There are indications that Kimathi hoped for something in the nature of an amnesty, and it is in any case doubtful whether his influence extends to more than a considerable proportion of the terrorist forces.[42]

The KIC advised the government that these significant developments represented a sincere wish by many Mau Mau to surrender. The army redeployed 39 and 70 Brigades, taking offensive action in the Aberdares and around south Mount Kenya to pressurise the gangs.[43] Baring and Erskine announced the start of the scheme on 24 August, with the Director of Information in charge of providing widespread publicity.[44] Leaflets were circulated by hand throughout the Emergency areas and dropped from KPR air wing aircraft. To make identifying surrendering Mau Mau easier, insurgents were instructed to carry green branches

[38] TNA, WO 276/200: Emergency Directive no. 9, Surrender Policy, signed Hinde, 28 July 1953.
[39] IWMD, Erskine papers, Report to the Secretary of State for War, 'The Kenya Emergency', signed Erskine, 2 May 1955, para. 35.
[40] TNA, CO 822/378: KICFA, 11 August 1953.
[41] TNA, CO 822/701: Signal from Erskine to CIGS, 12 August 1953.
[42] TNA, CO 822/378: KICFA 11/53, 25 August 1953.   [43] Ibid.
[44] TNA, WO 276/200: GHQ order, 20 August 1953.

with them as they came into government posts or security forces positions. The authorities hoped that widespread publicity, the instructions to troops on exactly why the policy mattered, and the green branch technique would all boost the surrender rate, which up to this point stood at only twenty-nine since October 1952.[45] The police took responsibility for the reception, feeding and accommodation of surrendered Mau Mau.[46]

Just over two weeks into the scheme, few surrendered Mau Mau sat in captivity. Instead the government possessed another letter from Dedan Kimathi. He requested negotiations with GHQ to arrange a conditional truce. What exactly happened to his proposal is unclear – there is no evidence to suggest his offer was taken up.[47] By 22 September sixty-two men had surrendered, mainly auxiliaries and porters rather than leadership figures. The government distributed more leaflets by air, and drove loud-hailer vans along the forest fringes.[48] During the next month, the scheme seemed most successful in the Rift Valley, and least persuasive around Mount Kenya. In the Central Province, administration officials disliked the policy, 'believing liquidation rather than capitulation to be the answer'.[49]

Although a worthwhile endeavour, the 'Green Branch' scheme ultimately failed, producing only 159 surrenders by 10 February 1954, at a time when Mau Mau numbered at least 10,000 in the forests of the Aberdares and Mount Kenya.[50] The scheme proved an important pedagogic tool for both the security forces – teaching them why and how surrender schemes operated – and for the insurgents – showing that government could be magnanimous. These messages mattered because local security forces and insurgents took time to adjust to negotiating with a hated enemy.

The 1954 'China' surrender scheme

The first major alteration in the government's fortunes happened on 15 January 1954, when a patrol captured Waruhiu Itote, otherwise known as the notorious General China, leader of the Mount Kenya insurgents.[51] Ian Henderson, a Special Branch officer with a deep knowledge of the Kikuyu language and culture, interrogated China at length,

[45] Heather, 'Counterinsurgency in Kenya', 114–16.
[46] TNA, CO 822/496: Memo by DDOps, Surrender Policy, 20 August 1953.
[47] TNA, CO 822/378: KICFA 12/53, 8 September 1953.
[48] TNA, CO 822/378: KICFA 13/53, 22 September 1953.
[49] TNA, CO 822/378: KICFA 15/53, 20 October 1953.
[50] Heather, 'Counterinsurgency in Kenya', 119.   [51] *Ibid.*, 145.

producing an invaluable forty-four-page summary report.[52] The report's contents, distributed by GHQ, detailed the Mount Kenya Mau Mau's order of battle, manpower strength, armaments and aims. Assessed alongside other evidence, the interrogation showed rising popular support for the Mau Mau over the preceding four months.[53] Thus intelligence recognised that the prospects for a mass surrender were limited unless those in the militant formations could be made to feel under stress.

China agreed to cooperate and Special Branch thought that his services might be exploited in contacting Mau Mau leaders. In early February Baring received British Cabinet approval for using China as a conduit for establishing top secret discussions with the insurgent leadership.[54] The operation's code name, chosen by someone with a sense of humour, would be Wedgewood; based at Nyeri and under Henderson's control it was launched on 13 February.[55] China addressed twenty-six letters to senior Mau Mau leaders imploring them to surrender and explaining the fair treatment he had received from the government. After a judge handed down the death sentence to China for his terrorist activities, Baring commuted the sentence to life imprisonment as a reward for his assistance.[56] This move also aimed at influencing the gang leaders in the forests. Special Branch 'paraded' China through certain troubled areas, such as Mathera, in an effort to appeal to militants. For some DOs, using China in this manner appeared to have a devastating effect on loyalist morale.[57]

Whereas the 'Green Branch' scheme targeted individual gang members, Operation Wedgewood's objective was to arrange mass surrenders. But like the previous effort, the scheme depended upon building confidence in the government's intentions, when most Mau Mau thought that any surrender efforts were an elaborate trap.[58] About three or four weeks after China distributed his letters the first replies were received from passive-wing leaders in the Reserves and militant-wing leaders in the forests.[59] While Special Branch tried to arrange a meeting with senior leaders, General Erskine tried to prevent the operation being

---

[52] See the full transcript in TNA, WO 276/512.
[53] TNA, WO 276/455: KISUM 4/54, issued by GHQ East Africa, 24 January 1954.
[54] Heather, 'Counterinsurgency in Kenya', 147.
[55] TNA, WO 216/967: Short History of the Wedgewood Operation, forwarded to VCIGS by Heyman, 20 April 1954, para. 2.
[56] Heather, 'Counterinsurgency in Kenya', 148–9.
[57] Royal Commonwealth Society Collection, Cambridge University Library: T. L. Edgar, RCMS 318/1/3.
[58] TNA, WO 216/967: Short History of the Wedgewood Operation, para. 2.
[59] Ibid., para. 4.

scotched by his own forces. On 8 March he issued a directive to all officers, so that there should be 'no misconception of my motives in the measures I have taken'. The object of the China scheme was to bring the Emergency to a quick end. So far the scheme had produced 'more information of a very useful kind in the course of a few weeks than we could ever have expected to have obtained by normal methods over a much longer period'. Loyal Kikuyu should not fear the prospect of surrendered Mau Mau being freely allowed back into the Reserves, as they would be put in detention. Erskine affirmed his intention to vigorously attack the Mau Mau movement.[60]

Security force operations continued in both Reserves and forests without change during the initial phases of Operation Wedgewood.[61] In receiving surrendering Mau Mau, separate tasks were assigned to the security forces. The army guarded surrendered Mau Mau, the police searched, interrogated and documented them, and the administration provided food and shelter. The army created surrender points and then transported people to reception centres; finally they went to detention camps.[62] 70 Brigade wished soldiers to receive surrenders in the forest where possible, 'so that no Home Guard or locals see the surrenders and attempt to interfere with them'.[63]

The lack of respite combined with fears over the settler and Home Guard reaction may have caused doubts in the Mau Mau leadership. A letter from the 'Mount Kenya Committee of Elders', generally favouring surrender, was tempered by the worry that the government might 'amend their policy'. Erskine hoped to assuage their fears by encouraging Michael Blundell, the settler Minister without Portfolio, to make a statement supporting the policy.[64] Intelligence reports informed Erskine that in key areas, such as Fort Hall, the population retained a 'deep seated sympathy with Mau Mau and hatred of Government'.[65] Sustained by these popular sentiments, would insurgents give up?

They did. On 28 March, General Kaleba surrendered to an army truck driving along a main road, and was taken for talks with the Chief Native Commissioner, the army Chief of Staff and Special Branch

[60] IWMD, Erskine papers, Commander-in-Chief's Directive no. 3, 8 March 1954.

[61] Heather, 'Counterinsurgency in Kenya', 151.

[62] TNA, WO 276/454: Letter from Brigadier J. R. H. Orr, CO 70 (EA) Infantry Brigade, to Major-General G. D. Heyman, Chief of Staff East Africa Command, 7 March 1954.

[63] TNA, WO 276/454: 70 (EA) Infantry Brigade Operational Instruction no. 2/54, Operation Wedgewood, 19 March 1954.

[64] TNA, WO 216/967: Letter from Erskine to VCIGS, 9 March 1954.

[65] TNA, WO 276/455: KISUM, 23 March 1954.

representatives, as well as the captured Generals Tanganyika and China. He was firmly convinced that the Mount Kenya groups wanted peace, and the Aberdares groups would follow their lead in any mass surrender. Special Branch released him into the Reserve at four in the morning the next day to try and contact the gangs and arrange another meeting.[66] Kaleba made quick progress, and a meeting took place in Nyeri on 30 March. Erskine wrote to his wife:

> The 'China' business is really most exciting. I have been in a state of high tension since we started this thing on the 14th Feb ... The thing has moved very slowly mainly because our operations are so effective that the Mau Mau can't get in touch with each other quickly. However today we got in four top leaders from Mt Kenya and two from the Aberdares. They accepted our terms without any serious difficulty. They have now gone back to the forest to convince their gangs to come in and surrender. I feel very hopeful that they will be able to do this. We shall now know within two weeks how we stand. Quite evidently the pressure on them has been too great and they do not want to go on fighting a hopeless battle.[67]

Present at the Nyeri meeting were Generals China, Tanganyika and Kaleba, five incognito Mau Mau leaders, the Chief Native Commissioner, army Chief of Staff, Head of Special Branch and Ian Henderson. The insurgents admitted their lingering doubts about the government's intentions, and requested more time to consult their followers before reaching a final agreement. The government allowed them to take Tanganyika back as a sign of good faith, and made five proposals if the Mau Mau leaders brought in large numbers of men with their arms. First, the security forces would not shoot at them while they were surrendering. Second, prisoners would be well treated. Third, no prosecutions would arise relating to possessing guns and ammunition. Fourth, the death penalty would be suspended for crimes committed prior to surrender. Fifth, those who surrendered would be placed in detention camps. The Mau Mau representatives agreed to these terms and discussion then focused on how best to bring the gang members together. Major-General Heyman, the Chief of Staff, promised to stop patrols and bombing in the forests, to help the leaders negotiate with their gangs. Military operations were to continue in the Reserves, and any Mau Mau attacks in the Reserves could be pursued into the forest if necessary. Heyman suggested another meeting on 10 April, to which the insurgents agreed. They then returned to the forest.[68]

---

[66] TNA, WO 216/967: Telegram from GHQ East Africa to War Office, 29 March 1954.
[67] IWMD: Erskine papers, letter from Erskine to his wife, 30 March 1954.
[68] TNA, WO 216/967: Short History of the Wedgewood Operation, paras. 5–8.

Although the government kept their promise on ceasing operations in the forests, nobody from the Mau Mau side turned up for the meeting on 10 April, bringing Operation Wedgewood to an end.[69] Unfortunately the whole scheme failed due to mere accident, elucidated by General Gatamuki, who fell into captivity on 7 April. Gatamuki arrested the leaders who met at Nyeri when they re-entered the forest, but changed his mind and released them (apart from Tanganyika), favouring surrender himself after other leaders and the passive wing made their case. The leaders decided to concentrate their gangs inside the forest boundary by the evening of 6 April. Around one thousand insurgents duly congregated at the specified point, with another six hundred en route with Kaleba from Meru and Embu and hundreds more expected from around Nanyuki. Some of this large number strayed across the boundary into the mile strip or Reserve near Gathuini, provoking army interest. On the morning of 7 April soldiers claimed they came under fire while on a sweep through the area. In the ensuing battle twenty-five Mau Mau were killed and seven captured. The remaining insurgents in the area fled, convinced that the whole thing was a trap.[70]

After the Gathuini battle the passive wing in the Reserves stopped passing letters from Special Branch to Mau Mau leaders and attempts to restore contacts were made in vain. A letter was found on 10 April from an insurgent leader declaring Mau Mau's complete distrust in government and that the leaders who met in Nyeri were all under arrest.[71] The government broadcast an appeal pleading innocence in breaking the agreement, stating: 'You fought our soldiers in the reserve, and this resulted in the Gathuini battle.' The broadcast went on to warn that operations would shortly recommence in the forests. The Wedgewood terms finally ended on 16 April.[72]

Gathuini destroyed the trust in government so carefully constructed over many months. The authorities quickly made the best of a bad situation, initiating Operation Overdraft, which lasted until 16 April. The security forces capitalised upon the information gathered during the negotiations, making numerous arrests and conducting sweeps through areas known to contain gangs.[73] At the same time the administration increased the pressure against the passive wing through 'intensified administrative and economic

---

[69] TNA, CO 822/774: Telegram from Acting Governor to Colonial Secretary, 11 April 1954.
[70] TNA, WO 216/967: Short History of the Wedgewood Operation, paras. 9–14.
[71] *Ibid.*, paras. 15–19.   [72] TNA, WO 276/515: Unheaded note, 10 April 1954.
[73] TNA, CO 822/774: Telegram from C-in-C East Africa to VCIGS, 12 April 1954.

measures', such as villagisation.[74] When Overdraft concluded, the security forces deployed in preparation for Operation Anvil and the subsequent offensives throughout the Emergency areas.

By 5 June 1954 a total of 191 Mau Mau had surrendered since 28 August the previous year.[75] A few days later, a surprise chance to renew the defunct mass surrenders emerged, when the Indian High Commissioner in Nairobi reported that local African elders had approached him requesting that he reopen the talks. The civil and military authorities rejected the Indian offer of mediation, and remained sceptical about the likely success of such talks. There is no evidence that anything came of the Indian communication.[76] However, it may have prompted a reconsideration of policy in late June. The War Council decided that the Wedgewood terms were still acceptable except for one important change. Immunity would no longer be extended for all previous crimes; murder would be prosecuted where sufficient evidence existed.[77] After an insurgent entered captivity, an investigation would determine the kind of penalty applied, such as imprisonment, detention or exile.[78] So in this sense the China surrender scheme made a lasting impact on the campaign, by pushing the government towards moderation instead of an annihilationist strategy. Twenty-three individuals gave up in North Tetu division in August. They cited hunger due to villagisation, bombing, harsh treatment by gang leaders and poor weather as motivating factors. Apparently further Mau Mau wanted to surrender if presented with the opportunity.[79] These signs kept the notion of surrender schemes alive in East Africa Command, despite the disappointing end to the China affair.

The 1955 'double amnesty' surrender scheme

The year 1955 witnessed the major surrender scheme in the Emergency, as the government tightened their grip on the gangs through offensives and the passive wing through villagisation. According to Erskine, the new scheme he planned for March 1955 was brought forward to January

---

[74] TNA, CO 822/774: Telegram from Acting Governor to Colonial Secretary, 11 April 1954.

[75] TNA, CO 822/774: Telegram from Acting Governor to Colonial Secretary, 12 June 1954.

[76] TNA, WO 216/967: Telegram from GHQ East Africa to War Office, 11 June 1954.

[77] TNA, CO 822/774: Telegram from Acting Governor to Colonial Secretary, 24 June 1954.

[78] TNA, WO 276/515: Surrender Terms, note by the Secretary of the War Council, 4 December 1954.

[79] KNA, VP/9/9: Nyeri district fortnightly intelligence report, 12 August 1954.

Handling prisoners[111]

Once Mau Mau came into custody the security forces possessed comprehensive guidelines for dealing with them, in addition to the directives
on good conduct. In a directive of 28 July 1953, Major-General Hinde
explicitly drew on the Malaya experience in advocating that: 'terrorists
should not be ill-treated. They may subsequently be our main propaganda weapon in encouraging further surrenders'.[112] Another directive
stressed how 'it is imperative that they should NOT be illtreated', and
ordered soldiers to follow the procedures outlined in Operational Intelligence Instruction no. 4: an immediate tactical interrogation for actionable information, then handing them over to the police. The police kept
them in interrogation centres 'until fully exploited', then passed the
prisoners over to the Commissioner of Prisons.[113] A later directive called
on soldiers to fill in a special proforma whenever they captured someone,
to help the police secure prosecutions.[114]

These basic, easily followed instructions remained in place until the
double amnesty in January 1955. Thereafter, all those surrendering were
sent to one place: Thika detention camp. In contrast to previous policy,
the CID refrained from conducting interrogations of surrendered Mau
Mau. Case files were compiled against those who were captured, in case
the Attorney-General decided upon prosecution.[115] On 1 February the
War Council altered the arrangements by extending the period for which
surrendered insurgents could be held in forward areas to up to a month
instead of the previous forty-eight hours. A week later the rules were
changed again, allowing Mau Mau to be held in operational areas
indefinitely in the charge of the local DO, under delegated detention
orders.[116] These modifications were intended to facilitate the use of
these men as pseudo-gang members, guides and trackers for the security
forces. The army reverted to the forty-eight-hour holding limit in

---

[111] Especially helpful sources amid the large literature on prisoners in wartime are:
N. Ferguson, 'Prisoner Taking and Prisoner Killing in the Age of Total War: Towards
a Political Economy of Military Defeat', *War in History*, 11 (2004), 148–92;
S. Scheipers (ed.), *Prisoners in War* (Oxford University Press, 2010); N. Wylie,
'Prisoners of War in the Era of Total War', *War in History*, 13 (2006), 217–33.

[112] TNA, CO 822/496: Emergency Directive no. 9, Surrender Policy, issued by GHQ East
Africa, 28 July 1953.

[113] TNA, CO 822/496: Emergency Directive no. 10, Directive on the treatment of
surrendered terrorists, issued by GHQ East Africa, 28 July 1953.

[114] TNA, WO 276/526: Emergency Directive no. 11, signed Rimbault, 20 August 1953.

[115] TNA, CO 822/775: Disposal of surrendered terrorists, Memorandum by the
Emergency Joint Staff, 17 January 1955.

[116] TNA, CO 822/775: Disposal of surrendered terrorists, memo by the Minister of
Defence, 25 February 1955.

October: prisoners could be used for two days, provided Special Branch were informed. Afterwards, they were sent to Special Branch for 'deliberate interrogation', and then subject to a delegated detention order, issued by the local DC, who could keep them in his district 'for the purpose of encouraging surrenders' for up to a month.[117]

In November 1955 the Kenya government issued new instructions. Surrendered insurgents were now the responsibility of Special Branch, but were to be handed over to the CID for prosecution where evidence existed. They could be held for ninety-six hours for operational purposes. The instructions defined the various categories of persons falling into government custody. A 'terrorist' was 'any person who in any way participates *actively* in the *Mau Mau* terrorist campaign'. A 'Surrendered Terrorist' was defined as any terrorist who willingly surrendered when they could have escaped. A 'Captured Terrorist' was an insurgent who capitulated in battle, in the course of a pursuit, or otherwise against their will. 'Suspects detained' were 'all persons taken into custody by the Security Forces other than captured or surrendered terrorists'. No time limit was placed on the use of surrendered insurgents provided a detention order was issued within twenty-eight days, and no prosecution was forthcoming. If the authorities decided to prosecute a surrendered terrorist the operational exploitation could still take place for up to twenty-eight days, after which he would have to be charged and taken before a magistrate.

In short, the policy for dealing with surrendered terrorists fell into six stages: immediate operational use, deliberate interrogation, further operational use, prosecution for crimes outside surrender immunity, detention and finally rehabilitation. For captured terrorists, the policy also comprised six parts: immediate operational use, deliberate interrogation, further operational use, extended operational use with the Attorney-General's authority, prosecution within thirty days of capture, and detention if no prosecution was instituted. Because prosecutions were needed within thirty days, investigations proceeded alongside interrogation and operational use.[118] There was a military imperative for only employing those who sincerely wanted to help the security forces, as coercion would have proved counterproductive. On some occasions the Attorney-General decided not to prosecute captured terrorists who gave exceptional service to the security forces. Whenever captured insurgents were due

---

[117] TNA, WO 276/430: Memo from Brigadier R. M. P. Carver, Chief of Staff, to all formations and units, 26 October 1955.

[118] TNA, CO 822/776: Booklet, 'War Council Instruction No. 18. The Treatment of Captured and Surrendered Terrorists'. Issued by Cabinet Office, Nairobi, 30 November 1955.

for prosecution on capital charges the government took their assistance into consideration when deciding whether to commute the death penalty.[119]

So much for the formal policy. The McLean Inquiry proceedings and oral histories offer insights into how soldiers viewed the enemy and thought about the surrender campaign. Ron Cassidy, with the Rifle Brigade in Kenya, remembered that his unit actively sought to take prisoners.[120] Trevor Matless, in theatre from 1954 to 1956, recalled Erskine's orders on treating prisoners well, which were obeyed in his experience.[121] Soldiers understood the need for restraint, providing an informed basis for acting beyond blind obedience. In one case, this resulted from previous experience in Malaya, where the reason for taking prisoners – to supply information – also applied.[122] An officer in 5 KAR explained how: 'it was quite clear from those who were in charge that there was a great deal of advantage in having a man caught alive. Because of the information he might be able to impart.'[123] Others perceived the policy to support screening operations.[124] The troops realised that surrenders were significant when, as Major Lithgow put it, 'a dead man cannot talk and we want prisoners because the prisoners will probably lead to further prisoners, and that is a very definite order in the company'.[125]

The procedures for dealing with prisoners proved valuable in leading troops to Mau Mau locations in the PAs. Major Squires from The Buffs expressed his satisfaction: 'We recently got three prisoners and the information we got was so good they led us to the hide'.[126] Two colonels had benefited from a prisoner's immediate tactical intelligence, and from taking prisoners on patrol as guides before handing them over to the police.[127] Other witnesses at the inquiry detailed giving prisoners a 'slight verbal interrogation' at their unit's headquarters.[128] Most soldiers

---

[119] TNA, CO 822/776: Telegram from Acting Governor to Secretary of State for the Colonies, 14 May 1956.

[120] IWMSA, R. Cassidy, 11138/4.   [121] IWMSA, T. R. Matless, 21020/4.

[122] TNA, WO 32/21720: McLean proceedings, 152 (Major N. Holroyd, 3 KAR).

[123] IWMSA, P. H. W. Brind, 10089/2.

[124] TNA, WO 32/21720: McLean proceedings, 180 (Fusilier R. Williams, Royal Northumberland Fusiliers); 214 (Lt.-Col. L. W. B. Evans, 5 KAR).

[125] Ibid., 367 (Major A. O. L. Lithgow, Black Watch), 182 (Fusilier G. A. G. Anderson, Royal Northumberland Fusiliers); 187 (Lt.-Col. E. H. W. Grimshaw, Royal Inniskilling Fusiliers).

[126] Ibid., 432 (Major S. J. Squire, The Buffs).

[127] Ibid., 52 (Lt.-Col. J. C. Bartlett, 23 KAR); 133 (Lt.-Col. J. O. Crewe-Read, 3 KAR).

[128] Ibid., 140 (CSM (Company Sergeant-Major) I. J. Day, 3 KAR); 188 (Lt.-Col. E. H. W. Grimshaw, Royal Inniskilling Fusiliers); 258 (2nd Lt. R. E. Ginner, 5 KAR); 359 (Lt.-Col. D. McN. C. Rose, Black Watch); 410 (Lt.-Col. J. F. Connolly, The Buffs).

who talked on the matter said that the police conducted interrogations,[129] and that they handed prisoners to them as soon as possible.[130]

Mistreating or torturing prisoners was thought 'foreign to our way of life'.[131] The medical officer in charge of the Nyeri native civil hospital saw numerous Kikuyu civilians and prisoners, none of whom had sustained injuries from mistreatment.[132] Major Huggan made the same point about the Nanyuki hospital, while Reverend Jerome had observed a large number of badly wounded Mau Mau well treated in various hospitals.[133] Wounded Mau Mau suspects were taken to hospital for treatment by men from diverse units, at times entailing the carrying of them for a fair distance.[134] Alternatively, doctors went to the wounded.[135] Humane treatment came in other forms, too. Lieutenant Marshall reckoned that prisoners normally put on a lot of weight, hardly surprising given the soldiers' tendency to hand over extra food, including slipping them the odd packet of biscuits.[136] Accounts can suggest that the troops almost fell over themselves doling out cigarettes and brewing up tea for all and sundry in an unstoppable reflex action.[137] To the less generous this smacked of spoiling the natives.[138] To the astute, though, it presented an effective alternative to torturing for information; Major Nepean stated how 'We have rather stressed the other way in that we find we have done extraordinarily well by producing a cigarette and a cup of tea.'[139]

Kindly behaviour towards prisoners certainly produced intelligence.[140] The troops' restraint also depended upon the ethical values

[129]   *Ibid.*, 75 (RSM E. P. Hodgkiss, 23 KAR); 319 (Major J. Bramston, 4 KAR).
[130]   *Ibid.*, 57A (Major H. F. Rawkins, 23 KAR); 69 (Major A. M. Hlawati, 23 KAR); 79 (WOPC Mtwamwari, 23 KAR); 107 (CSM H. Thomas, 7 KAR); 109 (WOPC F. Ojuka, 7 KAR); 202 (RSM J. Fillerty, Royal Inniskilling Fusiliers); 220 (Lt.-Col. L. W. B. Evans, 5 KAR); 295 (Major N. M. C. Cooper, Kenya Regiment); 305 (CSM J. F. Holland, Kenya Regiment); 389 (Private K. MacCash, Black Watch); IWMSA, J. F. Roberts, 18825/7; G. L. Potts, 23213/19.
[131]   TNA, WO 32/21720: McLean proceedings, 16–17 (Brig. J. R. H. Orr, 70 Infantry Brigade).
[132]   *Ibid.*, 124 (Surgeon Rear Admiral F. J. D. Twigg, RN retired).
[133]   *Ibid.*, 184 (Major J. T. Huggan, Royal Army Medical Corps); 269 (Reverend C. S. Jerome, Church of England Chaplain to Nanyuki Garrison).
[134]   *Ibid.*, 109 (WOPC F. Ojuka, 7 KAR); 227 (Major W. E. B. Atkins, 5 KAR); 410 (Lt.-Col. J. F. Connolly, The Buffs).
[135]   *Ibid.*, 163 (Reverend D. V. S. Asher, Church of England Chaplain to Royal Northumberland Fusiliers); 365 (Lieutenant L. G. Fallows, Royal Army Medical Corps, attached Black Watch).
[136]   *Ibid.*, 454 (Lt. J. R. Marshall, Kenya Regiment, attached Devons); 35 (2nd Lt. R. E. Campbell, 6 KAR); 419 (CSM J. R. J. Kemp, The Buffs).
[137]   *Ibid.*, 140 (CSM I. J. Day, 3 KAR); 210 (Major J. Bruce, 49 Infantry Brigade).
[138]   *Ibid.*, 401 (Major W. B. Thomas, 39 Infantry Brigade).
[139]   *Ibid.*, 447 (Major P. V. Nepean, Devons).
[140]   Clayton, *Counter-Insurgency in Kenya*, 35.

which General Erskine thought so vital to the army's self-respect and discipline. Studies on genocidal war show how seeing the enemy as an essentially different, inhuman foe greatly facilitates indiscriminate killing.[141] By contrast, 'humanizing, decategorizing, or personalizing others all create a powerful self-restraining effect'.[142] There is evidence for this effect in the McLean Inquiry testimonies. Prisoners held by the army – those in alternative captivity are another matter – were well treated in many cases.[143] Men related to the enemy, seeing similarities and treating them accordingly. An old soldier saw that the prisoners received the same care furnished to the Japanese and Germans in the Second World War.[144] Officers in the Inniskillings and The Buffs considered that captured or surrendered enemy personnel fared identically to their own men.[145] CSM Bailey noted his soldiers' attitude regarding the local population:

The majority of them are young and have just come out and this is their first time abroad and I think they treat them as human; they are quite prepared to be friendly with them.[146]

Officers worried about their soldiers being 'too kind'; or as one put it, 'the main difficulty is to stop the men being too nice'.[147] After all, the Mau Mau still needed defeating and concerns surfaced when niceness interfered with military effectiveness. The permanent dilemma for democratic armies, being able to motivate men to kill, yet needing them to check their aggression, was a consideration for commanders. Too little aggression could be as great a problem as too much. The Royal Northumberland Fusiliers noticed an aversion to shooting, especially at unarmed people evading capture, and attributed it to inexperience.[148]

---

[141] See, for example: O. Bartov, *The Eastern Front, 1941–45, German Troops and the Barbarisation of Warfare* (Basingstoke: Macmillan, 1985); C. R. Browning, *Ordinary Men: Reserve Police Battalion 101 and the Final Solution in Poland* (New York: HarperPerennial, 1993); G. Kassimeris (ed.), *The Barbarisation of Warfare* (London: Hurst, 2006); G. Kassimeris (ed.), *The Warrior's Dishonour: Barbarity and Morality in Modern Warfare* (Aldershot: Ashgate, 2006); M. Shaw, *War and Genocide: Organized Killing in Modern Society* (Oxford: Polity Press, 2003).

[142] J. Waller, *Becoming Evil: How Ordinary People Commit Genocide and Mass Killing* (Oxford University Press, 2002), 274.

[143] TNA, WO 32/21720: McLean proceedings, 455 (CSM M. Buckland, the Devons).

[144] *Ibid.*, 204 (Sgt. D. Bruce, Royal Inniskilling Fusiliers).

[145] *Ibid.*, 188 (Lt.-Col. E. H. W. Grimshaw, Royal Inniskilling Fusiliers); 416 (Major N. F. Gordon-Wilson, The Buffs).

[146] *Ibid.*, 177 (CSM J. Bailey, Royal Northumberland Fusiliers).

[147] TNA, WO 32/21720: McLean proceedings, 107 (CSM H. Thomas, 7 KAR); 167 (Major P. Bulman, Royal Northumberland Fusiliers).

[148] *Ibid.*, 161 (Lt.-Col. R. E. T. St. John, Royal Northumberland Fusiliers); 163 (Reverend D. V. S. Asher, Church of England Chaplain to the Fusiliers).

Some men eventually managed to overcome their initial hesitancy.[149] Others resisted by avoiding shooting, or taking prisoners instead.[150] The latter option proved particularly popular, with troops erring on the side of caution in interpreting Erskine's desire to take prisoners; soldiers chased down and captured escaping suspects when strictly speaking orders demanded they open fire.[151] Both Second Lieutenant Hall and Warrant Officer Abdipahaman in 3 KAR thought that their unit simply preferred capturing people to shooting them.[152]

The army followed comprehensive guidelines to ensure that prisoners were treated humanely, making the surrender offers more appealing to insurgents. Soldiers understood both the ethical and pragmatic reasons for following the rules and were quite capable of seeing their prisoners as fellow human beings. The testimony given by soldiers about their attitudes and behaviour towards non-combatants could be subject to a desire for self-exculpation. Claims about humane treatment must be weighed against the evidence of brutality assessed in the next two chapters. In the final analysis, soldiers were perfectly capable of offering one prisoner a friendly cigarette and another prisoner a slap with their rifle-butt.

Pseudo-gangs and special forces

In Kenya special forces methods came to the fore in the first half of 1954. Frank Kitson, one of the innovators, argues that they could not have started earlier because they depended on a considerable amount of background knowledge of an area, which took time to generate.[153] Two separate groups established pseudo-gangs in 1954: the Kenya Regiment, and Kitson's DMIO organisation. Bill Woodley described the Kenya Regiment's first operation:

As far as I know the idea of blacking one's face and dressing up as a terrorist to get close to a gang, came from a Kenya-born South African named Steve Bothma in 'I' Company. And the first time it was tried was in October 1954 when Steve and I went out with one of our trackers, a Kikuyu into the densely-populated Kiambu area. The tracker led the way with a shotgun and a revolver in his pocket, Steve and I following with Sten guns hidden under our overcoats. The tracker made an approach to the leader of a gang of eighteen

---

[149] *Ibid.*, 318 (Lt.-Col. D. H. Nott, 4 KAR); 420 (CSM J. R. J. Kemp, The Buffs).
[150] *Ibid.*, 215 (Lt.-Col. L. W. B. Evans, 5 KAR); 386 (Sgt. R. McPhail, Black Watch).
[151] *Ibid.*, 153 (Major N. Holroyd, 3 KAR); 257 (2nd Lt. R. E. Ginner, 5 KAR).
[152] *Ibid.*, 148 (2nd Lt. G. B. Hall, 3 KAR); 151 (WO Abdipahaman, 3 KAR).
[153] Interview with General Sir Frank Kitson.

and did the talking until at a given signal we all opened fire. It was a successful operation, and to my knowledge the first of its kind.[154]

General Erskine visited Kitson's establishment in June 1954 and soon afterwards Kitson was ordered to explain the pseudo system to all military intelligence personnel in the colony and then run a four-day course for all DMIOs and FIOs.[155] The pseudo-gangs were significant not only because of kill tallies and intelligence gathered. Soldiers accommodated former enemies, working alongside and even entrusting firearms to those who shortly before had sought to kill them. According to Kitson, the process for persuading Mau Mau to operate in the gangs was firstly to treat them harshly to 'put them in their place', then gradually involve them in the pseudo-community at the training centre, treating them as friends, then once they could be trusted with performing sentry duty and carrying arms, they were taken on patrol.[156] Kitson thought focusing on Mau Mau 'savagery' bad for intelligence and tried to understand the Mau Mau in order to turn them.[157] The pseudo-gangs and other special forces arguably succeeded because they treated the enemy with a degree of respect.[158] As Kitson explained, they normally aimed to take prisoners because 'You can't get much information out of a corpse.'[159] And these prisoners received good treatment because turning them without coercion would make them better and more reliable fighters for the government.[160]

In September and October 1954, prototype TCTs under Major Venn Fey tried out deep penetration tactics in the Aberdares, based on experience with the pseudo-gangs. Brigadier Taylor, commanding 49 Brigade, commended the teams to GHQ, as they were 'beginning to pay a good dividend'.[161] Erskine accepted Taylor's advice, authorising the creation of forest operation companies, each consisting of three TCTs.[162] These teams employed former Mau Mau as trackers; there were 205 of them distributed among the three brigades in June 1955.[163] Regiments had

---

[154] D. Holman, *Elephants at Sundown: The Story of Bill Woodley* (London: W. H. Allen, 1978), 80. Many thanks to General Sir Frank Kitson for bringing this source to my attention.
[155] Interview with General Sir Frank Kitson.
[156] Heather, 'Intelligence and Counter-Insurgency', 83.
[157] Lonsdale, 'Mau Maus of the Mind', 414.
[158] J. Newsinger, 'A Counter-insurgency Tale', 68.
[159] Kitson, *Gangs and Counter-gangs*, 95.   [160] IWMSA, R. Cassidy, 11138/4.
[161] TNA, WO 276/248: Letter from Brigadier G. Taylor, HQ 49 Bde, to GHQ East Africa, 12 October 1954.
[162] Heather, 'Counterinsurgency in Kenya', 238.
[163] TNA, WO 276/249: Letter from Lt.-Col. [illegible] GSO1 (East Africa) to Chief of Staff, 25 June 1955.

mixed opinions about their trackers. A staff officer touring units in June 1955 noted that 1 Glosters held 36 trackers, '(incl 11 ex MM) but also complain majority are NBG [no bloody good]'.[164] East Africa Command demanded that the teams operated in company groups under the direct control of a company commander, rather than independently in small teams, probably reflecting doubts about tracker reliability.[165]

TCTs primarily worked in the forests. Special methods teams, as pseudo-gangs became officially known, operated mainly in the Reserves. A GHQ staff appreciation recognised as early as November 1954 that as Mau Mau strength declined these special forces would be increasingly important in eliminating the surviving enemy.[166]

In December 1954 General Erskine issued orders for 1955, placing an emphasis on special forces. He directed each British and KAR battalion to raise its own 'special detachment for operational tasks in co-operation with FIOs and DMIOs', called 'Trojan teams'. While remaining under their parent battalion for administration, they would operate under the orders of the local area army commander, who directed them in consultation with the administration and police. Those selected for the teams required an aptitude for commando-type action and strict discipline. Teams comprised a Swahili-speaking leader, a non-commissioned officer, five other ranks and an interpreter. They sought to kill or capture identified individual Mau Mau.

The administration formed its own Trojan teams to work under military and Special Branch guidance.[167] At a meeting on 27 May 1955 the War Council agreed to the enlistment of up to fifty surrendered insurgents as Special Police constables, organised into five teams directed by Europeans. They underwent a month's training, and started operating in late July under the bland name of 'Special Force'. By November they had accounted for sixty-seven Mau Mau killed and much intelligence gathered. No members proved disloyal and the force suffered zero casualties.[168] In Naivasha district at least,

---

[164] TNA, WO 276/249: Tour Notes – GSO 2 [General Staff Officer, Grade 2] (Special Duties), 29 June 1955.

[165] TNA, WO 276/249: Letter from Major-General Heyman to Brigadier Orr, Commanding 70 Brigade, 30 December 1954.

[166] TNA, WO 276/460: Specialist Forces to Combat Mau Mau, memo to Chief of Staff by GSO1 (Ops) [General Staff Officer, Grade 1, Operations] Lt.-Col. (name illegible), 25 November 1954.

[167] TNA, WO 276/461: Emergency Directive no. 14, signed General Erskine, 6 December 1954.

[168] KNA, WC/CM/1/5: Operational use of surrendered terrorists. Memorandum by the Minister for Defence, Annex to WAR/C.789, 5 November 1955.

the special forces patrols received praise from the committees for improving operational and background intelligence.[169]

In May 1955 the new Commander-in-Chief, Lieutenant-General Sir Gerald Lathbury, gained War Council consent for establishing five special force teams (SFTs), each of ten ex-Mau Mau commanded by a European officer. These teams came under the authority of the Commissioner of Police, and attacked selected targets in the forests, killing over sixty Mau Mau during July and August. An additional fifty ex-Mau Mau were thus recruited as trackers for the army and police.[170] They undertook basic military training at the East Africa Battle School from May and the authorities enlisted them as tribal policemen, a step designed to bring them within the official disciplinary system.[171] By November, GHQ and the police together decided to create another SFT and to employ two Europeans in each team.[172]

On Operation Red Dog, from 26 October to 1 November 1955, Special Force Team no. 3 launched the first action in a new campaign aimed at killing key Mau Mau leaders. Red Dog targeted General Tanganyika in the settled area, making confidence-building contacts with passive-wing members to gather intelligence on his movements.[173] Lathbury thought that continued resistance relied overwhelmingly upon the power exerted by insurgent leaders.[174] Richard Catling, the Police Commissioner, issued detailed instructions on safety measures designed to ensure that team members were not mistaken for insurgents and killed. First, operations were cleared with all security force commanders in the area, the patrol leader himself making a double-check. Second, commanders identified boundaries on the map and by reconnaissance, issuing clear, comprehensive orders. Third, operations were carried out at night if possible. Fourth, sentries or scouts were always posted. Fifth, camp sites were chosen so as to avoid detection. Last, teams seen by other security forces retreated, establishing their identity by word of mouth if necessary.[175]

---

[169] KNA, MSS/128/123: Minutes of a meeting of the Naivasha district joint operations committee and DEC held on 27 September 1955.

[170] TNA, WO 236/20: Lathbury's final dispatch, paras. 25, 47.

[171] TNA, WO 276/460: Letter from GHQ to Officer Commanding, East Africa Battle School, 21 May 1955.

[172] TNA, WO 276/431: Letter from Catling (Commissioner of Police) to Carver (GHQ Chief of Staff), 24 October 1955; TNA, WO 276/431: Letter from Carver to Catling, 26 October 1955.

[173] TNA, WO 276/431: Special Force Patrol Report, Team no. 3, Operation Red Dog, Lt. J. G. Harper, 26 October 1955–1 November 1955.

[174] TNA, WO 236/20: Lathbury's final dispatch, para. 51.

[175] TNA, WO 276/431: Instruction on Pseudo-gang Operations and Patrols, signed Catling, 27 October 1955.

By now, connections between the passive wing and the insurgent gangs were largely broken by villagisation. On a patrol in November 1955, Captain Folliott noted that 'Liaison with Passives has been badly disrupted and now practically ceased.' In this context, the special force teams seemed better suited to destroying gangs than conventional military sweeps: 'Gangs have no fear of Military patrols which they say make so much noise in movement that their approach can be heard miles away.'[176] Patrols achieved considerable results; H. G. Clarke's patrol in December 1955 accounted for a Mau Mau general, a colonel, three lieutenant-colonels, two captains and an RSM.[177]

On 21 December Catling expanded the attack on the insurgent leadership:[178] SFTs 3, 4 and 5 were devoted to eliminating the leadership in Embu, Naivasha and South Nyeri districts respectively. Teams 1 and 2 won the prestigious missions of killing or capturing Stanley Mathenge and Dedan Kimathi. The sixth team remained on standby for emergencies. GHQ decreed that for teams one and two: 'By capturing and NOT killing terrorists, preliminary operations will be designed to secure information which will lead to the ultimate aim.' The teams began their task on 1 January 1956.[179] The job was long and tedious, frequently resulting in extended treks through the forests and mountains for little or no reward, and made harder by the gangs' increasing efficacy in hiding their movements.[180] After initial confusion and poor liaison between the SFTs and regular security forces, misunderstandings were soon ironed out.[181] By the end of January 1956, SFT 1 had undertaken Operation Dodo in the eastern Aberdares, SFT 2 Operation Albatross in the northeastern Aberdares, SFT 3 Operation Mamba on Mount Kenya, SFT 5 Operation Viking near Wanjora and SFTs 3 and 5 together Operations Baboon and Gorilla around the south of Mount Kenya.[182] On 3 February 1956 the SFTs reported having killed a hundred and captured two Mau Mau since their inception, accounting for two field-marshals, six

[176] TNA, WO 276/431: Special Force Patrol Report, Team no. 2, Capt. Folliott, 10th–20th November 1955. Operation [illegible].
[177] TNA, WO 276/431: Special Force patrol report. Team no. 5, Commander H. G. Clarke. Operation Antbear, 9th–13th December 1955.
[178] TNA, WO 276/431: Letter from R. C. Catling, Future employment of Special Force Teams, 21 December 1955.
[179] TNA, WO 276/431: GHQ Operation Instruction No. 35, dated December 1955.
[180] TNA, WO 276/431: Special Force patrol report. Team no. 2, Capt. R. J. Folliott, Operation Albatross, 19th–23rd January 1956. Task: Elimination of Dedan Kimathi.
[181] For example: TNA: WO 276/431: Cipher message from 70 Bde to 23 KAR, 23 January 1956.
[182] TNA, WO 276/431: Handwritten note, initialled by a major, GSO3 Ops (K) [General Staff Officer, Grade 3, Operations, Kenya], 23 January 1956.

generals, one major-general, two brigadiers, one colonel and one major.[183] This impressive tally coincided with decreases in Mau Mau activity and the resumption of primacy by the police and civil administration in several areas. But it also suggests that little effort was being made to capture insurgents.

Meanwhile, from early 1956 Special Branch Superintendent Ian Henderson ran Operation Blue Doctor. His teams cooperated closely with the other security forces; they closed Mount Kipipiri to all units from 23 February to 1 March in order to 'snatch additional material [i.e. personnel] for inclusion in our teams'. This action identified forty-four named Mau Mau members in the area, and gave the Gloucesters contact intelligence to launch their own operation.[184] Henderson sent four teams back onto the Kipipiri on 10 March, only contacting a gang on the fourth day:

one team ran face to face into a small party of two terrorists. As soon as guns were drawn to threaten the two into standing where they were, both made a break for it and were shot with a Patchett. Neither were terrorists of any calibre and their identities are being checked at Naivasha.

The incident made the Mau Mau jittery, so the team leaders decided to halt their activities for a few days to allow the gangs to calm down. When the Blue Doctor operations paused, normal military patrols resumed.[185] Back in the field on 25 March, the teams captured a Mau Mau brigadier, plus two guns, ammunition and documents.[186] Henderson kept in touch with the army and police commanders in his area, and arranged for Special Force units to function near his Blue Doctor teams.[187] In the last weeks of April, the teams came close to capturing Dedan Kimathi. At one stage they missed the main surviving Mau Mau leader by only thirty minutes, wounding and capturing Brigadier Thurura instead. He was made to endure 'a night of interrogation, when all information was extracted from the wounded man, who was being carried'.[188] Though the big leader remained elusive, his brother, Wambararia, fell into Henderson's hands in June.[189] Wambararia held the security forces up for a time by giving false information.[190]

---

[183] TNA, WO 276/431: Table of Special Force Operations Since Inception, 3 February 1956.
[184] TNA, WO 276/518: Letter from Ian Henderson, Special Branch HQ, to Director of Intelligence and Security (DIS), 28 February 1956.
[185] TNA, WO 276/518: Letter from Henderson to DIS, 15 March 1956.
[186] TNA, WO 276/518: Letter from Henderson to DIS, 27 March 1956.
[187] TNA, WO 276/518: Letter from Henderson to Brigadier Birkbeck, HQ 70 (EA) Infantry Brigade and Assistant Commissioner of Police, Nyeri, 5 April 1956.
[188] TNA, WO 276/518: Letter from Henderson to DIS, 23 April 1956.
[189] TNA, WO 276/518: CinC, Report from DIS, 4 Jun 56.
[190] TNA, WO 276/518: Letter from Henderson to DIS, 23 June 1956.

At this point, the security forces together employed 328 former Mau Mau as pseudo-gangsters, at least a hundred serving in teams run by the FIOs.[191] Henderson urged that 'unless greater pressure is applied by conventional forces to NON-FOREST areas to scare the terrorists back into the forest, our teams will become virtually defunct in two or three months time'.[192] Rather than special forces being viewed as a superior alternative to conventional tactics, the two were thought to rely upon each other. From late June, FIO Mr Leath ran three pseudo-gangs in the Rift Valley Province, under the provincial Special Branch commander's control.[193] On 7 November Assistant Superintendent Brans launched Operation Silver Doctor in the settled areas, running fifty pseudo-gangsters. They systematically searched all areas where Mau Mau had resided in the past, starting in Naivasha district. These teams suffered serious morale problems and Henderson had to intervene within a few weeks of them being established, changing their tactics.[194] The Commander-in-Chief's trust paid dividends, with Henderson's teams accounting for around 200 Mau Mau in the last nine months of the Emergency.[195] Special force operations finally came to a spectacular conclusion with the capture of Dedan Kimathi by Henderson on 21 October 1956.[196]

'If anything, we go out of our way to give them the odd cigarette and a cup of tea'[197]

Legal zoning, the surrender schemes, the humane handling of prisoners and the pseudo-gang operations may all be seen as important examples of restraint in British military policy. The legal distinction between PAs and Special Areas gave the troops, and the population, a clear understanding of what could be done, to whom, and where. At times, soldiers used less

---

[191] Witness statement number two of Huw Bennett, in the case of *Ndiku Mutua and others v. Foreign and Commonwealth Office*, Queen's Bench Division in the High Court of Justice, 1 April 2011 (hereafter Bennett witness statement 2), citing Hanslope document AA 45/48/1/1A: Disposal of captured and surrendered terrorists employed by the security forces, Memorandum by the Emergency Joint Staff, 19 May 1956.

[192] TNA, WO 276/518: Letter from Henderson to DIS, 27 July 1956.

[193] TNA, WO 276/518: Extensions of 'Blue Doctor' operations into the Rift Valley Province. Minutes of a meeting held in the office of the Director of Intelligence and Security, 19 June 1956.

[194] TNA, WO 276/518: Letter from Henderson to DIS, 24 November 1956.

[195] WO 236/20: Lathbury's final dispatch, para. 89.

[196] Anderson, *Histories of the Hanged*, 288. See also I. Henderson, *Man Hunt in Kenya* (New York: Doubleday, 1958); I. Henderson and P. Goodhart, *The Hunt for Kimathi* (London: Hamish Hamilton, 1958).

[197] TNA, WO 32/21720: McLean proceedings, 140 (CSM I. J. Day, 3 KAR).

force than was allowed, taking prisoners in PAs when they were permitted to shoot on sight. Inspired by Malaya, and carried out in close collaboration with Special Branch, the attempts at securing mass surrenders showed the army's preference for the accurate application of violence instead of overwhelming attrition. Working most effectively after the completion of villagisation, Erskine's personal role in pushing the schemes was significant, as was the way in which junior officers made their own local arrangements. This does not mean that all opportunities for taking surrenders were exploited, as Mau Mau initiatives to open negotiations were ignored more than once. Ordinary soldiers professed to understand and implement the need for restraint in handling non-combatants.

The army realised that treating prisoners well could produce intelligence dividends, which were at a premium in this war where so little was known about the Mau Mau. Pseudo-gangs were another form of the discriminate application of force in the Emergency, as they attempted to target the guilty. Whether only the guilty suffered at their hands is debatable, and impossible to judge on the presently available evidence. They were only able to operate a year into the campaign because they relied upon detailed human intelligence networks to function effectively. Besides their own successes, they had a wider impact on the army by promoting special force methods among regular troops, as seen in the TCTs and Trojan teams. They certainly required the surrender schemes and close cooperation from administration and police to work properly, and questions remain about their methods, as we shall see in the chapters to come. Despite their faults, they were perhaps better than large-scale sweeps or mass detentions, though they sometimes relied on these measures in their planning.

These policies pushed the army away from genocide or even attrition, when many settlers in Kenya called for harsher repression. However, while the nature of the force employed was enough to prevent the deaths of hundreds of thousands, it probably did result in the deaths of tens of thousands. Does such suffering deserve to be associated with the word minimal? The next chapter will explain the forces that drove the army to commit mass killings of non-combatants, torture, forced population movement and other indiscriminate acts when in many ways it tried to act with restraint.

7 'A lot of indiscriminate shooting': military repression before Erskine's arrival

There were strategic and disciplinary imperatives for the army in Kenya to avoid an all-out annihilationist campaign against the Kikuyu, Embu and Meru peoples. These logics compensated for the marginalisation of international law and the dangerous flexibility in national law and military doctrine. While the army certainly did not try to destroy the civilian populations in rebellious areas, they consistently sought to coerce them.[1] The form and extent of the violence used depended upon the identity, experiences and functions of different units, and the perceived strategic requirements. It included forced population movement, beatings, rape, torture and shootings. The political and military leaderships never issued direct orders for mass atrocities, but they created a permissive environment by failing to halt the abuses brought to their attention. Official policies such as the evictions from the Rift Valley, and later villagisation, radicalised the military and existed symbiotically with the pseudo-policies of atrocity which aimed at terrorising the population into supporting the government.[2]

Coercion of the entire Kikuyu population was the norm in the campaign's first phase, from October 1952 until July 1953. Force was exemplary, designed to be observed. As the commander of the Kenya Regiment wrote in 1955: 'The Kikuyu must be taught a lesson that will be remembered for generations and which will act as a warning to other tribes.'[3] From the available records a picture of beatings, torture and murder emerges, in addition to government collusion with vigilante

---

[1] For an overview of coercion theory, see P. J. Jakobsen, 'Pushing the Limits of Military Coercion Theory', *International Studies Perspectives*, 12 (2011), 153–70.

[2] For conceptual and empirical studies of state terror, see A. George (ed.), *Western State Terrorism* (London: Polity Press, 1991); R. Jackson, E. Murphy and S. Poynting (eds.), *Contemporary State Terrorism: Theory and Practice* (Abingdon: Routledge, 2009); A. Jones (ed.), *Genocide, War Crimes and the West: History and Complicity* (London: Zed Books, 2004); P. Wilkinson, *State Terrorism and Human Rights: International Responses since the Cold War* (Abingdon: Routledge, 2011).

[3] KRA, Vol. VIa. Guy Campbell papers. Typed papers, headed 'Narok 1955'.

groups. These actions did not result from poor command and control, or a breakdown in military discipline. Although the Emergency's early commanders were less effective than Erskine, they and the War Office in London approved the punitive approach. Discipline in general remained strong, with only violence against the Kikuyu allowed. The nexus between policy and discipline is examined by looking in detail at 'B' Company, 5 KAR. Revenge, racism, competition for kills and, perhaps most importantly, a culture of impunity allowed several atrocities to occur. Events in 'B' Company are considered in the light of the widespread violence against civilians for intelligence-gathering and terrorising purposes. Evidence suggests that 'B' Company's brutalities were far from unique.

The army's conduct towards civilians in the first phase

When the Emergency was declared in October 1952, the Kenya government wished to crush the rebellion quickly, using force to eliminate the threat to its authority from the Kikuyu tribe, while signalling resolve to Kenya's other tribal groupings. As we have seen in chapter 4, these decisions reflected long-standing traditions in British colonial practice and military thought. Military repression of civilians in this period may be examined with reference to four types of behaviour: beatings and torture, shootings, collaboration with ruthless vigilante groups and squatter evictions from the Rift Valley Province. In each of these cases, the army pursued the strategic objective of protecting the minority white-settler population as its main priority. Almost the entire Kikuyu population were considered troublemakers; the government estimated in August 1952 that 90 per cent were Mau Mau members. The army characterised the tribe's attitude as 'sullen and unco-operative' at best.[4] In consequence, the military means for combating the perceived threat were static defence of settler property, mobile patrols to kill Mau Mau groups, and measures to intimidate the population into moving away from vulnerable settler areas and changing their allegiance in favour of the government.

Beatings and torture

From the campaign's very start, the security forces were known to flog Mau Mau suspects, even though the government refused calls to legalise

[4] IWMD, Erskine papers, Booklet 'Notes for British Units Coming to Kenya', GHQ East Africa, no date, 5–6.

corporal punishment.[5] While there is no evidence of a direct military order authorising physical abuse, it is clear that large numbers of individuals decided to obtain intelligence about the Mau Mau through violence, leading one observer to describe it as 'almost a routine measure'.[6] General Erskine discovered the pattern when he arrived in Kenya, noting a 'tendency to take prisoners and interrogate them with a view to extracting information by force'.[7] Writing less euphemistically in a letter he said: 'I am quite certain prisoners were beaten to extract information.'[8]

The process known as screening achieved notoriety for the violence practised in these normally combined operations.[9] Official army doctrine stipulated that the troops form a cordon around the chosen area, move the people inside it into barbed wire enclosures, and guard them while the civil powers screened them for their political sympathies.[10] In Kenya the district administrations were formally responsible for organising the screening teams, for example by selecting 'hooded men' – disguised informers whose opinions on the reliability of suspects complemented any available police intelligence. Screening assumed that everyone was guilty until proved innocent; all Kikuyu over the age of about fourteen were probably screened at least once.[11] The process frequently involved beatings and torture.[12] Estimating the exact percentage who were beaten or tortured while being screened is impossible. However, Governor Baring recognised the violent nature of the process, describing how 'numbers of Africans were manhandled and the sympathies of loyal Kikuyu alienated'.[13]

The operational situation reports for the first few months are incomplete.[14] The surviving records clearly show that the army played an

---

[5] D. H. Rawcliffe, *The Struggle for Kenya* (London: Victor Gollancz, 1954), 67.
[6] *Ibid.*, 68.
[7] IWMD, Erskine papers, Report to the Secretary of State for War, The Kenya Emergency, signed Erskine, 2 May 1955, para. 18.
[8] TNA, WO 32/15834: Letter from Erskine to Secretary of State for War, 10 December 1953.
[9] Rawcliffe, *Struggle for Kenya*, 68.
[10] TNA, WO 276/138: War Office Booklet 'Imperial Policing and Duties in Aid of the Civil Power', issued by the Army Council, 1949, 37–41.
[11] G. Kershaw, *Mau Mau from Below* (Oxford: James Currey, 1997), 250, 325.
[12] Elkins, *Britain's Gulag*, 62–90; Branch, 'Loyalism during the Mau Mau Rebellion', 149; Evans, *Law and Disorder*, 205.
[13] TNA, CO 822/501: Note of a meeting held in the Secretary of State's room on 15 December 1952.
[14] The reports were compiled by two commands: Force Nairobi and Northern Area. Force Nairobi reports do not exist for the periods 9 January–3 February 1953, and 24 April–1 May 1953 (with two exceptions: sitreps 41 and 42 of 27 January 1953 and 30 January 1953 do survive). There are no reports for Northern Area before 1 February 1953.

important part in screening. During 1952 the 1 Lancashire Fusiliers, various battalions of the KAR and the Kenya Regiment rounded up at least 5,892 people.[15] Some reports simply recorded a 'large number [of] arrests'.[16] Army actions went beyond the cordoning and guarding outlined in the doctrine. The GOC noted how 'the Army had been used for carrying out certain functions that properly belonged to the Police, e.g. searching of huts and screening of Africans'.[17]

As an example of this type of operation, on 1 November a company of the Lancashires detained about a thousand suspects for screening in the Bahati forest area of Nyeri district. Soldiers may have found these experiences frustrating as, despite rounding up large numbers, few arrests were made. A raid on the African part of Nanyuki in November 1952 brought in 3,800 suspects, of whom only 87 were arrested.[18] Sometimes no arrests were made at all.[19] Even the 'hooded men' technique failed to compensate for prolonged under-investment in colony intelligence.[20] Force Nairobi rued how 'info restricts arrests on many occasions'.[21] Under conditions where the security forces were thwarted by the obstructive silence of so many, the temptation to lash out sometimes trumped the abstract demand for minimum force.

In the first three months of 1953 screening continued apace. The situation reports become even vaguer about the numbers concerned, sometimes merely recording that 'screening continues'.[22] At least 2,059 people were collected by the Kenya Regiment, Lancashire Fusiliers, 4 KAR, 6 KAR, 23 KAR, 26 KAR and East Africa Training Centre troops in both Central and Rift Valley Provinces. The problems with achieving a high screening to arrest ratio persisted.[23] Aside from identifying Mau Mau members, the process aimed at displaying government

[15] See the operational sitreps in TNA, WO 276/466.

[16] For example TNA, WO 276/466: Jock Scott sitrep from Force Nairobi to Mideast, 23 December 1952.

[17] Bennett witness statement 2, citing Hanslope document CAB MM/5/1: Note of a meeting held at Government House at 6.30 p.m. on Saturday, 1st November, 1952.

[18] TNA, WO 276/466: Jock Scott sitrep from Force Nairobi to Mideast, 2 November 1952.

[19] TNA, WO 276/337: Northern Area sitreps, Norbrig Nairobi to Force Nairobi, no date, c. 24 February 1953.

[20] Heather, 'Counterinsurgency and Intelligence in Kenya', 13.

[21] TNA, WO 276/466: Jock Scott sitrep from Force Nairobi to Mideast, 18 November 1952.

[22] TNA, WO 276/337: Northern Area sitreps, Norbrig Nairobi to Force Nairobi, no date, c. 15 February 1953.

[23] For examples see TNA, WO 276/466: Jock Scott sitrep from Force Nairobi to Mideast, 9 January 1953; TNA, WO 276/337: Northern Area sitreps, Norbrig Nairobi to Force Nairobi, no date, c. 24 February 1953.

power. A series of 39 Brigade sweeps in North Nyeri and Embu in late June/early July 1953 stated the object: 'to obtain info, screen labour and generally dominate the area'.[24] The army deployed at this point approximately 10,000 men in the Emergency areas, not all of whom were operational.[25] Dominating the whole area continuously in a physical sense was not infeasible.[26] Rather then, the mass intimidation of screening fulfilled a useful, if harrowing, purpose. To achieve this the army maintained a close working relationship with the police.[27] The police were notorious for using their rifles first and asking questions later.[28] Only eleven days into the Emergency, Christian leaders complained to the Colonial Secretary that the ordinary African had trouble in knowing who to be more afraid of – the Mau Mau or the police.[29] A 1954 parliamentary report noted the continuing reliance of the police upon 'brutality and malpractice'.[30] The KPR, rapidly recruited from settlers, were apparently the worst offenders.[31]

By 19 June 1953 the army and police in combined operations had screened at least another 11,933 people.[32] Forces involved included the Devons, the Lancashires, The Buffs, 4 KAR, 6 KAR, 7 KAR, 23 KAR and the Kenya Regiment. The KPR operated with the military on numerous occasions.[33] As mentioned above, doctrine required the army to round people up and the police and administration to conduct the screening. There are grounds for questioning whether this division of

[24] TNA, WO 276/202: GHQ East Africa Operational Instruction no. 2, 18 June 1953. 39 Brigade took control of operations in the Rift Valley Province on 7 April 1953, with EATC, East Africa Armoured Car Squadron, 1 Lancashire Fusiliers, 1 The Buffs and 1 Devons under command. See TNA, WO 276/436: 39 Brigade Jock Scott operational instruction, 4 April 1953.

[25] TNA, WO 276/55: Approximated distribution of military forces in East Africa Command by locations as at 30 April 1953.

[26] Branch, 'Loyalism during the Mau Mau Rebellion', 96.

[27] For further analysis of the politics of army–police relations, see chapter 9.

[28] Throup, 'Crime, Politics and the Police in Colonial Kenya', 147.

[29] TNA, CO 822/460: Verbatim report. Meeting of the Secretary of State [for the Colonies] and the Christian Council of Kenya, held at Government House on Friday, 31st October, 1952.

[30] TNA, PREM 11/696: Report to the Secretary of State for the Colonies by the Parliamentary Delegation to Kenya, January 1954, Cmd 9081.

[31] Clayton, Counter-Insurgency in Kenya, 45. A comprehensive account of the KPR has yet to be written.

[32] Figure compiled from sitreps in TNA, WO 276/466, TNA, WO 276/467, TNA, WO 276/468, and TNA, WO 276/337.

[33] An exact figure is unobtainable because the reports often do not identify the units involved. For examples of army–KPR operations, see TNA, WO 276/467: Jock Scott sitrep from Force Nairobi to Mideast, 24 March 53; TNA, WO 276/467: Jock Scott sitrep from Force Nairobi to Troopers and Mideast, 24/4/53; TNA, WO 276/337: Northern Area sitreps, Norbrig Nairobi to Force Nairobi, no date, c. 27 February 1953.

responsibility somehow vindicated the army. In the first place, the rounding up phase could involve as much violence as the later questioning, especially as time went on and the population realised what being caught in the net meant. Despite the doctrine, some army officers involved themselves in the questioning stage, as they were integrated into the intelligence structure via the JAPOIT system. A directive issued on 28 May 1953 banned the running of screening teams or the conducting of interrogations 'which are at present being carried out, in some cases, by JAPOIT officers'.[34] A retrospective appraisal by Erskine noted how some of the screening teams used methods of torture.[35] Of course these actions could not have taken place at all without military assistance.

The army directed the Emergency's largest screening effort: Operation Anvil. Even when abstaining from mistreating the people undergoing the process themselves, soldiers failed to uphold the law by preventing abuses by the administration and police. Whether screening achieved much is impossible to prove with any great certainty. A Special Branch assessment in May 1953 reported the 'beneficial effect' that screening operations produced in Naivasha district.[36] Yet in other cases, screening failed miserably – in the North Kinangop, farm labourers passed as reliable by screening were later discovered to be Mau Mau members.[37] In areas where the Mau Mau maintained a tight grip on the population, screening teams might find extracting denunciations 'almost impossible'.[38] Presumably the authorities thought the policy broadly effective, as it continued throughout the Emergency.

'Shot while attempting to escape'

Another way in which the civilian population suffered from security force terrorisation was by indiscriminate shootings, perhaps constituting deliberate murder. In January 1953 the Governor's Emergency Committee discussed the alarming prospect of security forces using too little force:

The General Officer Commanding stated that situation and press reports frequently referred to patrols making contact with Kikuyu gangs which then apparently

---

[34] TNA, WO 276/200: Emergency Directive no. 6, operational intelligence, 28 May 1953.
[35] TNA, WO 32/15834: Letter from Erskine to Secretary of State for War, 10 December 1953.
[36] TNA, CO 822/373: SBFIS 4/53, 1–15 May 1953.
[37] TNA, WO 276/243: Letter from Captain [name illegible], DMIO Naivasha, to the DEC, 5 December 1953.
[38] TNA, WO 276/243: Naivasha district operational intelligence report, 12 October 1953.

made off unharmed. He instanced a recent report of a KAR patrol 'chasing' a gang for 2½ miles, and questioned whether present tactics for dealing with these gangs were in fact correct ... *The Deputy Commissioner of Police* emphasised that the nature of the country was generally such that [it] made escape easy and tracking difficult. While, in Prohibited and Special Areas, patrols were not hindered by the need to challenge required by law, he believed that in Prohibited Areas more use could be made of sten and bren guns. *It was agreed* that the Commander, Northern Brigade, should issue orders accordingly.[39]

Soldiers were encouraged to make vigorous use of their firearms. As the previous chapter explained, the formal policy authorised lethal force in Special Areas only after two warnings were given. That so senior a figure as the Deputy Commissioner of Police could state that the Special Areas imposed no such restriction – and without being corrected by the colony's most senior military officer – is telling about official attitudes. After the Mau Mau massacred villagers at Lari in March 1953, the security forces took revenge, allegedly killing perhaps as many as four hundred civilians. Most accounts blame the Home Guard for the incident, although KAR troops may also have been involved.[40] The Hanslope intelligence papers record that the 'African Home Guard retaliated for Uplands massacre', killing eleven.[41] As the authorities failed to investigate, we cannot be sure about the extent of the reprisals. On 27 April a detachment of 7 KAR, who had repeatedly beaten and robbed labourers on a farm near Nyeri, killed four men who apparently ran when fired on. Their infuriated employer explained that running away was a natural reaction as the Mau Mau had launched several attacks in the area recently.[42] Major-General Hinde noted his regret and said that the Provincial Commissioner was looking into the murders, a curious decision as the KAR came under military law and should have been investigated by the SIB.[43] On 20 April 1953 Governor Baring informed Whitehall that:

430 Mau Mau terrorists or suspects have been shot while attempting to escape or while resisting arrest during the past six months. A number of these have been

---

[39] Bennett witness statement 3, citing Hanslope document EM COM 4 Vol. I: Record of a meeting of the Governor's Emergency Committee held at Government House on the 20th January, 1953.

[40] Evans, *Law and Disorder*, 170; Elkins, *Britain's Gulag*, 45; R. Edgerton, *Mau Mau: An African Crucible* (London: Collier Macmillan, 1989), 80.

[41] Bennett witness statement 3, citing Hanslope document INT 10/4/2/4/8A: Schedule of incidents and operations connected with the Emergency in Nairobi area during the period 30 March 1953–12 April 1953.

[42] ODRP, W. R. Hinde, MSS Afr.s.1580. Vol. I: Director of Operations Department correspondence, letter from H. T. D. Hickman to Hinde, 30 April 1953.

[43] ODRP, W. R. Hinde, MSS Afr.s.1580. Vol. I: Director of Operations Department correspondence, letter from Hinde to Hickman, 26 May 1953.

positively identified as wanted for murders and other criminal offences, apart from the circumstances in which they were contacted by the security forces.[44]

This telegram responded to a query from the Colonial Office ten days earlier, when a civil servant expressed an 'unpleasant feeling' about the number of reports in the daily telegrams mentioning Africans shot in this manner. Whitehall wondered whether the phrase was a euphemism for unnecessary, indiscriminate shooting.[45] Leonard Gill, a settler with wide experience from the beginning of the Emergency in the KPR, the Kenya Regiment, 3 KAR and 4 KAR, states that the phrase was common code for a suspect having been murdered.[46] Soldiers may have preferred to execute suspects rather than risk them being set free by a judicial system viewed as too lenient.[47] In any case, the figures supplied by Baring simply did not add up. The available situation reports show that by 20 April 1953 the security forces had shot a total of seventy-eight persons attempting to escape or resisting arrest. Of these the army killed seven, wounded three and shot four with unspecified consequences. The police or other civil forces killed seventeen, wounded one and shot five with unspecified consequences. A further forty-one people were shot by unknown security forces; twenty-four of these were shot dead, nine wounded and eight shot with unrecorded results.[48]

The Hanslope records provide another figure for those shot attempting to escape up to 20 April. These papers, largely concerned with intelligence assessments for Central Province, and thus only a partial record until all the intelligence papers for the Emergency become available, state that ninety people were shot escaping. Of these, the army was recorded as shooting dead twenty-eight and wounding three. In the week from 29 March 1953 soldiers from 23 KAR shot dead seven men who 'refused to halt' in Katamayu, two who 'refused to halt' in Kiambu, and four for 'failing to halt' in Uplands Kerita. In early April unspecified KAR units shot groups of two, five, another five and a single individual. All were killed.[49] The Hanslope

[44] TNA, CO 822/474: Telegram from Baring to Secretary of State for the Colonies, 20 April 1953. The figure was quoted by Colonial Secretary Oliver Lyttelton to the Commons. Edgerton, *Mau Mau: An African Crucible*, 159.
[45] TNA, CO 822/474: Civil servant's memo, signed P. Rogers, 10 April 1953.
[46] Gill, *Military Musings*, 43, 47.   [47] Rawcliffe, *Struggle for Kenya*, 108.
[48] Figures compiled from TNA, WO 276/466, TNA, WO 276/467, TNA, WO 276/337, TNA, WO 276/287.
[49] Bennett witness statement 3, citing Hanslope documents ADM 35/2/11/3/1A: Intelligence summary, signed Captain Ragg, Int. Section, Thomson's Falls, 18 February 1953; INT 10/4/2/4A Vol. I: Schedule of incidents and operations connected with the Emergency in Central Province for the fortnight 23 April to 7 May 1953; INT 10/4/2/4A Vol. I: Schedule of incidents and operations connected

papers list another seventeen people as shot attempting to escape between 20 April and the end of May 1953.[50]

Clearly this is a major discrepancy with the figure provided by Baring on 20 April, but the killings continued.[51] The archives give no indication as to how he arrived at the number of 430. The Colonial Office may have been equally curious, as in the next few days Baring provided additional statistics. Unfortunately they confused matters even further. Apparently the Home Guard had killed '47 Mau Mau terrorists' who were resisting arrest or attempting to escape, and another twelve were killed by the Home Guard and police on operations together.[52] Three days later Baring presented Whitehall with yet more information. The security forces killed twenty-nine people who failed to halt after being challenged in the PAs, created at the start of 1953. In the Special Areas the position was that:

335 persons have been shot under the provisions of Emergency Regulation No. 22B while resisting arrest or attempting to escape, 270 of them in native land units and forest reserves, and 65 in settled areas. Of this total of 364 persons shot [sic], 224 have been identified subsequently as persons wanted for murder or other serious Mau Mau crimes.[53]

These figures obviously do not add up to the number initially declared, or make sense in themselves. The statistics given by Erskine in his final report state that from 21 October 1952 up to 18 April 1953, the security forces killed 522 and captured wounded 125.[54] Could 430 of these really have been shot attempting to escape? The impression emerging from

---

with the Emergency in Central Province, no date; INT 10/4/2/4/8A: Central Province (South) Provincial intelligence committee summary, 15 April 1953; INT 10/4/2/4/8A: Schedule of incidents and operations connected with the Emergency in Nairobi area during the period 30 March 1953–12 April 53; INT 10/4/2/4/2A Vol. I: Nyeri district intelligence committee minutes, 4 April 1953, 10 April 1953, 24 April 1953; INT 10/4/2/4A Vol. I: Schedule of incidents and operations connected with the Emergency in Central Province for the fortnight 8th to 23rd April 1953.

[50] Bennett witness statement 3, citing Hanslope documents INT 10/4/2/4A Vol. I: Schedule of incidents and operations connected with the Emergency in Central Province for the fortnight 23rd April to 7th May 1953; INT 10/4/2/4A, Vol. I: Schedule of incidents and operations connected with the Emergency in Central Province for the fortnight 7th May to 21st May 1953; INT 10/4/2/4A; Vol. I: Schedule of incidents and operations connected with the Emergency in Central Province, no date; INT 10/4/2/4/2A, Vol. I: Nyeri district intelligence committee minutes, 22 May 1953, 29 May 1953.

[51] See, for example, TNA, WO 276/468: Jock Scott sitrep from Force Nairobi to Troopers and Mideast, 1 May 1953.

[52] TNA, CO 822/474: Telegram from Baring to Colonial Office, 22 April 1953.

[53] TNA, CO 822/474: Telegram from Baring to Secretary of State for the Colonies, 25 April 1953.

[54] IWMD, Erskine papers, Report to the Secretary of State for War, The Kenya Emergency, signed Erskine, 2 May 1955, Appendix B.

these reports is either one of confusion or of concealment. Quite possibly Baring issued the 430 figure in a bid to suggest the authorities had the situation under control, or because the real figure was substantially higher and he wished to play down the extent of the killings. Evidence submitted to the McLean Inquiry suggests illegal shootings. In a directive issued by Baring on 25 February to the security forces, he noted that despite an increased number of kills inflicted in recent weeks, precise details 'have not, however, been reported as promptly as they should have been'. He required all kills to be notified to the nearest police station, which would then pass the information up the chain of command.[55] The wording is vague here, but might mean kills were not being recorded at all in some cases. If this was the case, then the figure of 430 may be an underestimate.

Shootings might also have occurred through panic or misunderstanding. Whatever regulations stipulated about people standing still when being ordered to do so, many Kikuyu rightly feared the rough treatment or extended detention often awaiting them, so it is hardly surprising that people ran away. In late March 1953 a Kenya Regiment patrol shot dead a man seen carrying a panga who ran when challenged; they found a note from the authorities on his body permitting him to carry the item.[56] In another incident a man in the Thomson's Falls area was shot dead leaving the forest. The patrol subsequently discovered that he worked for the Forestry Department.[57] Thus the working assumption that running away denoted guilt was a dubious one. Compounding matters, hardly any soldiers spoke Kikuyu. Swahili was the KAR's lingua franca, and the official notes for British battalions gave a few key Swahili phrases, including 'simama' for stop, or halt.[58] In a raid in Kipipiri in December 1952 a Kenya Regiment soldier shot dead a man who 'ran away despite 3 orders to stop in Swahili'.[59] The fact that British Army units were instructed to call people to halt in a language foreign to them, and eschewed teaching soldiers any Kikuyu, perhaps helps explain why people were shot unnecessarily. Although the Kikuyu may quickly have learnt what the word meant, the refusal to teach soldiers basic Kikuyu phrases is telling of official

[55] TNA, WO 32/21721: Directive by the Governor: Reporting of Casualties, 25 February 1953.
[56] TNA, WO 276/337: Northern Area sitreps, Norbrig Nyeri to Force Nairobi, 25 March 1953.
[57] TNA, WO 276/337: Northern Area sitreps, Norbrig Nairobi to Force Nairobi, no date, c. 4 February 1953.
[58] IWMD, Erskine papers, Booklet, Notes for British Units Coming to Kenya, GHQ East Africa, no date, 42.
[59] TNA, WO 276/466: Jock Scott sitrep from Force Nairobi to Mideast, 9 December 1952.

attitudes. An intelligence report from November 1952 astutely noted the reluctance in certain quarters to restrict the use of firearms:

There is a strong feeling amongst coy comds [company commanders] and below that until they are allowed to fire on cordon breakers many of the worst elements will escape. The comds concerned do not appreciate the need for avoiding the deaths of these people who run away because they fear punishment for comparatively trivial offences. On the other hand there is something to be said for allowing rifle fire at cordon breakers in certain circumstances. In particular it is for consideration whether it should not be announced with effect from a certain day cordon breakers are liable to be fired at allowing sufficient time for the info to circulate throughout the reserve.[60]

Taken as a whole, the evidence on the opening phase shows that some soldiers shot first, and constructed justifications afterwards. Running away, escaping, cordon-breaking, failing to halt – how far these events happened and how far soldiers reconstructed them for their own benefit is debatable. While the full extent of the shootings will probably never be known, General Erskine soon realised the extent of the problem. After landing in Kenya, he undertook a systematic tour of the troubled areas, meeting officials, settlers and Kikuyu chiefs in the Rift Valley Province, Central Province and Nairobi.[61] These meetings caused him to issue his 23 June order on discipline, according to a letter to his wife. In the same letter, Erskine stated that 'There had been a lot of indiscriminate shooting before I arrived and one of the first things I did was to stop the casualty competition which was going on.'[62] Both the police and the army were implicated. In a letter to the Secretary of State for War in December 1953, Erskine was so concerned about the prospect of the McLean Inquiry examining the early months that he thought 'the revelation would be shattering'. The letter continued: 'There is no doubt that in the early days, i.e. from Oct 1952 until last June there was a great deal of indiscriminate shooting by Army and Police.'[63]

Collaboration with vigilantes

Critics condemned the army for associating with the brutal 'settlers in uniform', such as the KPR.[64] Soldiers also collaborated with illegal

---

[60] TNA, WO 276/239: Letter from G2(Int) [General Staff Intelligence Branch] to G(Ops) [General Staff Operations Branch], 21 November 1952.

[61] TNA, CO 822/693: Letter from Erskine to Harding, 14 June 1953.

[62] IWMD Erskine papers, Erskine in letter to wife, dated 28 November 1953.

[63] TNA, WO 32/15834: Letter from Erskine to Secretary of State for War, 10 December 1953.

[64] The phrase is Erskine's: TNA, WO 32/15834: Letter from Erskine to Secretary of State for War, 10 December 1953.

settler vigilante groups. The vigilantes practised 'counter-terror' in the first few months, when they thought the government too soft on the Mau Mau.[65] These groups murdered suspects on the spot on the slightest pretext.[66] The army colluded with groups such as 'Dobie Force' and the 'United Kenya Protection Association'.[67] The government anticipated that vigilantes might appear well before the Emergency's declaration. The November 1951 internal security working committee report warned that:

Europeans may affect internal security in three ways: (a) by acting as an abrasive to the other communities; (b) by propagating well meaning but impracticable or misguided advice to Africans; (c) by unlawful actions against the Government or other communities.[68]

As the army's purpose in Kenya was to restore law and order, it was legally obliged to prevent anyone breaking the law, including settlers. In practical terms though, policing settlers over widely dispersed areas would have seriously challenged government resources. Rather than wishing to stop vigilante activities, the army worried about keeping these matters secret. Writing in January 1953, the Commander-in-Chief of MELF, responsible for East Africa as part of his larger command, General Sir Brian Robertson, revealed his anxiety about news of vigilante actions becoming public knowledge. Fortunately, he wrote, such cases had so far been 'hushed up'.[69] Whitehall expressed surprise, having heard nothing on the matter before Robertson's report.[70] After visiting Kenya in February, CIGS Field Marshal Harding urged progress in 'curbing the European hotheads'.[71]

Situation reports demonstrate how the military may have collaborated with vigilante groups. One report refers to casualties inflicted by 'Kitale commando plus mil patrol'.[72] On 24 February a raid by '6 KAR plus 4 KAR and loyal army in west end of Chinga' resulted in forty-eight detentions and one man shot resisting arrest.[73] In the Nyeri/South Nanyuki area, police and military forces operating with a 'loyal army' shot one person dead and seriously injured another two.[74] An

---

[65] Evans, *Law and Disorder*, 81.   [66] Rawcliffe, *Struggle for Kenya*, 66.
[67] Anderson, *Histories of the Hanged*, 113.
[68] Cited in Percox, 'Counter-Insurgency in Kenya', 57.
[69] TNA, CO 822/468: Report from Robertson (C-in-C MELF) to CIGS, 12 January 1953. Also cited in Heather, 'Counterinsurgency and Intelligence', 41.
[70] TNA, CO 822/468: Civil servant's minute, signed P. Rogers, 11 February 1953.
[71] TNA, CO 822/442: Report by CIGS on his visit to Kenya, 19–24 February 1953.
[72] TNA, WO 276/337: Northern Area sitreps, Norbrig Nairobi to Force Nairobi, no date, *c.* 14 February 1953.
[73] TNA, WO 276/337: Northern Area sitreps, Norbrig Nairobi to Force Nairobi, no date, *c.* 25 February 1953.
[74] TNA, WO 276/337: Northern Area sitreps, Norbrig Nairobi to Force Nairobi, no date, *c.* 19 February 1953.

intelligence summary concerning Nyeri district congratulated 'Private Armies' on doing 'a very good job especially as regards extracting information from Mau Mau suspects'.[75] These vigilante groups proved themselves useful to the security forces and were allowed to exist at a time when the state suffered serious manpower shortages.

Forced population movement

Government support for squatter evictions from the Rift Valley accelerated the campaign's brutality, where fear played a political role. For many years, hundreds of thousands of Africans had worked on settler farms in the Rift Valley in return for small squatter leaseholds. Many Africans regarded the Europeans as the real temporary residents, and labour unrest grew in the years running up to the Emergency's outbreak.[76] In Kericho, and perhaps elsewhere, settler farmers wanted to retain Kikuyu labour, and publicly opposed the evictions.[77] But a substantial proportion took advantage of the Emergency to eject large numbers of people whom they considered a serious threat.[78] Settlers argued that Mau Mau violence was frightening off other sources of labour, and that evicting all Kikuyu, a process accelerated by screening, was the only solution.[79] Settler leader Michael Blundell advised farmers to get rid of the Kikuyu, and the police expedited the process.[80] The clamour for action against the Kikuyu burgeoned after each well-publicised, gruesome settler murder. When the Meiklejohn family were murdered in November 1952 the Lancashire Fusiliers helped remove 2,950 suspects from the area and sent them to the Reserves.[81] An intelligence summary for November noted a 'big influx' of Kikuyu women from the Fort Hall area into Nairobi, 'some of whom are spreading stories of rape by Police and Military askaris'.[82] In March 1953 police and soldiers in Laikipia were noted to be partaking in 'a certain amount of inevitable pilfering and molesting of women'.[83] The widespread abuses in the opening months aimed to intimidate the Kikuyu generally, and to

---

[75] TNA, WO 276/378: Information summary, Northern Area, 17 December 1952.
[76] The best general account is T. Kanogo, *Squatters and the Roots of Mau Mau 1905–63* (London: James Currey, 1987).
[77] KNA, PC/NKU/2/1/23: Monthly intelligence report, Kericho, 3 February 1953.
[78] Heather, 'Counterinsurgency and Intelligence', 41.
[79] Kanogo, *Squatters and the Roots of Mau Mau*, 138.
[80] Evans, *Law and Disorder*, 157.   [81] Anderson, *Histories of the Hanged*, 90.
[82] Bennett witness statement 3, citing Hanslope document ADM 35/2/11/1/5A: Political intelligence report – November 1952, Nairobi district, 4 December 1952.
[83] Bennett witness statement 3, citing Hanslope document ADM 35/2/11/3/1A: Laikipia special intelligence report, 15 March 1953.

encourage their departure to the Reserves in particular. Therefore, characterising the opening months as a 'phoney war', as several authors have done, is misleading for events in the Rift Valley Province.[84]

Situation reports for the other provinces under Emergency Regulations, Central and Nairobi, show troops carried out patrols, screening and static duties at a lower intensity than in the Rift Valley. Further murders of settlers created a febrile atmosphere. In late November, 4,324 Kikuyu were removed from the Thomson's Falls district after the Mau Mau murdered a European in Leshau.[85] On 15 December it became official policy to evict Kikuyu from areas where suspected Mau Mau offences had taken place.[86] One contemporary observer decried the 'frequent brutality with which the agents of law and order enforced the evictions'.[87] The already overcrowded Reserves offered little relief to the droves of people fleeing their ordeal.[88] By late April 1953 between 70,000 and 100,000 people had left the Rift Valley and Central Provinces for the Reserves, either through forced eviction or voluntarily.[89] Given what we know about the terrorisation of the population in this period, the word 'voluntarily' must be interpreted carefully.

The army aided the exodus, one witness noting the 'thousands of unwanted people' carried away in 'army lorries'.[90] A report from Nairobi recorded the army assisting in 'escorting Kikuyu expelled to Reserve from [the] Thomson Falls area'.[91] This continued into December along with sweeps and searches.[92] In February 1953 the Lancashire Fusiliers started to 'evacuate' Kikuyu from around Ol Kalou in the Rift Valley.[93] The operation lasted for several days, shifting hundreds.[94] Governor Baring wished to appease settler opinion. He was determined to avoid mass dismissals by farmers, by the

[84] Berman, *Control and Crisis*, 348; Heather, 'Intelligence and Counter-Insurgency in Kenya', 59; Percox, 'Counter-Insurgency in Kenya', 62.

[85] Furedi, *Mau Mau War*, 119–21.

[86] D. A. Percox, *Britain, Kenya and the Cold War: Imperial Defence, Colonial Security and Decolonisation* (London: I. B. Tauris Academic Studies, 2004), 53.

[87] Rawcliffe, *Struggle for Kenya*, 58.

[88] Furedi, *Mau Mau War*, 8; Berman, *Control and Crisis*, 349.

[89] Percox, 'Counter-Insurgency in Kenya', 69.

[90] T. F. C. Bewes, *Kikuyu Conflict: Mau Mau and the Christian Witness* (London: The Highway Press, 1953), 60.

[91] TNA, WO 276/466: Jock Scott sitrep from Force Nairobi to Mideast, 28 November 1952.

[92] TNA, WO 276/466: Jock Scott sitrep from Force Nairobi to Mideast, 5 December 1952.

[93] TNA, WO 276/337: Northern Area sitreps, Norbrig Nairobi to Force Nairobi, no date, *c.* 8 February 1953.

[94] TNA, WO 276/337: Northern Area sitreps, Norbrig Nairobi to Force Nairobi, no date, *c.* 10 February 1953.

commonly found in writings on the Emergency, which blame the army's involvement in excesses during the opening months on a weak command and control system.[111] The security forces are seen as 'a splintered group', each acting according to its own desires.[112] Are these charges well founded? Colonel G. A. Rimbault, appointed Personal Staff Officer to Baring at the end of December 1952, certainly lacked the seniority and staff to fully coordinate operations. Rimbault's appointment came after Baring's request for a Malaya-style director of operations was turned down by the Colonial Secretary and the Chiefs of Staff, who did not think the situation warranted it. Baring recognised Rimbault's ineffectiveness and next time went straight to the top, appealing to Churchill for a senior commander.[113]

Major-General W. R. N. Hinde, appointed Chief Staff Officer to the Governor on 1 February 1953 and promoted Director of Operations on 11 April, similarly failed to coordinate effectively.[114] Hinde initiated major policies, such as the mile strip, and influenced how Erskine understood the conflict. But he lacked sufficient authority, and a large and efficient staff organisation. Senior army commanders recognised the problem without making any rapid remedial moves. General Sir Brian Robertson thought lack of leadership and coordination were major problems.[115] The CIGS concurred after seeing the situation in Kenya for himself:

As regards the Army command organisation, one Brigadier with an attenuated staff and no signals cannot exercise effective command over five equivalent battalions deployed on a Company or Platoon basis over an area about 130 miles long and 120 miles wide.[116]

General Robertson at MELF and Lieutenant-General Cameron at East Africa Command seemed to take little interest in the Emergency. Guy Campbell, CO of the Kenya Regiment, was placed in charge of Nairobi City and the surrounding area on the Emergency's declaration. He noted in his diary meeting General Cameron at his headquarters on the morning of 20 October. The General informed him that Lieutenant-Colonel Gilbert Collins, from 7 KAR, was temporarily promoted to be Acting Brigadier commanding military forces. Five days later, General Cameron held a big conference for all battalion commanders.[117] At the

[111] Maloba, *Mau Mau and Kenya*, 81; Berman, *Control and Crisis*, 347; Heather, 'Of Men and Plans', 18.
[112] Elkins, *Britain's Gulag*, 44.   [113] Percox, *Britain, Kenya and the Cold War*, 55–6.
[114] Percox, 'Counter-Insurgency in Kenya', 70–1, 73.
[115] TNA, CO 822/468: Letter from General Sir Brian Robertson, C-in-C Middle East Land Forces, to CIGS, 12 January 1953.
[116] TNA, CO 822/422: Report by CIGS on his visit to Kenya, 19–24 February 1953.
[117] KRA: Vol. VII: Guy Campbell papers, Diary of Events.

end of the month, Cameron attended a meeting at Government House in Nairobi to discuss operations. The record for the meeting fails to note any verbal contribution by the General.[118] The MELF Chief of Staff, Major-General Douglas Packard, visited Kenya in November, dropping in on his old friend Guy Campbell. Campbell saw Cameron again on 8 November to 'put our case across'.[119]

By the year's end, Cameron decided to hold a conference every Saturday on Kenya operations. Unfortunately the records for these meetings are missing.[120] What records survive confirm that senior commanders adopted a hands-off approach, leaving a militarily inexperienced Governor to make decisions.[121] Cameron did write an influential report on 30 April; this combined with General Sir Cameron Nicholson's report on 16 May persuaded the War Office to appoint Erskine.[122] At the battalion level, KAR units were under strength, including in officers. The East African governments slowly started reinforcing units after prompting from the Colonial Office.[123] When Erskine assumed command in June 1953 he criticised the practice of attaching small army units to the police and administration, on the grounds that it removed soldiers from their senior officers, with 'evil results'.[124]

Does this mean that military discipline effectively collapsed during the first phase of the Emergency? Three sources illuminate the number and type of courts-martial held during the first phase. The first is a report produced by the Judge Advocate General's Office in response to a question asked in the House of Commons on the number of courts-martial in Kenya since January 1952.[125] The file gives the names of those tried, their units, the date and place of the trial, the charges and the sentence. The dates and places of the offences are omitted. Many of the

---

[118] TNA, CO 822/460: Record of a meeting held at Government House at 6.30 p.m. on the 29th October, 1952.

[119] KRA, Vol. VII: Guy Campbell papers, Diary of Events, 2 November 1952.

[120] TNA, WO 276/239: Memorandum from Lt.-Col. [name illegible], Acting Chief of Staff East Africa Command, to HQ Northern Area and East Africa Command Staff, 30 December 1952.

[121] Baring had never experienced military service. For a brief biographical sketch see Baring (Charles) Evelyn, first Baron Howick of Glendale (1903–1973), by A. Clayton, *Oxford Dictionary of National Biography* (Oxford University Press, 2004), online edition, at www.oxforddnb.com/view/article/30789, accessed 8 September 2006.

[122] Percox, *Britain, Kenya and the Cold War*, 57.

[123] TNA, CO 822/442: Extracts from Chiefs of Staff meeting held 10 April 1953.

[124] TNA, WO 32/15834: Letter from Erskine to Secretary of State for War, 10 December 1953.

[125] TNA, WO 93/56: Letter from [name illegible], AG3(A) 2 to Registrar, Judge Advocate General's Office, 13 January 1954.

Table 1 *Courts-martial in Kenya, 20 October 1952–1 July 1953*

Type of offence	Number of offences
Theft	14
Drunkenness	4
Indecency	1
Disobedience	1
Desertion	3
Absence	4
Threatening a superior	2
Violence to a superior	3
Escaping	3
Fraud	2
Sleeping on post	2
Housebreaking	2
Section 11 (neglect to obey orders)	1
Section 18(5)	4
Section 27(1) (false accusations)	1
Section 40	10
Total offences	57

charges are extremely vague, stating for example, 'Section 40', referring to the Army Act 1881. The report lists thirty-seven courts-martial held between 20 October 1952 and 1 July 1953, summarised in Table 1.

Of these, only the fourteen offences, those covered by Sections 18(5) and 40, might relate to violent crimes against civilians. They were committed by only ten individuals. Section 18(5) reads: 'any other offence of a fraudulent nature not before in this Act particularly specified, or of any other disgraceful conduct of a cruel, indecent, or unnatural kind'.[126] Section 40 offences were 'any act, conduct, disorder, or neglect, to the prejudice of good order and military discipline'.[127] There is no knowing whether these fourteen offences were committed against Africans, European settlers or fellow members of the security forces. The report is also problematic for only recording charges brought against two members of East African units, despite the fact that by 1 July 1953, six KAR battalions had been on operations since the start of the Emergency, plus the Kenya Regiment, East Africa Training Centre troops, the East Africa Armoured Car Squadron and the 156 (East African) HAA Battery. This must be an underestimation of the level of crime in these units.

[126] Army Act, 1881.   [127] Army Act, 1881.

On 11 December 1952, Sergeant G. Skinner was convicted in Nairobi of a Section 40 offence, and punished with a severe reprimand and forfeiture of seniority.[128] Sergeant W. Quayle suffered a reprimand and pay stoppages on 16 December in Gilgil for infringing Section 40.[129] A list submitted to the McLean Inquiry shows two cases where soldiers were punished for crimes against civilians. The commander of 70 Brigade reprimanded Second Lieutenant Green of the Kenya Regiment, attached to 7 KAR, for assaulting a postmaster at Mweiga. Major R. Sinclair-Scott, 23 KAR, was 'under investigation on a charge of bodily harm to an African on 29 Jan 53'. Interestingly:

The evidence was not sufficient to support the charge as there had been no clear directive from Higher Authority concerning disposal of prisoners. The C-in-C quashed the charge but saw the officer and impressed on him the importance of a correct attitude.[130]

In other words, the officer escaped punishment only because no order existed at the time prohibiting him from assaulting prisoners. This attitude is remarkable, and could explain why there were so few courts-martial in the opening phase. The Fort Hall district education officer complained to the authorities in March 1953, after the Kenya Regiment looted a school in Mioro, taking items worth 499 shillings.[131] Having investigated the allegations, Lieutenant-Colonel Campbell found them 'absolutely without foundation and a direct slur on my Regiment'. His mode of investigation was to ask the officer concerned: 'as he is an Officer not subject to telling lies I have accepted his denial'.[132] Though concerning a relatively trivial incident, the exchange offers an insight into the integrity of military justice during the Emergency. Commanding officers could effectively dismiss allegations about their men, which if investigated independently might threaten their personal reputations. For this precise reason the security forces strongly objected to the inquiries made into their actions by the police CID.

---

[128] TNA, WO 93/56: List of courts-martial in Kenya. He was very probably seconded to an East African unit, as his given regiment, the Wiltshires, were not in Kenya at the time.

[129] TNA, WO 93/56: List of courts-martial in Kenya; Quayle was from the Lancashire Fusiliers but specified as 'att. KAR'.

[130] TNA, WO 32/21721: McLean Inquiry Exhibit 22: List of cases brought to the notice of GHQ East Africa in which members of the Military Forces have been charged before Civil Courts, or Courts Martial, or Summarily for offences against Africans, compiled by Assistant AG, GHQ.

[131] KNA, DC/MUR/3/10/8: Letter from H. A. W. Shea, Fort Hall Education Officer, to DC, Fort Hall, 10 March 1953.

[132] KNA, DC/MUR/3/10/8: Letter from Lt.-Col. Guy Campbell, Commanding Kenya Regiment, to DC, Fort Hall, 2 April 1953.

The Kiambu DEC expressed 'the gravest concern at the severe loss of morale among Security Forces in the District, caused by the ceaseless CID enquiries'.[133] The morale of men fighting the Mau Mau assumed a greater importance than making sure they fought within the law. Winning mattered more than morality.

The available evidence suggests that while the military authorities wished to preserve discipline, by charging men for insubordination, drunkenness and the like, mistreating the Kikuyu population was permissible. Rather than there being an army out of control, policy permitted indiscriminate, terrorising violence against the Kikuyu population. Policies such as screening and evictions, combined with close collaboration with settler forces (uniformed and vigilante) impressed upon soldiers the idea that the Kikuyu should be coerced into dropping their support for Mau Mau. Often this required beatings, and sometimes torture and random killing. Exploring the behaviour of one particular KAR company gives an insight into how these brutalities took place at a lower level.

Mistreatment of the Kikuyu at a low level: the case of 'B' Company, 5 KAR

Understanding events in one unit will help understand the nature of the violence in Kenya and the culture of impunity in the army. Following this account, the next section analyses why these events took place and their significance for the army as a whole in the Emergency.

Major Griffiths

In mid-June 1953 Captain Gerald Selby Griffiths held the temporary rank of major, commanding 'B' Company in 5 KAR, a Kenyan battalion. A professional soldier with a service record stretching back to 1931, he owned a farm in Kenya for breeding horses.[134] 5 KAR spent a long time in the field, but it is unlikely that these soldiers committed atrocities as a result of combat fatigue, as the battalion enjoyed annual leave from 1 January to 1 April 1953.[135] On 11 June 'B' Company went on a typical Emergency operation, sweeping a cordoned area near Nyeri for insurgents. 'B' Company were supported by two platoons from 7 KAR and

---

[133] TNA, WO 276/170: Cited in CPEC minutes, 5 June 1953.
[134] Rubin, *Murder, Mutiny and the Military*, 256.
[135] TNA, WO 305/259: 5 KAR Annual Historical Report, 11–12.

part of the Armoured Car Squadron.[136] At the court-martial in November, CSM W. P. Llewellyn, temporarily under Griffiths's command from 7 KAR, stated that at a briefing beforehand, Griffiths said: 'You can shoot anybody you like – PWD [Public Works Department] or anybody.' Asked what he understood Griffiths to mean, Llewellyn said: 'I understood we could shoot anyone black … He said that his Company was expecting to leave for Malaya and he had to get a half century of kills before he left.'[137]

At about 7.30 am three Kikuyu forestry workers, Ndegwa son of Kagiri, Mutahi son of Gatutha and Gichuchi son of Kibira walked slowly towards a stop point manned by two 7 KAR askaris.[138] One of the askaris recalled having received orders only to fire in an emergency or with permission from CSM Llewellyn. Major Griffiths arrived in a jeep driven by Captain Joy, Royal Electrical and Mechanical Engineers, with two askaris in the back, and appeared to be 'in a great temper'. Demanding to know why the askaris had not killed the African civilians, he called the three men over to inspect their papers, telling the eldest 'you are too old to kill, go away'.[139] According to Private Kiptarus, Griffiths 'handed back the passes to the two younger Africans and told them they could go away. When the two Africans had got about 10 yds up the road Major Griffiths discharged a whole Bren gun magazine into their backs.'[140]

Nobody at the trial claimed that the men had provoked the shooting.[141] CSM Llewellyn and Lieutenant-Colonel Glanville, 6 KAR's commander, who also participated in the operation, recognised that the shooting took place in a Special – not a Prohibited – Area.[142] Griffiths left the scene with Captain Joy and the two askaris in his jeep. Some time later, Llewellyn arrived to find the two Kikuyu screaming and writhing in agony in the road, and diverted the traffic which one of them was trying to crawl under in a bid to kill himself.[143] Within half an hour of the shooting, Griffiths returned, remarking: 'You can scream, you bastards; when you killed my horse in Nanyuki he screamed a damned sight longer than you will scream.'[144] Griffiths shot one of the men in the

---

[136] Rubin, *Murder, Mutiny and the Military*, 260.
[137] TNA, WO 71/1218: Proceedings of the General Court Martial of G. S. L. Griffiths, for murder, 25–27 November 1953, 37.
[138] Rubin, *Murder, Mutiny and the Military*, 260.
[139] TNA, WO 71/1218: Proceedings of the General Court Martial of G. S. L. Griffiths, for murder, 25–27 November 1953, 15.
[140] *Ibid.*, 16.   [141] Rubin, *Murder, Mutiny and the Military*, 261.
[142] TNA, WO 71/1218: Proceedings of the General Court Martial of G. S. L. Griffiths, for murder, 25–27 November 1953, 49, 111.
[143] *Ibid.*, 16; Rubin, *Murder, Mutiny and the Military*, 261.
[144] TNA, WO 71/1218: Proceedings of the General Court Martial of G. S. L. Griffiths, for murder, 25–27 November 1953, 38.

head dead at close range with his revolver. The trial record states that he ordered Llewellyn to kill the other man, and that the CSM refused.[145] However, new evidence shows that Llewellyn did kill one of the men, and was granted immunity from prosecution in exchange for testifying against Griffiths. Information from the Director of Army Legal Services, East Africa, illustrates how after shooting one man in the head, Griffiths left the scene again:

and in the interval a Field Officer of the Buffs came on the scene and ordered CSM Llewellyn to despatch the remaining African, who was obviously in terrible agony and in extremis.

In addition to Llewellyn, Erskine and the Attorney-General granted immunity to Captain Joy and the officer from The Buffs.[146] As the Judge Advocate at the trial pointed out, mercy killing remained a crime under civilian and military law.[147] The civil and military leadership in Kenya clearly disagreed.

The Chuka massacre

The second atrocity committed by 'B' Company happened a few days later, near Chuka in Embu District.[148] On 13 June Griffiths set up a tactical headquarters at Embu with his two subalterns, Second Lieutenant Howard, who commanded 4 Platoon, and Second Lieutenant Innes-Walker, who commanded 5 Platoon. The battalion CO, Lieutenant-Colonel L. W. B. Evans, instructed the two subalterns to establish base camps at intervals and launch four patrols from them over a seven-day period. They would be accompanied by the DO, Mr Lakin, and the forest officer, Mr Gardner.[149] They were attached because 'it was

---

[145] *Ibid*; this is also stated by Rubin in *Murder, Mutiny and the Military*, 261.

[146] TNA, WO 32/21722: Extract from D.O. dated 31 Oct 53 from DALS East Africa to DALS War Office.

[147] TNA, WO 71/1218: Proceedings of the General Court Martial of G. S. L. Griffiths, for murder, 25–27 November 1953, 125.

[148] The only existing primary-source based analyses of the atrocity are D. Branch, *From Home Guard to Mau Mau: Ambiguities and Allegiances during the Mau Mau Emergency in Kenya, 1952–60* (University of Leiden: African Studies Centre, 2005), available at: asc. leidenuniv.nl/events/event-1259710325.htm, accessed 5 July 2006; Branch, 'Loyalism during the Mau Mau Rebellion', 121–2; Branch, *Defeating Mau Mau, Creating Kenya*, 98–9. Dr Branch's studies are based on information from the KNA; he has kindly shown me his original notes. For a short account published without footnotes see D. M. Anderson, H. Bennett and D. Branch, 'A Very British Massacre', *History Today*, 56 (2006), 20–2.

[149] TNA, WO 32/16103: 'Witness for the Prosecution 2/Lt. D. Innes-Walker (425231) Royal Warwicks attached 7 KAR [*sic*]' no date.

proposed to send out two patrols each day from each platoon thus there would be a European with each patrol'.[150] While Griffiths remained at the Tactical HQ, Innes-Walker and Howard were instructed to operate solely in the forested PA where Mau Mau groups were thought to train. Evans told the subalterns to treat anyone found in the forest as hostile, but under no circumstances to venture into the adjacent Reserve area. The local Home Guard were under strict instructions to stay out of the forest.[151] These Home Guards, under Chief Petro, attracted praise for their performance and reliability. They were to patrol the forest edge, arresting any Mau Mau flushed out by the army patrols.[152]

On 14 June Evans, Griffiths, Major Day (the battalion second-in-command), Howard and Innes-Walker collected two prisoners from Embu police station.[153] These men, Njeru son of Ndwega and Kavenji son of Njoka, acted as guides in the forest, leading the patrols to Mau Mau camps.[154] At about 6 pm Griffiths, Howard, Innes-Walker and Private Ali Segat led the two prisoners to the Tac HQ's perimeter for questioning.[155] Griffiths led the interrogation; he found the prisoners' answers unsatisfactory.[156] So he handed his Somali hunting knife to Segat, directing him to threaten Njeru with emasculation, after Innes-Walker removed his trousers.[157] When this failed to produce the right information, Griffiths ordered Segat to emasculate Njeru, but he refused.[158] It is disputed whether Griffiths ordered what happened next.[159] Segat said that Griffiths told him to use violence on the prisoner; Griffiths argued that he only wanted threats from his soldier.[160] Segat chopped off Njeru's right ear with the Somali knife. Questioned about his passivity, Innes-Walker, who left the scene after the mutilation, said he was 'in the habit of

---

[150] TNA, WO 32/16103: Signed statement of Lt.-Col. L. W. B. Evans, CO 5 KAR, 24 July 1953.

[151] TNA, WO 32/16103: Witness for the Prosecution 2/Lt. D. Innes-Walker (425231) Royal Warwicks attached 7 KAR [sic], no date; WO 32/16103: Signed statement of Lt.-Col. L. W. B. Evans, CO 5 KAR, 24 July 1953.

[152] Branch, From Home Guard to Mau Mau, 5–6.

[153] TNA, WO 71/1221: Second Trial of Captain Griffiths, 4–11 March 1954, second day, 11.

[154] TNA, WO 71/1221: Second Trial of Captain Griffiths, 4–11 March 1954, first day, 1; second day, 21.

[155] TNA, WO 71/1221: Second Trial of Captain Griffiths, 4–11 March 1954, second day, 11.

[156] TNA: WO 32/16103: Witness for the Prosecution 2/Lt. D. Innes-Walker (425231) Royal Warwicks attached 7 KAR [sic], no date

[157] TNA, WO 71/1221: Second Trial of Captain Griffiths, 4–11 March 1954, second day, 12.

[158] Ibid., 40.

[159] TNA, WO 71/1221: Second Trial of Captain Griffiths, 4–11 March 1954, second day, 40; third day, 4;

[160] TNA, WO 71/1221: Second Trial of Captain Griffiths, 4–11 March 1954, second day, 40; fourth day, 24.

accepting his [Griffiths's] actions'.[161] This is an important statement in light of the debate on the fine line between the need for military obedience and the duty to refuse manifestly illegal orders.

Ten to fifteen minutes after leaving the scene, Innes-Walker heard shots.[162] According to Griffiths, he had also left the prisoners, having interrogated the second man for a few minutes. Apparently Private Segat informed him that the mutilated prisoner had been shot while trying to escape.[163] The sergeant-major whom Griffiths claimed as an alibi denied having seen his company commander at this point.[164] Although the court-martial found Griffiths innocent of ordering the shooting, Innes-Walker recalled his commander saying: 'This man will have to be shot, otherwise he will bleed to death.'[165] In his statement before the earlier court of inquiry he told how the prisoner could not have been shot attempting to escape, because Njeru was handcuffed to a tree.[166]

The next day, the second prisoner suffered humiliation and pain at the hands of 'B' Company. In the morning, accompanied by Howard and Innes-Walker, Major Griffiths ordered Segat to pierce Kavenji's ear with a bayonet, passing wire through the bleeding hole to lead the prisoner as a guide for the day's operation. Nobody complained about the company commander's orders, then or later.[167] Later in the day, Innes-Walker allegedly told the prisoner to run, and ordered Private Segat and Lance-Corporal Harun to shoot him dead. They obeyed.[168] Other accounts suggest he may in fact have been killed 'escaping' on the night of 18 June instead.[169] The authorities never held anyone responsible for Kavenji's death.

Meanwhile the hunt for Mau Mau in the forest continued. On 17 June 'B' Company's reputation would descend even further. The local Home Guard leader, Chief Petro, heard that the KAR were camping near his headquarters in the Meru Reserve, so he met with 'the Major, Mr. Lakin DO Embu and the Forest Officer' at his camp, so that everyone would

---

[161] TNA, WO 32/16103: Witness for the Prosecution 2/Lt. D. Innes-Walker (425231) Royal Warwicks attached 7 KAR [sic], no date.

[162] Ibid.

[163] TNA, WO 71/1221: Second Trial of Captain Griffiths, 4–11 March 1954, fourth day, 25.

[164] Ibid., 59.

[165] TNA, WO 71/1221: Second Trial of Captain Griffiths, 4–11 March 1954, third day, 5.

[166] TNA, WO 32/16103: Witness for the Prosecution 2/Lt. D. Innes-Walker (425231) Royal Warwicks attached 7 KAR [sic], no date.

[167] TNA, WO 71/1221: Second Trial of Captain Griffiths, 4–11 March 1954, second day, 13.

[168] TNA, WO 71/1221: Second Trial of Captain Griffiths, 4–11 March 1954, third day, 44.

[169] TNA, WO 32/16103: Signed statements of Daudi s/o Maringa, 25 July 1953; Rueria s/o Samuel Ngeru, no date; Nthiri s/o Muruina Mwangi, 26 July 1953. All these men were civilian porters with 'B' Company on this operation.

know each other's location. The Home Guards were told about the military's operation in the forest, and were ordered to stay in the Reserve.[170] Petro agreed to supply food for the next day, taking meat, sugar cane, maize and bananas to the KAR base himself. Watching the sun set at his headquarters, a Home Guard told Petro that his men based at Karigine had been arrested. Shortly after, they heard rifle and automatic fire coming from the forest.[171]

Second Lieutenant Howard, never interviewed during the subsequent investigations, told Innes-Walker that one of his patrols had seen action. A patrol under WOPC Kipsigi captured ten or eleven men 'just in from the forest edge, in the forest'. Two of these 'members of the enemy' escaped. At about four o'clock, Howard asked Innes-Walker to interrogate the ten or so men, on account of his superior Swahili: 'They said that they were not Home Guard, but they were not Mau Mau. That they had been taken from their home and were being taken somewhere by the two men who escaped.' The assertion about the two escaped men seems unlikely given the lack of supporting evidence from any other witnesses. Innes-Walker was unsure whether Howard himself led the patrol that took the men prisoner. During interrogation the prisoners were all made to lie face down except for the individual being questioned, who was 'made to remove his shirt so that we could look for any Mau Mau markings'. No markings were discovered. Later, when Howard and Innes-Walker were in the forest camp, all ten or eleven men were shot dead. Innes-Walker denied having seen the shooting and conspiring with Howard to collect the victims from the Reserve. The ten askaris taking part in the patrol said that Innes-Walker led them, and another seven witnesses saw him leaving the camp with them.[172]

One of the young subalterns reported the killings to Griffiths. In the evening, a note arrived via a tribal police messenger from the DO, Mr Collins, inquiring whether anyone knew where missing local Home Guard men might be.[173] On 18 June, the DO received his reply:

Your note re H.G. received. No, as yet, we haven't run into any H.G. at all. Your chaps tell me they are looking for 35 of them, but I am afraid we have not seen anything like that. We have killed 22 in the past two days but these were all in or

---

[170] TNA, WO 32/16103: Witness for the Prosecution M'Ikingi s/o Ndegwa.
[171] KNA, DC/MRU/2/11/98: Statement of Chief Petro Njeru, 21 June 1953. Data kindly provided by Dr Daniel Branch.
[172] TNA, WO 32/16103: Witness for the Prosecution 2/Lt. D. Innes-Walker (425231) Royal Warwicks attached 7 KAR [sic], no date. The identity of the questioner is unknown.
[173] Ibid.

on the forest boundary and ran when challenged. Anyway, I have no doubt we will meet tomorrow. (sgd) D. Walker 2nd Lt. 5th K.A.R.[174]

The killing continued on 18 June. Events on this day are clearer because fifteen witnesses recounted their experiences when questioned by the authorities. At seven o'clock that morning, the Home Guard leader from Karigine entered Chief Petro's camp in Chuka and reported the previous day's events. This man, called M'Mathai, said that at about 2 pm the Home Guard were approached by 'many' KAR askaris, who ordered them to put down their bows and arrows, raise their hands, and lie down on the ground. The askaris beat the men with rifle butts, while M'Mathai was sent to fetch beer. Wisely he chose not to return, as did the man sent after him. Next the askaris went into the village, stealing honey and instructing a prisoner to find maize and sugar cane. To prevent another escape, the askaris threatened to kill all his companions if he failed to return. The threat worked. M'Mathai reported how 'The askaris seized the wife of [name withheld]. She screamed.'[175] This statement refers to a woman being raped. The file on the Chuka massacre contains eleven pages retained by the government until 2038. On 18 July 2006, Lord Steel asked a question in the House of Lords about the withheld pages. Baroness Crawley replied for the government that the pages contained 'statements by three Kenyan women raped by African soldiers. That information is sensitive personal data relating to the victims.'[176] Following the rapes, the askaris took the ten prisoners away into the forest, where they were shot dead.[177]

On the morning of 18 June, Innes-Walker and Howard decided upon sending four patrols into the forest; Innes-Walker would lead one patrol, Howard another, and WOPC Hussein a third.[178] The fourth patrol, commanded by Corporal Killis son of Kiyundu, went to fetch water.[179] Hussein's patrol left first, followed by Innes-Walker's, then Howard's, and finally Killis's.[180] Significantly, the available statements on the

---

[174] KNA, DC/MRU/2/11/98: Letter from D. Walker to D. T. Collins, District Officer, Kibwaga, 18 June 1953. Data kindly provided by Dr Daniel Branch.

[175] KNA, DC/MRU/2/11/98: Statement of Chief Petro Njeru, 21 June 1953. Data kindly provided by Dr Daniel Branch.

[176] The full text of the debate is available on the internet at the following address: www. publications.parliament.uk/pa/ld199900/ldhansrd/pdvn/lds06/text/60718-0999.htm.

[177] KNA, DC/MRU/2/11/98: Statement of Chief Petro Njeru, 21 June 1953. Data kindly provided by Dr Daniel Branch.

[178] TNA, WO 32/16103: Witness for the Prosecution 2/Lt. D. Innes-Walker (425231) Royal Warwicks attached 7 KAR [sic], no date.

[179] TNA, WO 32/16103: Signed statement of Cpl. Killis s/o Kiyundu, 'B' Company, 5 KAR, 13 August 1953.

[180] TNA, WO 32/16103: Witness for the Prosecution 2/Lt. D. Innes-Walker (425231) Royal Warwicks attached 7 KAR [sic], no date; WO 32/16103: Signed statement of Cpl. Killis s/o Kiyundu, 'B' Company, 5 KAR, 13 August 1953.

massacre in the forest only include five statements from those on the water patrol, and Innes-Walker's statement. There is no evidence from anyone on Howard's or Hussein's patrols, an anomaly due either to incompetence or a deliberate cover-up considering events on 18 June. At about 11 am, Kithumbi and his half-brother Njeru were in their village, Mogokulo, when around seven African civilians were escorted into the village by an askari. The soldier made Njeru join the group, but Kithumbi ran away and hid.[181] Shortly after, Kanambiu, a local Home Guard member, saw the group, including Njeru and another whom he recognised, walking through the village. The askari asked two other local men, Nkira and Muchiri, to join the group. In Kanambiu's view,

the Askari had come to obtain assistance in finding Mau Mau, as the Askari told them he wanted them to bring their weapons and go to the forest. The Askari and the party went in the direction of other nearby Bomas [enclosures].[182]

The patrols spent the morning in the Reserve, despite Lieutenant-Colonel Evans's distinct orders to the contrary. One of the motives for doing so was to steal. One villager, Moranga, recalled four askaris coming into his hut, making him lie on the floor as they emptied his money pouch of cash.[183] A man collecting water from a stream returned to his village of Karege an hour or so later to hear shooting. Walking closer, he hid in a shamba and saw an askari pointing 'a gun with a knife fixed to it' at a group of men, who were taking off their shirts. He recognised Njeru among them. The soldiers searched their pockets, taking money as the men lay on the ground. Then the villagers were told: 'Get your weapons we are going to find Mau Mau.' Having fetched bows, arrows, spears and pangas, the group were marched at bayonet point into the forest.[184] Another villager was sitting outside her hut with her husband when a soldier suddenly appeared. Having stolen money from the hut, the soldier took her husband away to the forest.[185]

Corporal Killis's water-collecting patrol later came across all these detained men. According to a civilian porter accompanying Killis, his group consisted of eight porters, the corporal and eight or nine askaris, and went into the Reserve to fetch water. As they approached a shamba, they noticed:

a line of civilians in this shamba. They were 500 or 600 yards away from us ... I saw an askari behind the line of civilians. He was holding a rifle with fixed bayonet and seemed to be pointing it at the civilians.[186]

[181] TNA, WO 32/16103: Signed statement of Kithumbi s/o Mbwani, no date.
[182] TNA, WO 32/16103: Signed statement of Kanambiu s/o M'Rugamba, 24 July 1953.
[183] TNA, WO 32/16103: Statement of Moranga s/o Wombongu, 25 July 1953.
[184] TNA, WO 32/16103: Signed statement of Muthuri s/o Mbiti, no date.
[185] TNA, WO 32/16103: Statement of Nkwane w/o Mutowarei, 24 July 1953.
[186] TNA, WO 32/16103: Signed statement of Nthiri s/o Muruina Mwangi, 26 July 1953.

The shamba belonged to a local teacher, Bore, and they passed the group on their way to get the water. The porter remembered how 'As we were walking towards the river I heard a single shot fired from the direction of the teacher's house.' On walking back to the forest, the party noticed Second Lieutenant Howard by the shamba.[187] Bore was the first person shot dead that day, outside his house.[188] As the water party re-entered the forest, they saw ten civilians carrying their bows, arrows, spears and pangas with two askaris.[189] The patrol's leader remembered the two soldiers as Lance-Corporal Idris and Private Makahe, members of WOPC Hussein's patrol.[190] Another water porter heard Corporal Killis say to the two askaris: 'You have taken these people from the Reserve. Why don't you let them go.' The soldiers replied: 'They are Mau Mau.'[191]

About half an hour after the water party returned to camp, Innes-Walker's and Howard's patrols came back.[192] Ten minutes to half an hour later, between two and four o'clock in the afternoon, those in the forest camp heard 'considerable fire'.[193] The shots sounded like rifle and automatic gunfire coming from the forest.[194] About half an hour later WOPC Hussein's patrol returned, carrying bows, arrows, pangas, spears and severed African hands. He reported the soldiers had shot dead a group of Africans in the forest who failed to halt when challenged; the hands were for identification purposes.[195] The Chuka massacre was at an end. Including the two guides, twenty-two men lay dead in the forest and one dead in the Reserve. Special Branch reported the incident as having resulted in 'a complete disintegration of the Meru Guard in the Southern part of the district'.[196]

---

[187] TNA, WO 32/16103: Signed statement of Cpl. Killis s/o Kiyundu, 'B' Company, 5 KAR, 13 August 1953.
[188] TNA, WO 32/16103: Medical Report, Chojina, 26 June 1953, signed Clive Irvine.
[189] TNA, WO 32/16103: Signed statement of Nthiri s/o Muruina Mwangi, 26 July 1953.
[190] TNA, WO 32/16103: Signed statement of Cpl. Killis s/o Kiyundu, 'B' Company, 5 KAR, 13 August 1953.
[191] TNA, WO 32/16103: Signed statement of Daudi s/o Maringa, 25 July 1953.
[192] TNA, WO 32/16103: Statement of Cpl. Cheserch s/o Kipobo, 'B' Company 5 KAR, 13 August 1953.
[193] TNA, WO 32/16103: Signed statement of Kanambiu s/o M'Rugamba, 24 July 1953; TNA: WO 32/16103: Witness for the Prosecution 2/Lt. D. Innes-Walker (425231) Royal Warwicks attached 7 KAR [sic], no date.
[194] TNA, WO 32/16103: Statement of Cpl. Cheserch s/o Kipobo, 'B' Company 5 KAR, 13 August 1953.
[195] TNA, WO 32/16103: Witness for the Prosecution 2/Lt. D. Innes-Walker (425231) Royal Warwicks attached 7 KAR [sic], no date.
[196] TNA, CO 822/373: SBFIS 7/53, 30 June 1953. Interestingly, the next fortnight's report, 8/53, was at pains to highlight a rapid recovery in morale and popular support for the security forces.

'B' Company's behaviour in context

Describing these horrific events helps understand both the specific causes of 'B' Company's behaviour, and their relationship with the campaign as a whole in the early period.

In his 1976 study, Anthony Clayton labelled Griffiths 'an embittered, passed-over officer'.[197] In a book about the British Army officer corps, he described Griffiths's actions as 'the excesses of one mentally unbalanced officer'.[198] The moral condemnation is absolutely warranted. The desire to think that only deranged individuals, people unlike us, can commit atrocious acts, is instinctively appealing. Unfortunately, the idea is rejected by research in social psychology.[199] In 1953 GHQ brought in a 'specialist psychiatrist' to examine Griffiths before his court-martial. Papers from the assessment survive. The specialist found Griffiths 'to be not a normal man', a view supposedly supported by his having been 'invalided home during the war as a Psycho-neurotic'.[200] This hardly condemns him for being a deranged homicidal maniac, especially given the incidence of combat fatigue during the Second World War. The British Army in the Second World War consistently suffered psychiatric battle casualties at the rate of 10–20 per cent of all casualties. At least 40,000 men were discharged from the army for mental disorders.[201]

Griffiths's battle stress, hardly unusual, should not be equated with long-term psychosis. If he were deranged, this could have been raised in his defence, as courts-martial were entitled to find a defendant 'guilty but insane'.[202] In neither of his two courts-martial did the defence team mention such arguments. The notion that Griffiths was insane reflects *ex post facto* disgust with his behaviour rather than providing an explanation of events. Designating someone sick ultimately denies him any responsibility for his actions; Griffiths never denied his responsibility.[203] An alternative explanation for events in mid-June 1953 comes from Branch's analysis. Branch suggests that Chief Petro's failure to supply the soldiers with as much food as they

---

[197] Clayton, *Counter-Insurgency in Kenya*, 41.

[198] A. Clayton, *The British Officer: Leading the Army from 1660 to the Present* (Harlow: Pearson Education, 2006), 194.

[199] Waller, *Becoming Evil*, 87; P. Zimbardo, *The Lucifer Effect: How Good People Turn Evil* (London: Rider, 2009), 3–22.

[200] TNA, WO 32/21722: Telegram from Governor's Deputy (Crawford) to Baring (in London), 1 December 1953.

[201] B. Shephard, *A War of Nerves: Soldiers and Psychiatrists 1914–1994* (London: Pimlico, 2002), 325–6, 328.

[202] See the list of cases in TNA, WO 93/54.   [203] Shephard, *War of Nerves*, 369.

wanted provoked the massacre.[204] But Petro did supply food to the KAR, cooperating closely with them alongside the local administration officials. Several witnesses recount the askaris stealing extra food without remonstration from their victims. The killings took place a time after the thefts. Any causal connection between the two seems fairly trivial.

What then caused the killings? Clearly Major Griffiths played a central part, most certainly in the shooting of the forestry workers. Rather than his mental health, his settler background, desire for revenge and racism towards the Kikuyu better explain his behaviour. Under cross-examination at the second trial, Griffiths admitted that he thought the Mau Mau were 'loathsome creatures'.[205] Other witnesses mentioned nothing about it, but he thought the two guides tortured and murdered a few days later 'hard-core'.[206] According to Innes-Walker, before the patrols in the forest started, his commander told the whole company that the men should kill Kikuyu (not Mau Mau). Griffiths apparently expanded:

if any Kikuyu was killed by a member of the company and that person was employed either by the Government or by a civilian firm that a panga could always be put in their dead hand. If the Kikuyu killed happened to be Home Guard then their armband if worn must be removed.[207]

General McLean's public report downplayed claims about competition between units in Kenya. However, McLean limited his inquiries to events after General Erskine arrived in June 1953. Competition played an important role in 5 KAR and other units in the early phase of the Emergency. CSM Llewellyn testified that a 'great rivalry' existed, with his unit encouraged to beat 23 KAR's record of over a hundred kills.[208] Griffiths himself admitted giving soldiers 5s 5d, in contrast to others who offered a 5s reward for kills. He thought the practice perfectly normal.[209] Innes-Walker recalled how these incentives were always for 'Kikuyu kills' and not 'Mau Mau kills'. On two occasions askaris received money in his presence; nobody ever questioned who the victims were.[210]

---

[204] Branch, *From Home Guard to Mau Mau*, 7, 9; Branch, 'Loyalism during the Mau Mau Rebellion', 122.

[205] TNA, WO 71/1221: Second Trial of Captain Griffiths, 4–11 March 1954, fourth day, 32.

[206] *Ibid.*, 21.

[207] TNA, WO 32/16103: Witness for the Prosecution 2/Lt. D. Innes-Walker (425231) Royal Warwicks attached 7 KAR [*sic*], no date.

[208] TNA, WO 71/1218: Proceedings of the General Court Martial of G. S. L. Griffiths, for murder, 25–27 November 1953, 48–9.

[209] *Ibid.*, 94.

[210] TNA, WO 32/16103: Witness for the Prosecution 2/Lt. D. Innes-Walker (425231) Royal Warwicks attached 7 KAR [*sic*], no date.

Several askaris remembered the company commander paying out rewards to those who presented him with severed hands, and that rewards were not made for taking prisoners.[211] Griffiths certainly boosted the competitive, indiscriminate killing culture, but other officers participated too.

From the evidence available, Innes-Walker and Howard at the least failed to challenge their superior's illegal actions, as military law required. The officer who questioned Innes-Walker suspected him of conspiring with Howard in collecting victims from the Reserve.[212] This seems likely as both Hussein and Howard entered the Reserve against orders when the positions were well demarcated with the Home Guard and administration beforehand.[213] Furthermore, Innes-Walker failed to inspect the bodies of the men killed on 18 June, while Griffiths took no action against Segat for mutilating a prisoner – and even placed him in charge of another prisoner afterwards.[214] No disciplinary action was taken over the alleged rapes either. The battalion's CO, Lieutenant-Colonel Evans, heard about the mutilation by 'rumour', but failed to investigate.[215]

The evidence suggests a general disdain for Kikuyu life, a keen competitive spirit encouraging kills and a culture of impunity within the unit. That this differed from a breakdown in command and control is illustrated by the officers' attitude towards theft during the latter operation. Several witnesses talk about how the 'tall thin officer' (one of the two subalterns) ordered askaris near the teacher's house to throw away maize they had stolen.[216] In the specific case of the two guides, the most straightforward explanation is that the men were killed because they witnessed the soldiers committing crimes.[217]

---

[211] TNA, WO 32/16103: Signed statement of Cpl. Killis s/o Kiyundu, 'B' Company, 5 KAR, 13 August 1953; TNA: WO 32/16103: Statement of Cpl. Cheserch s/o Kipobo, 'B' Company 5 KAR, 13 August 1953; TNA: WO 32/16103: Signed statement of CSM T. Kilgallon, 'B' Company, 5 KAR, 1 August 1953.

[212] TNA, WO 32/16103: Witness for the Prosecution 2/Lt. D. Innes-Walker (425231) Royal Warwicks attached 7 KAR [sic], no date.

[213] Ibid.; Branch, From Home Guard to Mau Mau, 6.

[214] TNA, WO 32/16103: Witness for the Prosecution 2/Lt. D. Innes-Walker (425231) Royal Warwicks attached 7 KAR [sic], no date; TNA: WO 71/1221: Second Trial of Captain Griffiths, 4–11 March 1954, fourth day, 27, 58; TNA, WO 71/1221: Second Trial of Captain Griffiths, 4–11 March 1954, fifth day, 29.

[215] TNA, WO 71/1221: Second Trial of Captain Griffiths, 4–11 March 1954, second day, 25.

[216] TNA, WO 32/16103: Signed statement of Daudi s/o Maringa, 25 July 1953; TNA, WO 32/16103: Signed statement of Rueria s/o Samuel Ngeru, no date; TNA, WO 32/16103: Signed statement of Nthiri s/o Muruina Mwangi, 26 July 1953.

[217] TNA, WO 32/16103: Witness for the Prosecution 2/Lt. D. Innes-Walker (425231) Royal Warwicks attached 7 KAR [sic], no date.

When Erskine discovered the Chuka massacre, he considered the prime cause to be a 'spirit of competition'.[218] The behaviour of 5 KAR should be seen in the context of the widespread beatings, torture and murder practised by security forces – including the army – in the opening phase of the Emergency. In the early months, the government prioritised coercing the civilian population through fear. Even after Hinde took over, the stick came first, with the carrot of a good life for the Kikuyu promised only after law and order were restored.[219] Erskine's arrival did not change everything. Troops were deployed in Kiambu district in late 1953, for example, 'with the max possible punitive effect'.[220] Rather than 5 KAR's experiences constituting a rare breakdown in discipline, they reflected an unofficial, widespread policy of brutality. As Erskine recognised:

I do not consider Griffiths case was exceptional before my appointment. That is why I issued my directive. I consider such conduct now would be exceptional and it is well recognized in that it would be punished.[221]

A problem for the argument made throughout this book, that the army participated in widescale killings of civilians short of genocide, is the lack of statistical evidence. Of course the army would hardly wish to keep records of those killed illegally. However, demographer John Blacker helps support the argument in addition to the qualitative evidence presented in this chapter. Based on a detailed statistical analysis of the census data from before and after the Emergency, Blacker concludes that a further 11,500 'excess deaths' were previously unaccounted for. The total figure of 24,000 is a 'best guess' of adult deaths. It is imprecise because of the nature of the available data, but probably the closest to a true figure possible.[222] The figure supports the argument that killings were widespread yet short of genocide.

Setting the pattern? Indiscriminate violence in the opening months

Atrocities were widespread in the first few months, with the aim of terrorising the population into supporting the government rather than

---

[218] TNA, WO 32/21722: Telegram from GHQ East Africa to War Office, 30 November 1953.

[219] TNA, WO 276/411: Appreciation of the Situation, by Major-General Hinde, 5 March 1953.

[220] TNA, WO 276/202: GHQ East Africa Operational Instruction no. 8, 30 October 1953.

[221] TNA, WO 32/21722: Telegram from C-in-C East Africa to Secretary of State for War, no date, *c.* late November 1953.

[222] J. Blacker, 'The Demography of Mau Mau: Fertility and Mortality in Kenya in the 1950s: A Demographer's Viewpoint', *African Affairs*, 106 (2007), 205–27. Thanks to Professor David Anderson for bringing this article to my attention.

the Mau Mau. Beatings, torture, murder, collaboration with vigilantes and mass evictions were indiscriminate, exemplary policies which targeted civilians. They were pursued not only to terrorise, but also to gather intelligence and to protect the white minority. These activities were more widespread than is normally allowed for, and the army played a central role. The conventional explanation that there were problems with the command and control system is only partially correct, and should not be conflated with a general breakdown in discipline, which was avoided. Soldiers who got into drunken fights with their comrades were punished; soldiers who thrust violence on Kikuyu, Embu and Meru civilians were less likely to face the consequences.

The weak command and control system suited those directing the campaign, who were happy to turn a blind eye to the increasing evidence that the army was acting with little regard to the tenet of minimum force. Looking at the experience of one particular unit, 'B' Company, 5 KAR, revealing new evidence on the events at Chuka in June 1953, helps explain conduct in Kenya. Racism, competition for kills and ignorance about the legal duty to stop criminal acts played a role, in addition to the intelligence-gathering and terrorisation purposes described before. There is strong evidence to suggest that 'B' Company was not unique. General Erskine's admission that the army was engaged in widespread beatings and shootings, and the demographic evidence suggesting around 11,500 excess killings of the total of 24,000, force us to further question the centrality of minimum force in Kenya. Before Erskine's arrival, soldiers were allowed to brutalise civilians with impunity. The military and civilian leaderships systemically allowed brutality because they thought it would bring the government success in crushing the rebellion. In the next chapter, we explore whether General Erskine managed to reform the system, or whether it gradually corrupted his initial desire for change.

8 'Severe repressive measures': the army under Erskine

> The Kikuyu tribe, as a whole, has been subjected to severe repressive
> measures. *Intelligence summary, December 1953*[1]

When General Erskine arrived in Kenya he genuinely wanted to improve
the security forces' treatment of Kikuyu civilians. Throughout his first
six months in the country he struggled to comprehend the extent of the
war's brutality, and then to control it. Receiving scant support from the
Governor, direct opposition from the settlers and mixed signals from his
own troops, he compromised. By January 1954 General Erskine
appeared to accept his inability to impose tight discipline on all the
forces under his command. There were two fundamental reasons for
this. By the time Erskine arrived in the country, the pattern of violence
was set. All the major players in the conflict had already decided how to
conduct themselves in this bitter fight. They were damned if a British
general was going to change that. So Erskine entered into an implicit
bargain with the security forces: he would only punish the very worst
offenders against his moral code.

General Erskine entered this deal because his strategy for defeating
the Mau Mau left him no other option. Although military strategy
evolved in several respects, such as the growing use of special forces,
the core tenet remained in place from start to finish. The army in Kenya
aimed to defeat the rebellion by repressing those elements of the
Kikuyu population perceived to be disloyal. Policies such as collective
punishment, villagisation and mass detention, and coercive interrogations were considered strategically vital. When soldiers abused and killed
civilians in efforts to enact those policies, their commanding officers
could hardly punish them for doing so. Soldiers warned their officers
that if discipline became too tight, they would effectively stop fighting. In
other words, the army negotiated flexible discipline in order to wage a
punitive war against a whole people.

[1] TNA, CO 822/378: KICFA 18/53, 1 December 1953.

194

Investigating military misconduct

Erskine discovered in Kenya that discipline was a negotiated outcome, not a simple matter of hierarchically imposed diktats.[2] There were severe limitations to the investigations launched into the army's misconduct. As these investigations dragged on, Erskine came to the view that military discipline should be applied selectively, ignoring numerous allegations. The directives and orders issued by Erskine on conduct, analysed in earlier chapters, have led scholars to conclude that he was 'committed to the investigation of all allegations of brutality by the Security Forces', while any failings of punishment were the fault of the courts.[3] Others have seen Erskine's desire to impose discipline as indicative of a wider trend in Britain's post-war counter-insurgencies, where authorities did not shy away from prosecuting criminals.[4] These views have been convincing because the evidence on military misconduct has been obscured by official secrecy until quite recently. Newly available evidence allows us to understand discipline as a dialogue between commander and troops, one where punishments imposed are contextualised against acts which go unpunished. As stressed in chapter 5, the army preferred informal, summary justice administered quickly by a battalion's own officers, rather than full formal court-martial proceedings. A hidden history of verbal reprimands and minor punishments within all the battalions in Kenya cannot yet be written.[5] This chapter argues these informal methods failed to stop abuses against civilians.

As Kaushik Roy has demonstrated in relation to the British Indian Army in the late nineteenth century, lenient military justice can be deemed essential when mutiny is a possibility.[6] General Erskine heard soldiers protesting against his push for greater humanity in Kenya, and stopped tightening discipline before disgruntlement turned into mutiny

---

[2] L. V. Smith, *Between Mutiny and Obedience: The Case of the French Fifth Infantry Division during World War I* (Princeton University Press, 1994), 3–19. For a study of officer–man relations in the British Army during the First World War, see G. D. Sheffield, *Leadership in the Trenches: Officer–Man Relations, Morale and Discipline in the British Army in the Era of the First World War* (Basingstoke: Macmillan, 2000).

[3] Heather, 'Counterinsurgency and Intelligence', 139.

[4] G. R. Rubin, 'Courts Martial from Bad Nenndorf (1948) to Osnabrück (2005)', *RUSI Journal*, 150 (2005), 53.

[5] On discipline within battalions, see G. A. Steppler, 'British Military Law, Discipline, and the Conduct of Regimental Courts Martial in the Later Eighteenth Century', *English Historical Review*, 102 (1987), 859–86.

[6] K. Roy, 'Coercion through Leniency: British Manipulation of the Courts-Martial System in the Post-Mutiny Indian Army, 1859–1913', *Journal of Military History*, 65 (2001), 937–64.

or a refusal to kill. Militaries abhor the word mutiny. Rose calls the idea 'a negation of the military essence'. Consequently the word is absent from the archival record, as its utterance would have tarnished any officer. But the threat lingered in the 'negotiating repertoire' of soldiers communicating to higher commanders.[7] In North Africa in 1942–3 the British Army used courts-martial to impose harsh discipline when commanders worried about crumbling morale.[8] In the Kenya Emergency commanders thought morale generally strong, and did not want to damage it by imposing tough discipline.

Unravelling events in 5 KAR

The nature of military justice in the Emergency soon became evident after the Chuka massacre. On the last day of the massacre, a DO in Meru, W. B. Raynor, reported to his superior, stating that fifteen Home Guards had been killed by 5 KAR, and that he might have to hold a post-mortem.[9] The local chiefs insisted that the authorities investigate. Chief Petro visited the massacre site with his headman, Home Guards and tribal police, finding the bodies of the ten men killed the day before. The bodies lay about 100 yards from the deserted forest camp.[10] DO Collins suspected a massacre even before the KAR operation finished, but prevented Petro investigating until 'B' Company had completed its mission.

Visiting Chuka, Chief Karawa also urged Collins to find out what had happened. The next morning Collins saw eleven bodies for himself, identified as Home Guard members by the tribal policemen accompanying him. That afternoon, Collins reported to his superior, the DC for Meru.[11] The Kenya police were called in, and Assistant Inspector Dennis Prior went with Chief Karawa's men to see ten bodies in the forest. The hands of six of them had been completely severed. He found a single body near the remains of a recently used campsite, and another in the Reserve. On 21 June, Prior, 'numerous African civilians', two policemen and Dr Clive Irvine visited the scene to identify, examine and bury

---

[7] E. Rose, 'The Anatomy of Mutiny', *Armed Forces and Society*, 8 (1982), 563, 573.

[8] M. Connelly and W. Miller, 'British Courts Martial in North Africa, 1940–3', *Twentieth Century British History*, 15 (2004), 217–42.

[9] KNA, DC/MRU/2/11/98: Letter from W. B. G. Raynor, DO, Meru to A. C. Small, DC, Meru, 18 June 1953. Data kindly provided by Dr Daniel Branch.

[10] TNA, WO 32/16103: Signed statement of Daudi s/o Maringa, 25 July 1953; KNA, DC/MRU/2/11/98: Statement of Chief Petro Njeru, 21 June 1953. Data kindly provided by Dr Daniel Branch.

[11] KNA, DC/MRU/2/11/98: Statement by D. T. Collins, DO (Meru Guard), 22 June 1953. Data kindly provided by Dr Daniel Branch.

the bodies.[12] Dr Irvine concluded that twelve men had been killed by rifle bullets a few days previously: ten in the forest, a man by the empty campsite, and Bore by a coffee shamba in the Reserve. Later in the day Irvine inspected another ten bodies at a different spot in the forest, some with gunshot wounds but most displaying bayonet wounds in the back. The local civilians and the police with him identified the victims.[13]

These investigations forced the military to abandon Evans's *laissez-faire* approach to overseeing the company. On 22 June a military court of inquiry began sitting at Embu. It was probably convened at brigade level because the presiding officer, Lieutenant-Colonel Collins, came from another battalion within 70 Brigade, 7 KAR. Major Rawkins from 23 KAR also sat on the inquiry. A few days later Lieutenant-Colonel Collins informed the administration that 'the court would be adjourned and re-constituted at a later date'.[14] If the court produced any report it does not survive in the archives. This may reflect its shortcomings, revealed when Innes-Walker admitted lying about leading Hussein's patrol when it opened fire in the forest. Griffiths told him to 'concoct a feasible story that would help to clear HUSSEIN [sic] and his men', and Innes-Walker similarly coached the WOPC and his men in what to tell the court of inquiry.[15]

The civilian authorities halted their investigation as the military police's SIB slowly collected evidence. Meanwhile, the authorities wished to draw a line under the affair by paying compensation to the victims' relatives, representing an official admission that the victims were innocent. On 14 July General Erskine wrote to the Chief Native Commissioner:

I have held a Court of Inquiry and investigations have completely satisfied me that whoever is to blame, it is not any of the persons killed, even though they were not in possession of the usual Home Guard arm bands and certificates at the time of the killings.[16]

Major-General Hinde's DDOps Committee considered a suggestion of paying £30 to each family 'quite inadequate nowadays'. Instead, £100 was deemed more appropriate, a sum eventually increased to £125 on

---

[12] TNA, WO 32/16103: Signed statement of Asst. Insp. Dennis Edward Prior, Kenya Police Force, Meru, 23 July 1953.

[13] TNA, WO 32/16103: Medical Report, Chojina, signed Clive Irvine, 26 June 1953.

[14] TNA, WO 32/16103: Signed statement of Roger Aubone Wilkinson, DC, Embu, 20 September 1953; TNA: WO 32/16103: Signed statement by Major N. F. Rawkins, 23 KAR, 2 November 1953. Collins commanded 7 KAR from 1 June to 27 July 1953. See TNA, WO 32/21721: McLean Court of Inquiry Exhibit 2, List of Comds wef 1 Jun.

[15] TNA, WO 32/16103: Witness for the Prosecution 2/Lt. D. Innes-Walker (425231) Royal Warwicks attached 7 KAR [sic], no date.

[16] KNA, DC/MRU/2/11/98: Letter from General Erskine to B. H. Windley, Chief Native Commissioner, 14 July 1953. Data kindly provided by Dr Daniel Branch.

21 July. In addition East Africa Command decided to increase the scale of officers in KAR battalions to two per platoon.[17] The administration advocated these payments as 'blood money ... prescribed by Meru tribal custom'. The matter should be resolved rapidly to reverse the 'disastrous effect which these killings have had amongst our supporters in the Meru District'.[18] DC A. C. Small finally paid out the compensation at a baraza in Chuka on 12 August.[19] In today's prices, the £125 paid equals about £2,337.[20]

The first court of inquiry was ineffective. Aside from letting Innes-Walker commit perjury, Erskine had to replace the officers responsible: the brigade commander, Lieutenant-Colonel Evans, and 5 KAR's second-in-command, Major Day.[21] Erskine's ability to prosecute those responsible for Chuka was impeded by personnel shortages. In early July he requested more men to support the sole legal officer in Kenya, the overworked Major J. C. Robertson.[22] The War Office sent only Lieutenant-Colonel R. H. Cowell-Parker in the short term, although the SIB received reinforcements by the year's end, the precise extent of which is unknown.[23] The SIB started interviewing witnesses in late July.[24] Sergeant Barton took statements from African witnesses, and CSM Hateley also participated in the investigations. In August the SIB interviewed 'B' Company's askaris, under close arrest in Nairobi's Buller Camp.[25] Cowell-Parker later revealed irregularities in CSM Hateley's questioning technique,

---

[17] ODRP, W. R. Hinde, MSS Afr.s.1580. Vol. IV: Director of Operations Committee Minutes, Meetings of DDOps. Cttee, 16 July 1953 and 21 July 1953.

[18] KNA, DC/MRU/2/11/98: Letter from Acting Chief Native Commissioner to Secretary of Treasury Compensation Committee, 17 July 1953. Data kindly provided by Dr Daniel Branch.

[19] KNA, DC/MRU/2/11/98: Statement of Payment of Compensation to Relatives of Meru Guard Killed by Security Forces at Chuka on 17th and 18th June, 1953, signed A. C. Small. Data kindly provided by Dr Daniel Branch.

[20] This figure was kindly calculated by S. J. Bennett using the following sources: Office of National Statistics, 'Retail Prices Index: Long Run Series' in Economic Trends 604 (London: ONS, 2004), 46; Office of National Statistics, Labour Market Trends 114/3 (London: ONS, 2006), Table J11. This figure does not account for the greater purchasing power in Kenya compared to Britain.

[21] IWMSA, M. C. Hastings, 10453/6; P. H. W. Brind, 10089/2; S. Maclachlan, 10010/3.

[22] TNA, WO 32/15556: Telegram from Erskine to VCIGS, 6 July 1953.

[23] TNA, WO 32/15556: Telegram from VCIGS to Erskine, 8 July 1953.

[24] TNA, WO 32/16103: Statement of Nkwane w/o Mutowarei, 24 July 1953; Statement of Moranga s/o Wombongu, 25 July 1953; Signed statement of Daudi s/o Maringa, 25 July 1953; Signed statement of Nthiri s/o Muruina Mwangi, 26 July 1953; Signed statement of Sarastino M'Chabari s/o Mukapo, 27 July 1953; TNA, CO 822/378: Telegram from Baring to Secretary of State for the Colonies, 31 July 1953.

[25] TNA, WO 32/16103: Signed statement of Njoka s/o M'Rosa, 27 July 1953; Signed statement of Cpl. Killis s/o Kiyundu, 'B' Company, 5 KAR, 13 August 1953; Statement of Cpl. Cheserch s/o Kipobo, 'B' Company, 5 KAR, 13 August 1953.

when he refused to write down certain things said by Hussein, such as Howard's threat to 'make trouble' if he mentioned that either of the subalterns were involved in the shootings.[26] Erskine's early attempts to impose tighter discipline were obstructed by officers in 5 KAR and perhaps even the brigade commander, and frustrated by overstretched investigators who were reluctant to record all the evidence about crimes committed by officers.

Sergeant Allen: 'doing my duty'

Investigations into allegations against Sergeant Jeremy Allen from the Kenya Regiment, accused of murder, illustrate how Erskine's determination to see Major Griffiths behind bars was an exception. At first the incident may have escaped Erskine's notice because he only informed London on 12 September that a summary of evidence was being taken. Sergeant Allen, Corporal Kibiwot and Lance-Corporal Lakurian were suspected of murdering two Kikuyu on 18 April.[27] During April, barrister Peter Evans took witness statements from those who observed the killings. Evans was extremely unpopular among officialdom for his role in defending Jomo Kenyatta at his trial. The Kenya government deported him on 16 June for working without a permit.[28] Before his departure, he passed on his concerns to the Kiambu police, who investigated in May and June.[29]

In 1953 Jeremy Allen, a 22-year-old dry cleaner, had two years' experience in the Kenya Regiment and training up to platoon commander level. He served on secondment to 23 KAR, running his own Kikuyu informer network.[30] On 17 April he and his askaris, acting on informer intelligence, arrested four men in the Ndeiya location. The local Home Guard unit brought him a fifth man later that evening. The prisoners spent the night in a corrugated iron shack in his camp, next to the Kikuyu police station. On the morning of 18 April Allen, the askaris and the five prisoners drove around the area in his truck, making inquiries. Allen wanted to obtain incriminating information about his

---

[26] TNA, WO 32/16103: Note by Lt.-Col. R. H. Cowell-Parker, ADALS, 23 December 1953.

[27] TNA, DO 35/5357: Letter from F. A. K. Harrison, Commonwealth Relations Office to V. C. Martin, Office of the High Commissioner for the United Kingdom, New Delhi, 26 September 1953.

[28] 'British barrister deported', *The Times*, 17 June 1953, 6.

[29] Bennett witness statement 2, citing Hanslope document CO 968/424: Summary of evidence concerning the Sergeant Allen case (hereafter Sergeant Allen summary).

[30] *Ibid.*

prisoners which might be used in their interrogation. After stopping off in several places, the truck halted in the countryside on the road from Nachu to Gicheru. The interrogations began. Allen checked the prisoners' identities then found, as was common in his experience, a reluctance to give information in front of others. So he sent one prisoner off with his corporal into the bush to be interrogated, the remainder staying in the vehicle. Allen recounted how:

Very shortly after the Corporal had left with this man, I heard firing and the Corporal came back to tell me that the prisoner had started running away, in an effort to escape, and that he had had to shoot him. I went into the bush, to find that the said man was in fact dead.[31]

Allen and the corporal went back to the truck. Allen interrogated the prisoner given to him by the Home Guard, who seemed ready to talk, so Allen sent him off with the corporal. This time the corporal was warned to shoot near the man if he tried to escape, to give a warning shot before aiming to kill. Allen selected Chege Kahembi to take into the bush for questioning himself. Shortly after, he heard a shot from the corporal's direction, and then turned to see Chege making a dash into the bush. Allen called on Chege to halt, and when he carried on running, shot him dead. Allen claimed that an askari fired simultaneously, so they could not be sure who killed Chege. The corporal fired at the man's feet when he 'had shown signs of escaping'. Allen then decided they should leave.[32] He reported the shootings to his battalion that night, and the surviving three prisoners were released a day or two later.[33]

In many respects the witness statements confirmed this account. The most significant witness was Mwangi son of Mbari, the prisoner who survived the warning shot. He recalled events along similar lines, except that he implicated Allen in both shootings. Mwangi said that Allen and three askaris took the first prisoner, Kimani, into the bush and shot him. Allen then ordered him out of the truck, to begin his questioning: 'The accused said that all Kikuyu were Mau Mau and if I did not admit that I was a member that he would kill me.' Having been taken into the bush, the corporal fired a shot near his feet, then taking Chege some distance away, ordered him to watch what would happen. Mwangi saw Allen, the corporal and perhaps the Lance-Corporal shoot Chege dead. According to his version, 'At no time before he was shot did Chege attempt to escape.'[34]

These events happened in April 1953, before Erskine's arrival, in the period when shootings were widespread. Indeed, a statement provided by the DO of Chura division, John Cumber, elucidates just how

---

[31] *Ibid.*   [32] *Ibid.*   [33] *Ibid.*, exhibit E.   [34] *Ibid.*, 2–3.

unexceptional the killings of Kimani and Chege were in the early phase. Cumber attempted to justify the case by arguing that the shootings took place in a Special Area, allowing the killing of suspects who attempted to escape. Tellingly, he boasted how 'I know that there was general rejoicing among the loyal Kikuyu at the decease of Chege and Kimani. I have shot men in similar circumstances myself and have been considered to have done my duty.'[35] Cumber's statement is important not only for what it reveals about violence in the early phase. The inquiries into the shootings arose under Erskine's tenure in command. Alongside the Chuka massacre and the Griffiths court-martial, the incident revealed to General Erskine a disciplinary situation beyond his expectations. How the inquiries were handled portrays in essence the army's attitude towards abuses of civilians. The evidence suggests a growing desire to swat allegations away.

Peter Evans took his witness statements to the Kiambu police in early May. Inspector R. S. Wilkinson led the investigation, taking witness statements and examining the crime scene.[36] An inquest held by the Kiambu magistrate on 14 August called for the case to be heard in court.[37] The army and the Kenyan Attorney-General considered the matter, and decided that the army held jurisdiction because Allen was on active service when the offence occurred, and thus subject to the Army Act.[38] Exactly when the SIB began their work is unclear, as none of their records on the case are available. They may have left the investigation entirely to the police.

The summary of evidence hearing took place in Nairobi on 11, 17, 18 and 19 September 1953, overseen by ADALS Lieutenant-Colonel R. H. Cowell-Parker.[39] Most time was spent on questioning a single witness, Mwangi. He gave a statement and was asked 227 questions by Mr W. J. Parry, the accused's counsel. Curiously, the prosecution counsel declined to ask him a single question. Parry challenged several aspects of Mwangi's account, but focused intensely on the distance between him and Chege when the latter was shot dead. There were discrepancies in Mwangi's three statements on this point, yet the hearing ignored the fact that the witness feared for his life at the time, and was without a tape measure.[40] Allen directly disputed Mwangi's evidence:

---

[35] *Ibid.*, 36.   [36] *Ibid.*, 28–30.

[37] TNA, DO 35/5357: Letter from F. A. K. Harrison, Commonwealth Relations Office to V. C. Martin, Office of the High Commissioner for the United Kingdom, New Delhi, 26 September 1953.

[38] Bennett witness statement 2, citing Hanslope document CO 968/424: Letter from [illegible], War Office, to P. Rogers, Colonial Office, 12 September 1953.

[39] Sergeant Allen summary.   [40] *Ibid.*

I say Mwangi is deliberately lying when he said in his evidence in this Summary of Evidence that he saw Chege shot. From the spot where I first sat Chege down I could just see the figures of Mwangi and the Corporal Askari through the foliage. I was not present when Kimani was shot ... My interrogation methods that day had previously proved successful. I have had no previous cases of attempted escape. This area was a Special Area. I knew that I was required in such an area, after all other means had failed, to shoot to kill.[41]

The two askari NCOs gave statements supporting this version. Neither the askaris nor Sergeant Allen himself were subjected to cross-examination.[42] That the three accused persons were exempted from questioning, when the hearing gave Allen's lawyer 227 chances to discredit Mwangi, says a great deal about the quality of military justice in Kenya. Other evidence which may have weighed against Allen was missed by the investigation. Statements were never taken from the remaining askaris accompanying Allen, a passing Indian lorry driver and a passing government veterinary officer. At the summary hearing itself, Cowell-Parker deliberately prevented nine persons who had given witness statements from giving oral evidence and being cross-examined. He excluded them because the accused did not want them there, and because they could not be brought 'by reason of the loss of time involved'. These people included witnesses who supported Mwangi's statement.[43]

On 21 September GHQ issued a statement on the Allen case. Having read the proceedings and witness statements, Erskine decided that part of the evidence was false. He accepted Allen's explanations. GHQ's statement concluded: 'Sergeant Allen was doing his duty and the investigation leaves no stain on his character.'[44] Allen's defence rested on three core claims. First, his successful anti-Mau Mau activities in the Ndeiya location made him many enemies among the local Kikuyu. By implication, all the Kikuyu witnesses were conspiring to smear him.[45] Secondly, Allen argued that he killed Chege within the rules of engagement. Chege was a known Mau Mau ring-leader, running away in a Special Area.[46] The implication for Erskine to ponder here was that if a soldier could not kill in these circumstances, the whole military campaign in Kenya became impossible. Thirdly, Allen claimed that his own self-interest would have been served by killing Mwangi too. In allowing an eye-witness to live, he could not therefore have done anything wrong.[47] This precluded alternative reasons: pure error, or the desire to instil fear into

---

[41] *Ibid.*, 31.   [42] *Ibid.*, 33–4.   [43] *Ibid.*, 30a.

[44] 'Murder charge dismissed: Kenya allegations disproved', *The Times*, 22 September 1953, 6.

[45] Sergeant Allen summary, exhibit E.   [46] *Ibid.*, exhibit D.   [47] *Ibid.*, exhibit D.

Mwangi, who would then divulge information and spread fear of the army in the area by talking about the episode.

Of course, these are all hypothetical explanations. As Peter Evans later pointed out, a summary hearing is only supposed to allow the Commander-in-Chief to decide whether there is a prima facie case. If there is enough evidence, the officer must commit the case for trial by court-martial. The officer is not supposed to weigh the evidence. Yet this is precisely what General Erskine did.[48] Without question, the witness statements contain contradictions. Whether some of the evidence was false should not have tarnished all the evidence as such. The summary hearing received a witness statement from Miss Katherine Hurst, a barrister at Crichton Chambers, Nairobi. She claimed that Peter Evans told her in early May of his intention to use faked statements to get a European hanged. She also said, in corroboration, that 'It is within my knowledge that Evans was anti-British and anti-British security forces in Kenya.'[49] Miss Hurst never thought to bring the confession to anyone's attention until the summary proceedings had begun.

Knowing whether Evans really tried to frame Sergeant Allen or whether Miss Hurst was lying would have required them to be cross-examined in court. By this time Evans had been deported, much to the Kenya government's relief. Permitting a full court-martial meant taking an African's word as seriously as a European's, allowing an ardent critic of the government back into the country, and carefully examining the rules of engagement. General Erskine was unwilling to risk it.

Punishing Major Griffiths

Meanwhile, in mid-August Major Griffiths was transferred to the East Africa Training Centre.[50] A month later the military police held a successful identification parade of the patrol members at Langata, and interviewed additional witnesses.[51] G. C. Dockeray conducted a pathology report on a victim's skull at the request of Sergeant Barton.[52] On 26 October Griffiths was promoted to substantive major, a peculiar

---

[48] Evans, *Law and Disorder*, 218–19.   [49] *Ibid.*, 35.
[50] TNA, WO 32/21722: WO civil service briefing note for Secretary of State on Griffiths, signed T. L. Binney, 4 December 1953.
[51] TNA, WO 32/16103: Statement of Daudi s/o Maringa, 14 September 1953; Signed statement of Rueria s/o Samuel Ngeru, 15 September 1953; Signed statement of Roger Aubone Wilkinson, DC, Embu, 20 September 1953.
[52] TNA, WO 32/16103: Pathology report by G. C. Dockeray, Medical Research Laboratory, Nairobi, 23 September 1953.

decision given the growing understanding about his central role in the murders.[53] Three days before his promotion, GHQ informed the War Office that Griffiths had been placed under close arrest for murder.[54] Although inquiries initially focused upon events at Chuka, by the end of October the authorities discovered Griffiths's shooting of the forestry workers with a Bren gun.[55]

Despite the months-long work by the SIB, Erskine only informed the War Office that he was holding ten askaris potentially for another court-martial 'on [a] murder charge' in late November.[56] The Kenyan authorities had already told London they would await the outcome of the Griffiths trial before deciding whether to prosecute others.[57] Ultimately none of the askaris involved nor Hussein, Innes-Walker, Howard, Day or Evans faced justice. In February 1953 Governor Baring lamented his inability to bring criminals in the security forces fully to justice because of a lack of evidence.[58] Baring lacked the investigative capacity and large body of evidence accumulated by Erskine by the end of December 1953. Erskine decided that the imposition of justice would be selective – to send a message to the troops – rather than comprehensive, punishing all rule-breakers. Court-martialling Griffiths alone would show his 'intention to stop unjustifiable methods'.[59] The conviction of an individual soldier promised to deter others from committing similar acts, but also implied Griffiths's singularity in an effort to vindicate the army as a whole and find a scapegoat. Erskine could make justice selective because the decision on whether to prosecute was not removed from the military chain of command until the creation of the independent Army Prosecuting Authority in 1997.[60] In Kenya, crimes committed by the security forces were referred to the Army Legal Services for a decision on whether to court-martial, to hand the case to the civil authorities or to dismiss it.[61]

---

[53] TNA, WO 32/21722: Record sheet of Griffiths's service history, no date.
[54] TNA, WO 32/21722: Telegram from GHQ East Africa to War Office, 23 October 1953.
[55] TNA, WO 32/21722: Extract from DO dated 31 October 1953 from DALS East Africa to DALS War Office.
[56] TNA, WO 32/21722: Telegram from GHQ East Africa to War Office, 30 November 1953.
[57] TNA, CO 822/378: Telegram from Deputy Governor to the Secretary of State for the Colonies, 25 November 1953.
[58] TNA, CO 822/471: Telegram from Baring to the Colonial Secretary, 11 February 1953.
[59] TNA, WO 32/21722: Telegram from C-in-C to Adjutant-General, War Office, no date (probably late November 1953).
[60] Rubin, *Murder, Mutiny and the Military*, 27.
[61] Bennett witness statement 2, citing Hanslope document CAB 19/4 Vol. I: Record of the CSCCC, 31 May 1954.

Erskine was extremely annoyed when the court-martial acquitted Griffiths in late November. The verdict should never have been returned given the Army Legal Service's assessment that the evidence 'is quite clear as to which African Major Griffiths despatched', when the court found that the victim's identity was in doubt.[62] The Deputy Governor thought the acquittal 'due to improper exclusion of evidence of identification of the body and even more improper admission of hearsay defence evidence on this point'.[63] This was an abnormal outcome, when around 90 per cent were found guilty in courts-martial during this period.[64] We should remember that a court-martial is composed of brother officers. Were those on the panel trying to protect Griffiths from punishment for what they regarded as acceptable behaviour? Unfortunately for the historian the court's clerks were prevented from transcribing the panel's discussion on the verdict. Erskine debated the possibility of a retrial with the Attorney-General and kept Griffiths 'on the Command' while alternative charges were explored.[65] The military proceeded taking a formal Summary of Evidence on the Chuka massacre on 3 December. Erskine realised that 'a good many members of the public' opposed the improvements in discipline being pursued by himself and the Attorney-General, and many still 'openly approve beatings and torture'. He claimed that his 'campaign for decent behaviour [was] being prosecuted relentlessly'.[66] However, the failure to punish all those implicated in Chuka already suggested that Erskine's rhetoric rang hollow.

Erskine recognised his weak position when he decided to try Griffiths for a second time on a lesser charge in January 1954. A second acquittal could seriously jeopardise his authority. Reflecting this weakness, Major Clemas in 23 KAR noted 'a distinction between the formal and the real, that it was necessary to ignore three out of four infringements of discipline and then jump on the fourth'.[67] The military authorities perhaps believed they could enforce tough discipline if only a small number of soldiers refused to obey orders.[68] The weaknesses in military prosecution reflected those in the civilian world, where the courts repeatedly took the side of the security forces. Judges cared little that confessions

---

[62] TNA, WO 32/21722: Extract from DO dated 31 Oct 53 from DALS East Africa to DALS War Office.

[63] TNA, WO 32/21722: Telegram from Governor's Deputy (Crawford) to Baring (in London), 1 December 1953.

[64] French, *Military Identities*, 185.

[65] TNA, WO 32/21722: Telegram from C-in-C East Africa to AG, War Office, 1 December 1953.

[66] TNA, WO 32/21722: Telegram from Erskine to War Office, 3 December 1953.

[67] Cited in Clayton and Killingray, *Khaki and Blue*, 239–42.

[68] French, *Military Identities*, 200.

were produced under duress, therefore tacitly approving torture.[69]
A case in point were the light sentences handed down to Keates and
Ruben, from the Kenya Regiment and KPR, for beating Elijah Gideon
Njeru to death: they got a collective fine of £150.[70] Erskine merely
dismissed them from the forces.[71] He told London that he regretted his
inability to control civil cases.[72] This misrepresented the formal position in Kenya. Shortly after arriving, Erskine and the Kenyan Attorney-
General discussed how they would handle alleged crimes committed by
the security forces. In theory, they were subject to both civilian and
military law. They agreed that in all crimes committed by the army
(including the Kenya Regiment), the normal procedure would be for a
court-martial to take place.[73] So the suggestion that the Kenyan government prevented Erskine from reining in his own forces is false.
Ruben at least only received a fine for beating a man to death because
the army supported him.

Erskine understood there to be a balance in the violence needed to
fight the Mau Mau. Too much violence would be 'most harmful to
bringing the loyal Kikuyu to our side'. Too many restrictions on violence
risked that 'many officers will go very carefully when they would be
entitled to fire'. Erskine promised the VCIGS: 'Naturally I shall do my
best to correct this.'[74] This short letter concisely captures the army's
position in Kenya. General Erskine realised, in a way his predecessors
did not, that discipline and operational policy were inseparable. The
different responses to the Allen and the Griffiths cases demonstrate the
flexible attitude taken by Erskine to letting soldiers use enough violence
to crush the rebellion, but preventing them from committing genocide.
The cost of this pragmatism was impartial justice, which became deeply
politicised. And the violence against civilians was allowed to continue.

Restricting inquiries into military misconduct

General Erskine proposed a court of inquiry on 5 December.[75] Four
days later the Prime Minister, Winston Churchill, informed the War

---

[69] Anderson, *Histories of the Hanged*, 101.   [70] Evans, *Law and Disorder*, 267.
[71] TNA, CO 822/471: Telegram from Governor's Deputy to Secretary of State for the
     Colonies, 12 December 1953.
[72] TNA, WO 32/21722: Telegram from Erskine to AG, General Sir Cameron Nicholson,
     War Office, 9 December 1953.
[73] Bennett witness statement 2, citing Hanslope document CO 968/424: Letter from
     (illegible), War Office, to P. Rogers, Colonial Office, 12 September 1953.
[74] TNA, WO 276/524: Letter from Erskine to Lieutenant-General Sir Harold Redman,
     VCIGS, 28 October 1953.
[75] TNA, WO 32/21722: Letter from Erskine to AG, 5 December 1953.

Office that he favoured the idea, as long as it was held in closed session, with a summary report presented to the Commons. Churchill opposed 'such wide terms of reference as "the general conduct of the army in Kenya"'. Instead, the inquiry should focus on the Griffiths case, the KAR and any other specifics thought strictly necessary.[76] Erskine confirmed that there would be no 'general enquiry'; the purpose of the 'strictly limited' court was primarily to 'clear [the] good name of [the] Army quickly'.[77] The Cabinet in London agreed three closely defined terms of reference: monetary rewards, scoreboards and competition, announcing them in the Commons on 10 December.[78] Thus the authorities missed the only opportunity to fully comprehend the extent of the widespread beatings, torture and killings taking place in Kenya in the early phase, and whether the new Commander-in-Chief had succeeded in eliminating these practices. More important was the chance to improve the military's public image, as Erskine warned London about the perils inherent in a thorough inquiry:

I strongly recommend McLean and any others should enquire on the terms of reference already signalled by me, if an enquiry on such wide terms of ref as you suggest is made it would give a completely distorted picture unless all security forces are included. It would be almost certain to lead to enquiries concerning police since many members of Army mostly Kenya Regt served with police. You realise it would bring before court the Governor who was prior to my arrival the Commander-in-Chief not only in name but in fact. I recommend a Court of Enquiry on terms already signalled as a first step and a full enquiry if HMG wish as a second step. The first by its terms will not clash with the second. HMG should consider very carefully whether the second step may not do more harm than good.[79]

Consequently, Erskine received approval for limiting McLean to events after 1 June 1953.[80] The culpability of officers from the Governor down would be protected. When Labour MP Fenner Brockway created a 'minor stink' about an article in the Devons' regimental journal, mentioning cash prizes for kills, the War Office ensured that McLean questioned the battalion on the allegation. This was a minor expansion from the original terms of reference, as the Devons operated before June

---

[76] TNA, PREM 11/696: Telegram from Churchill to Secretary of State for War, 9 December 1953.
[77] TNA, WO 32/21722: Telegram from Erskine to AG, War Office, 9 December 1953.
[78] TNA, WO 32/21722: Telegram from Troopers to GHQ East Africa (AG to C-in-C), no date.
[79] TNA, WO 32/21722: Telegram from GHQ East Africa to War Office (Erskine to AG), 10 December 1953.
[80] TNA, WO 32/21722: Telegram from Troopers (AG) to C-in-C East Africa, no date.

1953.[81] There are grounds for questioning the McLean Inquiry's effect-iveness as a tool of investigation within the military disciplinary regime. The terms of reference prevented investigation into events prior to 1 June, and the court stopped witnesses from discussing early phase events.[82] Several active units were absent from the proceedings, namely the 1 Lancashire Fusiliers (the first British regular battalion in action), the East Africa Armoured Car Squadron and the 156 (East African) HAA (deployed as infantry). What might the inquiry have thereby missed? Although clearly only a single incident, the recollections of a national serviceman serving in the Lancashire Fusiliers illustrate the point that these absences affected the inquiry's findings. He remembered participating in night-time raids in Kenya:

We'd creep up overnight and then first thing in the morning we'd suddenly go rushing in banging on the doors with the butts of our rifles to get them all out to see if any Mau Mau were hiding in amongst them. We'd just smash our way in and drag them out and one bloke got hold of this African woman and he raped her. I thought 'Oh my God.' Another one shot an African dead he said he was attacking him and he wasn't, the bloke had no chance.[83]

Besides providing a minimum number of witnesses, commanders were required to call for volunteer witnesses and provide adequate time for them to come forward. Only six volunteers turned up, and none provided any startling revelations. Partly this was due to commanders failing to give the stipulated forty-eight hours' notice.[84] The thin red line may have closed in, as soldiers recognised that telling tales on men in their own units would make life difficult for the rest of their time in Kenya. The phrase 'not in my unit' was repeated by witnesses who admitted hearing rumours about abuses, yet remained elusive on the details.[85] The insur-gency's geography meant that units had less contact with one another than in conventional wars and therefore witnesses may indeed have known little. There were flaws with the questioning procedure at

---

[81] TNA, WO 32/21722: Telegram from Troopers to East Africa, Exclusive for Heyman from AG, no date; TNA, WO 32/21722: Letter from Heyman to McLean, 22 December 1953.

[82] TNA, WO 32/21720: McLean proceedings, 1 (Lt.-Col. A. D. B. Tree, GHQ); 19 (Major I. G. Jessop, 70 Infantry Brigade); 154 (Capt. F. Flory, 3 KAR); 211 (Lt.-Col. L. W. B. Evans, 5 KAR).

[83] NAM, Anonymous, typescript of unpublished work, NAM.2002–07–358–1.

[84] TNA, WO 32/21720: McLean proceedings, 55 (Lt.-Col. J. Cowell Bartlett, 23 KAR); 189 (Lt.-Col. E. H. W. Grimshaw, Royal Inniskilling Fusiliers).

[85] TNA, WO 32/21720: McLean proceedings, 97 (Major D. L. Lloyd, Royal Northumberland Fusiliers); 146 (Major R. E. Stockwell, 3 KAR); 160 (Lt.-Col. R. E. T. St. John, Royal Northumberland Fusiliers); 200 (Lt. G. E. M. Stephens, Royal Inniskilling Fusiliers).

the McLean Inquiry. Witnesses were asked leading questions intended to allow them to prove their virtue.[86] The senior NCOs interviewed, some with extensive combat experience, were patronised, only asked simplistic questions and not encouraged to expand on their points, as officers were.[87] On one occasion, Colonel Rimbault declared his deep admiration for a witness, hardly conducive to an impartial assessment of his role in the campaign, especially as the man in question commanded the notorious 'I Force' from the Kenya Regiment.[88]

The security forces were accused on many occasions of raping African women.[89] Captain Wigram revealed two allegations stood against askaris in 5 KAR for rape, but the court of inquiry failed to investigate them, preferring to move swiftly on to other topics.[90] Later, when another witness mentioned rape, the court replied 'That is not the sort of thing we are concerned with.'[91] The Deputy Assistant Provost Marshal, responsible for the military police in Kenya, considered rape a minor crime in the same category as theft.[92] Rape appeared in the same section of the Army Act as treason, murder and manslaughter.[93] His attitude must largely explain the failure to prosecute alleged rapists. Five additional rape cases are brought to light in the Hanslope files. Curiously, in all of these cases, the Attorney-General or his Deputy Public Prosecutor decided whether to prosecute, despite the alleged crimes being committed by soldiers. Rape was treated differently from other military offences, almost with a lack of interest. Discussing an alleged rape at Embu at a meeting of the CSCCC the Crown Counsel announced that he was unlikely to press for prosecution even though he had yet to receive the police report on the incident.[94] Investigations into alleged rapes committed by soldiers from 3 KAR and 23 KAR in July 1954, 5 KAR in

---

[86] TNA, WO 32/21720: McLean proceedings, 13 (Brig. J. R. H. Orr, 70 Infantry Brigade); 155 (Capt. F. Flory, 3 KAR).

[87] For example TNA, WO 32/21720: McLean proceedings, 177 (CSM J. Bailey, Royal Northumberland Fusiliers).

[88] TNA, WO 32/21720: McLean proceedings, 292 (Major N. M. C. Cooper, Kenya Regiment); G. Campbell, *The Charging Buffalo: A History of the Kenya Regiment* (London: Leo Cooper, 1986), 55–6, 59.

[89] M. S. Clough, *Mau Mau Memoirs: History, Memory, and Politics* (London: Lynne Rienner, 1998), 156; Elkins, *Britain's Gulag*, 247–8, 254.

[90] TNA, WO 32/21720: McLean proceedings, 261 (Capt. G. F. Wigram, Kenya Regiment).

[91] TNA, WO 32/21720: McLean proceedings, 316 (in response to Lt.-Col. D. H. Nott, 4 KAR).

[92] TNA, WO 32/21720: McLean proceedings, 350 (Major C. J. Dawson, Deputy Assistant Provost Marshal).

[93] Army Act, 1881, Section 41.

[94] Bennett witness statement 3, citing Hanslope document CAB 19/4 Vol. I: CSCCC minutes, 31 May 1954.

September and an alleged indecent assault by a Royal Electrical and Mechanical Engineers soldier on a child in May 1955 were also deemed fit for 'No Further Action'. As the minutes record, these cases may genuinely have rested on 'insufficient evidence'.[95] Besides the earlier allegations made at the McLean Inquiry and those made in oral history interviews, these five incidents must be weighed against the fact only three men were convicted for rape and one for indecent assault during the Emergency. That the authorities exhaustively investigated and prosecuted sexual offenders seems unlikely.

By December 1953 the army command in Kenya was more concerned with the effect that all these investigations were having on morale than with justice being done. An intelligence officer in GHQ wrote an appreciation on the likely impact of the inquiries on morale. He argued that Africans in the security forces wanted to kill Mau Mau and were incapable of understanding the need for evidence and other legal niceties. Prosecutions, such as that of Griffiths, were interpreted by all Africans (whether in the security forces, fence-sitters or Mau Mau) as a sign of government weakness. The paper concentrated on the reaction in the KAR battalions. An askari 'kills Mau Mau because that is the job his officer has told him to do. If he is prosecuted for doing this, he feels that he has been let down by his officer.' So prosecuting askaris risked destroying officer–man relations in the KAR. The assessment then discussed the implications of prosecuting officers: 'it is possible some will align themselves with the more extreme settler type, who have already helped financially'. There were three potential outcomes: some kind of mutiny, growing political divisions within the officer corps ('This division already exists') or 'work to rule'. The assessment warned that investigations alone threatened to produce these results, let alone prosecutions.[96]

When the Griffiths case and the McLean Inquiry were taking place, General Erskine was being clearly warned that further investigations might have disastrous consequences for the army, including mutiny. Accounts of the Kenya Emergency, and indeed those of many wars, often explain crimes against civilians with reference to racism. In the army in Kenya, racist attitudes about its soldiers' inability to understand basic rules were equally prominent. Even when prosecutions went ahead, the punishments imposed were less than draconian. Sergeant

---

[95] Bennett witness statement 3, citing Hanslope document CAB 19/4 Vol. I: CSCCC minutes, 12 July 1954, 10 August 1954, 26 July 1954, 15 November 1954, 6 September 1954, 1 November 1954, 6 June 1955, 8 August 1955.
[96] TNA, WO 276/184: Untitled memo, signed (illegible) Major, GSO2(Int) [General Staff Officer, Grade 2, intelligence], 5 December 1953.

Pearson and Private Taylor, two Kenya Regiment soldiers, were convicted by court-martial on 10 December for 'assaulting an African and maliciously burning a house and occasioning bodily harm', with Pearson alone further convicted for 'maliciously wounding an African'. Pearson's award for these activities was a year in prison, while Taylor was sentenced to nine months.[97]

By early January, Erskine's thinking on the balance between morale and justice had clarified. He wrote to the CIGS outlining his desire to increase military powers in the Reserves. He found that 'The challenge before shooting is a great handicap when dealing with a known gang.' He hoped that the Attorney-General would agree to a new Emergency Regulation, allowing officers to immediately declare anywhere a PA. The solution to situations such as the Allen case was not to investigate, or tighten the rules, but to allow soldiers to shoot anyone, anywhere.[98] Fortunately for people living in the Reserves the proposal never transpired.

Negotiated discipline in practice

There seems to have been a remarkable transformation in Erskine's attitude towards civilian casualties between June and December 1953. Altruism gave way to pragmatism. To fully comprehend the reasons why Erskine compromised, and what the consequences were in practice, we need to explore events from the bottom up, in addition to top-level policy-making.

Resistance to Erskine's orders

The position on chopping hands off corpses showed the ineffectiveness in implementing policy. This common practice was proscribed on 1 August 1953, but did not disappear as quickly as Erskine wished. Whether soldiers continued the practice because the hands assumed a trophy value, because it intimidated Kikuyu civilians or simply because it became a ritual must remain a speculative point.[99] The McLean Inquiry discovered seven instances since the prohibition came into effect where soldiers mutilated dead bodies because, in their own explanation, they lacked fingerprinting equipment.[100] Another four people complained about too

---

[97] TNA, WO 32/21721: Exhibit 22: List of cases brought to the notice of GHQ East Africa.

[98] TNA, WO 276/524: Letter from Erskine to Harding, 4 January 1954.

[99] Edgerton, *Mau Mau: An African Crucible*, 167; Waller, *Becoming Evil*, 207.

[100] TNA, WO 32/21720: McLean proceedings, 45 (2nd Lt. Tawney, 6 KAR); 123 (Sgt. M. R. N. Tetley, Kenya Regiment); 252 (Major J. Gordon, 5 KAR); 372 (Major C. M. Moir, Black Watch); 413 (Major N. F. Gordon-Wilson, The Buffs); 433 (Major D. N. Court, The Buffs); 453 (Lt. J. R. Marshall, Kenya Regiment).

few fingerprinting kits.[101] Several units improvised with stamp pads, mud or pens instead.[102] Two officers pleading ignorance about the new orders highlighted how easily soldiers could violate orders.[103] Indeed, 23 KAR's CO stated that his brigade (70) and the higher command were in dispute because the fingerprinting kits proved impractical.[104]

The McLean Inquiry provides evidence of how soldiers communicated to the higher commanders that there was a limit to the amount of interference they would tolerate. The KAR felt that all the inquiries and investigations were a waste of time.[105] Worse still, witnesses stated how 'carping criticisms' and 'legal quibbles' hampered operations and damaged morale.[106] These last two complaints came from the Kenya Regiment, as did others. Captain Franklin thought the courts-martial confused the troops to the extent that they lamentably required instruction on the rules of engagement prior to operations.[107] Captain Guy, the regiment's 'operational adjutant', believed that the Griffiths case and related press criticism adversely affected them more than any other unit.[108]

The settler community pressured army commanders to hold back their investigations. In a letter to Major-General Hinde in September 1953, the European Elected Members' Organization protested against investigations into the conduct of Major Sinclair-Scott. The settlers thought that these threatened 'a very considerable effect on the morale of the security forces', and drew attention to the 'very limited advantage which might be gained from over-emphasising the meticulous care taken by the authorities in their treatment of individual rebels'. If the authorities were too zealous they risked 'losing the complete loyalty of Officers and men in the field'.[109] The KAR chaplain claimed that the Griffiths

[101] TNA, WO 32/21720: McLean proceedings, 156 (WOPC Kitur, 3 KAR); 167 (Major P. Bulman, Royal Northumberland Fusiliers); 176 (2nd Lt. W. D. H. Smith, Royal Northumberland Fusiliers); 187 (Lt.-Col. E. H. W. Grimshaw, Royal Inniskilling Fusiliers).

[102] TNA, WO 32/21720: McLean proceedings, 160 (Lt.-Col. R. E. T. St. John, Royal Northumberland Fusiliers); 193 (Major P. M. Slane, Royal Inniskilling Fusiliers); 200 (Lt. G. E. M. Stephens, Royal Inniskilling Fusiliers).

[103] TNA, WO 32/21720: McLean proceedings, 336 (Capt. I. Grahame of Duntrune, 4 KAR); 368 (Major A. O. L. Lithgow, Black Watch).

[104] TNA, WO 32/21720: McLean proceedings, 50 (Lt.-Col. J. Cowell Bartlett, 23 KAR).

[105] TNA, WO 32/21720: McLean proceedings, 65 (Capt. R. J. Symonds, 23 KAR).

[106] TNA, WO 32/21720: McLean proceedings, 406 (Capt. J. W. Turnbull, Kenya Regiment); 296 (Major N. M. C. Cooper, Kenya Regiment).

[107] TNA, WO 32/21720: McLean proceedings, 299 (Capt. S. E. Franklin, Kenya Regiment).

[108] TNA, WO 32/21720: McLean proceedings, 291 (Capt. R. K. Guy, Kenya Regiment).

[109] ODRP: W. R. Hinde, MSS Afr.s.1580. Vol. I: Director of Operations Department correspondence, letter from Wilfred Havelock of the European Elected Members' Organization, to Hinde, 4 September 1953.

court-martial caused battalions to exercise extra caution in treating prisoners; but they viewed the McLean Inquiry as a witch hunt.[110] Lieutenant-Colonel Windeatt, commanding the Devons, said that the troops saw the inquiries as 'making an awful lot of fuss out of nothing, they are beginning to wonder what they are sent out here to do'.[111]

Lieutenant-General McLean publicly vindicated the army's behaviour in Kenya. However, apart from the revelations about hand severing, the full proceedings contradicted his announcement in two respects. First, McLean uncovered systematic torture in 7 KAR in November 1953 – months after Erskine came to Kenya and supposedly cleaned up army conduct. Erskine knew about the case in early December, but possibly not the details.[112] Captain H. D. Hilborne-Clarke, commanding the signal platoon, apparently oversaw the abuse of three persons, Ndrango, Mutu Manyori and Kanumbi, between about 4 and 16 November. The methods employed included beatings, burning, 'water treatment' and unspecified techniques. McLean criticised the 'very inadequate' summary of evidence taken against Hilborne-Clarke, and stated that the SIB were conducting a full investigation. McLean looked into the matter no further, but warned that other 7 KAR personnel could be implicated.[113] A Freedom of Information Act request for further evidence on the matter failed to produce any results.[114]

Beatings and intimidation

The second series of discoveries made by McLean, expunged from the final report, concerned beatings and intimidation inflicted by soldiers. This was hardly surprising, as accusations of mistreatment by the security forces could be heard in the special Emergency assize courts right up until the end of 1956.[115] The CO of 6 KAR thought that his troops 'will give a chap a cuff over the head or give him a bang with the [rifle] butt if they do not do what they are told'. He considered this only 'slightly rough handling' rather than deliberate brutality.[116] In 23 KAR's 'C' Company, Major Rawkins described the clips round the ear he had seen

---

[110] TNA, WO 32/21720: McLean proceedings, 270 (Rev. C. S. Jerome, KAR Chaplain Nanyuki).
[111] TNA, WO 32/21720: McLean proceedings, 438 (Lt.-Col. J. K. Windeatt, Devons).
[112] TNA, WO 32/21722: Telegram from Erskine to AG, 9 December 1953.
[113] TNA, WO 32/21722: McLean Court of Inquiry Report and Findings.
[114] Letter to the author from Mr M. A. Wight, AG Secretariat, Ministry of Defence, 20 September 2006.
[115] Anderson, 'The Battle of Dandora Swamp', 164.
[116] TNA, WO 32/21720: McLean proceedings, 27 (Lt.-Col. R. C. Glanville, 6 KAR).

administered to civilians as 'no beating worse than I got as a boy'.[117] Another officer from the same unit defined the common euphemism, 'rough handling': 'I would not call it beating up in the way I visualise a beating up. It was just that they were a little bit over easy with a stick or a rifle butt.'[118] These low-level beatings seemed common in December 1953, but less so than at the start of the Emergency, when they were widespread.[119] Several witnesses failed to see anything wrong in giving a troublesome African a good 'clip across the head' to 'wake a fellow up'.[120] Sergeant Robertson, facing allegations of beating a person in Nyeri district in May 1954, 'admitted to slapping the complainant but gave as his excuse that the African was truculent under interrogation and it appeared he endeavoured to strike him'. The court hearing into the affair was postponed in July because Robertson was busy on duty with his unit, and eventually dropped, apparently 'at the request of the complainant'.[121] A prosecution brought against Sergeant Merril for allegedly committing assault causing actual bodily harm on labourers in October 1954 was postponed and then dropped as part of the 1955 double amnesty.[122]

The Kenya Regiment Afrikaners achieved special notoriety for their rough and tough outlook.[123] One Kenya Regiment soldier working with the Black Watch, prone to knocking civilians about, was reprimanded and instructed to conform to Black Watch standards.[124] On the other hand, Captain Grahame freely confessed to having beaten suspects on the bottom with a stick: 'That I have done quite frequently.' In fact, he went on, 'other Europeans have done exactly the same and it was one of the best ways of getting information, but so far as torturing is concerned I know nothing of it'.[125] The distinction between beating and torture is far from axiomatic, but the army seemed to differentiate between them and generally considered a little beating judiciously applied more helpful

---

[117] TNA, WO 32/21720: McLean proceedings, 57 (Major H. F. Rawkins, 23 KAR).

[118] TNA, WO 32/21720: McLean proceedings, 65 (Capt. R. J. Symonds, 23 KAR).

[119] TNA, WO 32/21720: McLean proceedings, 258 (2nd Lt. R. E. Ginner, 5 KAR).

[120] TNA, WO 32/21720: McLean proceedings, 261 (Capt. G. F. Wigram, Kenya Regiment); 291 (Capt. R. K. Guy, Kenya Regiment); 72 (2nd Lt. J. Y. Ellis, 23 KAR).

[121] Bennett witness statement 3, citing Hanslope documents CAB 19/4 Vol. I: CSCCC minutes, 10 May 1954, 31 May 1954, 14 June 1954, 26 July 1954, 20 September 1954.

[122] Bennett witness statement 3, citing Hanslope documents CAB 19/4 Vol. I: CSCCC minutes, 20 December 1954, 10 January 1955, 24 January 1955.

[123] TNA, WO 32/21720: McLean proceedings, 296 (Major N. M. C. Cooper, Kenya Regiment).

[124] TNA, WO 32/21720: McLean proceedings, 360 (Lt.-Col. D. McN. C. Rose, Black Watch).

[125] TNA, WO 32/21720: McLean proceedings, 337 (Capt. I. Grahame of Duntrune, 4 KAR).

than harmful. The infliction of corporal punishment by soldiers must be considered within the context of the times. Although banned in the British metropolitan armed forces by 1907 and African colonial units by late 1946, corporal punishment remained widespread within Britain and East Africa.[126]

Another productive method for obtaining information during tactical interrogations rested in the art of terrifyingly convincing intimidation. Second Lieutenant Muir from the Kenya Regiment recalled interrogators grabbing victims by the scruff of their neck when threatening them;[127] 3 KAR's Major Topham allowed frightening a prisoner immediately after capture in order to obtain information, including 'any means of frightening him which did not amount to, speaking quite honestly, torturing or maiming or in any way really impairing his possibility of life'.[128] Captain Russell's account of how he frightened a prisoner without physically hurting him is illuminating:

> I decided that he would not divulge any information he had unless I frightened him. I decided to frighten him by firing a shot from my pistol. I quite deliberately took my pistol, put the chamber of the pistol against his left ear and knowing that the barrel protruded behind the man's head I fired one shot into a sack lying on the ground behind. The man was very frightened. Further questioning elicited no information at all and I decided then that the man knew nothing whatsoever about this gang.[129]

Effectively torture from this point on became a short step, an even shorter one when intelligence was desperately wanted. The beatings, intimidation and torture instigated by British forces seem to have come in response to the intelligence drought with, for example, Kenya Regiment commander Guy Campbell conceding that soldiers used torture to extract information while denying knowing about any specific instances.[130] That a battalion commander conceded that torture was taking place, and yet no investigation followed, reveals how military justice in Kenya worked.

---

[126] On the situation in the African colonial forces, see D. Killingray, '"The Rod of Empire": The Debate over Corporal Punishment in the British African Colonial Forces, 1888–1946', *Journal of African History*, 35 (1994), 201–16.

[127] TNA, WO 32/21720: McLean proceedings, 115 (2nd Lt. I. K. Muir, Kenya Regiment).

[128] TNA, WO 32/21720: McLean proceedings, 136, 138 (Major R. N. Topham, 3 KAR).

[129] TNA, WO 32/21720: McLean proceedings, 278 (Capt. H. C. Russell, 7 KAR).

[130] TNA, WO 32/21720: McLean proceedings, 284 (Lt.-Col. G. T. H. Campbell, Kenya Regiment).

Killings

Numerous other examples of abuses of civilians and prisoners occurred during Erskine's tenure as commander in Kenya, disproving the notion that he cleaned up the army's conduct.[131] At the end of June 1953 a Home Guard unit perpetrated one of the war's worst atrocities.[132] A few days after his son Thigiru was killed in a Mau Mau attack, Chief Njiri took revenge on the local population at Mununga Ridge. In a two-day orgy of death and destruction, around four hundred people were killed.[133] Leonard Gill recounts what his KAR patrol discovered when they came across the scene in the following days:

We heard about it two days later, and were shocked. Our Company Commander, Major John Bramston, took a Land Rover with me and a fellow Kenya Regiment Sergeant up to the area. Before going to see Njiri, we drove across the Erati River Valley and up onto the ridge. We had to drive round bodies left lying everywhere.[134]

Virginia Blakeslee, a missionary doctor in the area, also witnessed events. She remembered that Njiri sent KAR askaris, as well as Home Guards, stationed at his village to 'kill every man on the ridge'.[135] In Anderson's view, the massacre represented the state's willingness to use 'surrogates' to 'deploy terror and violence within a culture of impunity'.[136] Although correct about the use of surrogate forces given the Home Guard's involvement, this explanation ignores Blakeslee's accusation against the KAR. It seems the authorities completely failed to investigate the massacre or the KAR's role in blatantly disregarding the orders on correct conduct issued by GHQ only days before. Towards the end of July, 5 KAR killed three Home Guards, 'thinking them terrorists', this time in Embu.[137]

People were 'shot while attempting to escape' beyond the first phase, although most likely to a reduced extent. Situation reports for August 1953 record two people killed escaping by unspecified units, and four killed escaping by the police.[138] A Special Branch summary stated that

---

[131] Clayton, *Counter-Insurgency in Kenya*, 40; Anderson, *Histories of the Hanged*, 258.

[132] Branch, 'Loyalism during the Mau Mau Rebellion', 103.

[133] D. M. Anderson, 'Surrogates of the State: Collaboration and Atrocity in Kenya's Mau Mau War', in G. Kassimeris (ed.), *The Barbarisation of Warfare* (London: Hurst, 2006), 164–5.

[134] Gill, *Military Musings*, 90.

[135] H. V. Blakeslee, *Beyond the Kikuyu Curtain* (Chicago: Moody Press, 1956), 254.

[136] Anderson, 'Surrogates of the State', 167.

[137] TNA, WO 276/179: Signal from 70 Infantry Brigade, Nyeri, to Force Nairobi, 27 July 1953.

[138] TNA, WO 276/287: Sitreps 121 to 144, from Force Nairobi to London, 01–24 August 1953.

five Mau Mau captured in Thika were handed over to the police, who subsequently shot them dead when they 'attempted to escape'. A sceptical reader underlined the words 'and were shot dead', writing in the margin 'all five?'[139] Patrols shot dead others attempting to escape: one person in November 1953,[140] one in January 1954,[141] one in February[142] and the final recorded instance in April.[143] The COs of The Buffs and 23 KAR thought that the Mau Mau themselves adapted to the changing context, noting a sensible tendency for 'terrorists in action to put their hands up when cornered instead of trying to run away'.[144] A soldier performing his national service in the East African Service Corps arrived in Kenya in January 1954. Even at this stage, he recalled:

It was very difficult to know who was a terrorist and who wasn't; I mean there was very much a shoot to kill policy at one stage ... I used to mess with 23rd KAR, and in the early days of the Emergency it was quite common to lay out the previous night's kill outside the Mess, and I remember going down to have breakfast at Karatina, where the 23rd KAR were, and there were 27 dead bodies laid out, most of them with bullets through the head.[145]

All those shots in the head might suggest execution rather than death in combat. Thomas Cashmore was a DO who transferred to Thika in early 1954. One day a young Kenya Regiment private stopped by his house for a meal with him and an assistant officer. The private was furious because another Kenya Regiment man had just been acquitted at court-martial of sexually assaulting a young Kikuyu woman. The soldiers in the regiment knew he was guilty, and the private despised him for it. Cashmore recalled how 'no doubt the judgment was thought to be good for morale and welcomed by many in the regiment'.[146]

The Hanslope intelligence files further demonstrate how the security forces carried on shooting people 'attempting to escape', despite General Erskine's orders to the contrary. Between 2 June 1953 and 31 October 1955 at least fifty-nine people were shot attempting to escape, eighteen

[139] TNA, CO 822/373: SBFIS 15/53, 20 October 1953.
[140] TNA, WO 276/293: 49 Brigade sitrep, 13 November 1953.
[141] TNA, WO 276/294: 49 Brigade sitrep, 13 January 1954.
[142] TNA, WO 276/294: 49 Brigade sitrep, 20 February 1954.
[143] TNA, WO 276/295: 49 Brigade sitrep, 13 April 1954.
[144] KNA, VP/2/22: Nyeri DEC minutes, 18 March 1954.
[145] NAM, Anonymous, oral history interview, NAM.1996–09–82–24.
[146] Royal Commonwealth Society Collection (RCMS), Cambridge University Library: T. H. H. Cashmore, 'Kenya Days', by T. H. H. Cashmore, memoirs written between January 1992 and January 1995, RCMS 175.

of them shot dead by the army.[147] Although incomplete, these records support the view that abuses persisted under Erskine, albeit at a reduced level from the Emergency's opening months. Groups of people still managed to get themselves shot on occasion: in June 1953 a KAR unit shot dead '11 prisoners who tried to escape'.[148] During a sweep in Chura division in April 1954, six Africans were shot having failed to halt.[149] Reports seldom explained the reasons for opening fire – there was no requirement for them to do so. Surviving justifications are revealing. A military patrol killed a man who failed to halt in January 1954: 'examination of his papers stated him to be a Masai, but there is reason to believe he was either a Kikuyu or an Embu'.[150] The notion that all Kikuyu, Embu or Meru were fair game endured after direct instruction to treat these tribes humanely and with respect. Mau Mau were probably among those shot escaping. A combined Kenya Regiment–Home Guard patrol found a home-made pistol on a man they killed when he 'attempted to flee'.[151] Another report noted how a woman the Black Watch killed attempting to 'evade capture' was a 'scout': in other words, a legitimate target.[152] These justifications are rare. While the evidence cannot prove all those shot to be either innocent victims or legitimate targets, the casual approach to making such a distinction indicates that Erskine's efforts to impose tighter discipline were half-hearted and ineffective.

---

[147] Bennett witness statement 3, citing Hanslope documents INT 10/4/2/4A Vol. I: Schedule of incidents and operations connected with the Emergency in Central Province, no date; INT 10/4/2/4A Vol. I: Schedule of incidents and operations connected with the Emergency in Central Province for the fortnight ending 23 June 1953; INT 10/4/2/4A Vol. I: Schedule of incidents and operations connected with the Emergency in Central Province for the fortnight 19 June 1953 to 2 July 1953; INT 10/4/2/2A Vol. I: Rift Valley provincial intelligence summary, 29 September 1953; INT 10/4/2/4/6A Vol. II: Kiambu district intelligence summary, 23 January 1954, 24 April 1954, 7 May 1954, 14 May 1954, 12 June 1954. 19 June 1954; INT 10/4/2/6A Vol. II: Nairobi City district intelligence committee summary, 29 January 1954, 2 April 1954, 4 November 1955; INT 10/4/2/4/5A Vol. I: Meru district intelligence committee summary, 18 February 1954, 11 March 1954, 25 March 1954, 13 May 1954, 24 June 1954, 8 July 1954, 15 July 1954; INT 10/4/2/1/4A Vol. II: District intelligence committee summary, Kisumu no. 14/54, 31 July 1954.

[148] Bennett witness statement 3, citing Hanslope document INT 10/4/2/4A Vol. I: Schedule of incidents and operations connected with the Emergency in Central Province for the fortnight 19 June 1953 to 2 July 1953.

[149] Bennett witness statement 3, citing Hanslope document INT 10/4/2/4/6A Vol. II: Kiambu district intelligence summary, 24 April 1954.

[150] Bennett witness statement 3, citing Hanslope document INT 10/4/2/6A Vol. II: Nairobi City district intelligence committee summary, 29 January 1954.

[151] Bennett witness statement 3, citing Hanslope document INT 10/4/2/4/6A Vol. II: Kiambu district intelligence summary, 19 June 1954.

[152] Bennett witness statement 3, citing Hanslope document INT 10/4/2/4/5A Vol. I: Meru district intelligence committee summary, 24 June 1954.

When soldiers were accused of murder they could, as we have seen in chapter 5, find themselves in the dock, though the punishments meted out were very lenient. Prosecutions could fail, or be blocked, before reaching the courtroom. An official from the Nightwatchmen, Clerks and Shopworkers' Union lodged a formal complaint after he was shot during a raid on union offices in Nairobi in April 1954. The Attorney-General personally decided not to launch criminal proceedings.[153] In June an investigation began into the assault and murder of a man at the Kingaro Home Guard post, where Home Guard and Kenya Regiment men were implicated. By August the Deputy Public Prosecutor was warning the investigation might be protracted, as forty-seven witnesses were involved. However, General Erskine ruled out court-martial proceedings, due to 'insufficiently clear evidence'. He and the Governor agreed that no proceedings would be taken against the Home Guard men either.[154]

Continuing coercion against the civilian population

General Erskine continued a number of policies which directly inflicted suffering on the civilian population. Captain John Farr, a staff officer at GHQ in Nairobi from 1954, recalled how 'The first aim, obviously, was the elimination of the Mau Mau, and we didn't worry too much about what the political scene was going to be afterwards.'[155] Erskine presided over a number of harsh policies designed to crush the insurgency. Some of these methods were carried over from the first phase, whereas others were new. Three policies are considered here. First, the oldest of these was collective punishment, normally under the administration's control, but strongly supported by the army.[156] Second, the army participated in the revolutionary villagisation scheme and helped guard certain prisons and detention camps. Third, prisoner abuses carried on despite the efforts taken to improve discipline. These abuses can be considered an informal policy because the command repeatedly failed to take measures sufficient to stop them.

---

[153] Bennett witness statement 3, citing Hanslope documents CAB 19/4 Vol. I: CSCCC minutes, 10 May 1954, 28 June 1954.
[154] Bennett witness statement 3, citing Hanslope documents CAB 19/4 Vol. I: CSCCC minutes, 26 July 1954, 10 August 1954, 23 August 1954, 15 November 1954.
[155] British Library Sound Archive: J. H. Farr, oral history interview, C409/042/01–04.
[156] For the administration's role in collective punishment, see the material in TNA, CO 822/501.

Collective punishment

A standard policy for armies of occupation by the end of the Second World War, collective punishment enjoyed a long history in the British Empire.[157] In Kenya collective fines formed part of the normal law since the days of the colony's creation.[158] Collective punishment brought about resentment and bitterness in the populations affected, caused by a policy that required no evidence of individual culpability.[159] The policy was first imposed in relation to the Mau Mau on 4 April 1952 in the form of £2,500 fines against the Aguthi and Thengenge locations.[160] Fines and property confiscation were the normal punishments, with assets sometimes distributed to loyalist chiefs in reward for their support.

The situation changed in November 1952 when the government made it easier for DCs to seize livestock, transport and crops.[161] 5 KAR soon exercised these powers, launching Operation Cowboy on 9–10 November; they confiscated 4,000 cattle and 5,000 sheep and goats, in reprisal for Mau Mau activity in the Githathi area.[162] A few days later the Lancashire Fusiliers rounded up livestock in the Nyeri area because the inhabitants proved 'uncooperative and hostile' towards police investigations.[163] Force Nairobi reported that these seizures had an 'excellent effect', deterring Kikuyu from cooperating with the Mau Mau, as they feared incurring collective punishments.[164] On some occasions forced evictions accompanied the imposition of fines and confiscations. At the end of November the authorities restricted these removals to areas where 'disturbances' happened, 'save in exceptional circumstances'.[165] A punitive fine was effectively extended to the entire Kikuyu, Embu and Meru tribes in December when the government declared an Emergency tax.[166] Confiscations carried on throughout December; for example

---

[157] M. Levene, Introduction in M. Levene and P. Roberts (eds.), *The Massacre in History* (Oxford: Berghahn, 1999), 25.

[158] Evans, *Law and Disorder*, 23; Castro and Ettenger, 'Counterinsurgency and Socioeconomic Change', 74.

[159] Castro and Ettenger, 'Counterinsurgency and Socioeconomic Change', 75; M. P. K. Sorrenson, *Land Reform in the Kikuyu Country: A Study in Government Policy* (Oxford University Press, 1967), 106; Rawcliffe, *Struggle for Kenya*, 58.

[160] Anderson, *Histories of the Hanged*, 46.

[161] Heather, 'Counterinsurgency and Intelligence', 38.

[162] TNA, WO 305/259: 5 KAR Annual Historical Report, 9.

[163] Heather, 'Counterinsurgency and Intelligence', 39.

[164] TNA, WO 276/466: Jock Scott sitrep from Force Nairobi to Mideast, 13 November 1952.

[165] Percox, *Britain, Kenya and the Cold War*, 53.

[166] Heather, 'Counterinsurgency and Intelligence', 39; loyalist chiefs and the Home Guard were eventually exempted from the tax; see Elkins, *Britain's Gulag*, 72, 273.

residents near Muiga had over 500 animals taken from them when the bodies of two askaris were discovered.[167] Governor Baring 'disliked punishments of this nature', but thought removing Kikuyu from farms where crimes had taken place preferable to large-scale punitive sweeps.[168]

Apart from fines, confiscations and evictions the army helped implement severe restrictions on movement, including curfews, identity checks and travel limitations.[169] In response to a large volume of cattle thefts by Mau Mau, the government instituted a 'barren earth' policy in the mile strip around the Aberdares forest. The army supported this move, resulting in evictions and property destruction in the strip. A long ditch in the mile strip was dug by forced labour.[170] In the forests themselves, the army played an important role in pushing for large areas to be designated PAs. According to the pre-eminent expert on the Kikuyu people, 'thousands of Kikuyu families ... live and have their homes – albeit temporary homes – in the forest reserves'.[171] Whether innocent people were killed as a result or were moved out before offensives began is unknown.

Army participation in collective punishment endured into 1953. On 25 February, 23 KAR made raids in the Kiambu/Thika area, confiscating 170 cattle and 420 sheep and goats in retaliation for Mau Mau mutilation of cattle.[172] Over the next couple of days cattle were seized following a panga attack on a loyalist.[173] A *Daily Chronicle* article published in October summarised the extent of confiscations up to that point. The government seized 6,047 cattle, 15,033 sheep and goats, 28 bicycles, a car, 52 donkeys and six pigs from Kikuyu in the Reserves. Additionally they took 245 cattle, 15,846 sheep or goats, 79 bicycles and 50 donkeys from forest squatters and farm labourers.[174] Asked if the policy could be revoked, the Chief Native Commissioner reportedly argued that:

communal fines were imposed after the most careful consideration within the most limited area possible in cases where the inhabitants had condoned

---

[167] TNA, WO 276/466: Jock Scott sitrep from Force Nairobi to Mideast, 20 December 1952.
[168] TNA, CO 822/501: Note of a meeting held in the Secretary of State's room on 15 December 1952.
[169] Castro and Ettenger, 'Counterinsurgency and Socioeconomic Change', 69–72.
[170] Heather, 'Counterinsurgency and Intelligence', 94; Percox, 'British Counter-Insurgency', 76.
[171] L. S. B. Leakey, *Mau Mau and the Kikuyu* (London: Methuen, 1952), 72.
[172] TNA, WO 276/337: Northern Area sitreps, Norbrig Nairobi to Force Nairobi, no date, *c*. 26 February 1953.
[173] TNA, WO 276/467: Jock Scott sitrep from Force Nairobi to Mideast, 27 February 1953.
[174] TNA, CO 822/501: Excerpt from the *Daily Chronicle*, 9 October 1953.

or assisted in serious crimes or brutal murders, or had refused to give information concerning such crimes.[175]

Whether people actually possessed any information to give is questionable. The definition of 'the most limited area' also invites scepticism. For example, in February 1954 all Kikuyu within a ten-mile radius of a settler's house burnt down in Njoro were removed, totalling about 3,000 people.[176] In the run-up to Operation Anvil in April 1954, Erskine advocated stricter administrative measures in the Reserves, including land confiscation, reductions in food stocks and a clampdown on travel and trade.[177] Months later Erskine asked Hinde to increase punishments in the Reserves; he refused to believe that the inhabitants were not fully aware of Mau Mau movements in their areas. Surprisingly, perhaps, Erskine thought the administration too lenient:

I have found considerable reluctance on the part of the Administration to inflict severe punishments on the population for those offences and I regard them as offences of harbouring gangsters. I spoke to H.E. on the subject on the 4th November and told him that I did not think that we were being sufficiently tough and I was convinced that unless we were much more tough we should not break the passive wing. I found H.E. quite sympathetic and ready to lower his standards on collective punishments.[178]

According to Sorrenson's calculations, by May 1956 the number of confiscations approached 200 bicycles, 200 donkeys, 12,000 cattle and 44,000 sheep and goats; to this should be added huge fines, mass evictions and draconian work, travel and trade restrictions.[179]

Army involvement in villagisation

The second policy which directly aimed at coercing disloyal elements of the civilian population was villagisation. Because the conflict quickly descended into a civil war among the Kikuyu, a key government objective was to promote and expand loyalist factions.[180] Loyalism fluctuated, with Kikuyu switching their allegiances from Mau Mau to government as the conflict evolved.[181] Villagisation was promoted by influential government social science advisers L. S. B. Leakey and J. C. Carrothers,

---

[175] *Ibid.*   [176] Kanogo, *Squatters and the Roots of Mau Mau*, 142.
[177] Heather, 'Counterinsurgency and Intelligence', 136.
[178] ODRP: W. R. Hinde, MSS Afr.s.1580. Vol. III: Personal correspondence, letter from Erskine to Hinde, 5 November 1954.
[179] Sorrenson, *Land Reform*, 103.   [180] *Ibid.*, 108.
[181] Branch, 'Loyalism during the Mau Mau Rebellion', 8.

who drew inspiration from the Malaya experience.[182] Villagisation existed alongside other social measures such as food control, oath-cleansing ceremonies and land consolidation, largely controlled by the administration.[183] Another policy, forced labour, was utilised in constructing the new villages.[184]

The first moves towards forming small villages preceded government policy, when loyalists and Christians concentrated to protect themselves from Mau Mau attacks.[185] Major-General Hinde observed this trend in January 1954, advising Erskine to encourage concentration without moving too fast in enforcing it.[186] Following Anvil, the authorities put a special emphasis on 'compelling' inhabitants of Central Province living near the forest edge or where uncooperative to move into new villages. By the end of July, over half those in South Nyeri, Fort Hall, Embu and Meru were in villages, whereas in Kiambu the figure was only about 2 per cent.[187] Throughout 1954 the administration rapidly advanced the projects, each village typically housing up to 500 people, and located near a Home Guard post both to deter Mau Mau attacks and to monitor the inhabitants.[188] By October 1954, 259 villages were complete.[189]

The administration and Home Guard's pursuit of the policy facilitated a shift in focus for military operations. Army forces were reduced in the Reserves to undertake offensives in the forests.[190] This coincided with a 2,500 per cent expansion in the number of detainees in the camp system over 1954.[191] Villagisation was completed in October 1955.[192] Over one million people now lived in 845 villages, dominated by the Home Guard, administration, police and a limited number of soldiers.[193] In Lieutenant-General Lathbury's final assessment, the scheme proved 'highly successful from the security point of view'.[194] The policy proved highly effective in denying Mau Mau access to food supplies and their passive wing support base, restricting resupply,

[182] Castro and Ettenger, 'Counterinsurgency and Socioeconomic Change', 82.
[183] Ibid., 88; Branch, 'Loyalism during the Mau Mau Rebellion', 15; Sorrenson, Land Reform, vii, 107.
[184] Castro and Ettenger, 'Counterinsurgency and Socioeconomic Change', 78–9.
[185] Ibid., 83.
[186] ODRP, W. R. Hinde, MSS Afr.s.1580. Vol. I: Director of Operations Department correspondence, Memo to C-in-C from Hinde, 7 January 1954.
[187] IWMD, Erskine papers, Report to the Secretary of State for War, The Kenya Emergency, signed Erskine, 2 May 1955, paras. 70–5.
[188] Branch, 'Loyalism during the Mau Mau Rebellion', 153–4.
[189] Heather, 'Counterinsurgency and Intelligence', 181.   [190] Ibid., 179.
[191] Elkins, Britain's Gulag, 131.   [192] Sorrenson, Land Reform, 112.
[193] Heather, 'Counterinsurgency and Intelligence', 271.
[194] TNA, WO 236/20: Lathbury's final report, 14 December 1956, para. 5.

communications and recruitment.[195] Villagisation was thought to promote government values and act as the first step in a longer-term programme of socio-economic development.[196]

There are grounds for questioning how far the villages contributed towards social progress. The inhabitants supposedly enjoyed extended community activities such as farming support, women's groups, youth clubs and sports teams.[197] One 3 KAR officer thought the Kikuyu welcomed the new villages with their 'creature comforts'.[198] An officer in 5 KAR remembered that after initial dissatisfaction, people soon appreciated the protection and 'accepted it quite happily'.[199] However, Elkins condemns the villages for being part of a bigger 'bogus and largely nonperforming program of liberal reform'.[200] She argues that the liberal paternalists in the administration's wish to reform the Kikuyu was well meaning, but ultimately compromised.[201] Rawcliffe attributed the failure to the overwhelming influence of settlers bent on punishment rather than persuasion.[202]

There were numerous disadvantages to living in the villages. The distinction between 'reward' and 'punitive' villages meant that those placed in the latter type were basically in a form of concentration camp. The security forces had physically to compel people into the new villages.[203] Compulsory communal labour formed part of the daily routine.[204] A 23 KAR officer recalled that people were 'pretty peeved' at being removed from homes they had lived in for many years. The villages were far more concentrated than traditional habitations in Kenya.[205] Health provisions often proved woefully inadequate. Crowding worsened sanitation problems, compounded by the fact that few villages had any medical facilities.[206] High infant mortality was another major issue, and in June 1956 the administration in Kiambu reported a 'starvation problem' in some villages.[207] The villages were largely occupied by children, women and the elderly, as the men were either working in the towns, in the forest, in detention or dead.[208] They became easy

---

[195] Castro and Ettenger, 'Counterinsurgency and Socioeconomic Change', 81, 88; Heather, 'Counterinsurgency and Intelligence', 209.
[196] Castro and Ettenger, 'Counterinsurgency and Socioeconomic Change', 82.
[197] Ibid., 86.   [198] IWMSA, T. G. Wilkinson, 10082/2.
[199] IWMSA, P. H. W. Brind, 10089/2.   [200] Elkins, Britain's Gulag, 119.
[201] C. Elkins, 'The Struggle for Mau Mau Rehabilitation in Late Colonial Kenya', International Journal of African Historical Studies, 33 (2000), 25–57.
[202] Rawcliffe, Struggle for Kenya, 109.   [203] Ibid., 83.
[204] Branch, 'Loyalism during the Mau Mau Rebellion', 155; Elkins, Britain's Gulag, 242.
[205] IWMSA, A. L. K. Liddle, 10091/4.
[206] Castro and Ettenger, 'Counterinsurgency and Socioeconomic Change', 85.
[207] Branch, 'Loyalism during the Mau Mau Rebellion', 154.
[208] Castro and Ettenger, 'Counterinsurgency and Socioeconomic Change', 84.

targets for the unscrupulous Home Guards watching over them, who were accused of 'routine sexual assaults'.[209] British soldiers may have committed rape and assault of women in the villages, according to interviews conducted with victims fifty years later.[210]

In sum, the villages inflicted great suffering on the Kikuyu population in an effort to coerce them into supporting the government instead of the Mau Mau.[211] Although the army played a peripheral part in executing the policy, Erskine advocated it, and even called for a more drastic implementation. The army needed villagisation in order to concentrate on destroying the gangs in the forests; thus the sufferings imposed should be considered partly the army's responsibility in a holistic understanding of the campaign's strategy.

Abusing prisoners

The huge network of prisons and detention camps in Kenya was the responsibility of the administration. However, the army was involved to an extent. The large numbers involved strained the detention system, prompting East Africa Command to deploy Pioneer Corps soldiers as warders at Mackinnon Road and Thika camps, a role later assumed by the RAF Regiment.[212] From June until October 1954 a company of 26 KAR guarded prisoners at the Manyani detention camp, as did 6 KAR later on.[213] The army remained at Manyani until at least 1955.[214] General Erskine had pressed for the expansion of Thika prison into a camp, and seconded a staff officer to advise the Prisons Department on the external defence of camps.[215] At least twenty-seven Kenya Regiment soldiers were seconded to the Prisons Department to act as warders, advise on external camp defences and train African warders.[216]

A soldier in 1 Royal Northumberland Fusiliers recalled his company performing guard duty on a train to McKinnon Road camp; soldiers

[209] Elkins, 'Detention and Rehabilitation during the Mau Mau Emergency', 11.
[210] BBC 2 television programme, *Correspondent: White Terror* broadcast 17 November 2002, reporter John McGhie, editor Karen O'Connor.
[211] Elkins, *Britain's Gulag*, 252.
[212] Bennett witness statement 3, citing Hanslope documents Chief Secretary, Vol. I: 40A, War Council minutes, 15 June 1954, WAR/C/MIN.23; Chief Secretary, Vol. I: 40A, War Council minutes, 25 May 1954, WAR/C/MIN.17.
[213] ODRP, P. Thompson, History of 26 KAR during the Emergency, MSS Afr. 1715.
[214] TNA, CO 822/775: Disposal of surrendered terrorists, Memorandum by the Emergency Joint Staff, 17 January 1955.
[215] Bennett witness statement 3, citing Hanslope document Chief Secretary, Vol. II: 40A, War Council minutes, 21 September 1954, WAR/C/MIN.48.
[216] Bennett witness statement 3, citing Hanslope document Chief Secretary, Vol. III: 40A, War Council minutes, 26 October 1954, WAR/C/MIN.58.

robbed cash and watches from prisoners, as did men from the Black Watch. In his words: 'everyone was doing it'.[217] Soldiers encountered opportunities to commit crimes against prisoners before they entered the detention system, shortly after capture. For this reason the Command attempted to place limits on the time a unit could hold prisoners before handing them to the police. These rules were frequently ignored. In August 1954 the Chief of Staff, Major-General Heyman, rebuked the brigades for holding surrendered prisoners 'for some considerable time', in certain cases up to five days.[218] Soldiers admit blatantly ignoring orders aimed at taking prisoners. An NCO recalled putting an oath-taker 'out of his misery'.[219] In an oral history interview, an officer with the Royal Inniskillings in Kenya in 1953–4 talked about having taken prisoners:

They were all dead by the time we'd finished with them. You didn't capture too many Mau Mau; a waste of money. Shouldn't say that should I, that's not politically correct ... The thing was, in Kenya you never, or very occasionally took prisoners because you didn't ... treachery; and they could be very treacherous if they had a weapon.[220]

Leonard Gill's commanders Bramston and Harris often took into the forest prisoners who never returned. They were never punished for these murders. Gill himself lectured his askaris on the importance of taking prisoners. The talk fell on deaf ears, and as he often lost sight of his men during skirmishes in the forest, the killing of prisoners could not always be prevented.[221] Judging from the anecdotal evidence, mistreatment of prisoners occurred more often than murder. A Kenya Regiment sergeant attached to 4 KAR used torture to obtain information. Iain Grahame, an officer in the same unit, sheds light on the great influence exercised by the Kenya Regiment on those with little experience in Kenya:

Three months back I could not possibly have sympathised with his point of view, but a lot of things had happened in the last three months, and now, somehow, it seemed different. I was beginning to understand and to share in that fanatical love of Kenya which characterised the best type of Kenya settler and often made him so unscrupulous in trying to achieve his aim.[222]

When the army interrogated prisoners with a view to finding Mau Mau hides in the forests, they 'did not always adhere to the principles of the

---

[217] IWMSA, T. L. Hewitson, 11159/3.

[218] TNA, WO 276/430: Letter from Major-General Heyman, to 39, 49 and 70 Bdes, 17 August 1954.

[219] IWMSA, J. F. Pickering, 21054/3.   [220] IWMSA, G. L. Potts, 23213/19.

[221] Gill, *Military Musings*, 49, 61.

[222] I. Grahame, *Jambo Effendi: Seven Years with The King's African Rifles* (London: J. A. Allen & Co., 1966), 46.

Geneva Convention'.[223] Sometimes threats sufficed instead of actual physical abuse.[224] An officer who worked with pseudo-gangs acknowledged that pseudos were threatened, remaining rather elusive on the details.[225] Officially, Mau Mau insurgents who were turned into pseudo-gang members were not required to appear before a magistrate to state their willingness to assist the security forces. The government insisted that only volunteers ever proved of any value, but as there was no oversight of how their cooperation was secured, threats and intimidation may have been common.[226]

Taken together, these numerous examples suggest that the informal policy of terrorising the population continued after Erskine arrived in Kenya. The government and army Command certainly knew what was happening and seemed unwilling to take sufficient steps to halt the abuses. A July 1954 report on interrogation methods in Meru district sheds light on the interrogation methods used:

The occasional beating is administered in the form of a tanning on the backside in a cold and calculated manner, and above all without any rancour ... Sometimes initial interrogations may be unproductive, and it is found necessary to provoke an incident in order to secure the first witnesses. This is done by going to work on the family of a known gangster away from home. His hut is destroyed, his family – always first oathers – are given the maximum sentence, crops are destroyed and stock impounded. Reaction of some sort is usually swift, and from the resulting incident the first witnesses may be obtained.[227]

The above paper was a formal military report acknowledging assaults on prisoners and the desire to provoke Mau Mau action by harming civilians. Such practices hardly conform to the orthodox understanding of British restraint in counter-insurgency. Whether beatings were always in fact administered 'without any rancour' seems unlikely.

'Severe repressive measures' and the army in Kenya

Under General Erskine the army's fundamental approach to defeating the Mau Mau went unchanged. The continuities can clearly be traced back to the Emergency's opening months, and indeed back into Britain's colonial past. Collective punishment, inflicting pain on the whole tribe because the state refused to distinguish between innocent and guilty,

---

[223] *Ibid.*, 51.   [224] L. Gill, *More Military Musings* (Victoria, BC: Trafford, 2004), 4.

[225] IWMSA, Anonymous, 11162/3.

[226] TNA, CO 822/776: Telegram from Acting Governor to Secretary of State for the Colonies, 14 May 1956.

[227] ODRP, W. R. Hinde, MSS Afr.s.1580. Vol. II: personal correspondence, Appendix 'A' to Paper on Meru Interrogation Teams, compiled by CPEC, Nyeri, 5 July 1954.

remained the hallmark policy. As the Emergency dragged on, the security forces took less and less interest in attempting to separate guilty from innocent. Many people fighting the Mau Mau, including many men in the British Army, convinced themselves that all Kikuyu, Embu and Meru were contributing to the rebellion. That such a totalising mentality should prevail so soon after the Second World War is hardly surprising. What is surprising is that an army which prided itself on being better than the Germans and Japanese came to compromise its own standards.

In June 1953 General Erskine set out high moral standards for the army in Kenya. He sincerely wanted to change the widespread brutality evident when he arrived. The McLean Inquiry and the investigations into 5 KAR, 7 KAR and the Kenya Regiment changed his thinking about what was possible. Through these investigations and trials the army communicated to General Erskine the need for a compromised settlement on appropriate behaviour towards civilians and prisoners. At first Erskine tried to impose his way through prosecutions. He failed when his subordinates failed to investigate military crimes properly and when they acquitted Major Griffiths. The general would assert his authority in seeing Griffiths eventually convicted and imprisoned for his horrific murders. But the signals were, by December 1953, quite clear. Erskine had to choose between impartial military justice or damaged military morale, threatening his ability to conduct the campaign. Erskine chose to negotiate, and thus politicise, military justice and discipline. His precise reasoning is a mystery.

As a consequence, numerous military crimes against civilians went unpunished. In many cases, allegations were levied which went unproven in the courts. By protecting those involved in the Chuka massacre, Sergeant Allen and his askaris, and those accused of rape, murder, beatings and torture at the McLean Inquiry and elsewhere, General Erskine prevented a mutiny in the security forces. He also denied the British Army an opportunity to clear its name.

9 'An essential part of the campaign': civil-military alliances

In the fight against the Mau Mau, the British Army in Kenya worked alongside civilians on a daily basis. These politicians, administration officials, policemen and settlers all had their own political agendas, which threatened to clash with the army's goals. As we have seen, the common desire to crush the rebellion quickly and formalised cooperation through the committees tended to minimise disputes. This book is concerned with exploring how the army used force to defeat Mau Mau, so we need to move beyond the institutions to examine policy implementation. Some of the policies explored in this chapter have been analysed as contributing towards restraint or coercive force. Here policies are analysed for a distinct purpose: to assess how army behaviour was shaped by external groups, and how the army in turn influenced civilians.

Each policy area is analysed with reference to three modes of interaction: civilian control, military influence and consensus. In the first case, a civilian group imposed its view on the army and decisively affected policy. In the second, the military influenced a civilian group to behave in a certain way, thus changing policy. In the third category, policy was discussed and a consensus reached between the military and one or more civilian group. By applying this conceptual device to each policy area in turn, the army's political power and degree of subjection to civilian control may be understood in practice. A wide range of policy fields could be explored in this manner. This book restricts itself to the three most salient fields for the campaign in Kenya from 1952 to 1956: intelligence, administration and the use of force. In the intelligence arena, the police Special Branch dominated, but the army sought to ensure its interests by meshing the police and military intelligence structures together. Even though the police broadly controlled intelligence-gathering, the army assumed primacy in exploiting the product, using this higher-status position to pressurise the police to collect intelligence in a form soldiers deemed suitable. Special forces teams and pseudo-gangs effectively merged intelligence-gathering and exploitation in independent, self-sustaining units. The police and army both ran their own teams, but these played a relatively minor role in the overall strategy until 1955.

The army wanted to exert sustained pressure on the Kikuyu population, and to encourage loyalism in order to defeat Mau Mau. As such, the military frequently intervened in what were, strictly speaking, administration policy areas. The army supported Home Guard expansion and assisted them through training and joint operations designed to augment their offensive capability. The army advocated population control measures and helped the administration enforce them. In denying food to the insurgents, the army occasionally advocated tighter food control than DOs, and actively pushed the policy's extension. Finally, the chapter analyses military policy itself. In terms of offensive operations, soldiers were willing to mount small patrols at the request of civilians, but when planning and conducting large-scale operations stayed firmly in command. In this field, the army were trusted by their civilian masters to conduct a core professional activity without external interference. During the Emergency the British Army operated with minimal government supervision. When it did intervene the Cabinet tended to support the army, and East Africa Command exerted its own potent political influence on counterparts in Kenya. Cooperation was granted when intensified military effectiveness was promised, as in the intelligence realm, but soldiers preserved their autonomy when they thought civilians were mistaken.

Intelligence

For the first few months, the army, police and administration maintained their own separate intelligence systems. But the potential for squabbling and duplicated efforts was quickly thwarted and a remarkable degree of cooperation achieved. While existing studies emphasise the central importance of formalised structures in bringing about such harmony, this chapter argues that military necessity and a shared purpose forged close relationships. The core intelligence-gathering methods in Kenya were screening, interrogations and informers. All three required the army to collaborate with at least one civilian partner organisation to produce useable intelligence suitable for launching operations. And this was the army's highest priority – to locate and destroy the Mau Mau gangs. Infighting with the other organisations and preserving intelligence autonomy could only hinder these efforts. Collaboration, by contrast, produced results.

Intelligence collection and analysis

Captured Mau Mau papers were the least prominent source of information for the security forces. In December 1953 a Buffs patrol encountered a hide containing a large amount of documents and a printing machine. These papers were rated as being 'exceedingly valuable'.[1] The Royal Northumberland Fusiliers recovered 'two hides and valuable documents', also without stating their impact.[2] Conversely, documents obtained in South Nyeri district indicated where a gang meeting was scheduled to take place, and identified a previously unknown leader and his area of responsibility.[3] A lucky patrol captured a Mau Mau cameraman in Fort Hall, and rather than documents, found five spools of film showing members of General Matenjagua's gang.[4] So there is evidence that documentary sources gave the security forces at least some useful intelligence. The quantity of documents captured rose in 1955 and 1956, and informed the security forces about Mau Mau membership, records of movements and order of battle.[5]

Screening comprised a major security policy during the Emergency and required cooperation from the administration, police and army to function efficiently. By November 1953 the security forces had made 147,830 arrests for screening.[6] The standard procedure was for the army to cordon an area, the police to arrest suspects for screening, and the administration to question suspects with the aid of Special Branch, Home Guard, local chiefs and headmen, MIOs and hooded informers. Screening operations took place in the field – in villages, towns and on farms – and in detention camps. The term referred to two objectives. For those running the detention camps, screening formed part of a rehabilitation process whereby all detainees were forced to confess. These forced confessions sought to purge the infected mind and usher in a psychologically renewed life. For the police, Home Guard and army, screening meant a form of mass interrogation, where everybody caught in the cordon would be questioned. The questioning encompassed both political loyalties (Mau Mau or pro-government), and knowledge about

---

[1] KNA, VP/9/9: Nyeri district weekly intelligence report, 3–9 December 1953.

[2] TNA, WO 305/211: Royal Northumberland Fusiliers historical record, 1 April 1954 to 1 April 1955, entry for 22 December 1954.

[3] KNA, VP/9/9: South Nyeri Reserve district intelligence committee summaries for 20–26 November 1954 and 4–10 December 1954.

[4] TNA, CO 822/373: SBFIS 11/53, 12–25 August 1953.

[5] For examples of translated captured documents, see TNA, WO 276/376 and WO 276/412.

[6] Bennett witness statement 3, citing Hanslope document CO 968/266: Civil servant's minute, signature illegible, 15 December 1953.

gangs in the area. So in practice there was substantial overlap between screening and interrogation. Many people found themselves screened on numerous occasions. A memorandum for the War Council confirmed the evidence obtained by screening was inadmissible in court, as such 'confessions' were 'not voluntary'.[7]

There is emerging evidence that the army participated in screening in the camps. Previously, it had been assumed the army only gathered intelligence for operational purposes outside the detention camps. A few indicative examples show how this understanding needs to be revised. In August 1954, two army FIAs were temporarily sent to serve on the interrogation teams at Manyani screening camp. The FIAs worked as 'recorders' alongside six 'crackers'.[8] Another document explains what these terms meant. After preliminary sorting into black, grey and white categories by the Home Guard, short dossiers on suspects were compiled. A Mr McLeod then 'reduces these down to a workable percentage (about 2 per cent) of customers likely to merit his attention. These are then handed over to the "crackers" to prepare them for the recorders who in turn record and pass the information so gleaned to Mr. McLeod to use and disseminate.'[9] This document thus suggests military involvement in a systematic process designed at softening up suspects during interrogation in a screening camp.

Major Harington, the PMIO for the Rift Valley, described the screening teams as 'One of our main sources of intelligence'. The army briefed all teams on the type of information they needed.[10] Rift Valley Province Special Branch laid out eight categories of information which screening should obtain. They wanted to know about the names of gang leaders, transit routes used by gangs and so forth. Any intelligence gleaned was passed via Special Branch in Nakuru to the DMIO and PMIO officers.[11] During January 1953, Operation Yellow Hackle screened about 500 people in the Wonjohi Valley, leading to 250 detentions. On 15 January, the native locations in Nakuru were subjected to screening, with about 2,700 undergoing the process, resulting in

[7] Bennett witness statement 3, citing Hanslope document Chief Secretary, Vol. VIII: 40B: Prosecution of detainees – C.I.D. investigations. Memorandum by the Minister for Defence, WAR/C.710, 11 August 1955.

[8] Bennett witness statement 2, citing Hanslope document AA 45/26/3/2A Vol. I: Letter from Secretary for Defence to Secretary for African Affairs, 30 August 1954.

[9] Bennett witness statement 2, citing Hanslope document AA 45/26/3/2A Vol. I: Letter from Col. T. H. Henfrey to Minister for African Affairs, 11 August 1954.

[10] TNA, WO 276/404: Letter from Major J. T. Harington, PMIO Rift Valley Province, to Special Branch Rift Valley Province headquarters, 7 November 1953.

[11] Bennett witness statement 2, citing Hanslope document: SEC 5, Notes for Screening Teams, Special Branch Rift Valley Province, Nakuru, 23 October 1953.

350 detentions.[12] On 5 July Major Willcocks of the 1 Devons led another such operation in Nakuru, assisted by the KPR, East Africa Training Centre troops, local Home Guards and the 'Township Force'.[13]

A situation report from August stated that the Devons, 5 KAR and the police cordoned and screened Karatina, placing twenty-one under arrest, including 'murderer one oath administrator members of gang [sic]'.[14] Throughout October the 1 Royal Inniskillings, the police and the Home Guard screened hundreds in Nairobi.[15] Sometimes the military ran the screening – such as Operation Hoover in Kahaha, organised by Captain Frank Kitson.[16] Military personnel also integrated into civilian teams – Meru district lent Kenya Regiment men from their own interrogation teams to screen labour in Nanyuki.[17]

As noted in earlier chapters, the screening teams were notoriously brutal. A telegram from Governor Baring to London in January 1955 referred to the immunity from prosecution for 'One Kenya Regiment Sergeant and one Field Intelligence Assistant, assault by beating up and burning of two Africans during screening operations on 19 September 1954'.[18] Their competence also came into question at times. The team based in Kericho district were sent back to Kiambu after the police received allegations of bribery and assault. The DC ensured that the replacement team worked under closer supervision.[19] Months later in the same district, the team gathered an intelligence product out of keeping with expectations. The DC opined how 'the proportion of "clean" Kikuyu is disturbingly high', and recruited new screeners who could find the desired result.[20]

The committee system thus failed to weed out such distortions of the intelligence cycle, where the product was made to fit preconceptions. However, they were at least a forum for coordinating screening operations. In December 1955 the Senior Assistant Commissioner of Police and the Commander of 70 Brigade agreed on multiple screening

---

[12] TNA, WO 276/378: Jock Scott intelligence summary, 21 January 1953.
[13] TNA, WO 276/453: 'B' Company 1st Devon Operations Order no. 4. Code Word – Op 'Clean Up', 4 July 1953.
[14] TNA, WO 276/291: 39 Infantry Brigade operational sitrep, 16 August 1953.
[15] TNA, WO 276/342: 1 Royal Inniskillings war diary, October 1953.
[16] TNA, WO 276/437: 39 Infantry Brigade Jock Scott operational instruction no. 21, 30 July 1954.
[17] Bennett witness statement 2, citing Hanslope document EMER 45/69/2A: CPEC, Post Phase II Operations, October 1954–April 1955.
[18] Bennett witness statement 2, citing Hanslope document E 16/3/8A: Telegram from Baring to Secretary of State for the Colonies, 17 January 1955.
[19] KNA, PC/NKU/2/1/23: Monthly intelligence report – Kericho, from DC Kericho to PC Nyanza, 12 November 1953.
[20] KNA, PC/NKU/2/1/23: Monthly intelligence report – Kericho, from DC Kericho to PC Nyanza, 7 April 1954.

operations throughout Central Province during a committee meeting.[21] The committees permitted those involved to comment on the *modus operandi*. The commander of 70 Brigade complained about screening arrangements in Othaya to the CPEC, who referred the matter to the appropriate DEC for resolution.[22] The commander of 39 Brigade informed the committee his troops wished to know the fate of those they picked up during screening. Following his request, the DCs and Special Branch told brigade commanders the details of those arrested, such as their being placed on a detention order.[23] The committees thus helped in the practical implementation of screening and in minimising frictions between the army and civil powers by resolving complaints.

A third source of intelligence on the insurgency came from interrogating suspects, either those detained on screening or captured during offensive operations. The evidence shows a rising quantity and quality of this source in the second half of 1953 and throughout 1954. By August 1953 an FIA reported that interrogations had stated that Dedan Kimathi commanded Mau Mau forces in the Aberdares and on Mount Kenya, and provided details on the gang structures in these areas.[24] An East Africa Command analysis of an interrogation report, 'believed to be reliable', elaborated on Kimathi's command hierarchy, stressing the links between forest gangs and a support organisation in the Reserves. The importance attached to disseminating this single interrogation report to all military and police units suggests that this kind of source was still fairly atypical by December 1953.[25] A further report several weeks later distilled valuable intelligence gathered from an insurgent captured in the Bahati Forest:

DEDAN KIMATHI has ordered certain gangs out of the reserve and East Aberdares ... Enemy are in the habit of lighting a decoy fire when they hear a plane coming over and then sit back watching bombs being wasted. They have little fear of Harvards but the rear gunners 'spraying' from the Lincolns worries them most of all ... Morale of enemy very high. Look well fed and contented. Convinced that Mau Mau is the best thing for the African in Kenya.[26]

---

[21] TNA, WO 276/415: CPEC minutes, 16 December 1955.

[22] TNA, WO 276/438: CPEC minutes, 22 December 1954.

[23] TNA, WO 276/438: CPEC minutes, 19 November 1954.

[24] TNA, WO 276/383: Report on Mau Mau tactics, Sergeant J. Dykes, Kenya Regiment attached Special Branch, 19 August 1953.

[25] TNA, WO 276/385: Mau Mau Organisation – Analysis of Interrogation Report, from Major Holmes for Chief of Staff, East Africa Command, to brigades and police, 8 December 1953.

[26] TNA, WO 276/404: Enemy methods and intention, from D. Stewart for PMIO, Rift Valley, to Special Branch Nakuru, 28 December 1953.

The report shows how prisoner interrogations gave vital information on gang movements, tactics and morale impossible to obtain elsewhere. This particular document indicates that the police and military enjoyed less integration in practice than suggested by the formal mechanisms introduced in May 1953. The MIO responsible for the Rift Valley Province sent information to the Special Branch in Nakuru, a district in his province. According to the official policy, collection was supposedly centralised through the Special Branch. There are plenty of examples in the archive files of the army sending captured suspects to the police for interrogation, such as when The Buffs handed a detainee to Muthaiga police in February 1954.[27] Yet the army also gave suspects to the administration and Home Guard for interrogation – as at Kandara, Ichichi and Othaya during January and February 1954.[28]

Through the committees information was circulated on Mau Mau command arrangements, tactics and strength during 1954. Information obtained in May from suspects captured separately indicated that the Mau Mau leader Kibera had taken over the Othaya area.[29] Prisoners taken in South Nyeri explained how gangs evaded sweeps by the security forces through forested areas.[30] A prisoner from Mayuru's gang placed Mau Mau strength in South Tetu division at about a hundred in December.[31] These examples illustrate how information from relatively low-level insurgents could be quickly disseminated through the committee system and inform offensive operations.

Occasionally the intelligence system achieved a *coup* by capturing a leading Mau Mau figure who proffered a deep understanding of the movement. The most important individual was General China (Waruhiu Itote), captured in January 1954 and interrogated for at least sixty-eight hours in Nairobi by Special Branch Assistant Superintendent Ian Henderson, in Kikuyu.[32] Henderson described him as 'a complete fanatic ... an arrogant and ill-tempered Kikuyu, possessed of a good brain and remarkable memory'. China remained fully committed to the Mau Mau, but Henderson claimed that he brought him to inadvertently reveal a lot about the movement by

---

[27] TNA, WO 276/290: 39 Infantry Brigade operational sitrep, 1 February 1954.
[28] TNA, WO 276/290: 39 Infantry Brigade operational sitreps, 6 January 1954, 23 January 1954, 7 February 1954.
[29] KNA, VP/9/9: Weekly intelligence report, 13–19 May 1954.
[30] KNA, VP/9/9: South Nyeri Reserve district intelligence committee summary, 20–26 November 1954.
[31] KNA, VP/9/9: South Nyeri Reserve district intelligence committee summary, 4–10 December 1954.
[32] See also W. Itote, *'Mau Mau' General* (Nairobi: East African Institute Press, 1967); Anderson, *Histories of the Hanged*, 230–5.

exciting him through discussing Kikuyu aspirations. China explained the command and control structure in his Mount Kenya area, the order of battle of the units under his command, and Mau Mau militant strength in his region alone as standing at 7,500.

British intelligence had previously divided the movement into passive and militant wings. China added that three organisations sat between them: the couriers, the scouts and the special police. The special police collected intelligence in the Reserve, and conveyed it to the nearest militant unit. The Mount Kenya command thought they were winning the conflict, their only major hindrance being the shortage of ammunition. Chiefs, headmen and the Home Guard were the movement's top priority targets. China argued that Kikuyu joined the Mau Mau voluntarily when their friends had been shot, and thought surrender efforts unlikely to succeed on Mount Kenya, where morale was strong. He stated that aerial attacks were feared and had caused forty-six deaths, but that the gangs adapted by staying in the Reserve (where bombing was normally forbidden). This provided a critical insight into an ill-understood military method. China explained that major attacks in the Reserves were discouraged because they brought communal punishment on the people, again giving valuable evidence on the impact of a major policy.[33]

Other captured insurgents proved valuable. Aram Ndirango, captured in July 1954, gave details on hide locations, sentry methods and offensive tactics. Support in the Reserves was buoyant because the security forces annoyed people by destroying crops. The Mau Mau actively sustained their backing by eliminating criminals and paying money to the relatives of killed insurgents. Ndirango reinforced China's assertion about government policy:

> There is a policy which is being increasingly enforced and observed, of attacking only carefully selected targets in the reserves. Indiscriminate attacks may have indirect repercussions on the passive wing because Government imposes communal punishment on areas in which incidents have taken place.[34]

Another form of intelligence came from informers in the Kikuyu population, some from the passive wing of the movement.

As early as December 1952 the police offered monetary rewards to informers – with little effect.[35] What motivated people to inform is a

---

[33] TNA, WO 276/412: Interrogation of WARUHIU S/O ITOTE (Alias) 'GENERAL CHINA', conducted at Special Branch HQ, Nairobi, 26 January 1954.

[34] TNA, WO 276/455: Miscellaneous information obtained from the interrogation of Aram Ndirango s/o Joseph Kawoi, 6 July 1954.

[35] TNA, WO 276/378: Information summary, HQ Northern Area, Nairobi, 1 December 1952.

mystery, although the security forces had their suspicions. A report on the subject thought many would willingly give information under the right conditions. A staff officer pondered the nature of these enigmatic, yet vital, figures:

(a) He will not in the first instance give information to anyone he does not know, nor will he do so unless he has absolute confidence in his contact.
(b) If these conditions are fulfilled permanently he becomes not only a good informer, but he is loyal to his contact.
(c) Despite (b) above money is a powerful factor, and in its absence the informer's enthusiasm wanes.
(d) Providing (a) is initially fulfilled, the informer can be introduced to a contact of lesser calibre, but he will work satisfactorily to the latter for a limited period only. After that he has to be re-visited by the original contact.[36]

Military intelligence reported a 'fairly established informer service', growing steadily despite Mau Mau intimidation and reprisals. Where the police or army based themselves, 'informers are more ready to be of service'.[37] In contrast to the screening process, which forcibly squeezed information out of hundreds at a time, informers volunteered by approaching Special Branch and 'making enquiries as to how they can make themselves useful'.[38] Yet in other areas, commanders vented their frustration when people refused to offer information.[39] The correlation between security force presence and information from informers seemed clear. When a British platoon occupied a farm in the Ngare Ndare area for a fortnight, the labour force gave information leading to a successful ambush. Surrounding areas provided nothing: 'The Committee deduce from this that the labour on this farm only consider themselves safe from reprisals.'[40] The committee's interpretation was vindicated a week later when a reduction in gang activity in Nanyuki township corresponded with a rise in denunciations to the security forces from 'fence sitters'.[41]

[36] TNA, WO 276/231: Minute on 'Covert Intelligence', from Major [name illegible] GSO2 (Int) to GSO1 (Ops and Int) [General Staff Officer, Grade 1, Operations and Intelligence], 3 February 1954.
[37] TNA, WO 276/378: Intelligence summary, from HQ Northern Area to East African Independent Armoured Car Squadron, 4 KAR, 5 KAR, 7 KAR, 23 KAR, 156 HAA Battery, East Africa Training Centre, Troops Fort Hall, Officer Commanding Troops Mombasa and Kenya Regiment, 17 December 1952.
[38] KNA, DC/NKI/3/12/32: Nanyuki district intelligence committee summary for the week ending 13 August 1954.
[39] KNA, VP/9/9: Nyeri district weekly intelligence report, 16–23 December 1953.
[40] KNA, DC/NKI/3/12/32: Nanyuki district intelligence committee summary for the week ending 3 September 1954.
[41] KNA, DC/NKI/3/12/32: Nanyuki district intelligence committee summary for the week ending 10 September 1954.

The Mau Mau deliberately tried to discourage the giving of information to the state, murdering a police informer in Njoro in November 1952, and severely injuring another man, who barely escaped with his life.[42] In April 1954 soldiers found a dead body with a note attached threatening death to all informers.[43] The security forces tried to counteract Mau Mau threats by improving the protection afforded to informers. Police Commissioner O'Rorke faced a challenge in having insufficient policemen at his disposal to physically guard every informer. Instead, he wanted to stop further murders by safeguarding informer identities, holding meetings with them discreetly and giving instruction on personal security measures – such as varying routines and times of meetings.[44] Major-General Heyman reminded the police of their responsibilities, following an incident where a police officer in Fort Hall ordered all informers out of a police station, which resulted in the murder of a high-value informer two months later.[45]

While prisoner interrogations indicated that collective punishment reduced violence in the Reserves, they also produced a negative side-effect. Ian Henderson complained about the Ragati sub-location, where collective punishments destroyed crop cultivation and villagisation was in full swing. The informer network in the area almost completely ceased functioning because the informers were employed on compulsory construction work most of the time. Not only did this give them little chance to circulate and collect information, but Henderson thought compulsory labour a poor reward for helping the government.[46] South Nyeri district intelligence committee observed the same problem in September 1955; close administrative control prevented agents from easily contacting informers without their identities being compromised. The intelligence collected duly declined, as did the number of Mau Mau killed in the area, 'rapidly'.[47] The relationship between administrative control and intelligence collection varied, however.

[42] TNA, CO 822/376: KCPIS 19/52, 15 November 1952.

[43] TNA, WO 276/295: 49 Brigade sitrep, 8 April 1954.

[44] TNA, WO 276/231: Letter from M. S. O'Rorke, Commissioner of Police, to Assistant Commissioners of Police for Nairobi and Nyeri, and Senior Superintendents of Police for the Rift Valley Province, Coast Province, Nyanza Province and Northern Province, 11 March 1953.

[45] TNA, WO 276/231: Letter from Chief of Staff to Commissioner of Police, 23 April 1954.

[46] TNA, WO 276/384: Operational intelligence Mt. Kenya and Aberdare Areas, 23rd – 25th Sept. 1953, report from Ian Henderson to Special Branch HQ, 29 September 1953.

[47] KNA, VP/9/9: South Nyeri Reserve district intelligence committee summary, 9–23 September 1955.

Following total villagisation in the Gikondi area, information from the populace on the gangs multiplied.[48] Frank Kitson, who ran an informer network as a DMIO, argues that the system truly came into its own during 1954. By the summer of 1954 Kitson's organisation in Kiambu, Thika and Nairobi districts ran over two hundred informers.[49]

The FIAs started off building up background information on their areas, which was generally inappropriate for launching offensive operations. Gradually they compiled records based on a card index system cataloguing all Mau Mau members in a given area.[50] According to Special Branch training materials, the FIAs needed to rely on handlers as intermediaries between themselves and informers because they lacked sufficient manpower to deal with all their informers directly. By operating two handlers in each location, each responsible for six informers, Special Branch planned to maintain at least thirty-six informers in every division.[51] Ian Henderson ran an informer network and used agents from within the Mau Mau movement, providing an insight into their thinking and planning.

In October 1953 Henderson's agents in Nyeri district indicated that General Erskine's offensives in the Aberdares were 'pinching the terrorist very hard', and warned that murders of loyalists were imminent.[52] Informers alerted their handlers to an impending attack on the Imenti mission in Chuka district, even naming the assigned killers.[53] This kind of detail gave the security forces something to act on. But informers came at a cost. DO George Nightingale noted their reputation for cruelty, and thought that they planted ammunition on suspects to collect a cash reward for a Mau Mau court conviction.[54] A Kenya Regiment FIA in Embu district resorted to visiting informers at night to protect their identity. He recalled how: 'The ultimate inducement to co-operate was to point out to the man concerned the fate that befell suspected informers and turncoats at the hands

---

[48] KNA, VP/9/9: Nyeri district fortnightly intelligence report, 15–29 July 1954.

[49] F. Kitson, *Bunch of Five* (London: Faber and Faber, 1978), 30.

[50] *Ibid.*, 32, 49–50.

[51] TNA, WO 276/231: Training pamphlet for the Operational Element of Special Branch, *c.* 1954.

[52] TNA, WO 276/384: Notes on information obtained from agents whilst on tour of Nyeri district on 15.10.53, from Ian Henderson to Commissioner of Police and GSO2 (Int), GHQ, 16 October 1953.

[53] TNA, WO 276/384: Intrep from Ian Henderson to GHQ East Africa, forwarded to Brigades, 17 November 1953.

[54] RCMS, Cambridge University Library: G. Nightingale: Memoirs of George Nightingale, RCMS 113/44.

of their fellow terrorists.'[55] Informer handlers relied on a blend of voluntarism and menace to extract the intelligence they wanted.

Intelligence exploitation

'Contact' information could be used to launch operations. As 70 Brigade's commander said: 'This Brigade must kill the gangs. This can only be achieved by getting sound information of their movements and and [sic] whereabouts.'[56] In September 1953 a Buffs patrol based on information from a prisoner found a small camp, but it appeared to have been deserted for about five days.[57] Information supplied by prisoners rapidly diminished in value after capture, showing the need for prompt exploitation. A patrol by the Black Watch 'on info received' engaged the enemy in a fire-fight and recovered a large number of documents.[58] The Kenya Regiment and Home Guard arrested an oath administrator in Kiambu after receiving a tip-off.[59] The security forces used information received from surrendered and captured insurgents to reduce Njiraini Warui's gang to 'negligible proportions' in Mathira division.[60] Village women in Thegenge location supplied information leading to thirteen captured Mau Mau, including General Waichuhi.[61] The security forces frequently took informers and captured or surrendered insurgents with them as guides. When informers changed their minds and tried to flee, they risked death, such as the individual shot fleeing in August 1953.[62] A Devons patrol guided by prisoners in the same month killed a sentry and captured a rifle and ammunition.[63] The historical record of 3 KAR shows how a prisoner-led patrol might unfold:

On the 23rd of December a composite force of A and B Coys entered the forest guided by a prisoner in an effort to locate the camp of the local terrorist leader, known as 'Matenjago'. Approaching the suspected area they met three terrorists and opened fire, without inflicting any casualty. Realising that the sound of shots

[55] KRA, vol. XXVI: Emergency – other KR roles: Recollections of D. H. McCabe concerning some of his activities combating the Mau Mau rebellion from 1953–1955, no date.
[56] Military Intelligence Museum: Letter from HQ 70 Bde to Bde formations, 24 August 1953.
[57] TNA, WO 276/292: 39 Infantry Brigade operational sitrep, 26 September 1953.
[58] TNA, WO 276/294: 49 Brigade sitrep, 15 February 1954.
[59] TNA, WO 276/298: 49 Brigade sitrep, 28 August 1954.
[60] KNA, VP/9/9: South Nyeri Reserve district intelligence committee summary, 26 March 1955–12 April 1955.
[61] KNA, VP/9/9: South Nyeri Reserve district intelligence committee summary, 10–24 June 1955.
[62] TNA, WO 276/287: GHQ operational sitrep to War Office, 20 August 1953.
[63] TNA, WO 276/287: GHQ operational sitrep to War Office, 22 August 1953.

would raise the alarm they pressed on with all speed. Almost immediately they were fired upon by an enemy sentry. The troops returned the fire, and then rushed the camp, but only to find that the occupants had made good their escape. The camp consisted of some hundred shelters, which were destroyed. A quantity of gunpowder, fuses and detonators were recovered.[64]

These operations were precarious, dependent on the fading utility of prisoners after capture. A patrol on 19 December led by a prisoner found a camp for a hundred insurgents, and could have inflicted a substantial loss on the enemy, had they not vacated the camp three days before.[65] Ideally, units taking prisoners on patrol interrogated them immediately and acted on the information at once. A patrol on 24 March 1954 accidentally bumped into a gang of about fifty insurgents, killing seven and capturing five. One of the prisoners indicated that three gangs were in the area, under General Rui's command. Based on his information and that supplied by an insurgent who surrendered in Nyeri, the security forces killed the leader of the second gang and his deputy, and went searching for the third gang.[66] In one instance, women in Thegenge went beyond merely supplying intelligence for the security forces to exploit – they captured Mau Mau themselves and handed them over, complete with home-made guns and ammunition.[67]

Friction between the military and police arose over intelligence exploitation. By March 1954, GHQ noticed that a surge in manpower meant that the military element working alongside Special Branch now outnumbered those from the police force itself. The imbalance prompted separation in certain areas, forcing Major-General Heyman to remind army officers to work with the police organisation at all times.[68] A deeper tension existed between the competing imperatives to either kill or prosecute the maximum number of insurgents. From the Special Branch perspective, the best option was to do neither of these things, but rather to cultivate insurgents as agents or informers for developing the longer-term intelligence picture. In June 1953 GHQ noted poor liaison between army and police when Mau Mau were captured in action. Units were required to guarantee that whoever captured the insurgent made a statement outlining the circumstances,

---

[64] TNA, WO 276/491: 3 KAR historical record, 10 August 1953 – 31 March 1954.
[65] TNA, WO 276/293: 49 Brigade sitrep, 21 December 1953.
[66] KNA, VP/9/9: Nyeri district weekly intelligence report, 24–30 March 1954.
[67] KNA, VP/9/9: South Nyeri Reserve district intelligence committee summary, 25 June 1955 – 11 July 1955.
[68] TNA, WO 276/427: Operational Intelligence Instruction no. 9, issued by Major-General Heyman, GHQ East Africa Command, 11 March 1954.

that this form was handed to the police rapidly, and that commanders made those involved available for court appearances.[69]

The CPEC informed the military that convictions were difficult to obtain against suspects found possessing only one round of ammunition. They asked commanders to provide a witness to each search of an arrested person.[70] This suggests that the committee suspected that single rounds were being planted on suspects to boost the conviction rate. An even graver concern arose in November 1955, when the Kenyan Attorney-General raised the procedures for handling captured and surrendered insurgents in the War Council. He recognised the need to make use of prisoners as guides and so forth, but reminded those present that fifteen days was the maximum period prisoners could be held without charge. He proposed to increase this period to thirty days, which the Commander-in-Chief and the Commissioner of Police supported. The Commissioner for the Rift Valley Province argued that captured insurgents were more helpful than those who surrendered, and noted that some had been used for over twenty-eight days to great effect.[71] The final revised guidelines were published later in the month in booklet form. Discussing them in the War Council, the Attorney-General said that legal action would not necessarily be taken against a commander who kept a prisoner in the field for longer than four days after their initial capture or surrender, for example if taking him to a police post entailed breaking off a contact. The police would then have discretion, but the fact should not be advertised in case it encouraged officers to think the rules could be broken with impunity.[72] The rules were allowed to be broken.

Intelligence also prompted friction over resources. In September 1953 Nyeri district asked their provincial committee to secure more FIAs as the two available were insufficient to interrogate insurgents, preventing rapid information exploitation.[73] Despite a close relationship between army and police, the commander of 39 Infantry Brigade complained in January 1955 about Special Branch producing irrelevant intelligence. He particularly wanted information about where Mau Mau obtained their food.[74] The brigadier griped again

[69] KNA, DC/NKI/3/1/14: Letter from Colonel G. A. Rimbault, Chief of Staff GHQ, to 39 Infantry Brigade and 70 (East African) Infantry Brigade, 18 June 1953.
[70] TNA, WO 276/170: CPEC minutes, 4 December 1953.
[71] KNA, WC/CM/1/3: Minutes of a meeting of the War Council (hereafter War Council minutes) held on 8 November 1955.
[72] KNA, WC/CM/1/3: War Council minutes, 22 November 1955.
[73] KNA, VP/2/22: Nyeri DEC minutes, 25 September 1953 and 29 September 1953.
[74] KNA, VP/2/23: CPEC minutes, 14 January 1955.

later in the year when Special Branch in Nyeri failed to quickly translate documents captured by his troops. The police representative on the committee agreed to pursue the matter, showing that the committees tried to resolve disputes.[75]

Expediting intelligence: pseudo-gangs and special forces

The army and police achieved a high level of cooperation and mutual understanding in forging an effective intelligence system. Transmitting information from the collecting organisation (primarily the police) to the organisation which exploited it (primarily the army) hindered efficiency. When all information had a limited shelf-life, the transmission process took time and made successful follow-on action less likely. The key to overcoming this in Kenya was to merge intelligence collection, analysis and exploitation for operational purposes into a single team – either pseudo-gangs or special forces. These small units operated in the field for protracted periods and circumvented the need for intelligence to be bureaucratically processed before exploitation, thus saving time. Chapter 5 explained the evolution of pseudo-gang and special forces methods. This chapter considers their position insofar as they were affected by the politics of civil-military relations.

The two organisations running pseudo-operations differed in their objectives – the Kenya Regiment teams aimed to kill Mau Mau, whereas the DMIO teams sought information about the gangs and the situation in the Reserves. The teams operated independently under cover in the field, but they coordinated with the local committees to avoid friendly-fire accidents. One FIA who ran a pseudo-gang in Meru recalled nearly being killed by the Home Guard on his first mission, after being taken for a genuine Mau Mau gangster.[76] Pseudo-gangs cleared proposed missions through DEC operations rooms, which then ensured that no other security force units operated in the area concerned.[77] Pseudo-gangs either acted on contact intelligence themselves when circumstances made this necessary, or they passed it to nearby security force units directly or through DECs as appropriate.[78]

These forces brought their own special problems. The Attorney-General discovered in November 1955 that the use of captured and surrendered

---

[75] TNA, WO 276/439: CPEC minutes, 21 October 1955.
[76] KRA, 'Kenya Regiment. Field Intelligence Assistants', by F. J. McCartney, formerly Kenya Regiment sergeant, 26 July 1996.
[77] Interview with General Sir Frank Kitson.
[78] Interview with General Sir Frank Kitson.

Mau Mau breached the law. Out of 252 Mau Mau captured between 10 July and 17 October, 110 were prosecuted. The Attorney complained about the legal distinction between capture and surrender being ignored. Captured terrorists should only have been held without prosecution for operational purposes, with the Attorney's permission. The army 'completely disregarded' this stipulation. Captured people were supposed to be in police custody within four days. In reality, of the sixty-six held for 'operational reasons' on 1 November 1955, one had been held since May 1953, about twelve since dates in 1954, and 'many' for several months in 1955. The Attorney-General stated: 'No one is going to believe that this is operationally necessary or otherwise justifiable; it is indeed a shocking state of affairs.' He called for a report on each case, and threatened disciplinary or criminal action against those responsible.[79] The military and police took these concerns rather lightly. On the same day that the Attorney-General presented his strenuous objections, the Commissioner of Police proposed creating another SFT. The Commander-in-Chief agreed with him on a total strength of sixty-two Africans and fourteen Europeans.[80]

This exchange demonstrates the combined power of the army and police in resisting control by the political authorities. In the War Council, the Commander-in-Chief warned that he might need to keep surrendered pseudo-gangsters in the field for longer than the thirty days allowed by law.[81] In late January 1956 the Attorney-General objected again: because European officers were absent from some pseudo-gang operations, securing prosecutions based on the evidence of former insurgents became problematic. Despite the Attorney's worries about prosecutions, the War Council upheld the army's view of pseudo-gangs as primarily intended to induce surrenders rather than arrests.[82] In a concession to his concerns about the legal distinction between capture and surrender – which after all could mean the difference between the death penalty and detention – fresh instructions were issued in February.

Operation Instruction no. 36 ordered European officers to participate in operations intended to capture high-value targets, to satisfy the legal requirements for having the person classified as captured and thus subject to prosecution. By contrast, missions without European officers

[79] KNA, WC/CM/1/5: Memorandum by the Minister for Legal Affairs. Captured and surrendered terrorists, WAR/C.784, 5 November 1955.
[80] KNA, WC/CM/1/5: Operational use of surrendered terrorists. Memorandum by the Minister for Defence, Annex to WAR/C.789, 5 November 1955.
[81] TNA, WO 276/19: War Council minutes, 27 January 1956.
[82] TNA, WO 276/19: War Council minutes, 31 January 1956.

classified anyone taken into custody as having surrendered.[83] While this adjustment in operating procedures was a compromise to placate the Attorney-General, it had a minimal impact. Deciding whether someone taken into custody during an operation had surrendered or been captured before the operation even started made a mockery of the law. The episode showed how little concern the army and police had for abiding by the law's spirit. Thus the War Council largely left the army and police to run pseudo-gangs and special forces as they saw fit, an approach imitated by subordinate committees. Apart from the odd instance, such as a request to inquire whether long-serving pseudos needed replacing, the committees left them to their own devices.[84]

When the end of the military campaign against the Mau Mau came into sight, Lieutenant-General Lathbury pressed the War Council to take an interest in the welfare of former pseudo-gang members. These men, he argued, having proved their loyalty to the Crown, deserved to be saved from the hardships of lengthy rehabilitation and detention. Lathbury rejected the Emergency Joint Staff's proposal to send them to Manyani Camp. Instead, they were go through a 'sorting process' at the Mau Mau interrogation centre before being sent to a settlement anonymously, to protect them from reprisals. Special instructions should be issued to the officer-in-charge at the interrogation centre to treat the ex-pseudos 'firmly but sympathetically', as any abuses could jeopardise future recruitment prospects to the pseudo-gangs.[85]

Although the army and civilians clashed during the Emergency over intelligence matters, the general impression is of widespread cooperation and efficiency. Soldiers valued the expertise of the Special Branch and the local knowledge of the administration. Both these groups provided actionable intelligence to go out and kill the enemy, so harmony suited the army's requirements. The informer networks and prisoner interrogations gradually improved in span and quality, and probably as quickly as could be expected in the circumstances. Special operations and pseudo-gangs proved highly effective, but only because they fed into and flourished on the wider intelligence system then established. Pushing their use earlier on, when background information was lacking, would have produced negligible results. A notable feature of the intelligence aspect of the campaign is the manner in which the Special Branch

[83] TNA, WO 276/529: GHQ Operation Instruction no. 36, issued by GHQ, 18 February 1956.
[84] TNA, WO 276/416: Minutes of a meeting of the CPEC (South) held on 17 May 1956.
[85] Bennett witness statement 3, citing Hanslope document Chief Secretary, Vol. VI: 40A, War Council minutes, 23 May 1956, WAR/C/MIN.169.

and army unified to stymie and successfully resist outside interference, such as the Attorney-General's attempts to control the handling of captured insurgents. Apart from advising on reforms, by sending Percy Sillitoe, the British and Kenyan governments abstained and allowed the police and army almost complete autonomy in how they ran the intelligence war.

Administration

The army realised early on in the Emergency that it could only win with assistance from local security forces. The Home Guard was the decisive organisation, providing manpower and local knowledge. As a result, the army conducted numerous operations with the growing force throughout the Emergency.[86] But the army played a more active part than merely receiving assistance from the Home Guard and administration. East Africa Command advocated Home Guard expansion, supplied essential training, including on operations, and pushed the committees to strengthen them. The army's drive to restrain Home Guard brutality was lacklustre and sporadic. Despite local initiatives to prevent them from beating, torturing and killing Kikuyu suspects, at the highest level the army acquiesced in the Kenya government's immoral bargain. Brutality became acceptable as the price worth paying for collaboration. When it came to governing the Kikuyu, the army sought to influence administration policies. Soldiers used the committee system to push for faster villagisation and wider food denial. When DOs or settlers moved too slowly for the army's liking, they reported on them through the committees. On collective punishment, the three legs of the stool reached a consensus on viewing policy as normally beneficial, and cooperated closely in imposing fines and other measures.

Helping the Home Guard

Home Guards emerged early on in the Emergency as militias supporting chiefs, and sometimes known as 'resistance groups', for their opposition to the insurgency. Intelligence assessments understood the connection between Home Guard recruitment and popular backing for the government. Reports as early as December 1952 drew succour from their growing numbers, but expressed concern lest Mau Mau members join

---

[86] Heather, 'Counterinsurgency and Intelligence in Kenya', 77.

them surreptitiously.[87] Major-General Hinde formally established the Kikuyu, Embu and Meru Home Guards in March 1953, primarily to deny Mau Mau free movement in the Reserves and enable the military to concentrate on destroying the gangs.[88] The second task allotted to the Guard was gathering information on Mau Mau for the other branches of the security forces.[89] Members were enrolled as special tribal police, under the district administration, with Colonel P. A. Morcombe acting as their colony-wide coordinator.[90] According to Paget's figures, they killed 4,686 Mau Mau, amounting to 42 per cent of the total.[91] Clearly then, they played a major role in the campaign.

One British Army subaltern remembers protecting Home Guard posts as being a high priority for his battalion. In return for availability in a crisis, the Home Guards looked after the villages and workers in the fields, allowing the army to concentrate on offensive patrols.[92] An intelligence appreciation observed that the Home Guard possessed an offensive spirit – up to a point. On taking casualties they lost heart, so five Kenya Regiment men and some police askaris were attached to them from February 1953 to improve matters.[93] By May the 6 KAR took the North Tetu Home Guard with them on sweeps and night ambushes.[94] In June Operation Royal Flush proceeded in the Aberdares, aimed mainly at boosting Home Guard confidence.[95] The DO for North Tetu organised the operation in conjunction with the army. Starting on the morning of 18 June, 1,200 Home Guards from North Tetu and 600 from Othaya participated. Few Mau Mau were accounted for, but the District Committee considered the 'information and experience gained was most useful'. The army boosted Home Guard morale, and derived many tactical lessons from the experience themselves.[96] Combined actions occurred in Nyeri throughout mid-1953, such as Operation Mission utilising 400 Home Guards, police, aircraft and armoured cars under Lieutenant-Colonel Glanville's command.[97] Operation Scatter,

[87] TNA, CO 822/376: KCPIS 21/52, for the period ending 15 December 1952; TNA, CO 822/376: KCPIS 22/52, for the period ending 31 December 1952.
[88] TNA, WO 276/411: Appreciation of the situation, by Major-General Hinde, 5 March 1953.
[89] TNA, WO 276/200: Emergency Directive no. 3, Kikuyu Guard, 22 April 1953.
[90] TNA, WO 276/510: Office of the Director of Operations, Emergency Directive no. 3: Kikuyu Guard, 23 April 1953.
[91] Cited in Maloba, *Mau Mau and Kenya*, 90.
[92] Interview with Chapman, McFrederick and Moore.
[93] TNA, WO 276/378: Jock Scott intelligence summary, 19 February 1953.
[94] KNA, VP/2/22: Nyeri DEC minutes, 25 May 1953.
[95] TNA, WO 305/265: Historical record of 26th KAR, 18–19 June 1953.
[96] KNA, VP/2/22: Nyeri DEC minutes, 10 June 1953, 13 June 1953, 27 June 1953.
[97] KNA, VP/2/22: Nyeri DEC minutes, 9 June 1953 and 10 June 1953.

commanded by Major Wilkins, deployed troops from 5 KAR, 7 KAR, 26 KAR, the police and 500 Home Guards from North Tetu.[98] These operations conformed to a pattern: the forces involved, the tactical plan and the commander were all agreed at the district committee. The army officer generally held command; at times, such as during Operation Wimbledon in Mahiga on 30 June, the DO commanded.[99]

In July GHQ formalised army–Home Guard relations, directing that 'Full use should be made of K.G. [Kikuyu Guard] units at all times by Police/Military Commanders.'[100] Relations developed well enough in Nyeri for the district committee to record the killing or capturing of fifty-five Mau Mau in an eight-day period, and a distinct surge in Home Guard morale.[101] At this time, 39 Infantry Brigade incorporated the militia into their thinking. Their plans called for army, police and Home Guard to intensify offensive action together in the forests, Reserves and settled areas.[102] In a series of operations in September, the army swept through the forests, forcing Mau Mau into a line of posts on the forest fringe manned by the police and Home Guard.[103] After Operation Anvil, 39 Brigade's mission focused on supporting the administration and Home Guard even more. Operation Pugilist, an offensive against Mau Mau in Kiambu, Thika and Fort Hall districts, aimed to create a 'strong, stable Administration Police org and KG/HG network capable of maint law and order when the Districts are no longer the scene of maj mil ops'.[104] Thus operating with the Home Guard and boosting the administration's authority became a central part of the military strategy.

Instead of viewing these units as an organisational rival, the army sought to promote them. At a CPEC meeting, the commander of 70 Brigade called on all forces to make 'maximum use of the Kikuyu Guard' in the settled area.[105] Right down to platoon level, soldiers worked together with the Home Guard, often relying on them as guides.[106] Apart from planned combined operations, the militia acted on their

[98] KNA, VP/2/22: Nyeri DEC minutes, 25 June 1953.
[99] KNA, VP/2/22: Nyeri DEC minutes, 29 June 1953.
[100] TNA, WO 276/200: Emergency Directive no. 8, Role of and cooperation with the Kikuyu, Embu and Meru Guards, 15 July 1953.
[101] KNA, VP/2/22: Nyeri DEC minutes, 18 September 1953.
[102] TNA, WO 276/437: 39 Infantry Brigade Jock Scott operational instruction no. 10, 29 August 1953.
[103] TNA, WO 276/437: 39 Infantry Brigade Jock Scott operational instruction no. 11, 10 September 1953.
[104] TNA, WO 276/437: 39 Infantry Brigade Jock Scott operational instruction no. 20, 11 May 1954.
[105] TNA, WO 276/171: CPEC minutes, 23 July 1954.
[106] Interview with Chapman, McFrederick and Moore.

own initiative, informing the committees where this might conflict with other forces in the area, such as following up stock thefts into the mile strip.[107] The crisis support role could vary in size from a single platoon going to the aid of a post under attack, as happened at Guruaini on the night of 20 November 1953, to complex reactions.[108] An example of the latter occurred in April 1955, when 3 KAR responded to a request from the administration for help after intelligence indicated a gang in the area. Two KAR companies, police units and a thousand Home Guards leapt into action, capturing two Mau Mau found hiding in a compost heap.[109]

The Home Guard needed substantial training, and the army was the only organisation in a position to offer it. At first, the DOs commanding Home Guards consulted local military units, a piecemeal arrangement which led to complaints, like 'too much drill and not enough field craft and use of weapons'.[110] By December 1953, regiments such as The Buffs were providing sustained support to Home Guard posts. In Nyeri, the committee urged the army to station platoons at posts overnight.[111] The Kenya Regiment assumed a leading position in training the Home Guard; they often commanded them on secondment as DOs Kikuyu Guard (DOKG). They constructed ranges and gave shooting lessons.[112] The committees advocated maintaining Kenya Regiment support because they increased morale and made the units capable enough for regular forces to be deployed elsewhere.[113] Central Province Committee monitored the DOKGs, recommending the War Council to authorise 108 for the province, and attempted to rectify shortfalls.[114] When Kenya Regiment support for Home Guards in Nyeri was withdrawn in July 1954, the commander of 70 Brigade deplored the marked loss in efficiency.[115]

So the army vocally supported the Home Guard, and helped develop them for tasks beyond static defence and population control. When the Fort Hall committee proposed raising two Kikuyu Guard units for operations in the forests, the commander of 39 Brigade agreed to help run the experiment.[116] The Devons trained the Othaya Kikuyu Guard Combat Unit (KGCU), The Buffs the North Tetu unit, 70 Brigade Mathira

---

[107] KNA, VP/2/22: Nyeri DEC minutes, 29 May 1953.
[108] TNA, WO 276/491: 3 KAR historical record, 20 November 1953.
[109] TNA, WO 276/493: 3 KAR historical record, 23 April 1955.
[110] KNA, VP/2/22: Nyeri DEC minutes, 13 June 1953.
[111] KNA, VP/2/22: Nyeri DEC minutes, 10 December 1953 and 24 December 1953.
[112] KNA, VP/2/22: Nyeri DEC minutes, 2 February 1954.
[113] KNA, VP/2/22: Nyeri DEC minutes, 9 March 1954.
[114] TNA, WO 276/171: CPEC minutes, 23 April 1954.
[115] TNA, WO 276/171: CPEC minutes, 2 July 1954.
[116] TNA, WO 276/171: CPEC minutes, 29 January 1954.

KGCU, and 3 KAR the South Tetu team.[117] By August 70 Brigade deemed the training in Nyeri district to be 'progressing very satisfactorily'.[118] 39 Brigade ran courses through to at least April 1955.[119] The sessions covered subjects such as wireless transmission, field craft and patrol drill.[120] In the settled areas, farmers who employed African labour formed parallel forces to the Home Guards, called the Special Farm Guards; 39 and 70 Brigades helped train them in Central Province from August 1955, in consultation with the local DO concerned.[121]

The commander of 39 Brigade at one point pressed the administration to retain good Guards in their own locations.[122] A week later the commander of 70 Brigade 'recommended that Kikuyu Guard should be given increased responsibility and definite areas for which they would be entirely responsible'.[123] The commander of 49 Brigade urged that posts be strengthened with loyalists from other areas – a point accepted by the Central Province (South) Committee.[124] The Commander of 70 Brigade advised an overlap period when DOKGs changed.[125] So besides operating closely with the Home Guards, all three brigade commanders felt compelled to interfere in their management – strictly speaking, an administration responsibility. What is notable is not only that they often managed to influence administration policy here, but that they faced almost no resistance. By contrast, Daniel Branch argues that the Home Guard provided the administration 'with substantial influence over the nature of the counterinsurgency effort in the localities. The Administration was fiercely protective of this hard-won stake in the military campaign.'[126] The evidence presented here suggests the army exerted an influence over the Home Guard's development, and that a consensus between army and administration held good at most times.

When it came to discipline and the treatment of civilians and prisoners, the Home Guard presented the army with problems. Scholars have rightly condemned the Home Guard's reputation for ruthlessness and brutality, not to mention looting and personal

[117] KNA, ARC(MAA)2/5/310: Nyeri DEC minutes, 23 February 1954.
[118] TNA, WO 276/438: CPEC minutes, 20 August 1954.
[119] KNA, VP/2/23: CPEC minutes, 22 April 1955.
[120] TNA, WO 305/264: 23 KAR historical records, 1 April 1954 to 31 March 1955.
[121] TNA, WO 276/439: CPEC minutes, 19 August 1955, 2 September 1955, 7 October 1955, 18 November 1955.
[122] TNA, WO 276/171: CPEC minutes, 29 January 1954.
[123] TNA, WO 276/171: CPEC minutes, 5 February 1954.
[124] TNA, WO 276/438: Minutes of a meeting of the CPEC (South) held on 2 November 1954.
[125] KNA, VP/2/23: CPEC minutes, 10 February 1955.
[126] Branch, *Defeating Mau Mau, Creating Kenya*, 71.

enrichment.[127] Caroline Elkins describes Home Guard posts as 'the epicenters of torture'.[128] Bruce Berman's research shows how the Guard benefited from numerous cover-ups by a protective administration, according them a 'semi-official acceptance' which only encouraged their harsh treatment of civilians.[129] Arguably the government reduced and then disbanded the Home Guard in late 1955 because they were unreliable and brutal.[130] This may be true, but underestimates the essential terrorising function fulfilled by the Home Guard in 1953 and 1954. In these years it grew in strength from around 8,000 to about 25,000, at a time when allegations of abuses were rife.[131] If the army truly deplored the notorious behaviour, then it would not have actively supported such an expansion knowing full well what the consequences would be.

In truth, the army fundamentally relied upon the Home Guard for the campaign to succeed. While Kitson argues that the Home Guards simply failed to understand British standards, the decision to wilfully ignore their misdeeds was a decisive factor in high-level military policy.[132] An intelligence summary neatly captured the situation: 'it is only Kikuyu Gd who are committed to govt.'[133] General Erskine's orders on discipline applied to these units, yet they persisted in inflicting beatings and torture until the end of the Emergency.[134] Some British units in the field physically halted Home Guard abuses in train.[135] Senior commanders occasionally tried to restrain the Home Guard, such as the Commander of 39 Brigade's call for improved control on operations in November 1953.[136] Ultimately the responsibility rested with the Director of the Kikuyu Guard. When the KGCUs were formed, he explicitly prohibited them from indulging in independent or 'private Army' activity, hinting at the tendency to violently settle personal vendettas.[137] In June 1954, General Erskine explained his view on the subject to the War Council, after learning of plans to prosecute several Home Guard members for murder:

---

[127] Anderson, *Histories of the Hanged*; Elkins, *Britain's Gulag*; Maloba, *Mau Mau and Kenya*, 93.
[128] Elkins, *Britain's Gulag*, 244.   [129] Berman, *Control and Crisis*, 358.
[130] Anderson, *Histories of the Hanged*, 271; Heather, 'Intelligence and Counter-Insurgency', 79.
[131] Maloba, *Mau Mau and Kenya*, 89.
[132] Kitson, *Gangs and Counter-gangs*, 46; Edgerton, *Mau Mau: An African Crucible*, 165.
[133] TNA, WO 276/406: KISUM 31, 21 August 1953.
[134] Anderson, 'The Battle of Dandora Swamp', 164.
[135] Edgerton, *Mau Mau: An African Crucible*, 168.
[136] TNA: WO 276/170: CPEC minutes, 13 November 1953.
[137] KNA, ARC(MAA)2/5/310: Letter from Colonel Morcombe to Provincial Commissioner, Central Province, 16 February 1954.

The Kikuyu Guard are not a disciplined force – their European supervision is inadequate – their standards are not the standards of regular disciplined troops or police. They are not paid – they are not clothed – they are inadequately fed. They do a very good job because they do it from the heart and with faith in the Kenya Government. I have always warned the Government that by accepting the Kikuyu Guard and arming them the Government were accepting the aid of irregular auxiliaries who were not under my disciplinary control and that they must not expect the disciplinary standards which I should require from regular troops and police. As I understand it the Government have accepted this risk because of the obvious advantages to be derived from a loyal local force. I am convinced they are an essential part of the campaign ... But it now appears to me that the Government are proposing to try for murder some of these men because they do not come up to the standard of conduct they would expect from their regular forces. It is important that the whole case should be studied before a decision is taken ... I must warn the War Council that my opinion is that if these men are tried for murder they may be faced with a deterioration in morale and perhaps some desertion from the Kikuyu Guard.[138]

The army understood the ethical trade-off inherent in incorporating the Home Guard in their strategy, and were willing for the rule of law to be sacrificed. Whether abrogating the responsibility to intervene in halting Home Guard abuses was either morally or legally excusable is a contentious question. War Council minutes demonstrate General Erskine's pivotal role in protecting the Home Guard from prosecution for their abuses. In December 1954 the Minister for African Affairs raised concerns about the 'numerous criminal charges' facing Home Guard members. A week later, General Erskine suggested these prosecutions be considered alongside the matter of 'amnesty and surrenders'. In other words, General Erskine invented the idea behind the 1955 double amnesty, to encourage more Mau Mau to surrender, and to give the Home Guard immunity for their crimes.[139] This was the logical evolution from his suggestion six months earlier that 'breaches of discipline' committed by the Home Guard 'in good faith' should result in dismissal, rather than prosecution.[140] To senior soldiers these compromises were inevitable in a bitter civil war, an unsavoury fact which 'must be accepted'.[141]

---

[138] TNA, WO 276/474: Kikuyu Guard. Note by the Commander-in-Chief. WAR/C.114, 9 June 1954.

[139] Bennett witness statement 3, citing Hanslope documents Chief Secretary, Vol. III: 40A, War Council minutes, 7 December 1954, WAR/C/MIN.69; Chief Secretary, Vol. III: 40A, War Council minutes, 14 December 1954, WAR/C/MIN.72.

[140] Bennett witness statement 3, citing Hanslope document Chief Secretary, Vol. I: 40A, War Council minutes, 11 June 1954, WAR/C/MIN.22.

[141] TNA, WO 32/21722: Telegram from C-in-C to AG, War Office, no date (probably late November 1953).

Policy in the Reserves

Another area technically the preserve of the DOs, soldiers expressed a view on how to govern the Reserves. As chapter 8 argued, General Erskine supported collective punishments, villagisation and mass detentions without trial. These were combined policies, depending on army, police and administration consensus for a maximum impact. During Operation Kneel, on 26 November 1952, the army helped transport 2,500 Kikuyu to the Reserves and impounded stock, crops and grain. When used rapidly after a Mau Mau crime on the nearby inhabitants, the effect was thought 'markedly salutary'.[142] Police intelligence concurred with this assessment, the Commissioner advising applying communal punishments 'heavily and swiftly ... with even greater force'.[143] By mid-December 1952 the police regarded collective punishments as having a 'definite effect'.[144]

The committees reminded their members to inflict swift and severe punishment in areas where information on gangs was withheld.[145] The commander of 39 Brigade emphasised the matter at the CPEC.[146] In the Fort Hall district, the Mau Mau adapted to this common government tactic, evacuating all stock and people from the area where they had murdered two policemen on Christmas Eve 1952.[147] Although police, administration and army normally agreed on the policy, occasional doubts surfaced. Intelligence officers in Nanyuki found 'no obvious beneficial results from the imposition of collective punishment on Kikuyu, Meru and Embu squatters'. The squatters possessed less to feed the gangs with, but the passive wing enjoyed high morale and militant units retained their freedom of movement.[148]

The policy to compulsorily move almost all members of the Kikuyu, Embu and Meru tribes into villages was conceived as a punitive measure. Investigating for the War Council in July 1954, Michael Blundell discovered only two such villages in the vital Kiambu district. Rather than building villages, the DC thought that declaring PAs was a better

---

[142] TNA, WO 276/378: Table of Mau Mau Incidents and collective punitive measures taken from 26 NOV to 9 DEC 52, signed Captain O. H. Waring, Intelligence Officer HQ Northern Area.

[143] TNA, WO 276/378: Situation appreciation. Week ending the 4th December, 1952, signed M. S. O'Rorke, Commissioner of Police.

[144] TNA, WO 276/378: Situation appreciation. Week ending the 17th December, 1952, signed M. S. O'Rorke, Commissioner of Police.

[145] KNA, VP/2/22: Nyeri DEC Minutes, 10 November 1953.

[146] TNA, WO 276/170: CPEC minutes, 6 November 1953.

[147] TNA, WO 276/378: Jock Scott intelligence summary, 31 December 1952.

[148] KNA, DC/NKI/3/12/32: Summary for the Nanyuki district intelligence committee, for week ending 6 August 1954.

punitive measure, contrary to War Council policy. By doing so, he removed all people and stock from rebellious areas. The army strongly opposed the DC's approach. Moving the PAs around only shunted the insurgents from one area to another. The army considered villages a better 'psychological and disciplinary shock', and apt for controlling the population with the Home Guard.[149] The strong disagreement between DC and army in this case appears to be exceptional; the administration generally favoured villagisation, cohering with the War Council's objectives. The police and army cooperated in finding ways to make the policy more effective. In Central Province, they jointly called on all district committees to draw up nominal rolls in all villages as a means of imposing tighter control.[150] A few months later the police and army commanders in the province concurred on the need for individual identity certificates, fencing and punji (sharpened bamboo) moats around villages.[151]

The War Council issued broad directives on villagisation, ordering the policy to be completed in all Kikuyu and Embu areas by the end of August 1955.[152] As elsewhere in the committee system, the army monitored policy compliance by their counterparts. In March 1955 two staff officers from headquarters in Nairobi visited Chuka division, in Meru district, an administrative unit spanning nearly 300 square miles. Only three DOs oversaw the division, a comparatively sparse share. The staffers criticised the DC, Rayner, and Bamber, the DO for Chuka, quite severely. They thought Bamber 'confused about the villagisation policy', and 'more interested in short term measures to kill terrorists than he is in long term closer administration of the population'. To their surprise, Bamber had presided over limited devillagisation in Chuka. In contrast to the uniformed police and Special Branch officers, these two administration officials opposed villagisation. The DC favoured declaring PAs in Chuka and bombing them to induce surrenders – an idea supported by the army and provincial committee.[153] Extrapolating from this report on a single area must be attended by due caution. In Meru at least the military appeared more closely aligned with the police than the administration, and to favour tighter population control against

---

[149] TNA, WO 276/474: Report by European Minister without Portfolio. Administrative Control, Kiambu, Appendix to WAR/C.154, 1 July 1954.

[150] TNA, WO 276/438: CPEC minutes, 22 October 1954.

[151] KNA, VP/2/23: CPEC minutes, 7 January 1955.

[152] TNA, WO 276/90: War Council directive no. 5, Emergency Policy, 22 June 1955.

[153] TNA, WO 276/461: Situation in MERU district and in particular in CHUKA Division, memo from Lieutenant-Colonel (name illegible), GSO1 Ops(K), to Chief of Staff, East Africa Command, 11 March 1955.

the administration preference for attrition. East Africa Command took an interest in administration policies beyond Chuka in 1955, writing to 49 Brigade in April about Naivasha district. The Commander-in-Chief was unhappy with progress there, instructing the brigadier to send weekly updates: 'You should report if you consider adequate action is not being taken by the Administration.'[154]

Food denial

A third area where the army participated in and influenced administration policy was on the denial of food to the insurgents. The army began assisting in May 1953, when 6 KAR and the Devons helped lift crops in the Zute and Gura valleys.[155] During a three-day operation imaginatively entitled 'Spud' in June, 26 KAR lifted 379 bags of potatoes.[156] Replicating the monitoring undertaken over villagisation, the MIO in Nakuru informed his superiors about the failure to complete food denial.[157] Military forces based in Central Province in August directed their greatest efforts on dominating formerly Mau Mau territory.[158] But 70 Brigade gave explicit instructions on how to deny food, including clearing all forest shambas, preventing crop planting in the forests, concentrating labour near farms and enclosing cattle.[159] In Nairobi, General Erskine pressed on Governor Baring the great need to deny the Mau Mau food supplies.[160]

Out in the country, the army insisted that squatters and settlers comply with the policy. The Commander of 39 Brigade informed the CPEC that farmers in Mweiga had not done enough to prevent the Mau Mau stealing cattle. DO Beyts refuted the charge, imploring the committee to bear in mind the severe financial losses suffered by the farmers, who deserved compensation. Sympathising somewhat, the committee agreed to station troops near the concentrated stock to protect them.[161] Notwithstanding the difficulties faced in applying the policy widely,

---

[154] TNA, WO 276/461: Letter from Chief of Staff, East Africa Command, to 49 Independent Infantry Brigade, 4 April 1955.
[155] KNA, VP/2/22: Nyeri DEC minutes, 17 May 1953.
[156] TNA, WO 305/265: 26 KAR historical record, 13–15 June 1953.
[157] TNA, WO 276/404: Appreciation of the Situation by PMIO – NAKURU, 10 June 1953.
[158] TNA, WO 276/453: Rift Operations Instruction no. 12, 26 August 1953.
[159] KNA, DC/NKI/3/1/18: Letter from HQ 70 (East African) Brigade to 5 KAR, 6 KAR, 7 KAR, OC Troops Nanyuki, DEC Nanyuki, DEC Nyeri, DEC Embu, Provincial Executive Officer and Assistant Commissioner of Police, 30 August 1953.
[160] KNA, AH/5/2: Memorandum from Evelyn Baring to Deputy Governor, Chief Secretary, Chief Native Commissioner et al., 8 August 1953.
[161] TNA, WO 276/170: CPEC minutes, 11 September 1953.

by mid-September Mau Mau redeployments favourable to the security forces appeared to be caused by food denial.[162] In November 1953, 39 Brigade placed greater emphasis on the policy, making it the second priority, after destroying the gangs.[163] Brigade commanders watched for policy compliance, and when they found aberrations notified the provincial committees, which then nominated a subordinate committee or an officer to correct things.[164] Administration officials largely took the lead in effecting the farmers' cooperation, when necessary gently warning them that the police would assiduously check labour and food controls on farms.[165]

Meanwhile the army conducted combined operations with the police and Home Guard, including 'maj food denial ops' throughout July 1954 in Fort Hall.[166] 49 Brigade placed food denial on the same footing as destroying gangs in late February 1955, when gangs were dispersed and depended on stealing food to survive.[167] The hope was that starving Mau Mau would attack farms in a desperate bid to survive. Naivasha district anticipated such an eventuality by organising mobile patrols ready to reinforce any labour line or farm coming under attack.[168] Over the summer of 1955 the new Commander-in-Chief, Lieutenant-General Lathbury, took a direct interest in food denial, meeting farmers to explain the policy's rationale.[169] He became involved in tactical aspects, insisting on the Naivasha potato crop being lifted. He argued that food denial affected all other security policies.[170] Lathbury persuaded the administration to tighten up control measures in Nakuru, Laikipia and Naivasha, although the DCs concerned varied their intensity depending on local circumstances.[171]

At the War Council's meeting on 12 July, Lieutenant-General Lathbury attempted to impose uniformity on all Emergency districts.

---

[162] TNA, WO 276/287: GHQ Operational sitrep to War Office, 14 September 1953.
[163] TNA, WO 276/437: 39 Infantry Brigade Jock Scott Operations Instruction no. 13, 2 November 1953.
[164] TNA, WO 276/170: CPEC minutes, 6 November 1953.
[165] KNA, PC/NKU/2/15/62: Letter from W. N. B. Loudon, DC for Uasin Gishu, to all farmers and employers of Kikuyu, Embu and Meru in the district, 23 July 1954.
[166] TNA, WO 276/437: Signal from HQ 39 Infantry Brigade to GHQ East Africa, 1 July 1954.
[167] TNA, WO 276/461: Appreciation of the situation, by Brigadier G. Taylor, CO 49 Brigade, 25 February 1955.
[168] KNA, MSS/128/123: Minutes of a meeting of the Naivasha joint district operations committee and the Naivasha DEC held on 3 May 1955.
[169] KNA, WC/CM/1/2: War Council minutes, 9 June 1955.
[170] KNA, WC/CM/1/2: War Council minutes, 24 June 1955.
[171] KNA, PC/NKU/2/15/62: Letter from G. C. M. Dowson, DC for Nakuru, to all farmers in the Subukia and Solai areas, 1 July 1955.

However, the War Council resisted his more severe recommendations, leaving the PECs leeway to decide their own precise measures.[172] The War Council appointed a committee under Major-General Hinde's chairmanship to consider future policy.[173] He reported in September that the farmers had heeded the Commander-in-Chief's appeal for help over the summer months. Hinde recommended maintaining food denial, and especially stock controls, until the end of the year. Illegal squatter stock should be removed urgently, and the squatters banned from possessing stock or crops on any farm without a resident European. The government should move to fully reimburse farmers for the expense accrued in employing Special Farm Guards. Hinde advocated taking 'sanctions' against the 'small number of farmers whose failure to maintain a reliable labour force is their own fault'.[174] Ultimately the War Council decided to relax food denial everywhere from 1 January 1956.[175]

Taken as a whole, the army exerted a significant influence on administration policies pertinent to the campaign. Cooperation entailed more than simply notifying partner organisations about one's own projects: for the army it meant ensuring that the right policies were pursued with sufficient vigour. When this was not the case, the army resorted to the committees as a means to leverage settlers and administration to push food denial and villagisation faster. Yet in other policy areas, such as relations with the Home Guard and collective punishment, the administration and army essentially agreed and worked together effectively.

The use of force

The army attempted to destroy the Mau Mau movement through violent force and by encouraging surrenders. When it came to armed combat, the proximity of the Second World War magnified the British Army's credibility and ability to function autonomously. To avoid indulging in an exterminatory campaign, and to strategically weaken Mau Mau as quickly as possible, army commanders strongly advocated surrender schemes, sometimes despite opposition in Kenya. Soldiers adopted a more compromising attitude when out on patrol in the field. A large proportion of military activity during the Emergency consisted in small

---

[172] KNA, WC/CM/1/3: War Council minutes, 12 July 1955.
[173] KNA, WC/CM/1/5: Commander in Chief's appreciation of the operational situation in Kenya at the beginning of August 1955, Annex to WAR/C.704, 4 August 1955.
[174] KNA, WC/CM/1/5: Committee on food denial measures in the period following 30th September, 1955. Report by the DDOPs, WAR/C.742, 17 September 1955.
[175] KNA, WC/CM/1/3: War Council minutes, 5 October 1955.

patrols, which frequently meant army and civil powers patrolling together. Commanders willingly agreed to suggestions from their civilian colleagues and the committees because they might help locate enemy formations to engage in combat. Soldiers did resist ideas from outsiders at times. Again reflecting the impact of the Second World War, the administration and police left the army alone to conduct large-scale operations. These were deemed effective and the civil authorities never interfered in their conduct.

Small-scale patrols

Throughout the Emergency the army conducted thousands of small-scale patrols, in settled areas, Reserves and forests. A very substantial proportion, perhaps the majority, were carried out alongside either the Home Guard, the police or both. Immediately following Governor Baring's declaration of the Emergency the army patrolled through Nairobi and all troubled areas, imposing a temporary calm.[176] Within days 4 KAR, based at Nakuru, were 'carrying out a very strenuous programme of anti-terrorist patrols' in the Rift Valley, often supporting the 'hard pressed police forces'.[177] 5 KAR likewise embarked on 'a campaign of intensive patrolling', from the declaration until the end of the year.[178] Apart from simply killing Mau Mau, these patrols sought to demonstrate government dominance and to break up political gatherings, such as the patrols by the Inniskillings in Pumwani, Shauri Moyo, Kaloleni, Bahati and Makongeni in October 1953.[179] During the surrender schemes, offensive patrols assumed a low profile. During the 1954 scheme, for example, 70 Brigade authorised only platoon-size patrols, ordering them to call on insurgents to surrender before shooting. Patrols concentrated on collecting intelligence ready for when offensive actions resumed.[180]

These locally arranged patrols could be larger than platoon size: on 16 May 1954, 'B' Company of 5 KAR plus the Home Guard contacted a gang placed at a hundred in strength in the Aguthi Location, killing

[176] TNA, WO 276/287: Jock Scott operational sitreps, GHQ to War Office, 21 October 1952 and 22 October 1952.
[177] TNA, WO 305/257: 4 KAR historical record, 1 April 1952 to 31 March 1953.
[178] TNA, WO 305/259: 5 KAR historical record, 22 August 1952 to 27 March 1954.
[179] TNA, WO 276/342: Situation reports from 1 Royal Inniskillings to GHQ, 1 October 1953 and 3 October 1953.
[180] TNA, WO 276/454: Letter from Brigadier Orr, CO 70 (East Africa) Infantry Brigade, to 3 KAR, 5 KAR, 7 KAR, 23 KAR, Kenya Regiment, GHQ East Africa, Provincial Commissioner, Assistant Commissioner of Police, 2 April 1954.

four and capturing one. Five days later in Aguthi, 5 KAR joined two companies of 23 KAR, police and Home Guard in a running battle, inflicting twenty-eight kills on the Mau Mau.[181] During late October, 'Y' Company from the Royal Northumberland Fusiliers and a police General Service Unit engaged a hundred-strong gang in the Nairobi river bed, cordoning the area, firing in mortars, and then sweeping through. The engagement killed fifteen enemy and captured forty-two.[182] 23 KAR, based in Mathira division, ran 'continual' patrols and ambushes from April 1954 to March 1955. Small patrols tended to be speculative, but when specific intelligence about a Mau Mau concentration arrived, the whole battalion went out.[183] So these ad hoc, locally arranged operations could be quite large in scale.

The committees helped arrange these patrols, and presented the forum for DOs and policemen to request army action. An Inniskillings subaltern based in Chuka met his administration and police counterparts every few days to arrange operations in the division, finding both individuals easy to work with.[184] Quite aside from the constitutional duty to aid the civil power, the army liked operating alongside the police for the simple reason that they carried effective radios, unlike the poor army sets.[185] These informally arranged missions remain for the most part undocumented. However, the influence exerted by the official committees is, to a certain degree, observable from the surviving records. The PECs suggested subordinate committees launch operations, such as Central Province's proposition to Nyeri district for operations in the Kabage area in May 1953.[186]

District committees passed concerns about military matters up to the provincial level, Nyeri district warning the single company allocated to control South Tetu division was inadequate, for example.[187] District committees asked their military representatives to mount specific operations. The Devons and The Buffs agreed to 'lay on a weekly blitz' in requested places, as did 23 KAR.[188] Army representatives sometimes received these appeals with alacrity, jumping at the chance to attack Mau Mau based on specific intelligence. When Mr Gerald Burton asked 70 Brigade to assault gangs based in the Burguret and Naro Moru river beds, the brigadier accepted the opportunity to mount 'a series of river

---

[181] TNA, WO 305/259: 5 KAR historical record, 16 May 1954.
[182] TNA, WO 276/300: 49 Brigade sitrep, 26 October 1954.
[183] TNA, WO 305/264: 23 KAR historical record, 1 April 1954 to 31 March 1955.
[184] Interview with Chapman, McFrederick and Moore.
[185] Interview with Chapman, McFrederick and Moore.
[186] TNA, WO 276/170: CPEC minutes, 15 May 1953.
[187] KNA, VP/2/22: Nyeri DEC minutes, 30 March 1954.
[188] KNA, VP/2/22: Nyeri DEC minutes, 26 November 1953 and 15 December 1953.

bed blitzes'.[189] Committees influenced where the army located its unit headquarters, calling for those in Central Province to sit adjacent to administration and police headquarters within divisions wherever possible.[190] The Nairobi committee induced the units in the city to launch a 'show of Force' by three battalions in June 1954.[191] In Central Province in November 1955, the Commander of 70 Brigade went so far as to place one company from every battalion permanently at the disposal of the local DEC.[192]

Despite the general willingness to help, at several points the army asserted a right to act independently and resist external advice. When the CPEC recommended troops patrol around the forest fringes rather than inside them, the major representing 70 Brigade 'asked for his dissent with this opinion to be recorded'.[193] An attempt by settler member Briggs to have the army conduct major offensives in the North Aberdares was brushed off with reassurances about reinforcements in the area, and no change in policy.[194] Another settler member, Mr Welwood, complained about army policy in the Rift Valley in May 1954. He wanted 'smaller and more independent hunting patrols'. The commander of 39 Brigade informed the committee that the extant patrol system functioned perfectly well. His subordinate Major Huth promptly changed the subject.[195]

Other tactics for resisting outside pressures emerged. The major representing 39 Brigade deflected a police request to deal with a troublesome area by referring the matter to the (absent) brigadier.[196] The brigadier agreed the next month to combined operations requested by the police, on condition that an army officer commanded them. The Commander of 70 Brigade dissolved opposition to his forest basing policy by explaining its merits.[197] The army on the whole willingly submitted to the influence of others in conducting small-scale patrols, and even fairly large ones up to battalion size. But they retained the ability to resist external pressure where they thought the suggestions incorrect, and employed various methods short of outright refusal to obstruct those perceived flawed ideas. Away from the large set-piece operations, officers in the field enjoyed considerable latitude to conduct operations in their allocated areas as they

[189] TNA, WO 276/171: CPEC minutes, 21 May 1954.
[190] TNA, WO 276/171: CPEC minutes, 15 January 1954.
[191] TNA, WO 276/64: Minutes of a meeting of the Nairobi Emergency Committee held on 9 June 1954.
[192] TNA, WO 276/439: CPEC minutes, 18 November 1955.
[193] TNA, WO 276/170: CPEC minutes, 29 May 1953.
[194] TNA, WO 276/170: CPEC minutes, 6 November 1953.
[195] TNA, WO 276/63: Minutes of a meeting of the Rift Valley PEC held on 7 May 1954.
[196] TNA, WO 276/439: CPEC minutes, 24 June 1955.
[197] TNA, WO 276/439: CPEC minutes, 1 July 1955.

saw fit.[198] The implication for civil-military relations was that commanders went along with the other members of their local committee depending on circumstance and personality.

Major offensive operations

Finally, the army carried out large-scale operations involving several battalions. On these occasions, the roles allotted to the respective security forces were more rigidly laid down than for the ad hoc patrols. Because planning multiple-unit offensives was the very stuff of the professional soldier, little outside interference was accepted. Indeed, in a campaign fought within living memory of the Second World War, few attempted to shape how the army managed these operations. Large sweeps through the forest were supposed to fragment the gangs and demoralise them. The police and administration were often involved, and thus had some indirect influence. During Operation Plover, a sweep through the Rift Valley in July 1953, the police advised Mobile Column 'A' on cordons, searches and roadblocks, leaving only 'Killing Ops' entirely at the military's discretion.[199] Operation Silver Doctor, a three-company Black Watch sweep through the Rift Valley in August, attached a Home Guard unit to assist clearing the area of militants.[200] By contrast, Operation Carnation II, mounted in July, involved The Buffs, the Devons, the Kenya Regiment and 7 KAR, with only minimal police participation.[201]

On some occasions, the army brought outsiders into the heart of the planning process. Before Operation Scythe, an Aberdares forest mission organised by 39 Brigade, the brigadier personally briefed the police and DCs alongside his assembled battalion and brigade officers. The operation followed a pattern seen repeatedly in the future, where the army moved through the forest to flush out any Mau Mau towards stop lines on the forest fringe manned by police and Home Guard.[202] The impression that large-scale forest operations were always purely speculative and different to the intelligence-based small patrols is misleading. 70 Brigade launched Operation Thunder in November 1954 using six battalions and the whole RAF Kenya contingent. They attacked specific areas in

---

[198] Interview with Chapman, McFrederick and Moore.
[199] TNA, WO 276/453: Rift Operations Instruction no. 6, 16 July 1953.
[200] TNA, WO 276/453: Operation Silver Doctor, letter dated 19 August 1953.
[201] TNA, WO 276/437: 39 Infantry Brigade Jock Scott Operations Instruction no. 8, 20 July 1953.
[202] TNA, WO 276/437: Confirmatory notes on bde comds O Gp held at Sagana 15 Oct 53, by HQ 39 Infantry Brigade.

the south-west Mount Kenya forest identified by Mau Mau leader Kaleba during interrogation as containing gangs.[203]

Similarly, the Mau Mau leader Mackenyanga, interrogated after his capture by the Northumberlands, disclosed the location of Dedan Kimathi's hide in January 1955. 70 Brigade quickly launched Operation Nutcracker to 'kill or capture all terrorists within a 1000 yd radius' of the hide, drawing forces away from the long-planned (and bigger) Operation Hammer.[204] Reflecting on the lessons of Hammer, Brigadier Taylor believed 'that a given density of troops patrolling a given area which the enemy does not wish to vacate easily will obtain good results as long as the offensive effort is kept up for a good period of time'. Taylor contrasted this effective method with the twenty-four-hour long cordon and sweep, which proved futile in the forests.[205] As the Emergency's military phase neared its end, the army encouraged mass participation in large offensive operations.

During late November 1955, Operation Schemozzle I, mounted by the commander of 7 KAR, the DC for Meru and the local police chief, deployed three KAR companies, the Meru police, two tribal police units, and three police general service units, to sweep through the Meru forests and moorland. About 75,000 Meru tribesmen searched allocated sectors. Although few Mau Mau casualties resulted, the operation succeeded in demonstrating Meru loyalty and cooperation with the security forces.[206] The army high command certainly judged these large operations as worthwhile, and could point to around 700 insurgent deaths inflicted during large forest operations between 1 January and 10 August 1955.[207] So the army brooked outside influence concerning the small-scale patrols, and relied upon Cabinet and Special Branch support for the surrender schemes, but claimed autonomy on large-scale operations and the right to decide and implement the rules of engagement.

Civil-military relations in the Emergency

Personalities, organisations and structures set the context for civil-military relations during the Emergency. But nothing rocked the three-legged stool in Kenya more than the formation and practice of policy measures

---

[203] TNA, WO 305/264: 23 KAR historical record, for 1 November 1954 to 10 November 1954.
[204] TNA, WO 276/450: GHQ East Africa Operation Instruction no. 26, 22 January 1955.
[205] TNA, WO 276/461: Lessons from Op Hammer, Appendix 'A' to Appreciation of the situation, by Brigadier G. Taylor, CO 49 Brigade, 25 February 1955.
[206] TNA, WO 305/261: 7 KAR historical record, 1 April 1955 to 31 March 1956.
[207] TNA, WO 276/450: GHQ Operational Instruction no. 34, 16 August 1955.

designed to defeat the Mau Mau. The army exerted remarkable influence over the police, administration and settlers, establishing the organisation's political power within the conflict. Spared government oversight and control in vast policy fields, officers followed their training and took the initiative. In doing so, they interfered with the police intelligence-gathering and exploitation mechanisms, and the administration's decisions on how to control the Kikuyu population. Sidestepping attempts by the Attorney-General to change policy on handling captured insurgents, the army only willingly submitted to civilian influence in areas like small patrols, when it proffered enhanced combat effectiveness.

This power was exercised by the army to defeat the enemy as quickly as possible, when necessary resulting in interference in strictly non-military affairs. Collective punishments, food control, villagisation, intelligence collection – these all represented fields where the army changed policy implementation by civilians because they thought their ideas a superior way to end the Emergency. Yet in some core military activities, such as patrols and intelligence exploitation, soldiers allowed civilians to influence them, recognising they had no monopoly of expertise and certainly insufficient manpower. Conducting screening, interrogations and most local patrols demanded a collaborative approach. Resisting external settler influence because it clashed with their strategic ideas, the high command none the less incorporated settlers into their plan and their forces.

Moderating settler extremism was absolutely essential, as Lyttelton made clear at the outset; but brutality had a place in the campaign plan. Settlers in the Kenya Regiment and KPR and loyalist Africans in the Home Guard committed brutal acts with impunity because the army underwrote the political bargain that placed them above the law. Indeed, when the law ill-suited military demands, such as holding insurgents with pseudo-gangs, the army simply ignored it. And the Kenya government's refusal to prosecute these cases meant that the law only provided an internal control on the army, through the court-martial system, rather than an external political control, as constitutionally dictated. The evidence presented in this chapter thus coheres with the wider conclusion drawn in this study that the army exercised restraint in handling the Kikuyu population when doing so made strategic sense. As with the law, civilian control played only a severely limited part in restraining soldiers.

Conclusion

> Whilst I may have to take stern measures to restore respect for the law
> nobody need doubt that I believe in justice. I desire to see this country
> returned to a normal process of Government where justice and progress
> for all races and creeds can be developed in an atmosphere of peace.[1]

British soldiers in Kenya understood the Mau Mau uprising as deriv-
ing, to a certain extent, from injustices within the colony. The
inequalities were obvious to any soldier who saw how many settlers
treated their labourers. Some young men asked to kill strangers in an
exotic country aimed wide of those they were supposed to shoot. Other
soldiers physically stopped local security forces from committing murder
and torture. When thinking about the British Army's behaviour in the
Kenya Emergency, we must remember that a large proportion of soldiers
conducted themselves honourably. In this sense, the orthodox understanding of British counter-insurgency has a point. Clear elements of
restraint were present in military policy from 1952 to 1956. These were
thoroughly dependent upon the army's ability to field a disciplined force
against the Mau Mau. Without this discipline, commanders could not
have used violence in an instrumental fashion to defeat the insurgency.
Repeated efforts were made by GHQ to instil and maintain a disciplined
fighting force.

Restraint was evident in military policies such as legal zoning, the
surrender schemes, the humane handling of prisoners and the pseudo-
gang operations. The influence of the minimum force concept can certainly be traced in actual practice on operations. Clear rules prevented the
conflict from degenerating into genocide. Aside from constituting formal
policy, there is evidence that ordinary soldiers appreciated that restraint
and humanity would help win the campaign. Hundreds of Mau Mau
surrendered in the knowledge that they would not instantly be put to

[1] General Erskine, June 1953. IWMD, Erskine papers, Broadcast by C-in-C about 24 hrs
after arrival in evening at about 9 pm after BBC news.

death. Prisoners in military hands could often expect to receive humane treatment. After incrementally piecing together a sophisticated intelligence appreciation of the insurgency special forces were able to target militant gangs so as to minimise the suffering of ordinary people. As General Erskine declared the day after arriving in Kenya, he believed in justice.

How to achieve justice when confronted with insurgency is a fundamental challenge to the military which is unlikely ever to disappear. General Erskine's determination to conduct the campaign in a civilised manner was opposed from the moment he stepped off the aeroplane at Eastleigh Airport in Nairobi. But he brought with him preconceptions about the methods likely to be needed at East Africa Command. These were the 'stern measures' mentioned in the same radio speech calling for justice. The security forces would have to break, or at least bend, the law in order to achieve 'an atmosphere of peace'. Notions about how to respond to the Mau Mau reflected a long tradition in British imperialism, as prominent as minimum force. Soldiers, colonial administrators and policemen alike believed that trouble needed to be nipped in the bud, crushing rebellion quickly and ruthlessly. Anything less would be seen by the tribe concerned, and critically by tribes watching from the sidelines, as pathetic weakness. The mentality derived from rational fears about the precarious basis of British imperialism, reliant on very limited manpower to impose government, and racist beliefs about natives only reacting to tough measures.

From these beliefs collective punishments, mass detentions and the indiscriminate use of firearms resulted. Formal doctrine allowed great leeway to the commander on the spot in deciding how to treat suspected rebels. The Emergency laws within which the army operated during counter-insurgencies were highly permissive. Minimum force was inapplicable in the colonies and in insurrections, and in any case lacked rigorous oversight mechanisms. The international legal environment enabled soldiers to view the use of force against civilians in Kenya as perfectly legal. To a certain degree, they were correct, as international rules generally avoided giving extensive protections in internal conflicts. But the British government took measured steps to ensure that repression could take place in the colonies unhindered. Soldiers in Kenya therefore may have thought that there were no higher, universal rules on how they could behave. There was insufficient instruction about their duty to refuse superior orders to kill or torture civilians. Of course knowing whether training on this principle would have changed actual conduct is impossible. But evidence has been presented in this book showing instances where soldiers obeyed orders to commit atrocities. So these legal considerations had a direct bearing on events during the campaign itself.

This book has explored the considerable part played by the British Army in the Emergency, which has not received sufficient attention thus far. Involved in security policy from the very start, the army took the lead in June 1953 when General Erskine arrived. From then on, the campaign would be conducted with growing success, and with greater efforts to control violence. The systematic clearance of Nairobi, Operation Anvil, combined with the villagisation of most Kikuyu, Embu and Meru in 1954 to significantly change the war's dynamics. Living in the shadow of the Second World War, army officers were granted the authority to conduct operations as they saw fit. Much writing on British counter-insurgency assumes that close civilian control and supervision exerted a prominent influence in restraining the armed forces. Sketching the civil-military architecture, the major political groups and their political priorities were explained. Parliament, the media, the settlers, the Kenya administration and police all had an opinion about how the army should use force. The Cabinet was perhaps the most influential body outside the army, but even so only intervened on a few occasions to alter policy. In Kenya, the army regularly disagreed with its civilian counterparts. These minor disputes should not distort the bigger picture. Soldiers, policemen, administrators and settlers generally agreed on the need to cooperate in repressing the Mau Mau. The civilian groups in Kenya broadly assisted the army because they needed its help and appreciated its presence. As a result, civilians had little influence on the army's conduct.

Examining civil-military relations in detail, police, administration and military policies were analysed. When looking at intelligence activities, the military and police pursued a highly integrated approach. Cooperation on pseudo-gang methods played an increasingly important part in the campaign, especially its concluding stages from 1955 onwards. The army recognised that the rebellion could only be defeated by strengthening colonial government in the Kikuyu locations. To this end, soldiers supported the administration in exerting their control, and took active measures to physically support them. This included training and operational support for the Home Guard, open to numerous allegations of systematic brutality. But the army went further, interfering in administration policies and pushing for tighter population control. Here, as in the police sphere, the army influenced civilian policies. In terms of military policy, the British Army pushed through three surrender schemes despite considerable opposition. Soldiers mounted small patrols at the request of civilians, but retained full control over large-scale offensives. During the Emergency, the army normally operated without much political supervision. Significantly, some attempts to restrict the army, such as the Attorney-General's concerns about prisoner handling, were easily ignored.

Indiscriminate violence was widespread in the first few months, aimed at terrorising the population into supporting the government rather than Mau Mau. Beatings, torture, murder, collaboration with vigilantes and mass evictions were exemplary policies which targeted civilians. They were pursued not only to terrorise, but to gather intelligence and protect the settlers. The army played a central role in these actions, a fact normally denied or downplayed in writings on the Emergency. Commanders and politicians turned a blind eye to the mounting evidence that the army was acting brutally. Exploring what happened in 'B' Company, 5 KAR, allowed for new insights into the events at Chuka in June 1953. This helped to explain wider conduct in Kenya. Racism, competition for kills and disregard for the legal duty to stop criminal acts played a role, in addition to the intelligence-gathering and terrorisation purposes. 'B' Company were not unique. The military and civilian leaderships systemically allowed brutality in order to rapidly crush the revolt.

General Erskine genuinely wished to reform the army's conduct when he assumed command in June 1953. Obstacles were thrown in his path. The general gradually came to accept how things were done in Kenya. At source, there were two main reasons why he changed his initial position. First, soldiers in the country were already habituated to conducting the conflict in a certain way. They proved resistant to adopting a more discriminate approach. Second, General Erskine came to accept the argument that a large proportion of the civilian population supported the insurgency, and were thus fair targets. He came to believe, as many others did, in the strategic effectiveness of repression. As a result, policies such as collective punishment were continued and even intensified. This book has shown how the investigations into the conduct of 5 KAR, 7 KAR, the Kenya Regiment, and then the McLean Inquiry, fundamentally changed General Erskine's attitude towards discipline and brutality. These inquiries forged a compact between commanders and troops. Brutality was accepted, in exchange for soldiers continuing to fight the Mau Mau until they were beaten.

Our ability to assess military policy and discipline in Kenya has been constrained by the government's retention of files on the British Empire after the Second World War, the Hanslope archive, comprising in total some 8,800 files. This book has drawn on files pertaining to Kenya to assess the army's conduct. New evidence has been presented, in particular on people being 'shot attempting to escape', interrogation, torture, the intelligence system and policy-making in the War Council. Four Kenyans who claim to have endured torture at British hands have been pursuing legal action against the British government in the High Court since April 2011.[2] Whatever the outcome to the case, the belief that Britain waged its decolonisation wars with a greater degree of civility than other governments is no longer convincing, if it ever was. A vast archival record suggests that the British Empire in Kenya created a systematically repressive regime to try and eliminate the Mau Mau.

This book supports a wider emerging scholarship which shows that the British Army followed most others in reacting to internal rebellions with severe repression. Much writing on counter-insurgency is based on the belief that a soft hearts and minds approach can bring success. Experience in Kenya and elsewhere suggests that such a stance is merely a delusion. Because intelligence about who insurgents are, and shifting political loyalties, cannot be surmounted, it may be that counter-insurgencies will always be brutal. There are implications for contemporary and future military thought and practice, because the current debate in military circles tends to assume that warfare is perfectible to a humane standard. The evidence in this book suggests that there are internal forces within an army which make this impossible, in addition to the normally expected brutality of insurgents and terrorists.

What is quite clear is that significant variations in violence arise between locations in insurgencies. Normally this is presumed to be the function of political patterns in distinct local populations. While probably true, the Kenya Emergency shows how variations in military subcultures can fuse with different local conditions to prompt very diverse patterns of violence. The implications for understanding the limits on rational policy-making are important. Senior policy-makers and commanders may not understand the local variations, let alone be able to control them in any meaningful fashion. By implication, future studies need to focus more upon the dynamics of military subcultures interacting with localised insurgent violence. The Hanslope archive,

---

[2] D. M. Anderson, 'Mau Mau in the High Court and the "Lost" British Empire Archives: Colonial Conspiracy or Bureaucratic Bungle?', *Journal of Imperial and Commonwealth History*, 39 (2011), 699–716; H. Bennett, 'Soldiers in the Court Room: The British Army's Part in the Kenya Emergency under the Legal Spotlight', *Journal of Imperial and Commonwealth History*, 39 (2011), 717–30; C. Elkins, 'Alchemy of Evidence: Mau Mau, the British Empire, and the High Court of Justice', *Journal of Imperial and Commonwealth History*, 39 (2011), 731–48.

which is being deposited at the National Archives in Kew, is likely to allow these local dynamics to be thoroughly explored.

Senior commanders and politicians were aware, however, of soldiers in the field interpreting the rules of engagement variably. At critical junctures, when the leadership in Kenya were alerted to the rules being ignored, decisions were taken to 'turn the blind eye'. Police and military investigations into persons being 'shot attempting to escape' highlighted how easy it was for soldiers to commit murder and construct a *post facto* justification. The opportunities for challenging these actions were missed because commanders feared that if they faced criticism, soldiers would simply refuse to open fire at all. When it came to torture, substantial and frequent information was sent to the top levels of government describing the brutalities taking place. Prosecutions were instituted by the army to punish some of those responsible. The signal sent was not enough, as crimes against civilians carried on throughout the Emergency. General Erskine managed to reduce military participation in abuses by increasingly withdrawing soldiers from the Reserves and pushing for expansion in the non-military security forces. This meant supporting the Home Guards at the very time when widespread abuses by them were at their height. The army wished to wash their hands of the Home Guards, to ignore the methods used to extract intelligence from a suspect around the back of a hut or in a detention camp. Torture and lesser suffering were intrinsic to the wider government strategy advocated by the army in Kenya, and the high command successfully protected many security force personnel from prosecution for their abuses. Military morale would not stand for the systematic prosecution of soldiers for abuses which were, ultimately, the logical consequence of the government's own policy.

Bibliography

PRIMARY SOURCES

UNPUBLISHED SOURCES

British Library Sound Archive, London
Farr, J. H., C409/042/01–04.

British Library, London
Hume, A., Mss Eur D724/84.

Imperial War Museum, Department of Documents, London
Erskine, General Sir G., 75/134/18.
Windeatt, Lieutenant-Colonel J. K., 90/20/1.

Imperial War Museum, Sound Archive, London (IWMSA)
Anonymous, 11162/3.
Brind, P. H. W., 10089/2.
Burdick, P., 11143/3.
Burini, E. B., 19630/18.
Cainey, A., 26864/14.
Carriage, R. J., 18267/3.
Cassidy, R., 11138/4.
Gay, A. W., 10258/2.
Hastings, M. C., 10453/6.
Hewitson, T. L., 26853/12.
Liddle, A. L. K., 10091/4.
Maclachlan, S., 10010/3.
Matless, T. R., 21020/4.
Pickering, J. F., 21054/3.
Potts, G. L., 23213/19.
Randle, J. P., 20457/34.
Roberts, J. F., 18825/7.

Stockwell, R. Z., 10065/2.
Wilkinson, T. G., 10082/2.

Inniskillings Museum, Enniskillen
Regimental Diary of the Royal Inniskilling Fusiliers, Vol. VII: March
    1952 to January 1962.

Interviews
Chapman, J., J. McFrederick and R. Moore, formerly Royal Inniskilling
    Fusiliers, Windsor, 27 February 2010.
Kitson, General Sir Frank, Devon, 5 July 2010.

Joint Services Command and Staff College Library,
Shrivenham (JSCSC)
Army Staff College syllabus, 1945–60.
Erskine, General Sir G. 'The Mau Mau Rebellion', lecture given to the
    1955 Course, Army Staff College, Camberley.

Kenya National Archives, Nairobi (KNA)
African Affairs: ARC(MAA).
Chief Secretary: CS.
Defence: AH.
DC, Fort Hall: DC/MUR.
DC, Lamu: DC/LAMU.
DC, Meru: DC/MRU.
DC, Nanyuki: DC/NKI.
DC, Nyeri: VP.
Naivasha district emergency committee: MSS/128.
Officer-in-Charge, Nairobi Extra-Provincial District: RN.
Provincial Commissioner, Rift Valley Province: PC/NKU.
War Council: WC/CM.

Kenya Regiment Archive, to be deposited at the Imperial War Museum,
London (KRA)
Vol. VI: Material on Mau Mau Emergency.
Vol. VIa: Material on Mau Mau Emergency.
Vol. VII: Guy Campbell papers.
Vol. XXVI: Emergency – other Kenya Regiment roles.
Miscellaneous papers: Recollections of F. J. McCartney.

Military Intelligence Museum, Bedfordshire
Letters from 70 (East Africa) Infantry Brigade, 1953.

National Archives of the United Kingdom, Kew (TNA)
Cabinet Office: CAB 128, 130, 195.
Colonial Office: CO 822.
Dominions Office: DO 35.
Home Office: HO 45.
Law Officers' Department: LO 2.
Lord Chancellor's Office: LCO 2.
Ministry of Labour: LAB 13.
Prime Minister's Office: PREM 11.
Treasury Solicitor: TS 46.
War Office: WO 32, 71, 93, 163, 216, 236, 276, 279, 291, 305.

National Army Museum, Department of Archives, Photographs, Film and Sound, London (NAM)
Anonymous, oral history interview, NAM.1996–09–82–24.
Anonymous, typescript of unpublished work, NAM.2002–07–358–1.
Unknown author, letter from 'Neil' to Mr and Mrs W. Cannell, NAM.2001–10–124–2.

Oxford Development Records Project, Bodleian Library of Commonwealth and African Studies, Rhodes House, University of Oxford (ODRP)
Clemas, H. N., MSS Afr. 1715.
Hinde, W. R., MSS Afr.s.1580.
Langford, P. E., MSS Afr. 1715.
Nott, D. H., MSS Afr. 1715.
Thompson, P., MSS Afr. 1715.
Wallis, C. St. J., MSS Afr. 1715.

Royal Commonwealth Society Collection, Cambridge University Library (RCMS)
Cashmore, T. H. H., RCMS 175.
Edgar, T. L., RCMS 318/1/3.
Nightingale, G., RCMS 113/44.

Royal Courts of Justice, London
Witness statement number two of Huw Bennett, in the case of Ndiku Mutua and others *v.* Foreign and Commonwealth Office, *Queen's Bench Division in the High Court of Justice, 1 April 2011, citing the following Hanslope Archive documents*
AA 45/26/3/2A Vol. I: Letter from Col. T. H. Henfrey to Minister for African Affairs, 11 August 1954.
Letter from Secretary for Defence to Secretary for African Affairs, 30 August 1954.

AA 45/48/1/1A: Disposal of captured and surrendered terrorists employed by the security forces, Memorandum by the Emergency Joint Staff, 19 May 1956.

CAB MM/5/1: Note of a meeting held at Government House at 6.30 pm on Saturday, 1st November, 1952.

CAB 19/4 Vol. I: Record of the Chief Secretary's Complaints Co-ordinating Committee, 31 May 1954.

CO 968/424: Summary of evidence concerning the Sergeant Allen case.

CO 968/424: Letter from (illegible), War Office, to P. Rogers, Colonial Office, 12 September 1953.

DO 3/2: Reorganisation of Intelligence in Kenya Colony. Progress Report August 1953 Part I, by the Intelligence Adviser.

E 16/3/8A: Telegram from Baring to Secretary of State for the Colonies, 17 January 1955.

EMER 45/69/2A: CPEC, Post Phase II Operations, October 1954–April 1955.

SEC 5: Notes for Screening Teams, Special Branch Rift Valley Province, Nakuru, 23 October 1953.

Witness statement number three of Huw Bennett, in the case of Ndiku Mutua and others *v.* Foreign and Commonwealth Office, *Queen's Bench Division in the High Court of Justice, 25 May 2012, citing the following Hanslope Archive documents*

AA 45/79/7A Box 148: Summary of CPEC (South) Plan in response to War Council Directive no. 10, 10 September 1956.

ADM 35/2/11/1/5A: Political intelligence report – November 1952, Nairobi district, 4 December 1952.

ADM 35/2/11/3/1A: Intelligence summary, signed Captain Ragg, Int. Section, Thomson's Falls, 18 February 1953.

Laikipia Special Intelligence Report, 15 March 1953.

CAB/MM/7/7: 'Mau Mau and the Kamba', by R. D. F. Ryland, April 1959.

CAB 19/4 Vol. I: Savingram from the Officer Administering the Government of Kenya to the Secretary of State for the Colonies, Parliamentary Question, 28 July 1955.

Chief Secretary's Complaints Co-ordinating Committee minutes, 10 May 1954, 31 May 1954, 14 June 1954, 28 June 1954, 12 July 1954, 26 July 1954, 10 August 1954, 23 August 1954, 6 August 1954, 20 September 1954, 4 October 1954, 1 November 1954, 15 November 1954, 6 December 1954, 20 December 1954,

10 January 1955, 24 January 1955, 7 February 1955, 7 March 1955, 2 May 1955, 6 June 1955, 11 July 1955, 8 August 1955.

Chief Secretary, Vol. I: March 40A, War Council minutes, 25 May 1954, 11 June 1954, 15 June 1954.

Chief Secretary, Vol. II: 40A, War Council minutes, 21 September 1954.

Chief Secretary, Vol. III: 40A, War Council minutes, 26 October 1954, 7 December 1954, 14 December 1954, 1 February 1955.

Chief Secretary, Vol. VI: 40A, War Council minutes, 23 May 1956, WAR/C/MIN.169.

Chief Secretary, Vol. VIII: – 40B, 'Long term requirements of District Officers (Kikuyu Guard) and Field Intelligence Officers. Report by the Emergency Joint Staff', 9 July 1955.

Prosecution of detainees – C.I.D. investigations. Memorandum by the Minister for Defence, WAR/C.710, 11 August 1955.

CO, 968/266: Colonial Political Intelligence Summary no. 12, December 1953.

Civil servant's minute, signature illegible, 15 December 1953.

EM COM 4 Vol. I: Record of a meeting of the Governor's Emergency Committee held at Government House on the 20th January, 1953.

INT 10/4/2/1/4A Vol. II: district intelligence committee summary, Kisumu no. 14/54, 31 July 1954.

INT 10/4/2/2A Vol. I: Rift Valley provincial intelligence summary, 29 September 1953.

INT 10/4/2/2/9A: Naivasha District Intelligence Committee Summary, 27/11/53.

INT 10/4/2/4/2A Vol. I: Nyeri District Intelligence Committee Minutes, 4 April 1953, 10 April 1953, 24 April 1953, 22 May 1953, 29 May 1953.

INT 10/4/2/4A Vol. I: Schedule of incidents and operations connected with the Emergency in Central Province, no date.

Schedule of incidents and operations connected with the Emergency in Central Province for the fortnight 8th to 23rd April 1953.

Schedule of incidents and operations connected with the Emergency in Central Province for the fortnight 23rd April to 7th May 1953.

Schedule of incidents and operations connected with the Emergency in Central Province for the fortnight 7th May to 21st May 1953.

Schedule of incidents and operations connected with the Emergency in Central Province for the fortnight ending 23rd June 1953.

Schedule of incidents and operations connected with the Emergency in Central Province for the fortnight 19 June 1953 to 2 July 1953.

INT 10/4/2/4/5A Vol. I: Meru District Intelligence Committee Summaries, 18 February 1954, 11 March 1954, 25 March 1954, 13 May 1954, 24 June 1954, 8 July 1954, 15 July 1954.

INT 10/4/2/4/6A Vol. II: Kiambu district intelligence summaries, 23 January 1954, 24 April 1954, 7 May 1954, 14 May 1954, 12 June 1954, 19 July 1954.
  Nairobi City district intelligence committee summaries, 29 January 1954, 2 April 1954, 4 November 1955.
INT 10/4/2/4/8A: Schedule of incidents and operations connected with the Emergency in Nairobi area during the period 30 March 1953–12 April 1953.
  Central Province (South) provincial intelligence committee summary, 15 April 1953.
  Central Province South – Provincial Intelligence Summary, 24 November 1955.

The Sandhurst Collection, Royal Military Academy Sandhurst, Surrey
Sandhurst initial officer training syllabus, 1945–60.

Staffordshire Record Office, Stafford
Unett, R., D3610/21/7/1–30.

Communications
E-mail from Thomas B. Smyth, Black Watch Archivist, 4 October 2006.
E-mail from Captain J. Knox, Curator of the Royal Ulster Rifles Museum, 12 October 2006.
Letter from Mr M. A. Wight, Adjutant General Secretariat, Ministry of Defence, 20 September 2006.
Obituary in the Duke of Cornwall's Light Infantry journal *The Silver Bugle*, Summer 2006. Information kindly provided by Major T.W. Stipling, Regimental Secretary and Curator of the DCLI Museum.

PUBLISHED SOURCES

Memoirs
Blundell, M. *So Rough a Wind* (London: Weidenfeld and Nicolson, 1964).
Brockway, F. *African Journeys* (London: Victor Gollancz, 1955).
Carver, M. *Out of Step: Memoirs of a Field Marshal* (London: Hutchinson, 1989).
Catterall, P. (ed.). *The Macmillan Diaries: The Cabinet Years, 1950–1957* (London: Macmillan, 2003).
Franklin, D. *A Pied Cloak: Memoirs of a Colonial Police Officer (Special Branch)* (London: Janus, 1996).
Gill, L. *Military Musings* (Victoria, BC: Trafford Publishing, 2003).
  More Military Musings (Victoria, BC: Trafford, 2004).
Grahame, I. *Jambo Effendi: Seven Years with The King's African Rifles* (London: J. A. Allen & Co., 1966).

Henderson, I. *Man Hunt in Kenya* (New York: Doubleday, 1958).

Henderson, I. and P. Goodhart. *The Hunt for Kimathi* (London: Hamish Hamilton, 1958).

Hewitt, P. *Kenya Cowboy: A Police Officer's Account of the Mau Mau Emergency*, (Weltevredenpark, South Africa: Covos Day Books, 2001).

Itote, W. *'Mau Mau' General* (Nairobi: East African Institute Press, 1967).

Kitson, F. *Gangs and Counter-gangs* (London: Barrie and Rockliff, 1960).
Bunch of Five (London: Faber and Faber, 1987).

Lyttelton, O. *The Memoirs of Lord Chandos* (London: Bodley Head, 1962).

Meinertzhagen, R. *Kenya Diary 1902–1906* (London: Welbeck Street, 1957).

Trench, C. C. *Men who Ruled Kenya: The Kenya Administration, 1892–1963* (London: Radcliffe Press, 1993).

Official publications, manuals and parliamentary records

Army Act, 1881.

Corfield, F. D. *The Origins and Growth of Mau Mau: A Historical Survey* (London: HMSO, 1960).

Office of National Statistics, 'Retail Prices Index: Long Run Series', *Economic Trends* 604 (London: ONS, 2004).
Labour Market Trends 114/3 (London: ONS, 2006).

House of Lords debate on retained section of file WO 32/16103: http://www.publications.parliament.uk/pa/ld199900/ldhansrd/pdvn/lds06/text/60718–0999.htm, accessed 3 November 2006.

War Office, *Notes on Imperial Policing* (London: HMSO, 1934).
Manual of Military Law, 1929, Amendments No. 34, Notified in Army Orders for April 1944 (London: HMSO, 1944).
The King's Regulations for the Army and the Royal Army Reserve, 1940, reprint incorporating Amendments nos. 1 to 44 (London: HMSO, 1945).
Imperial Policing and Duties in Aid of the Civil Power (London: HMSO, 1949).
The Army List, April 1953 (London: War Office, 1953).
Manual of Military Law, Part II, 8th edn (London: HMSO, 1958).
The Law of War on Land, being Part III of the Manual of Military Law (London: HMSO, 1958).

Reference works and newspaper articles

Alexander, Harold Rupert Leofric George, first Earl Alexander of Tunis (1891–1969), by D. Hunt, rev. *Oxford Dictionary of National Biography* (Oxford University Press, 2008), online edition, at www.oxforddnb.com/view/article/30371, accessed 7 July 2010.

Baring (Charles) Evelyn, first Baron Howick of Glendale (1903–1973) by A. Clayton *Oxford Dictionary of National Biography* (Oxford University Press, 2004), online edition, at www.oxforddnb.com/view/article/30789, accessed 8 September 2006.

'British barrister deported', *The Times*, 17 June 1953, p. 6.

Callwell, Sir Charles Edward (1859–1928), by T. R. Moreman, *Oxford Dictionary of National Biography* (Oxford University Press, 2008), online edition, at www.oxforddnb.com/view/article/32251, accessed 31 May 2011.

'Embarrassing colonial files hidden for years were Foreign Office's "guilty secret"', *The Times*, 6 May 2011, p. 20.

Erskine, Sir George Watkin Eben James (1899–1965), by H. Bennett, *Oxford Dictionary of National Biography* (Oxford University Press, 2011), online edition, at www.oxforddnb.com/view/article/97289, accessed 1 June 2011.

Fraser, Sir Hugh Charles Patrick Joseph (1918–1984), by J. Biggs-Davison, rev. *Oxford Dictionary of National Biography* (Oxford University Press, 2004), online edition, at www.oxforddnb.com/view/article/31122, accessed 7 July 2010.

Gwynn, Sir Charles William (1870–1963), by G. Sinclair, *Oxford Dictionary of National Biography* (Oxford University Press, 2010), online edition, at www.oxforddnb.com/view/article/98221, accessed 31 May 2011.

Head, Antony Henry, first Viscount Head (1906–1983), by J. Colville, rev. *Oxford Dictionary of National Biography* (Oxford University Press, 2008) online edition, at www.oxforddnb.com/view/article/31214, accessed 7 July 2010.

Lathbury, Sir Gerald William (1906–1978), by J. Hassan, rev. *Oxford Dictionary of National Biography* (Oxford University Press, 2004), online edition, at http://www.oxforddnb.com/view/article/31335, accessed 1 June 2011.

Lloyd, (John) Selwyn Brooke, Baron Selwyn-Lloyd (1904–1978), by D. R. Thorpe, *Oxford Dictionary of National Biography* (Oxford University Press, 2009), online edition, at www.oxforddnb.com/view/article/31371, accessed 7 July 2010.

Macmillan, (Maurice) Harold, first earl of Stockton (1894–1986), by H. C. G. Matthew, *Oxford Dictionary of National Biography* (Oxford University Press, 2009), online edition, at www.oxforddnb.com/view/article/40185, accessed 7 July 2010.

Monckton, Walter Turner, first Viscount Monckton of Brenchley (1891–1965), by M. Pugh, *Oxford Dictionary of National Biography* (Oxford University Press, 2008), online edition, at www.oxforddnb.com/view/article/35061, accessed 7 July 2010.

'Murder charge dismissed: Kenya allegations disproved', *The Times*, 22 September 1953, p. 6.

'Obituary: Gen. Sir Richard Goodbody, Former Adjutant-General to the Forces', *The Times*, 6 May 1981, p. 19.

SECONDARY SOURCES

Abbott, K. W. 'International Relations Theory, International Law, and the Regime Governing Atrocities in Internal Conflicts', *American Journal of International Law*, 93 (1999), 361–79.

Anderson, D. M. 'Policing the Settler State: Colonial Hegemony in Kenya, 1900–1952' in D. Engels and S. Marks (eds.), *Contesting Colonial Hegemony: State and Society in Africa and India* (London: British Academic Press, 1994), 248–64.

'The Battle of Dandora Swamp: Reconstructing the Mau Mau Land Freedom Army October 1954', in E. S. Atieno Odhiambo and J. Lonsdale (eds.), *Mau Mau and Nationhood: Arms, Authority and Narration* (Oxford: James Currey, 2003), 155–75.

Histories of the Hanged: Britain's Dirty War in Kenya and the End of Empire (London: Weidenfeld and Nicolson, 2005).

'Surrogates of the State: Collaboration and Atrocity in Kenya's Mau Mau War', in G. Kassimeris (ed.), *The Barbarisation of Warfare* (London: Hurst, 2006), 159–74.

'Mau Mau in the High Court and the "Lost" British Empire Archives: Colonial Conspiracy or Bureaucratic Bungle?', *Journal of Imperial and Commonwealth History*, 39 (2011), 699–716.

Anderson, D. M., H. Bennett and D. Branch, 'A Very British Massacre', *History Today*, 56 (2006), 20–2.

Anglim, S. 'Orde Wingate and the Special Night Squads: A Feasible Policy for Counter-terrorism?', *Contemporary Security Policy*, 28 (2007), 28–41.

Anon. 'Hints on Internal Security', *British Army Review*, 1 (1949), 54–61.

'Obedience to Lawful Commands', *RUSI Journal*, 96 (1951), 71–3.

'A Senior Officer to Young Officers'; 'The Duties of an Officer', *British Army Review*, 3 (1950), 46–8.

Aylwin-Foster, N. 'Changing the Army for Counterinsurgency Operations', *Military Review*, November–December issue (2005), 2–15.

Barclay, C. N. 'The Training of National Armies in War', *Army Quarterly*, 58 (1949), 98–108.

Barnett, C. *Britain and Her Army 1509–1970: A Military, Political and Social Survey* (London: Allen Lane, 1970).

Barnett, D. L. and K. Njama, *Mau Mau from Within: Autobiography and Analysis of Kenya's Peasant Revolt* (London: MacGibbon and Kee, 1966).

Bartlett, C. J. 'The Military Instrument in British Foreign Policy', in J. Baylis (ed.), *British Defence Policy in a Changing World* (London: Croom Helm, 1977), 30–51.

Bartov, O. *The Eastern Front, 1941–1945: German Troops and the Barbarisation of Warfare* (London: Macmillan, 1985).

Baylis, J. *British Defence Policy: Striking the Right Balance* (Basingstoke: Macmillan, 1989).

Baylis, J. and A. Macmillan, 'The British Global Strategy Paper of 1952', *Journal of Strategic Studies*, 16 (1993), 200–26.

BBC 2 television programme *Correspondent: White Terror* broadcast 17 November 2002, reporter John McGhie, editor Karen O'Connor.

Beach, J. 'Soldier Education in the British Army, 1920–2007', *History of Education*, 37 (2008), 679–99.

Beckett, I. F. W. 'Robert Thompson and the British Advisory Mission to South Vietnam, 1961–1965', *Small Wars and Insurgencies*, 8 (1997), 41–63.

Modern Insurgencies and Counter-Insurgencies: Guerrillas and their Opponents since 1750 (London: Routledge, 2001).

Beckett, I. F. W and J. Pimlott (eds.), *Armed Forces and Modern Counter-Insurgency* (London: Croom Helm, 1985).

Bennett, H. 'The British Army and Controlling Barbarization during the Kenya Emergency', in G. Kassimeris (ed.), *The Warrior's Dishonour: Barbarity, Morality and Torture in Modern Warfare* (Aldershot: Ashgate, 2006), 59–80.

'The Other Side of the COIN: Minimum and Exemplary Force in British Army Counter-insurgency in Kenya', *Small Wars and Insurgencies*, 18 (2007), 638–64.

'"A very salutary effect": The Counter-Terror Strategy in the Early Malayan Emergency, June 1948 to December 1949', *Journal of Strategic Studies*, 32 (2009), 415–44.

'Detention and Interrogation in Northern Ireland, 1969–75', in S. Scheipers (ed.), *Prisoners in War* (Oxford University Press, 2010), 187–205.

'Minimum Force in British Counterinsurgency', *Small Wars and Insurgencies*, 21 (2010), 459–75.

'Soldiers in the Court Room: The British Army's Part in the Kenya Emergency under the Legal Spotlight', *Journal of Imperial and Commonwealth History*, 39 (2011), 717–30.

Berman, B. *Control and Crisis in Colonial Kenya: The Dialectic of Domination* (London: James Currey, 1990).

'Bureaucracy and Incumbent Violence: Colonial Administration and the Origins of the "Mau Mau" Emergency', in B. Berman and J. Lonsdale, *Unhappy Valley: Conflict in Kenya and Africa. Book 2: Violence and Ethnicity* (London: James Currey, 1992).

Berman, B. and J. Lonsdale, *Unhappy Valley: Conflict in Kenya and Africa* (London: James Currey, 1992).

Best, G. *Humanity in Warfare: The Modern History of the International Law of Armed Conflicts* (London: Weidenfeld and Nicolson, 1980).

'Making the Geneva Conventions of 1949: The View from Whitehall', in C. Swinarski (ed.), *Studies and Essays on International Humanitarian Law and Red Cross Principles in Honour of Jean Pictet* (Geneva/The Hague: International Committee of the Red Cross/Martinus Nijhoff, 1984), 5–17.

War and Law since 1945 (Oxford: Clarendon Press, 1994).

Betz, D. and A. Cormack, 'Iraq, Afghanistan and British Strategy', *Orbis*, 53 (2009), 319–36.

Bewes, T. F. C. *Kikuyu Conflict: Mau Mau and the Christian Witness* (London: Highway Press, 1953).

Black, J. *Rethinking Military History* (London: Routledge, 2004).

Blacker, J. 'The Demography of Mau Mau: Fertility and Mortality in Kenya in the 1950s: A Demographer's Viewpoint', *African Affairs*, 106 (2007), 205–27.

Blackett, J. 'Superior Orders – the Military Dilemma', *RUSI Journal*, 139 (1994), 12–17.

Blakeslee, H. V. *Beyond the Kikuyu Curtain* (Chicago: Moody Press, 1956).

Blaxland, G. *The Regiments Depart: A History of the British Army, 1945–1970* (London: Kimber, 1971).

Bloxham, D. '"The Trial That Never Was": Why there was no Second
     International Trial of Major War Criminals at Nuremberg', *History*, 87
     (2002), 41–60.
  'British War Crimes Trial Policy in Germany, 1945–1957: Implementation
     and Collapse', *Journal of British Studies*, 42 (2003), 91–118.
Bobbitt, P. *The Shield of Achilles: War, Peace and the Course of History* (London:
     Penguin, 2003).
Bogdanor, V. (ed.), *The British Constitution in the Twentieth Century* (Oxford
     University Press for the British Academy, 2003).
Bond, B. *British Military Policy between the Two World Wars* (Oxford: Clarendon
     Press, 1980).
Bourke, J. *An Intimate History of Killing: Face-to-Face Killing in Twentieth Century
     Warfare* (London: Granta, 2000).
  'New Military History', in M. Hughes and W. Philpott (eds.), *Palgrave
     Advances in Modern Military History* (Basingstoke: Palgrave, 2006),
     258–80.
Branch, D. 'Loyalism during the Mau Mau Rebellion in Kenya, 1952–60'
     (doctoral thesis, University of Oxford, 2005).
  *From Home Guard to Mau Mau: Ambiguities and Allegiances during the Mau
     Mau Emergency in Kenya, 1952–60* (University of Leiden: African Studies
     Centre, 2005), available at: http://asc.leidenuniv.nl/events/event-
     1259710325.htm, accessed 5 July 2006.
  *Defeating Mau Mau, Creating Kenya: Counterinsurgency, Civil War, and
     Decolonization* (Cambridge University Press, 2009).
  'Footprints in the Sand: British Colonial Counterinsurgency and the War in
     Iraq', *Politics & Society*, 38 (2010), 15–34.
Brand, G. 'The War Crimes Trials and the Laws of War', *British Year Book of
     International Law* (1949), 414–27.
Browning, C. R. *Ordinary Men: Reserve Police Battalion 101 and the Final Solution
     in Poland* (New York: HarperPerennial, 1993).
Buijtenhuijs, R. *Mau Mau: Twenty Years After: The Myth and the Survivors*
     (The Hague: Mouton, 1973).
  Essays on Mau Mau: Contributions to Mau Mau Historiography (Leiden: African
     Studies Centre, 1982).
Bulloch, G. 'The Application of Military Doctrine to Counter Insurgency
     (COIN) Operations – A British Perspective', *Small Wars and Insurgencies*, 7
     (1996), 165–77.
Burleigh, M. *The Third Reich: A New History* (London: Pan Books, 2001).
Busch, P. 'Killing the "Vietcong": The British Advisory Mission and the
     Strategic Hamlet Programme', *Journal of Strategic Studies*, 25 (2002),
     135–62.
Byers, M. *Custom, Power and the Power of Rules: International Relations and
     Customary International Law* (Cambridge University Press, 1999).
Callwell, C. E. *Small Wars: Their Principles and Practice*, 3rd edn (London:
     University of Nebraska Press, 1996).
Campbell, G. *The Charging Buffalo: A History of the Kenya Regiment* (London:
     Leo Cooper, 1986).

Cann, J. P. 'Low-Intensity Conflict, Insurgency, Terrorism and Revolutionary War', in M. Hughes and W. J. Philpott (eds.), *Palgrave Advances in Modern Military History* (Basingstoke: Palgrave, 2006), 107–30.

Carruthers, S. L. 'Two Faces of 1950s Terrorism: The Film Presentation of Mau Mau and the Malayan Emergency', *Small Wars and Insurgencies*, 6 (1995), 17–43.

Winning Hearts and Minds: British Governments, the Media and Colonial Counter-Insurgency 1944–1960 (London: Leicester University Press, 1995).

'Being Beastly to the Mau Mau', *Twentieth Century British History*, 16 (2005), 489–96.

Carver, M. *Harding of Petherton* (London: Weidenfeld and Nicolson, 1978).

Britain's Army in the Twentieth Century (London: Pan Books/Imperial War Museum, 1999).

Castro, A. P. and K. Ettenger, 'Counterinsurgency and Socioeconomic Change: The Mau Mau War in Kirinyaga, Kenya', *Research in Economic Anthropology*, 15 (1994), 63–101.

Chandler, D. and I. F. W. Beckett (eds.), *The Oxford History of the British Army* (Oxford University Press, 1994).

Chappell, S. 'Air Power in the Mau Mau Conflict: The Government's Chief Weapon', *RUSI Journal*, 156 (2011), 64–70.

Charters, D. A. *The British Army and Jewish Insurgency in Palestine, 1945–47* (London: Macmillan, 1989).

'From Palestine to Northern Ireland: British Adaptation to Low-Intensity Operations' in D. A. Charters and M. Tugwell (eds.), *Armies in Low-Intensity Conflict: A Comparative Analysis* (London: Brassey's, 1989), 169–249.

Chickering, R., S. Förster and B. Greiner, *A World at Total War: Global Conflict and the Politics of Destruction, 1937–1945* (Cambridge University Press, 2005).

Chin, W. 'Why Did It All Go Wrong? Reassessing British Counterinsurgency in Iraq', *Strategic Studies Quarterly*, 2 (2008), 119–35.

'The United Kingdom and the War on Terror: The Breakdown of National and Military Strategy', *Contemporary Security Policy*, 30 (2009), 125–46.

Clark, I. *Waging War: A Philosophical Introduction* (Oxford: Clarendon Press, 1988).

Clayton, A. *Counter-Insurgency in Kenya: A Study of Military Operations against Mau Mau* (Nairobi: Transafrica Publishers, 1976).

The British Empire as a Superpower, 1919–39 (London: Macmillan, 1986).

'Deceptive Might: Imperial Defence and Security, 1900–1968', in W. R. Louis, J. M. Brown and A. Low (eds.), *Oxford History of the British Empire*. Vol. IV: *The Twentieth Century* (Oxford University Press, 1999), 280–305.

The British Officer: Leading the Army from 1660 to the Present (Harlow: Pearson Education, 2006).

Clayton, A. and D. Killingray, *Khaki and Blue: Military and Police in British Colonial Africa* (Athens, OH: Ohio University Center for International Studies, 1989).

Cleary, A. S. 'The Myth of Mau Mau in its International Context', *African Affairs*, 89 (1990), 227–45.

Clough, M. S. *Mau Mau Memoirs: History, Memory, and Politics* (London: Lynne Rienner, 1998).

Cohen, E. A. *Supreme Command: Soldiers, Statesmen and Leadership in Wartime* (London: Simon and Schuster, 2003).

Collett, N. *The Butcher of Amritsar: General Reginald Dyer* (London: Hambledon and London, 2005).

Connelly, M. and Miller, W. 'British Courts Martial in North Africa, 1940–3', *Twentieth Century British History*, 15 (2004), 217–42.

Corbally, M. J. P. M. 'The Education and Employment of Senior Subalterns', *Army Quarterly*, 52 (1946), 223–6.

Cork and Orrery, Earl of, 'Obedience to Lawful Command', *RUSI Journal*, 96 (1951), 258–62.

Corum, J. S. and W. R. Johnson, *Airpower in Small Wars: Fighting Insurgents and Terrorists* (Lawrence, KS: University Press of Kansas, 2003).

Crang, J. *The British Army and the People's War 1939–1945* (Manchester University Press, 2000).

Crawford, N. C. 'Individual and Collective Moral Responsibility for Systemic Military Atrocity', *Journal of Political Philosophy*, 15 (2007), 187–212.

Crawford, W. K. B. 'Training the National Service Army Officer at Eaton Hall', *RUSI Journal*, 96 (1951), 134–8.

Creveld, M. van 'The Clausewitzian Universe and the Law of War', *Journal of Contemporary History*, 26 (1991), 403–29.

Croft, S. *The End of Superpower: British Foreign Office Conceptions of a Changing World, 1945–51* (Aldershot: Dartmouth, 1994).

Croft, S., A. Dorman, W. Rees and M. Uttley, *Britain and Defence 1945–2000: A Policy Re-evaluation* (Harlow: Pearson Education, 2001).

Cullen, A. 'Key Developments Affecting the Scope of Internal Armed Conflict in International Humanitarian Law', *Military Law Review*, 183 (2005), 66–109.

Curtis, M. *The Ambiguities of Power: British Foreign Policy since 1945* (London: Zed Books, 1995).
  Web of Deceit: Britain's Real Role in the World (London: Vintage, 2003).
  'Britain's Real Foreign Policy and the Failure of British Academia', *International Relations*, 18 (2004), 275–88.

Danchev, A. 'The Reckoning: Official Inquiries and the Iraq War', *Intelligence and National Security*, 19 (2004), 436–66.
  'Accomplicity: Britain, Torture and Terror', *British Journal of Politics and International Relations*, 8 (2006), 587–601.

Darby, P. *British Defence Policy East of Suez 1947–1968* (Oxford University Press, 1973).

Darwin, J. *The Empire Project: The Rise and Fall of the British World-System, 1830–1970* (Cambridge University Press, 2009).

Detter, I. *The Law of War*, 2nd edn (Cambridge University Press, 2000).

Devereux, D. R. *The Formulation of British Defence Policy towards the Middle East, 1948–56* (London: Macmillan, 1990).

Dewar, M. *Brush Fire Wars: Minor Campaigns of the British Army since 1945* (London: Robert Hale, 1990).

Dixon, P. 'Britain's "Vietnam syndrome"? Public Opinion and British Military Intervention from Palestine to Yugoslavia', *Review of International Studies*, 26 (2000), 99–121.

Dockrill, M. *British Defence since 1945* (Oxford: Basil Blackwell, 1988).

Douglas-Home, C. *Evelyn Baring: The Last Proconsul* (London: Collins, 1978).

Dower, J. *War without Mercy: Race and Power in the Pacific War* (New York: Pantheon Books, 1986).

Draper, G. I. A. D. *The Red Cross Conventions* (London: Stevens & Sons, 1958).
   'The Place of the Laws of War in Military Instruction', *RUSI Journal*, 111 (1966), 189–98.
   'The Ethical and Juridical Status of Constraints in War', *Military Law Review*, 55 (1972), 169–85.

Dunbar, N. C. H. 'The Responsibility of Junior Officers to the Laws of War', *RUSI Journal*, 97 (1952), 164–76.

Durkheim, E. 'The Normal and the Pathological', reprinted in E. J. Clarke and D. H. Kelly (eds.), *Deviant Behaviour: A Text-Reader in the Sociology of Deviance*, 6th edn (New York: Worth, 2003), 80–4.

Edgerton, R. *Mau Mau: An African Crucible* (London: Collier Macmillan, 1989).

Egnell, R. 'Explaining US and British Performance in Complex Expeditionary Operations: The Civil-Military Dimension', *Journal of Strategic Studies*, 29 (2006), 1041–75.

Elkins, C. 'The Struggle for Mau Mau Rehabilitation in Late Colonial Kenya', *International Journal of African Historical Studies*, 33 (2000), 25–57.
   'Detention and Rehabilitation during the Mau Mau Emergency: The Crisis of Late-colonial Kenya' (doctoral thesis, Harvard University, 2000).
   Britain's Gulag: The Brutal End of Empire in Kenya (London: Jonathan Cape, 2005).
   'Alchemy of Evidence: Mau Mau, the British Empire, and the High Court of Justice', *Journal of Imperial and Commonwealth History*, 39 (2011), 731–48.

Ellis, D. 'The Nandi Protest of 1923 in the Context of African Resistance to Colonial Rule in Kenya', *Journal of African History*, 17 (1976), 555–75.

Ellis, J. *The Social History of the Machine Gun* (London: Pimlico, 1993).

Evans, M. *Algeria: France's Undeclared War* (Oxford University Press, 2012).

Evans, M. M. *Encyclopedia of the Boer War, 1899–1902* (Oxford: ABC-Clio, 2000).

Evans, P. *Law and Disorder, or Scenes of Life in Kenya* (London: Secker and Warburg, 1956).

Falk, R. 'Telford Taylor and the Legacy of Nuremberg', *Columbia Journal of Transnational Law*, 37 (1999), 693–724.

Feaver, P. D. *Armed Servants: Agency, Oversight, and Civil-Military Relations* (London: Harvard University Press, 2003).

Ferguson, N. 'Prisoner Taking and Prisoner Killing in the Age of Total War: Towards a Political Economy of Military Defeat', *War in History*, 11 (2004), 148–92.

Ferris, J. R. *The Evolution of British Strategic Policy, 1919–26* (London: Macmillan, 1989).
    'Power, Strategy, Armed Forces and War', in P. Finney (ed.), *Palgrave Advances in International History* (Basingstoke: Palgrave, 2005), 58–79.
Fitzpatrick, D. 'Militarism in Ireland, 1900–1922', in T. Bartlett and K. Jeffery (eds.), *A Military History of Ireland* (Cambridge University Press), 379–406.
Foran, W. R. *The Kenya Police 1887–1960* (London: Hale, 1962).
Freeman, M. D. A. *Lloyd's Introduction to Jurisprudence*. 7th edn (London: Sweet and Maxwell, 2001).
French, D. 'Have the Options Really Changed? British Defence Policy in the Twentieth Century', *Journal of Strategic Studies*, 15 (1992), 50–72.
    Military Identities: The Regimental System, the British Army, and the British people, c. 1870–2000 (Oxford University Press, 2005).
    'Big Wars and Small Wars between the Wars, 1919–39', in H. Strachan (ed.), *Big Wars and Small Wars: The British Army and the Lessons of War in the Twentieth Century* (London: Routledge, 2006), 36–53.
    'History and the British Army, 1870–1970: Where Are We and Where Might We Go?' Keynote lecture given at the 'Britons at War: New Perspectives' conference, University of Northampton, 21 April 2006.
    The British Way in Counter-Insurgency, 1945–1967 (Oxford University Press, 2011).
    Army, Empire, and Cold War: The British Army and Military Policy, 1945–1971 (Oxford University Press, 2012).
Furedi, F. 'The Social Composition of the Mau Mau Movement in the White Highlands', *Journal of Peasant Studies*, 1 (1974), 486–505.
    The Mau Mau War in Perspective (London: James Currey, 1989).
    Colonial Wars and the Politics of Third World Nationalism (London: I. B. Tauris, 1994).
Fussell, P. *Wartime: Understanding and Behaviour in the Second World War* (Oxford University Press, 1989).
Garnier, M. A. 'Changing Recruitment Patterns and Organizational Ideology: The Case of a British Military Academy', *Administrative Science Quarterly*, 17 (1972), 499–507.
George, A. (ed.), *Western State Terrorism* (London: Polity Press, 1991).
Gilbert, M. *Never Despair: Winston S. Churchill 1945–1965* (London: Heinemann, 1988).
Gittings, C. J. 'The Bertrand Stewart Prize Essay, 1949', *The Army Quarterly*, 59 (1950), 161–77.
Goldsworthy, D. *Colonial Issues in British Politics 1945–1961: From 'Colonial Development' to 'Wind of Change'* (Oxford: Clarendon Press, 1971).
Gray, C. S. *Modern Strategy* (Oxford University Press, 1999).
    Strategy and History: Essays on Theory and Practice (London: Routledge, 2006).
Green, L. C. *The Contemporary Law of Armed Conflict*. 2nd edn (Manchester University Press, 2000).
    'Superior Orders and Command Responsibility', *Military Law Review*, 175 (2003), 309–84.

Grenfell, R. 'This Question of Superior Orders', *RUSI Journal*, 96 (1951), 263–6.

Grossman, D. *On Killing: The Psychological Cost of Learning to Kill in War and Society* (London: Little, Brown and Company, 1996).

Gwynn, C. W. *Imperial Policing*, 2nd edn (London: Macmillan, 1939).

Hack, K. 'Screwing Down the People: The Malayan Emergency, Decolonisation and Ethnicity', in H. Antlöv and S. Tonnesson (eds.), *Imperial Policy and Southeast Asian Nationalism* (London: Curzon, 1995), 83–109.

'"Iron Claws on Malaya": The Historiography of the Malayan Emergency', *Journal of Southeast Asian Studies*, 30 (1999), 99–125.

Hart, P. *The I.R.A. and Its Enemies: Violence and Community in Cork, 1916–1923* (Oxford: Clarendon Press, 1999).

The I.R.A. at War 1916–1923 (Oxford University Press, 2003).

Harvey, A. D. 'Who were the Auxiliaries?', *The Historical Journal*, 35 (1992), 665–9.

Heather, R. W. 'Intelligence and Counter-Insurgency in Kenya, 1952–56', *Intelligence and National Security*, 5 (1990), 57–83.

'Counterinsurgency and Intelligence in Kenya: 1952–56' (doctoral thesis, Cambridge University, 1993).

'Of Men and Plans: The Kenya Campaign as Part of the British Counterinsurgency Experience', *Conflict Quarterly*, 13 (1993), 17–26.

Hennessy, P. *The Prime Minister: The Office and its Holders since 1945* (London: Allen Lane, 2000).

Having It So Good: Britain in the Fifties (London: Allen Lane, 2006).

Hickman, T. *The Call-Up: A History of National Service* (London: Headline, 2004).

Hoffman, B. and J. M. Taw, *Defense Policy and Low-Intensity Conflict: The Development of Britain's 'Small Wars' Doctrine during the 1950s* (Santa Monica, CA: RAND, 1991).

Holden Reid, B. 'Introduction: Is There a British Military "Philosophy"?', in J. J. G. Mackenzie and B. Holden Reid (eds.), *Central Region vs. Out-of-area: Future Commitments* (London: Tri-Service, 1990), 1–16.

Holland, R. 'Britain, Commonwealth and the End of Empire', in V. Bogdanor (ed.), *The British Constitution in the Twentieth Century* (Oxford University Press for the British Academy, 2003).

Holman, D. *Elephants at Sundown: The Story of Bill Woodley* (London: W. H. Allen, 1978).

Holmes, R. *Acts of War: The Behaviour of Men in Battle* (London: Weidenfeld and Nicolson, 2003).

Hopkinson, M. *The Irish War of Independence* (Dublin: Gill and Macmillan, 2002).

Howard, M. 'Civil-Military Relations in Great Britain and the United States, 1945–1958', *Political Science Quarterly*, 75 (1960), 35–46.

'The Use and Abuse of Military History', *RUSI Journal*, 107 (1962), 4–10.

War and the Liberal Conscience (London: Temple Smith, 1978).

Howard, M., G. J. Andreopoulos and M. R. Shulman (eds.), *The Laws of War: Constraints on Warfare in the Western World* (London: Yale University Press, 1994).

Howe, S. *Anticolonialism in British Politics: The Left and the End of Empire, 1918–1964* (Oxford: Clarendon Press, 1993).

Hudson, W. M. 'Book Reviews. "Obeying Orders: Atrocity, Military Discipline and the Law of War"', *Military Law Review*, 161 (1999), 225–36.

Hughes, M. 'The Banality of Brutality: British Armed Forces and the Repression of the Arab Revolt in Palestine, 1936–39', *English Historical Review*, 124 (2009), 313–54.

'A History of Violence: The Shooting in Jerusalem of British Assistant Police Superintendent Alan Sigrist, 12 June 1936', *Journal of Contemporary History*, 45 (2010), 725–43.

Huntington, S. P. *The Soldier and the State: The Theory and Politics of Civil-Military Relations* (London: Belknap Press of Harvard University Press, 1985).

Hyam, R. *Britain's Declining Empire: The Road to Decolonisation, 1918–1968* (Cambridge University Press, 2006).

Jackson, R., E. Murphy and S. Poynting (eds.), *Contemporary State Terrorism: Theory and Practice* (Abingdon: Routledge, 2009).

Jacobsen, M. '"Only by the Sword": British Counter-Insurgency in Iraq, 1920', *Small Wars and Insurgencies*, 2 (1991), 323–63.

Jakobsen, P. J. 'Pushing the Limits of Military Coercion Theory', *International Studies Perspectives*, 12 (2011), 153–70.

James, L. *Warrior Race. A History of the British at War from Roman Times to the Present* (London: Abacus, 2002).

Janowitz, M. *The Professional Soldier: A Social and Political Portrait* (London: Collier-Macmillan, 1960).

Jeffery, K. 'The British Army and Internal Security 1919–1939', *The Historical Journal*, 24 (1981), 377–97.

The British Army and the Crisis of Empire 1918–22 (Manchester University Press, 1984).

'Intelligence and Counter-Insurgency Operations: Some Reflections on the British Experience', *Intelligence and National Security*, 2 (1987), 118–49.

'Colonial Warfare 1900–39', in C. J. McInnes and G. Sheffield (eds.), *Warfare in the Twentieth Century: Theory and Practice* (London: Unwin Hyman, 1988), 24–50.

Jenkins, R. *Churchill* (London: Macmillan, 2001).

Jochnick, C. A. and R. Normand, 'The Legitimation of Violence: A Critical History of the Laws of War', *Harvard International Law Journal*, 35 (1994), 49–95.

Joes, A. J. *Resisting Rebellion: The History and Politics of Counterinsurgency* (Lexington, KY: University Press of Kentucky, 2004).

Johnson, F. A. *Defence by Committee: The British Committee of Imperial Defence 1885–1959* (Oxford University Press, 1960).

Johnson, J. T. *Can Modern War Be Just?* (New Haven: Yale University Press, 1984).

Jones, A. (ed.), *Genocide, War Crimes and the West: History and Complicity* (London: Zed Books, 2004).

Jones, P. D. 'Nazi Atrocities against Allied Airmen: Stalag Luft III and the End of British War Crimes Trials', *The Historical Journal*, 41 (1998), 543–65.

Jones, T. 'The British Army, and Counter-Guerrilla Warfare in Transition, 1944–1952', *Small Wars and Insurgencies*, 7 (1996), 265–307.

Judd, D. and K. Surridge, *The Boer War* (London: John Murray, 2003).

Kanogo, T. *Squatters and the Roots of Mau Mau 1905–63* (London: James Currey, 1987).

Kassimeris, G. (ed.), *The Barbarisation of Warfare* (London: Hurst, 2006).

The Warrior's Dishonour: Barbarity and Morality in Modern Warfare (Aldershot: Ashgate, 2006).

Kelly, J. B. 'Legal Aspects of Military Operations in Counterinsurgency', *Military Law Review*, 21 (1963), 95–122.

Kennedy, D. 'Constructing the Colonial Myth of Mau Mau', *International Journal of African Historical Studies*, 25 (1992), 241–60.

Kerr, R. 'A Force for Good? War, Crime and Legitimacy: The British Army in Iraq', *Defense and Security Analysis*, 24 (2008), 401–19.

The Military on Trial: The British Army in Iraq (Nijmegen: Wolf Legal Publishers, 2008).

Kershaw, G. *Mau Mau from Below* (Oxford: James Currey, 1997).

Kiernan, V. G. *Colonial Empires and Armies 1815–1960* (Stroud: Sutton Publishing, 1998).

Killingray, D. 'The Idea of a British Imperial African Army', *Journal of African History*, 20 (1979), 421–36.

'"A Swift Agent of Government": Air Power in British Colonial Africa, 1916–1939', *Journal of African History*, 25 (1984), 429–44.

'The Maintenance of Law and Order in British Colonial Africa', *African Affairs*, 85 (1986), 411–37.

'Race and Rank in the British Army in the Twentieth Century', *Ethnic and Racial Studies*, 10 (1987), 276–90.

'"The Rod of Empire": The Debate over Corporal Punishment in the British African Colonial Forces, 1888–1946', *Journal of African History*, 35 (1994), 201–16.

Kitson, F. *Low Intensity Operations: Subversion, Insurgency, Peace-keeping* (Harrisburg, PA: Stackpole Books, 1971).

Kudaisya, G. '"In Aid of Civil Power": The Colonial Army in Northern India, c.1919–42', *Journal of Imperial and Commonwealth History*, 32 (2004), 41–68.

Kyle, K. *The Politics of the Independence of Kenya* (Basingstoke: Macmillan, 1999).

Lathbury, G. Foreword in R. Meinertzhagen, *Kenya Diary 1902–1906* (London: Welbeck Street, 1957), vii–viii.

Leakey, L. S. B. *Mau Mau and the Kikuyu* (London: Methuen, 1952).

Leeson, D. M. *The Black and Tans: British Police and Auxiliaries in the Irish War of Independence* (Oxford University Press, 2011).

Levene, M. and P. Roberts (eds.), *The Massacre in History* (Oxford: Berghahn, 1999).

Lewis, J. '"Daddy Wouldn't Buy Me a Mau Mau": The British Popular Press and the Demoralization of Empire', in E. S. Atieno Odhiambo and J. Lonsdale (eds.), *Mau Mau and Nationhood: Arms, Authority and Narration* (Oxford: James Currey, 2003), 227–50.

Lewis, J. and P. Murphy, 'The Old Pals' Protection Society? The Colonial Office and the British Press on the Eve of Decolonisation', in C. Kaul (ed.), *Media and the British Empire* (Basingstoke: Palgrave Macmillan, 2006), 55–69.

Lloyd, N. *The Amritsar Massacre: The Untold Story of One Fateful Day* (London: I. B. Tauris, 2011).

Lonsdale, J. 'Mau Maus of the Mind: Making Mau Mau and Remaking Kenya', *Journal of African History*, 31 (1990), 393–421.

   'Kenya: Home County and African Frontier' in R. Bickers (ed.), *Settlers and Expatriates: Britons over the Seas* (Oxford University Press, 2010), 74–111.

Lopez, L. 'Uncivil Wars: The Challenge of Applying International Humanitarian Law to Internal Armed Conflicts', *New York University Law Review*, 69 (1994), 916–62.

Lovell-Knight, A. V. *The Story of the Royal Military Police* (London: Leo Cooper, 1977).

Lowry, D. (ed.), *The South African War Reappraised* (Manchester University Press, 2000).

Lynn, J. A. 'Patterns of Insurgency and Counterinsurgency', *Military Review* (July-August 2005), 22–7.

MacKenzie, S. P. *Politics and Military Morale: Current-affairs and Citizenship Education in the British Army, 1914–1950* (Oxford: Clarendon Press, 1992).

Majdalany, F. *State of Emergency: The Full Story of Mau Mau* (Boston: Houghton Mifflin, 1963).

Malanczuk, P. *Akehurst's Modern Introduction to International Law*. 7th rev. edn (London: Routledge, 1997).

Maloba, W. *Mau Mau and Kenya: An Analysis of a Peasant Revolt* (Bloomington: Indiana University Press, 1993).

Mao Tse-Tung, *On Guerrilla Warfare. Translated and introduced by Samuel B. Griffith* (New York: Anchor Press/Doubleday, 1978).

Marshall, S. L. A. *Men against Fire: The Problem of Battle Command* (Norman, OK: University of Oklahoma Press 2000).

Matson, A. T. *Nandi Resistance to British Rule 1890–1906* (Nairobi: East African Publishing House, 1972).

McCoubrey, H. 'From Nuremberg to Rome: Restoring the Defence of Superior Orders', *International and Comparative Law Quarterly*, 50 (2001), 386–94.

McInnes, C. J. *Hot War, Cold War: The British Army's Way in Warfare 1945–95* (London: Brassey's, 1996).

   'The British Army's New Way in Warfare: A Doctrinal Misstep?', *Defence and Security Analysis*, 23 (2007), 127–41.

Miller, S. M. 'Duty or Crime? Defining Acceptable Behaviour in the British Army in South Africa, 1899–1902', *Journal of British Studies*, 49 (2010), 311–31.

Mockaitis, T. R. *British Counterinsurgency, 1919–60* (New York: St Martin's Press, 1990).

   'Minimum Force, British Counter-Insurgency and the Mau Mau Rebellion: A Reply', *Small Wars and Insurgencies*, 3 (1992), 87–9.

   'Low-Intensity Conflict: the British Experience', *Conflict Quarterly*, 13 (1993), 7–16.

'Winning Hearts and Minds in the "War on Terrorism"', *Small Wars and Insurgencies*, 14 (2003), 21–38.

Moir, L. *The Law of Internal Armed Conflict* (Cambridge University Press, 2002).

Moreman, T. R. '"Small Wars" and "Imperial Policing": The British Army and the Theory and Practice of Colonial Warfare in the British Empire, 1919–1939', *Journal of Strategic Studies*, 19 (1996), 105–31.

The Army in India and the Development of Frontier Warfare, 1849–1947 (Basingstoke: Macmillan, 1998).

Morgan, K. O. 'Imperialists at Bay: British Labour and Decolonization', *Journal of Imperial and Commonwealth History*, 27 (1999), 233–54.

Moyse-Bartlett, H. *The King's African Rifles: A Study in the Military History of East and Central Africa, 1890–1945* (Aldershot: Gale and Polden, 1956).

Mulligan, W. 'Review Article: Total War', *War in History*, 15 (2008), 211–21.

Mumford, A. 'Unnecessary or Unsung? The Utilisation of Airpower in Britain's Colonial Counterinsurgencies', *Small Wars and Insurgencies*, 20 (2009), 636–55.

Murphy, P. *Party Politics and Decolonization: The Conservative Party and British Colonial Policy in Tropical Africa, 1951–1964* (Oxford: Clarendon Press, 1995).

Alan Lennox-Boyd: A Biography (London: I. B. Tauris, 1999).

Nagl, J. A. *Counterinsurgency Lessons from Malaya and Vietnam: Learning to Eat Soup with a Knife* (London: Praeger, 2002).

Learning to Eat Soup with a Knife: Counterinsurgency Lessons from Malaya and Vietnam (London: University of Chicago Press, 2005).

Narain, S. *The Historiography of the Jallianwalla Bagh Massacre* (South Godstone: Spantech and Lancer, 1998).

Nasson, B. 'Waging Total War in South Africa: Some Centenary Writings on the Anglo-Boer War', *Journal of Military History*, 66 (2002), 813–28.

Neiberg, M. S. 'War and Society', in M. Hughes and W. J. Philpott (eds.), *Palgrave Advances in Modern Military History* (Basingstoke: Palgrave, 2006), 42–60.

Newbery, S. 'Intelligence and Controversial British Interrogation Techniques: The Northern Ireland Case, 1971–2', *Irish Studies in International Affairs*, 20 (2009), 103–19.

Newsinger, J. 'Revolt and Repression in Kenya: The "Mau Mau" Rebellion, 1952–1960', *Science and Society*, 45 (1981), 159–85.

'A Counter-insurgency Tale: Kitson in Kenya', *Race and Class*, 31 (1990), 61–72.

'Minimum Force, British Counter-Insurgency and the Mau Mau Rebellion', *Small Wars and Insurgencies*, 3 (1992), 47–57.

British Counterinsurgency: From Palestine to Northern Ireland (Basingstoke: Palgrave, 2002).

'English Atrocities', *New Left Review*, 32 (2005), 153–60.

Nissimi, H. 'Illusions of World Power in Kenya: Strategy, Decolonization, and the British Base, 1946–1961', *International History Review*, 23 (2001), 824–46.

'Mau Mau and the Decolonisation of Kenya', *Journal of Military and Strategic Studies*, 8 (2006), 1–35.

Norris, J. 'Repression and Rebellion: Britain's Response to the Arab Revolt in Palestine of 1936–39', *Journal of Imperial and Commonwealth History*, 36 (2008), 25–45.

Norton, P. (ed.), *Dissension in the House of Commons: Intra-Party Dissent in the House of Commons' Division Lobbies 1945–1974* (London: Macmillan, 1975).

O'Brien, W. V. 'The Rule of Law in Small Wars', *Annals of the American Academy of Political and Social Sciences*, 541 (1995), 36–46.

O'Connell, D. P. 'The Nature of British Military Law', *Military Law Review*, 19 (1963), 141–55.

Ó Dochartaigh, N. 'Bloody Sunday: Error or Design?', *Contemporary British History*, 24 (2010), 89–108.

Ogot, B. A. 'Review Article: *Britain's Gulag*', *Journal of African History*, 46 (2005), 493–505.

Ogot, B. A. and W. R. Ochieng (eds.), *Decolonization and Independence in Kenya, 1940–93* (London: James Currey, 1995).

Omissi, D. 'Britain, the Assyrians and the Iraq Levies, 1919–1932', *Journal of Imperial and Commonwealth History*, 17 (1989), 301–22.

  Air Power and Colonial Control: The Royal Air Force 1919–1939 (Manchester University Press, 1990).

  'Technology and Repression: Air Control in Palestine 1922–36', *Journal of Strategic Studies*, 13 (1990), 41–63.

  The Sepoy and the Raj: The Indian Army, 1860–1940 (London: Macmillan, 1994).

Oppenheim, L. *International Law: A Treatise*. Vol. II: *Disputes, War and Neutrality*. 7th edn, revised and edited by H. Lauterpacht (London: Longmans, Green and Co., 1952).

Osiel, M. J. 'Obeying Orders: Atrocity, Military Discipline, and the Law of War', *California Law Review*, 86 (1998), 1–127.

Otley, C. B. 'The Social Origins of British Army Officers', *Sociological Review*, 18 (1970), 213–39.

  'The Educational Background of British Army Officers', *Sociology*, 7 (1973), 191–209.

  'Militarism and Militarization in the Public Schools, 1900–1972', *British Journal of Sociology*, 29 (1978), 321–39.

Overy, R. *Interrogations: Inside the Minds of the Nazi Elite* (London: Penguin, 2002).

  'The Nuremberg Trials: International Law in the Making', in P. Sands (ed.), *From Nuremberg to The Hague: The Future of International Criminal Justice* (Cambridge University Press, 2003), 1–29.

Page, M. *A History of the King's African Rifles and East African Forces* (London: Leo Cooper, 1998).

Paget, J. *Counter-insurgency Campaigning* (London: Faber and Faber, 1967).

Pakenham, T. *The Boer War* (London: Abacus, 2003).

Pal, D. 'Limits to Obedience', *Army Quarterly*, 72 (1956), 81–3.

Parker, I. *The Last Colonial Regiment: The History of the Kenya Regiment (T.F.)* (Kinloss: Librario Publishing, 2009).

Parsons, T. 'Book Review: David Anderson. Histories of the Hanged: The Dirty War in Kenya and the End of Empire; Caroline Elkins. Imperial Reckoning:

The Untold Story of Britain's Gulag in Kenya', *American Historical Review*, 110 (2005), 1295–7.

Parsons, T. H. *The African Rank-and-file: Social Implications of Colonial Military Service in the King's African Rifles, 1902–1964* (Oxford: James Currey, 1999).

Paxman, J. *The English: A Portrait of a People* (London: Michael Joseph, 1998).

Percox, D. A. 'British Counter-Insurgency in Kenya, 1952–56: Extension of Internal Security Policy or Prelude to Decolonisation?', *Small Wars and Insurgencies*, 9 (1998), 46–101.

'Internal Security and Decolonization in Kenya, 1956–63', *Journal of Imperial and Commonwealth History*, 29 (2001), 92–116.

'Mau Mau and the Arming of the State', in E. S. Atieno Odhiambo and J. Lonsdale (eds.), *Mau Mau and Nationhood: Arms, Authority and Narration* (Oxford: James Currey, 2003), 121–54.

Britain, Kenya and the Cold War: Imperial Defence, Colonial Security and Decolonisation (London: Tauris Academic Studies, 2004).

Peterson, D. R. 'The Intellectual Lives of Mau Mau Detainees', *Journal of African History*, 49 (2008), 73–91.

Pimlott, J. 'The British Army: The Dhofar Campaign, 1970–1975', in I. F. W. Beckett and J. Pimlott (eds.), *Armed Forces and Modern Counter-Insurgency* (London: Croom Helm, 1985), 16–45.

Popplewell, R. '"Lacking Intelligence": Some Reflections on Recent Approaches to British Counter-Insurgency, 1900–1960', *Intelligence and National Security*, 10 (1995), 336–52.

Presley, C. A. 'The Mau Mau Rebellion, Kikuyu Women, and Social Change', *Canadian Journal of African Studies*, 22 (1988), 502–27.

Kikuyu Women, the Mau Mau Rebellion, and Social Change in Kenya (Oxford: Westview Press, 1992).

Priya, S. 'The Defense of Inhumanity: Air Control and the British Idea of Arabia', *American Historical Review*, 111 (2006), 16–51.

Rabkin, J. 'Nuremberg Misremembered', *SAIS Review*, 19 (1999), 81–96.

Raghavan, S. 'Protecting the Raj: The Army in India and Internal Security, c. 1919–39', *Small Wars and Insurgencies*, 16 (2005), 253–79.

Ramakrishna, K. *Emergency Propaganda: The Winning of Malayan Hearts and Minds 1948–1958* (Richmond: Curzon Press, 2002).

Rangwala, G. 'Counter-Insurgency amid Fragmentation: The British in Southern Iraq', *Journal of Strategic Studies*, 32 (2009), 495–513.

Rant, J. W. *Courts-Martial Handbook: Practice and Procedure* (Chichester: John Wiley and Sons, 1998).

Ratner, S. R. and J. S. Abrams, *Accountability for Human Rights Atrocities in International Law: Beyond the Nuremberg Legacy* (Oxford University Press, 2001).

Rawcliffe, D. H. *The Struggle for Kenya* (London: Victor Gollancz, 1954).

Razzell, P. E. 'Social Origins of Officers in the Indian and British Home Army: 1758–1962', *British Journal of Sociology*, 14 (1963), 248–60.

Reis, B. 'The Myth of British Minimum Force in Counterinsurgency Campaigns during Decolonisation (1945–70)', *Journal of Strategic Studies*, 34 (2011), 245–79.

Reynolds, D. *Britannia Overruled: British Foreign Policy and World Power in the Twentieth Century* (London: Longman, 1991).

Roberts, A. 'The British Armed Forces and Politics: A Historical Perspective', *Armed Forces and Society*, 3 (1977), 531–56.

'Doctrine and Reality in Afghanistan', *Survival*, 51 (2009), 29–60.

Roberts, A. and R. Guelff (eds.) *Documents on the Laws of War*. 3rd edn (Oxford University Press, 2000).

Rogers, A. P. V. 'War Crimes Trials under the Royal Warrant: British Practice 1945–1949', *International and Comparative Law Quarterly*, 39 (1990), 780–800.

Law on the Battlefield. 2nd edn (Manchester University Press, 2004).

Rosberg, C. G. and J. Nottingham, *The Myth of 'Mau Mau': Nationalism in Kenya* (London: Pall Mall Press, 1966).

Rose, E. 'The Anatomy of Mutiny', *Armed Forces and Society*, 8 (1982), 561–74.

Rosecrance, R. N. *Defense of the Realm: British Strategy in the Nuclear Epoch* (London: Columbia University Press, 1968).

Roy, K. 'Coercion through Leniency: British Manipulation of the Courts-Martial System in the Post-Mutiny Indian Army, 1859–1913', *Journal of Military History*, 65 (2001), 937–64.

Royle, T. *National Service: The Best Years of Their Lives* (London: André Deutsch, 2002).

Rubin, G. R. 'Courts Martial from Bad Nenndorf (1948) to Osnabrück (2005)', *RUSI Journal*, 150 (2005), 52–3.

Murder, Mutiny and the Military: British Court Martial Cases, 1940–1966 (London: Francis Boutle, 2005).

Santoru, M. E. 'The Colonial Idea of Women and Direct Intervention: The Mau Mau Case', *African Affairs*, 95 (1996), 253–67.

Satia, P. 'The Defense of Inhumanity: Air Control and the British Idea of Arabia', *American Historical Review*, 111 (2006), 16–51.

Sayer, D. 'British Reaction to the Amritsar Massacre 1919–1920', *Past and Present*, 131 (1991), 130–64.

Scheipers, S. (ed.) *Prisoners in War* (Oxford University Press, 2010).

Schmoeckel, M. 'Review of Best, "War and Law since 1945" and Andreopolous "The Laws of War"', *Journal of Modern History*, 69 (1997), 570–3.

Scott, L. V. *Conscription and the Attlee Governments: The Politics and Policy of National Service 1945–1951* (Oxford: Clarendon Press, 1993).

Shaw, M. *War and Genocide: Organized Killing in Modern Society* (Oxford: Polity Press, 2003).

Sheehan, W. *A Hard Local War: The British Army and the Guerrilla War in Cork, 1919–1921* (Stroud: The History Press, 2011).

Sheffield, G. D. *Leadership in the Trenches: Officer–Man Relations, Morale and Discipline in the British Army in the Era of the First World War* (Basingstoke: Macmillan, 2000).

Shephard, B. *A War of Nerves: Soldiers and Psychiatrists 1914–1994* (London: Pimlico, 2002).

Shoul, S. 'In Aid of the Civil Power: The British Army's Riot Control Operations in India, Egypt, and Palestine, 1919–1939', paper presented at the 'Britons at War: New Perspectives' conference, University of Northampton, 21 April 2006.

'Soldiers, Riots, and Aid to the Civil Power, in India, Egypt and Palestine, 1919–1939' (doctoral thesis, University College London, 2006).

'Soldiers, Riot Control and Aid to the Civil Power in India, Egypt and Palestine, 1919–39', *Journal of the Society for Army Historical Research*, 346 (2008), 120–39.

Simpson, A. W. B. *Human Rights and the End of Empire: Britain and the Genesis of the European Convention* (Oxford University Press, 2001).

Singh, N. *The Defence Mechanism of the Modern State: A Study of the Politico-Military Set-up of National and International Organisations with Special Reference to the Chiefs of Staff Committee* (New York: Asia Publishing House, 1964).

Smith, H. A. 'The Defence of Superior Orders', *RUSI Journal*, 96 (1951), 617–19.

Smith, J. H. 'Njama's Supper: The Consumption and Use of Literary Potency by Mau Mau Insurgents in Colonial Kenya', *Comparative Studies in Society and History*, 40 (1998), 524–48.

Smith, L. V. *Between Mutiny and Obedience: The Case of the French Fifth Infantry Division during World War I* (Princeton University Press, 1994).

Smith, M. L. R. 'Guerrillas in the Mist: Reassessing Strategy and Low Intensity Warfare', *Review of International Studies*, 29 (2003), 19–37.

Smith, P. (ed.), *Government and the Armed Forces in Britain 1856–1990* (London: Hambledon Press, 1996).

Snyder, W. P. *The Politics of British Defense Policy, 1945–1962* (Columbus, OH: Ohio State University Press, 1964).

Sorrenson, M. P. K. *Land Reform in the Kikuyu Country: A Study in Government Policy* (Oxford University Press, 1967).

Spiers, E. M. *The Late Victorian Army 1868–1902* (Manchester University Press, 1992).

Strachan, H. *The Politics of the British Army* (Oxford: Clarendon Press, 1997).

'Total War in the Twentieth Century', in A. Marwick, C. Emsley and W. Simpson (eds.), *Total War and Historical Change: Europe 1914–1955* (Buckingham: Open University Press, 2001), 255–83.

'Making Strategy: Civil-Military Relations after Iraq', *Survival*, 48 (2006), 59–82.

'Training, Morale and Modern War', *Journal of Contemporary History*, 41 (2006), 211–27.

(ed.), *Big Wars and Small Wars: The British Army and the Lessons of War in the Twentieth Century* (London: Routledge, 2006).

Steppler, G. A. 'British Military Law, Discipline, and the Conduct of Regimental Courts Martial in the Later Eighteenth Century', *English Historical Review*, 102 (1987), 859–86.

Stewart, J. G. 'Towards a Single Definition of Armed Conflict in International Humanitarian Law: A Critique of Internationalized Armed Conflict', *International Review of the Red Cross*, 85 (2003), 313–50.

Stone, D. 'The Domestication of Violence: Forging a Collective Memory of the Holocaust in Britain, 1945–6', *Patterns of Prejudice*, 33 (1999), 13–29.

Stubbs, R. *Hearts and Minds in Guerrilla Warfare: The Malayan Emergency 1948–1960* (Oxford University Press, 1989).

Surridge, K. '"All you soldiers are what we call pro-Boer": The Military Critique of the South African War, 1899–1902', *History*, 82 (1997), 591–3.

'Rebellion, Martial Law and British Civil-Military Relations: The War in Cape Colony 1899–1902', *Small Wars and Insurgencies*, 8 (1997), 35–60.

Tamarkin, M. 'Mau Mau in Nakuru', *Journal of African History*, 17 (1976), 119–34.

Thompson, A. *The Empire Strikes Back? The Impact of Imperialism on Britain from the Mid-Nineteenth Century* (Harlow: Pearson Education, 2005).

Thompson, J. (ed.), *The Imperial War Museum Book of Modern Warfare: British and Commonwealth Forces at War 1945–2000* (London: Pan Books/Imperial War Museum, 2003).

Thompson, R. *Defeating Communist Insurgency: Experiences from Malaya and Vietnam* (London: Chatto and Windus, 1966).

Thornton, A. P. *The Imperial Idea and its Enemies: A Study in British Power* (London: Macmillan, 1959).

Thornton, R. 'Understanding the Cultural Bias of a Military Organization and its Effect on the Process of Change: A Comparative Analysis of the Reaction of the British and United States Armies to the Demands of Post-Cold War Peace Support Operations in the Period, 1989–1999' (doctoral thesis, University of Birmingham, 2001).

'The British Army and the Origins of its Minimum Force Philosophy', *Small Wars and Insurgencies*, 15 (2004), 83–106.

'"Minimum Force": A Reply to Huw Bennett', *Small Wars and Insurgencies*, 20 (2009), 215–26.

Throup, D. W. *Economic and Social Origins of Mau Mau 1945–53* (London: James Currey, 1987).

'Crime, Politics and the Police in Colonial Kenya, 1939–63', in D. M. Anderson and D. Killingray (eds.), *Policing and Decolonisation: Politics, Nationalism and the Police, 1917–65* (Manchester University Press, 1992), 127–58.

Tidrick, K. *Empire and the English Character* (London: I. B. Tauris, 1990).

Towle, P. *Pilots and Rebels: The Use of Aircraft in Unconventional Warfare 1918–1988* (London: Brassey's, 1989).

Townshend, C. *The British Campaign in Ireland 1919–1921: The Development of Political and Military Policies* (Oxford University Press, 1975).

Britain's Civil Wars: Counterinsurgency in the Twentieth Century (London: Faber and Faber, 1986).

Tusa, A. and J. Tusa, *Nuremberg Trial* (London: BBC Books, 1995).

Valentino, B. A. *Final Solutions: Mass Killing and Genocide in the Twentieth Century* (London: Cornell University Press, 2004).

Vandervort, B. *Wars of Imperial Conquest in Africa, 1830–1914* (London: UCL Press, 1998).

Wade, D. A. L. 'A Survey of the Trials of War Criminals', *RUSI Journal*, 96 (1951), 66–70.

Waller, J. *Becoming Evil: How Ordinary People Commit Genocide and Mass Killing* (Oxford University Press, 2002).

Walton, C. 'British Intelligence and Threats to National Security, c. 1941–1951' (doctoral dissertation, Cambridge University, 2006).

Walzer, M. *Just and Unjust Wars. A Moral Argument with Historical Illustrations* (New York: Basic Books, 2000).

Warhurst, F. 'Training Army Officers', *Army Quarterly*, 52 (1946), 252–61.

Weaver, L. 'The Kenya Regiment', in M. Page, *A History of the King's African Rifles and East African Forces* (London: Leo Cooper, 1998), 239–49.

Weitz, E. D. *A Century of Genocide: Utopias of Race and Nation* (Oxford: Princeton University Press, 2003).

Wessels, A. 'Afrikaners at War', in J. Gooch (ed.), *The Boer War: Direction, Experience and Image* (London: Frank Cass, 2000), 73–106.

White, L. 'Separating the Men from the Boys: Constructions of Gender, Sexuality, and Terrorism in Central Kenya, 1939–1959', *International Journal of African Historical Studies*, 23 (1990), 1–25.

White, V. C. *The Story of Army Education 1643–1963* (London: George G. Harrap, 1963).

Wilkinson, P. *State Terrorism and Human Rights: International Responses since the Cold War* (Abingdon: Routledge, 2011).

Wylie, N. 'Prisoners of War in the Era of Total War', *War in History*, 13 (2006), 217–33.

Zimbardo, P. *The Lucifer Effect: How Good People Turn Evil* (London: Rider, 2009).

Zugbach, R. G. L. von *Power and Prestige in the British Army* (Aldershot: Avebury, 1988).

Index

3 King's African Rifles (KAR)
  arrival in Kenya, 22
  discipline, 110
  and the Home Guard, 249, 250
  and legal zones, 132
  and the McLean Inquiry,
    120, 121
  officers, 111, 224
  and political oversight, 50
  and prisoners, 152, 215, 240
  rape allegations, 209
4 King's African Rifles and the
    McLean Inquiry
  operations, 163, 164, 258
  and vigilantes, 171
5 King's African Rifles
  'B' Company, 112, 119, 125,
    180–93
  and the Home Guard, 248
  officers, 117, 224
  operations, 220, 233, 258
  and prisoners, 149
  rape allegations, 209
  shootings, 216
  see also Griffiths, Major Gerald S.
6 Division, 101
6 King's African Rifles
  beatings, 213
  and detention camps, 225
  and the Home Guard, 247
  officers, 106, 181
  operations, 163, 164, 255
  orders, 118
  and vigilantes, 171
7 Armoured Division, 12
7 King's African Rifles
  and the Home Guard, 248
  investigations into abuses, 117, 119,
    166, 213
  mutilation, 122
  officers, 106, 197
  operations, 164, 261, 262

17 Lancers, 101
23 King's African Rifles
  beatings, 213
  and committees, 57
  discipline, 110, 179, 205
  and legal zones, 130
  officers, 197, 224
  operations, 15, 18, 163, 164, 221, 259
  rape allegations, 209
  shootings, 167, 217
26 King's African Rifles
  and detention camps, 225
  discipline, 110
  and the Home Guard, 248
  looting, 58
  operations, 163, 255
  and surrenders, 146
39 Corps Royal Engineers, 22
39 Infantry Brigade
  and committees, 56, 57, 131,
    234, 253
  deployment, 18, 20, 22, 164, 256
  and the Home Guard, 248, 249
  orders on conduct, 114, 123, 133
  planning, 53, 261
  and settlers, 39, 255, 260
  and Special Branch, 242
49 Independent Infantry Brigade, 22–3,
    121, 153, 255, 256
70 (East Africa) Infantry Brigade
  and committees, 56, 233
  commander replaced, 115
  deployment, 18, 20, 22–3, 261–2
  discipline, 179
  and the Home Guard, 248, 249
  intelligence collection, 240, 258
  orders on conduct, 113, 118
  security breaches, 58
  and settlers, 40, 255, 259
  successes, 25
156 (East African) Heavy Anti-Aircraft
    Artillery (HAA), 13, 14, 208

Abdipahaman, Warrant Officer (WO), 152
Act of Indemnity, 89
aerial bombing, 49, 129, 236
    see also air control
Afghanistan, 4
air control, 93
    see also aerial bombing
Alexander, Earl, 43, 45
Allen, Sergeant Jeremy, 199–203
Amritsar massacre, 87, 97
Anderson, David, 216
Arab revolt, 103
arms and ammunition
    sale to Mau Mau, 58
Army Act, 63, 110, 178, 201, 209
Army Council, 67
Army Legal Services, 75, 120, 182, 201, 204
Army Prosecuting Authority, 204
Army Quarterly, 74
Army Staff College
    Charles Gwynn as commandant, 91
    General Lathbury as commandant, 28
    teaching about Palestine, 66
    teaching of law, 62, 73
    teaching of minimum force, 85–6,
        88–9
Arnhem, 28
arrests
    on declaration of the Emergency, 13, 45
    prior to declaration of Emergency, 12
    statistics, 19, 21
    see also military operations, Anvil;
        Overdraft
assaults, 119, 124, 179, 211, 214, 219, 227
Assistant Chief Secretary, 54
Attlee, Clement, 117
Auxiliary Division, 99, 100

Bahati, 163
Bailey, Company Sergeant Major (CSM)
    J., 151
Baring, Sir Evelyn
    awareness of abuses, 162, 167–9, 204, 233
    declares state of Emergency, 12
    directives on discipline, 111
    and evictions, 19, 173, 221
    introduces Emergency tax, 15
    meeting with Kenya Regiment, 41
    reorganisation of government machinery,
        52
    requests director of operations, 15, 176
    and surrender schemes, 134, 136,
        141, 144
    views on military commanders, 47
Barratt, Colonel G., 120, 121

Barton, Sergeant, 198, 203
basic training, 109
beatings, 102, 161, 162, 166, 213–15, 233
Benn, Anthony Wedgwood, 48
Berman, Bruce, 34, 37, 251
Best, Anthony, 69
Beyts, District Officer (DO), 255
Black and Tans, 99, 101
Black Watch
    arrival in Kenya, 22
    experience with the Kenya Regiment,
        214
    officers, 106, 121
    operations, 240, 261
    robberies, 226
    shot attempting to escape, 218
Blacker, John, 192
Blakeslee, Virginia, 216
Blundell, Michael
    and evictions, 172
    on Governor's Committee, 52
    and surrender schemes, 137, 143
    views on military policy, 40, 44
    on War Council, 53, 54, 253
Boer War, 71, 87, 95–7
Bond, Brian, 100
Bore, 188, 197
Bothma, Steve, 152
Boxer Rebellion, 102
Bramston, Major John, 216, 226
Branch, Daniel, 189, 250
Brans, Assistant Superintendent, 158
Briggs, Group Captain L. R., 39, 260
British Army of the Rhine, 64
British Army Review, 72, 74, 86
British Command Japan, 79
British Empire, 4
Brockway, Fenner, 49, 119, 207
Buffs, The *see* Royal East Kent Regiment
Buller Camp, Nairobi, 113
Burdick, Lieutenant Peter, 111
Burini, Captain Eric, 111
Burton, Gerald, 259

Cabinet
    and the Amritsar massacre, 98
    appointment of Erskine, 35
    discussions about the Emergency,
        42–7
    and the Geneva Conventions, 67
    and the Irish War of Independence, 100
    and the McLean Inquiry, 118, 207
    and surrender schemes, 136, 144
Cabinet Defence Committee, 44
Cabinet Secretary, 39

Callwell, Charles, 90, 92, 102
Cameron, Lieutenant-General Sir
     Alexander, 20, 52, 176
Campbell, Lieutenant-Colonel Guy, 41,
     42, 176, 177, 179, 215
Campbell-Bannerman, Sir Henry, 95
Carrothers, J. C., 222
Carruthers, Susan, 87
Carver, Field Marshal Lord, 52–3
Cashmore, Thomas, 217
Cassidy, Ron, 149
Castle, Barbara, 49
casualty statistics, 19, 25, 27, 121, 192, 247
     see also shot attempting to escape
Catling, Sir Richard, 155, 156
cattle confiscation, 91, 93, 102–3, 105,
     220–1
Cavendish Bentick, F. W., 52
Central Province Emergency Committee
     (CPEC), 39, 131, 242, 248, 249,
     253, 255
Chief Native Commissioner, 54, 137, 138,
     197, 221
Chief of Staff, East Africa Command, 137,
     138, 142
Chief of the Imperial General
     Staff (CIGS) see Harding, Field
     Marshal Sir John
Chief Secretary, 52, 57, 142
Chief Secretary's Complaints Co-ordinating
     Committee (CSCCC), 124–5, 209
Chief Staff Officer to the Governor
     see Hinde, Major-General William
chiefs, 16
China, General, 23, 46, 135–40, 235–6
Christian Council of Kenya, 120
Christian Missionary Society, 115
Chui, Major, 27, 142
Chuka massacre, 182–9, 196–9
Churchill, Sir Winston, 39, 43, 45–8, 64,
     176, 206
civilian control, 31, 42, 47, 59, 229,
     244, 263
civil-military relations
     theory, 31–2
Clarke, H. G., 156
Clayton, Anthony, 56, 189
Clemas, Major H. N., 205
Cold War, 65
collective punishment
     in doctrine, 89, 91
     in India, 97
     in international law, 78
     in Kenya, 194, 220–2, 227, 238, 253
     in Palestine, 103

Collins, D. T., 185, 196
Collins, Lieutenant-Colonel R. G. T., 112,
     176, 197
Colonial Office, 48, 80, 88, 167, 168, 177
Colonies, Secretary of State for see Lennox-
     Boyd, Alan and Lyttelton, Oliver
Colony Emergency Committee, 18,
     24, 51
command ammunition depot, 38
command and control, 17, 18, 20, 39,
     51–4, 176–7
command responsibility, 70
commander-in-chief see Erskine, General
     Sir George; Lathbury,
     Lieutenant-General Sir Gerald
Commissioner for Central Province, 46
Commissioner for Rift Valley Province,
     174, 242
Commissioner of Prisons, 147
committee system, 32, 39, 51–4, 56,
     233, 254
     see also intelligence committees
common law, 1, 70, 84, 87
compensation, 198
concentration camps, 96
Congress of Peoples Against
     Imperialism, 49
Conservative Party, 48, 94
Cooke, Second Lieutenant M., 132
Cooke, Sergeant, 124
Cooper, Major N. M. C., 132
Cornah, Brigadier Donald, 41, 112
Council of Ministers, 23, 54
Court of Inquiry, 112, 115, 117, 197, 198
courts-martial, 110, 117, 119, 124, 177–9,
     204, 212
Cowell-Parker, Lieutenant-Colonel R. H.,
     198, 201, 202
Craigie, Sir Robert, 66, 67
Crawford, Frederick, 52, 54, 116, 205
Criminal Investigation Department (CID),
     27, 141, 147, 179–80
Cromwell, Oliver, 1
Crossman, Richard, 123
Crown Counsel, 209
Crozier, Brigadier-General Frank, 100
Cullen, A., 78
Cumber, John, 200
curfew, 221
customary international law, 79, 80

Daily Chronicle, 221
Daily Herald, 119
Daily Mail, 50
Daily Mirror, 50

Davies, Lieutenant, 58
Day, Major F. W. J., 183, 198, 204
death penalty, 44, 46, 101
decolonisation, 3, 77, 82, 83, 94, 268
delegated detention orders, 147
Denning, R. E. V., 37
Department of Information, 145
Deputy Assistant Provost Marshal, 209
Deputy Commissioner of Police, 166
Deputy Director of Operations Committee, 197
Deputy Governor *see* Crawford, Frederick
Deputy Public Prosecutor, 209, 219
detention camps, 39, 146, 147, 223, 225, 232
detention policy, 49, 56, 144
Devonshire Regiment
  arrival in Kenya, 17
  and committees, 259
  deployment, 18
  and food denial, 255
  and the Home Guard, 249
  killing competitions, 119, 121, 207
  officers, 110, 123, 130, 132, 213
  operations, 164, 233, 261
  and prisoners, 240
Director of Information, 134, 141, 144
Director of Intelligence and Security, 144
Director of Operations, 15
Director of Operations Committee, 18
district committees, 52, 56, 259
district intelligence committees, 54
District Officers Kikuyu Guard, 249
district operations committee, 52
district operations room, 52
Dobie Force, 171
Dockeray, G. C., 203
doctrine, 5, 88, 105, 107
  see also minimum force
Donlea, Lieutenant-Colonel Basil J., 106
double amnesty, 27, 252
Draper, Gerald, 73, 75, 78
Dyer, Brigadier-General Reginald, 98

East Africa Armoured Car Squadron, 13, 208
East Africa Battle School, 155
East Africa Command
  attempt to disband the Kenya Regiment, 42
  and detention camps, 225
  directives, 132
  at the Emergency's outset, 176
  and the Home Guard, 246
  interest in administration policy, 255

and political oversight, 125
reinforcement of KAR, 198
representation on the Emergency Joint Staff, 54
and special forces, 154
staff officers, 1, 120
status, 51, 59
and surrender schemes, 140, 144
East Africa Training Centre, 115, 163, 203, 233
East African Service Corps, 217
East Lancashire Regiment, 101
Easter Rising, 99
economic reform, 49, 224
Eden, Anthony, 43
Edye, Mr, 44
Egypt, 12, 13
Elkins, Caroline, 35, 224, 251
Ellis, John, 88
Embu Guard *see* Home Guard
Emergency Joint Staff, 54, 245
Emergency regulations
  creation of legal zones, 129, 211
  draconian nature, 87
  Erskine's view, 1
  powers granted to administration, 34
  and surrender schemes, 141
Emergency tax, 15, 220
Erskine, General Sir George
  assumption of command, 19, 46, 177
  attitude towards the Council of Ministers, 54
  awareness of abuses, 162, 165, 170, 192, 197, 251–3
  career, 11
  concept of operations after Anvil, 26
  departure from Kenya, 39
  early campaign directives, 39
  influence of Hinde on his strategy, 17
  lecture to Army Staff Course, 1
  and military justice, 182, 195, 202–3, 204–6, 219, 228
  orders on discipline, 111, 114, 117, 118, 195, 211–13
    see also Griffiths; Major Gerald S.
  protection of Home Guard from prosecution, 251–3
  relations with settlers, 39, 40
  replacement of officers over Chuka massacre, 198
  request for reinforcements, 21, 46
  support for special forces, 153, 154
  support for surrender schemes, 133, 136, 138, 140, 143
  understanding of the Mau Mau, 22, 33

Erskine, General Sir George (cont.)
  use of coercive measures, 219–25, 227
European Convention on Human Rights,
  60, 70, 80–1
European Elected Members' Organization,
  212
Evans, Lieutenant-Colonel L. W. B., 117,
  182, 187, 191, 197, 198, 204
Evans, Peter, 199, 201, 203
evictions, 14, 18, 19, 22, 172–5
excessive force, 86
exemplary force, 2, 76, 193
  at the start of the Emergency, 161
  in theory, 95
  in the wider British Empire, 102
  see also India

Farm Guards, 26, 250, 257
Farr, Captain John, 219
Fawcett, Millicent, 96
Fey, Major Venn, 153
Field Intelligence Assistants (FIAs), 41, 55,
  158, 232, 239, 242
fines, 102, 131, 220
First World War, 72, 87, 93
Folliott, Captain R. J., 156
food denial, 22, 28, 38, 255–7
Forced Labour Convention,
  60, 77
Foreign Office, 65, 66, 67–9, 80
Foreign Secretary, 68
forest tracks, 21
forest warfare school, 27
Forestry Department, 169
Franklin, Captain S. E., 212
Fraser, Hugh, 45, 115, 174
Freedom of Information Act, 5, 213
French, David, 4, 109

Gardner, Forest Officer, 182
Gatamuki, General, 23, 139
Gathuini, 23, 142
Gay, Major A. W., 110
General Service Unit, 259, 262
Geneva Conventions, 60, 73, 75,
  77, 227
Geneva Conventions, Additional Protocols,
  79
Geneva Conventions, Common Article 3,
  61, 65, 77–8
Geneva Conventions Bill, 69
genocide, 108, 128
Genocide Convention, 67
Gichuchi son of Kibira, 181
Gill, Leonard, 167, 216, 226

Glanville, Lieutenant-Colonel R. C., 106,
  118, 181, 247
Gloucestershire Regiment, 154, 157
Gold Coast, 103
Goodbody, General Sir Richard, 119
Governor see Baring, Sir Evelyn
Governor's Emergency Committee, 18, 51,
  53, 165
Grahame, Captain I., 214, 226
Green, Second Lieutenant, 179
Griffiths, Major Gerald S., 47, 115–18,
  125–6, 180–5, 189–91, 203–6
Guantanamo Bay, 4
Guelff, Richard, 79
Guy, Captain R. K., 212
Gwynn, Charles, 91, 102, 106

Hague Convention, 89
Haldane, General Sir Aylmer, 102
Hale, Leslie, 49
Hall, Second Lieutenant G. B., 152
Hampshire Regiment, 101
Hanslope papers, 166, 167, 209, 217
Hanslope Park, 3
Harding, Field Marshal Sir John, 17, 22,
  53, 114, 171, 176
Harington, Major J. T., 232
Hart, Peter, 101
Harun, Lance-Corporal, 184
Hateley, Company Sergeant Major, 113,
  198
Head, Antony, 39, 44, 46
headmen, 16
Heather, Randall, 39
Henderson, Ian, 23, 135–6, 138, 157–8,
  235, 238–9
Heyman, Major-General G. D., 47, 52,
  143, 226, 238, 241
Hilborne-Clarke, Captain H. D., 213
Hinde, Major-General William
  arrival in Kenya, 17
  awareness of abuses, 166, 197
  and command arrangements, 18,
    51, 176
  as Deputy Director of Operations, 52
  and evictions, 174
  and food denial, 257
  orders on prisoner handling, 147
  orders on Prohibited Areas, 130
  position after Erskine's arrival, 20, 52
  promotion, 17
  relationship with settlers, 38, 212
  and villagisation, 223
Hobhouse, Emily, 96
Hobson, John, 126

Home Guard
  abuses, 166, 168, 216, 218–19, 225,
    250–3
  attacked by Mau Mau, 17, 216
  desertions, 57, 141
  disbandment, 27
  disruption of surrenders, 137
  expansion, 23, 24, 251
  origins, 16, 246
  patrols, 18, 57, 247, 258
  relationship with the army, 113,
    247–53, 259
  role, 16, 25, 247, 251
  security breaches, 57
  training, 249–50
  see also Chuka massacre; double amnesty
    surrender scheme; Farm Guards,
    surrenders, tribal police; Watch
    and Ward
Home Office, 67, 68
hooded men, 162, 163
Howard, Second Lieutenant J. M., 113,
    182–3, 184–8, 191, 199, 204
Huggan, Major J. T., 150
Hunter Committee, 98
Huntington, Samuel, 31
Hurst, Katherine, 203
Hussein, Warrant Officer Platoon
    Commander, 186, 188, 191, 197,
    199, 204
Huth, Major P. H., 260

Idris, Lance-Corporal, 188
Imperial Defence College, 75
Imperial Policing and Duties in Aid of the Civil
    Power, 85, 87
indecent assault, 124, 210
India, 12, 56, 97–9, 102
Indian High Commissioner, 140
Indian Mutiny, 97
Indian Ocean, 94
informers, 26, 162, 199, 236–40
  see also intelligence
Innes-Walker, Second Lieutenant D.,
    115, 182–7, 188, 190, 197–8,
    204
intelligence
  on aerial bombing, 236
  assessments of the Mau Mau, 26, 136,
    145, 161, 234, 235–6
  collection and analysis, 231–40
  on collective punishment, 253
  committees, 54–6, 235
  comparing offensive and defensive
    operations, 38

deficiencies, 15, 29, 163
  on evictions, 174
  exploitation, 240–3
  general assessments, 11, 19
  on legal zones, 130
  Military Intelligence Officers (MIO), 232
  Operational Intelligence Organisation, 55
  on post-Anvil operations, 26
  reforms, 18, 55
  on screening, 165
  on special forces, 154
  on surrender schemes, 140, 142, 146
  on villagisation, 26
  see also informers; interrogation;
    pseudo-gangs; screening; Special
    Branch
Intelligence Adviser, 54, 55
Internal Security Working Committee, 171
International Committee of the Red Cross
    (ICRC), 66, 77
International Criminal Tribunal for the
    Former Yugoslavia, 78
international law, 60
  army understanding of, 60, 62–6, 73–5,
    80, 81
  British government attitude towards,
    64–5, 66–9
  see also non-international armed conflicts
International Military Tribunal at
    Nuremberg, 61, 74
interrogation, 148, 227
  of Brigadier Thurura, 157
  of General China, 23, 136, 235–6
  instructions, 113, 147, 148
  as an intelligence source, 234–6
  by Major Griffiths, 183
  by Second Lieutenant Innes-Walker, 185
  by Sergeant Allen, 200
  see also beatings; screening prisoners
intimidation, 215, 227
investigations of allegations, 111, 195–6
  see also Chief Secretary's Complaints
    Co-ordinating Committee, McLean
    Court of Inquiry; rape; Special
    Investigations Branch
  concerning 5 KAR, 196–9
  concerning Captain Hilborne-Clarke,
    213
  concerning Sergeant Allen, 199–203
Iraq, 4, 102
Ireland, 12, 87
Irish Republican Army, 101
Irish War of Independence, 87, 93, 99–102
Irvine, Dr Clive, 196
Itote, Waruhiu see China, General

Janowitz, Morris, 32
Jerome, Reverend C. S., 150
Jochnick, C. A., 76
Joint Army–Police Operational Intelligence
    Teams, 55, 165
joint operations committees, 18, 36
Journal of the Royal United Services Institute,
    63, 72, 74
Joy, Captain, 115, 116, 181
Judge Advocate General, 177

Kahembi, Chege, 200–2
Kaleba, General, 137, 138,
    139, 262
Kanambiu son of M'Rugamba, 187
Kanji, Field Marshal, 146
Kanumbi, 213
Karawa, Chief, 196
Karigine, 185, 186
Kavenji son of Njoka, 183, 184
Keates, Richard, 206
Kenya African Union, 11, 13
Kenya garrison, 51
Kenya government, 1, 13
Kenya Intelligence Committee (KIC), 54,
    55, 133
Kenya Police
    abuses, 164
    acceptance of bribes, 58
    combined operations with the army, 13,
        23, 55, 174, 256, 258–62 *see also*
        screening
    Criminal Records Office, 122
    expansion, 20
    presence in the Reserves, 15
    see also law and order, responsibility
        for; Special Branch
Kenya Police Reserve (KPR), 37, 164, 170,
    174, 206, 233
Kenya Police Reserve Air Wing,
    129, 134
Kenya Regiment
    acquittals, 124, 217
    assaults committed by, 119, 179, 211,
        219, 233
    beatings, 206
    composition, 38, 40, 41
    deployment, 13
    and the Home Guard, 247, 249
    indecent assault by, 124
    interrogations, 215, 233
    looting, 179
    need for rest, 21, 114
    operations, 163, 164, 261
    pseudo-gangs run by, 29, 152, 243

    relations with British battalions, 41–2
    reluctance to shoot women, 132
    secondment to Prisons Department,
        225
    security breaches, 58
    shootings by, 124, 169, 218
    status within the chain of command, 13,
        40
    torture, 226
    views about the Emergency, 41, 160,
        212, 214, 217
    see also Allen, Sergeant Jeremy
Kenyan Attorney-General
    and captured Mau Mau, 148, 242
    on the Colony Emergency Committee,
        51
    disagreement with Lathbury, 1
    and Major Griffiths, 117, 182, 205
    and military law, 206, 209, 219
    and Sergeant Allen, 201
    and special forces, 243–5
    and surrenders, 147, 242
    view of War Council, 54
Kenyatta, Jomo, 11, 15, 36, 199
Keohoe, Sapper, 124
Kiambu district emergency committee
    (DEC), 180
Kibiwot, Corporal, 199
Kikuyu Central Association, 11
Kikuyu Guard Combat Units, 24, 249, 251
killing competitions, 119, 121, 122, 190–1,
    192
Killingray, David, 93
Killis son of Kiyundu, Corporal, 186, 187
Kimani, 200
Kimathi, Dedan
    capture, 29, 158
    command of Mau Mau forces, 234
    rewards for killing him, 121
    special forces search for, 27, 156, 157
    split from Mathenge, 28, 142
    surrender negotiations, 27, 134–5, 142,
        143
Kimathi, Wambararia, 157
King's African Rifles (KAR)
    operations before the Emergency,
        103–5
    overstretch, 177
King's Own Yorkshire Light Infantry, 38
King's Regulations, 62, 73, 109
King's Royal Rifle Corps, 41
Kipsigi, Warrant Officer Platoon
    Commander (WOPC), 185
Kiptano son of Kaptinge, Private, 124
Kiptarus, Private, 181

Kirkwood, Lieutenant-Colonel J. H. M.,
    100
Kitchener, Lord, 96
Kithumbi, 187
Kitson, Frank, 41, 55, 152–3, 233, 239,
    251
Koinage wa Mbiyu, 11
Korea, 16, 63, 79
Kriegsraison, 76, 92

Labour Party, 49
Lakin, District Officer, 182
Lakurian, Lance-Corporal, 199
Lancashire Fusiliers
    absence from McLean Inquiry, 208
    arrival in Kenya, 13, 45
    departure from Kenya, 22
    operations, 14, 163, 164, 172–3, 220
Landregan, Reverend J. F., 121
Lari massacre, 18, 166
Lathbury, Lieutenant-General
        Sir Gerald, 1
    background and arrival in Kenya, 28
    launches offensives, 29
    support for food denial, 256
    support for nipping trouble in the bud,
        93
    support for special forces, 155
    view of villagisation, 223
Lauterpacht, Professor Hersch, 62
law and order, responsibility for, 27,
    28, 36
laws of war, 61, 73, 77
Leakey, L. S. B., 222
Leath, Mr, 158
legal zones, 108, 129–33
Lennox-Boyd, Alan, 47, 49
Liddle, Second Lieutenant A. L. K., 130
Llewellyn, Company Sergeant Major W. P.,
    115, 116, 181, 182, 190
Lloyd, Selwyn, 43
Lloyd George, David, 100
Lonsdale, John, 33, 39
looting, 58, 95, 101, 110, 179, 250
Lord Chancellor's Department, 68
loyalism, 17, 20, 128, 136, 222
Lyttelton, Oliver, 23, 33, 44–7, 53, 263

M'Mathai, 186
Mackenyanga, 262
Mackinnon Road detention camp, 225
Macmillan, Harold, 43
Macready, General Sir Nevil, 100
Mad Mullah of Somaliland, 104
Makahe, Private, 188

Malayan Emergency
    and British overstretch, 16
    and Geneva negotiations, 67
    harsh security measures, 37
    influence on policy in Kenya, 52, 133,
        147, 223
    military experience in, 56, 149
    mutilation, 114
man on the spot, 43, 46, 47
Manchester Regiment, 101
manifest illegality, 71, 184
manslaughter, 124
Manual of Military Law, 62, 70, 73, 75, 79,
    87, 88
Manyani detention camp, 225,
    232, 245
Manyori, Mutu, 213
Marshall, Lieutenant J. R., 150
Marshall, S. L. A., 72
martial law, 1, 35, 101
Masai, 105
Matenjagua, General, 231
Mathenge, Stanley, 27, 28, 142, 143,
    145, 156
Mathu, Mr, 45
Matless, Trevor, 149
Mau Mau
    attacks on informers, 238
    early violence, 12
    extent of popular support, 13, 25, 137, 175
    female membership, 132
    movement into the forests, 16, 25, 26
    movement into the Reserves, 23
    origins of rebellion, 8–11
    passive wing, 26, 145, 155, 253
    split in leadership, 28, 139, 142
    spread of the movement, 19
    violence, 14, 16, 25–6, 27, 172–3, 175
    see also casualty statistics; intelligence;
        prisoners
Mau Mau Interrogation Centre, 55, 245
McInnes, Colin, 76
McKinnon Road detention camp, 225
McLean, Lieutenant-General Sir Kenneth,
    119, 121
McLean Court of Inquiry, 47, 118–23,
    190, 206–8, 211–13
McLeod, Mr, 232
Meiklejohn family, 14, 172
Meinertzhagen, Richard, 92, 104
Member for Agriculture, 52
Member for Finance, 52
Merril, Sergeant, 214
Meru Guard *see* Home Guard
MI5, 54, 67

Middle East Land Forces (MELF), 19, 51, 171, 177
Military Intelligence Officers (MIOs), 41, 55, 152, 235, 239
military law, 73, 110, 166, 206
military necessity, 75–7, 89, 114
military obedience, 65, 71–3, 75, 81, 109, 184
military operations
  Albatross, 156
  Anvil, 24–5, 165
  Baboon, 156
  Beatrice, 29
  Blitz, 16, 129
  Blue Doctor, 157
  Broom, 25
  Buttercup, 20
  Carnation I, 20
  Carnation II, 21, 261
  Chui, 142, 143
  Columbus, 23
  Cowboy, 220
  Dante, 29
  Dodo, 156
  First Flute, 27, 29
  Gimlet, 28, 143
  Gorilla, 156
  Grouse, 20
  Hammer, 27, 262
  Hoover, 233
  Hungerstrike, 28, 57
  Jock Scott, 13
  Kneel, 253
  Mamba, 156
  Mission, 247
  Nutcracker, 262
  Overdraft, 24, 139
  Plover, 20, 261
  Primrose, 22
  Pugilist, 26, 248
  Rat Catcher, 21
  Red Dog, 155
  Royal Flush, 247
  Scatter, 247
  Schemozzle I, 262
  Scythe, 261
  Silver Doctor, 158, 261
  Spud, 255
  Thunder, 261
  Viking, 156
  Wedgewood, 136, 137, 139, 140
  Wimbledon, 248
  Yellow Hackle, 232
military police, 58, 113
Miller, Stephen, 96

minimum force, 2–3, 5, 76, 83
  balanced with exemplary force, 91, 105
  conceptual weaknesses, 87
  origins and nature of the concept, 84–7
Minister for African Affairs, 142, 145, 252
Minister for Legal Affairs see Kenyan Attorney-General
Minister of Defence, 43
Ministry for Internal Security and Defence, 54
Ministry of African Affairs, 54, 144
Mobile Column A, 20, 261
  see also East Africa Armoured Car Squadron
Mockaitis, Thomas, 84, 87, 88, 97
Monckton, Walter, 43
Moplah rebellion, 102
morale, 180, 196, 210–11, 217
Moranga son of Wombongu, 187
Morcombe, Colonel P. A., 247
Moreman, Timothy, 87
Morning Post, 98
Mount Kenya Committee of Elders, 137
Moyse-Bartlett, Hubert, 103
Muchiri, 187
Muir, Second Lieutenant I. K., 215
Mununga Ridge, 216
murders
  by Home Guard, 219, 251
  by Mau Mau, 12, 16, 50, 172, 173, 238, 253
  by soldiers, 116, 124–5, 166, 199, 208, 226
  by vigilantes, 171
  see also Chuka massacre; shot attempting to escape
Murphy, Philip, 39
Murray, Sergeant, 124
Mutahi son of Gatutha, 181
mutilation, 114–15, 122, 191, 211
mutiny, 195
Mwangi son of Mbari, 200, 201–3

Nandi uprising, 104
National Archives, 106
National Service, 62, 109, 110, 120
NATO, 94
Ndegwa son of Kagiri, 181
Ndirango, Aram, 236
Ndrango, 213
Nepean, Major P. V., 150
Newsinger, John, 5, 125
Nicholson, General Sir Cameron, 177

Nigeria, 104
Nightingale, George, 239
Nightwatchmen, Clerks and Shopworkers'
    Union, 219
nipping trouble in the bud, 88, 92, 93
Njeru, 187
Njeru, Elijah Gideon, 206
Njeru son of Ndwega, 183, 184
Njiri, Chief, 216
Nkira, 187
non-international armed conflicts, 78
    see also Geneva Conventions, Common
    Article 3
Norfolk Regiment, 102
Normand, R., 76
Northern Area, 51
Northern Brigade, 41, 51, 166
Notes on Imperial Policing, 87, 93
Nott, Lieutenant-Colonel D. H., 110
Nuremberg Principle, 62–4, 65, 70, 72,
    75, 81
Nyeri Emergency Committee, 58
Nyeri Native Civil Hospital, 150

O'Rorke, Commissioner of Police M. S.,
    238
Ogot, Bethwell, 104
one-mile strip, 20, 130, 131, 139,
    176, 221
operations committee, 52, 54
Orr, Brigadier J. R. H., 118, 132
Osiel, Mark, 71
Ottoman Empire, 92

Packard, Major-General C. D., 177
Palestine, 37, 48, 66–7, 103, 106
Palestine Police, 103
Parliament, 33
    debates about Kenya, 47, 49
    delegation to Kenya, 23
    interest in colonial policy, 48
    scrutiny of military operations, 48,
    49–50, 117, 177
Parry, W. J., 201
Parsons, Timothy, 109
passive wing see Mau Mau, passive wing
Pearson, Sergeant, 119, 211
Personal Staff Officer see Rimbault,
    Colonel G.
Petro, Chief, 183, 184, 186,
    189, 196
phoney war, 14, 173, 175
Pioneer Corps, 225
planted evidence, 242
population control, 21

Potter, H. S., 52
press coverage of operations, 50
Prior, Dennis, 196
prisoners
    military conduct towards, 149–52, 215,
    226–7
    prisoner handling, 113, 147–52, 226,
    242, 244–5
    and Sergeant Allen, 199
    use on operations, 1, 240–1
    see also surrenders
prisoners of war, 79
Prisons Department, 225
property destruction, 91, 93, 96, 102–5,
    130, 131
Provincial Administration
    influence on military operations, 34, 35,
    131, 250
    military interference in policy, 253–7
    role in the Emergency, 34–5
    see also law and order, responsibility for
Provincial Emergency Committees
    (PECs), 52
provincial intelligence committees, 54
pseudo-gangs, 29–30, 147, 152–8, 227,
    229, 243–5
psychological warfare, 134, 146
Public Works Department, 181
punitive columns, 102, 104
punitive force, 91–3, 98, 194

Quayle, Sergeant W., 179

racism, 190
Raghavan, Srinath, 86, 87
rape, 124, 172, 186, 191, 208–10, 225
Rawcliffe, D. H., 224
Rawkins, Major N. F., 112, 197, 213
Raynor, W. B. G., 196
reinforcements, 17, 21, 22
reprisals, 85–6, 91, 100–1, 103, 166, 220
Restoration of Order in Ireland Act, 101
Richardson, Sapper, 124
Rifle Brigade, 41, 124, 149
Rift Valley Province, 14, 36, 39, 172, 173
Rimbault, Colonel G., 15, 120, 121,
    176, 209
riots, 84, 86, 87, 88, 98
robbery, 186, 190, 226
Roberts, Adam, 79
Robertson, General Sir Brian, 171, 176
Robertson, Major J. C., 198
Robertson, Sergeant, 214
Rose, E., 196
Rose, Lieutenant-Colonel David, 106

Roy, Kaushik, 195
Royal Air Force, 20–1, 28, 124, 129,
    144, 261
Royal Air Force Regiment, 225
Royal East Kent Regiment (The Buffs)
    arrival in Kenya, 17
    deployment, 18
    and the Home Guard, 249
    intelligence collection, 231
    and legal zones, 132
    operations, 164, 240, 259, 261
    and prisoners, 149, 151, 235
    shootings, 217
Royal Electrical and Mechanical Engineers,
    181, 210
Royal Inniskilling Fusiliers
    arrival in Kenya, 22
    and committees, 259
    and legal zones, 130, 131
    operations, 23, 233, 258
    and political oversight, 50
    and prisoners, 151, 226
Royal Irish Constabulary, 99
Royal Irish Fusiliers, 124
Royal Military Academy Sandhurst, 62, 73,
    88, 111
Royal Northumberland Fusiliers
    arrival in Kenya, 22
    aversion to shooting, 151
    departure from Kenya, 28
    intelligence collection, 231, 262
    manslaughter, 124
    operations, 259
    robberies, 225
Royal United Services Institute (RUSI), 63
Ruben, Sergeant Jack, 206
Ruck family, 16, 37
Rui, General, 241
Russell, Captain H. C., 215

scorched earth, 95, 96
screening
    by army in detention camps, 232
    nature of, 15, 231
    operations, 20, 26, 162–5, 233
    statistics, 19, 163, 164, 231
    see also military operation, Anvil
Second World War, 44, 57, 81, 189,
    257, 261
Security Liaison Officer, 54
Segat, Private Ali, 125, 183, 184, 191
settlers
    agitation for tough action, 12, 16, 29, 36,
        44, 224
    attempts to disrupt surrenders, 141

evictions of Kikuyu squatters see evictions
influence on military operations, 34,
    36–40, 47, 212, 260, 263
protection from Mau Mau attack, 14, 16,
    26, 175
unofficial members on committees, 18
see also food denial; vigilantes
shootings, 124, 151
shot attempting to escape, 101, 125,
    165–70, 184, 200, 216–19
Shoul, Simeon, 98
Sillitoe, Sir Percy, 54, 246
Simpson, Brian, 77, 80, 87
Sinclair-Scott, Major R., 179, 212
Sinn Fein, 100
Sitrep Committee, 51
Skinner, Sergeant G., 179
sky shouting aircraft, 144, 145
Slim, Field-Marshal Sir William, 74
Small, A. C., 198
Small, Major G. W., 132
small-scale patrols, 17, 22, 27, 258–61
small wars, 90
Soloman, Justice, 71
South Nyeri district intelligence committee,
    238
Southern Province, 36
Special Branch, 27
    advice to halt evictions, 175
    Assistant Commissioner for, 54
    involvement in surrender talks, 133,
        135–7, 141, 142
    presence on intelligence committees, 54
    relations with army, 19, 55, 232, 234,
        235, 241, 242
    role, 15
    use of General China, 23
    see also informers; interrogations
special forces, 29,
    cooperation with regular forces, 158
    operations, 155
    origins in Kenya, 152–3
    significance in the campaign, 153, 154,
        156, 158
    Special Branch units, 154, 158
    special force teams (SFTs),
        155, 156
    special methods teams, 154
    tracker combat teams (TCTs), 27,
        153–4
    Trojan teams, 154
    see also pseudo-gangs
Special Investigations Branch (SIB)
    and 5 KAR, 113, 115, 118, 197, 204
    and 7 KAR, 117, 213

reinforcement, 198
and Sergeant Allen, 201
special methods teams, 29
special night squad, 103
squatters, 8, 253
Squires, Major S. J., 149
Stalag Luft III, 64
Steel, Lord, 186
Suez, 12
summary execution, 95, 102, 105
summary of evidence, 117, 201, 203, 205, 213
summary punishments, 110
Sunday Pictorial, 123
Supreme Headquarters; Allied Expeditionary Force, 12
surrender propaganda, 134–5, 141, 144, 145, 146
Surrender Propaganda Committee, 144
surrenders
China surrender talks, 23, 46, 135–40
double amnesty surrender scheme, 27, 28, 47, 140–5
'Green Branch' surrender scheme, 22, 23, 133–5, 136, 143, 144, 146
statistics, 22–3, 135, 141, 143–4, 145, 146
see also prisoners
Swahili, 154, 169, 185

Tanganyika, General, 138, 139, 155
Taylor, Brigadier G., 153, 262
Taylor, Private, 119, 211
Thigiru, 216
Thika detention camp, 225
Thompson, Robert, 2
Thornton, Rod, 84
Thurlow, Brigadier The Lord, 47
Thurura, Brigadier, 157
Tibet, 102
Topham, Major R. N., 215
torture
by Home Guard, 251
and screening, 162, 165
by soldiers, 117, 213, 215, 226
Townshend, Charles, 84
Township Force, 233
Treasury Department, 37, 54
tribal police, 27, 155, 185, 196, 262
Trojan teams *see* special forces
Tudor, Major-General Hugh, 100
Tweedie, Brigadier J. W., 122, 132, 133

Uganda, 104, 105, 120
Unett, Captain Richard, 38
Union of Soviet Socialist Republics, 44, 69
United Kenya Protection Association, 171
Universal Declaration of Human Rights, 60, 67, 77
unofficial members *see* settlers, unofficial members on committees

Vasey, E. A., 52
Vice-Chief of the Imperial General Staff (VCIGS), 116
vigilantes, 170–2
villagisation, 25–6, 144, 146, 156, 222–5, 253–4

Wachanga, Kahinga, 142, 143
Waichuhi, General, 240
Wallace, Charles, 110
War Council
creation, 24, 53, 126
directives, 54
and Emergency Joint Staff, 54
and food denial, 256, 257
and the Home Guard, 249, 251
and prisoners, 242
relationship to Council of Ministers, 54
and special forces, 154, 244, 245
and surrender schemes, 27, 140, 142, 143–4, 145, 147
and villagisation, 253, 254
war crimes, 115
Warui, Njiraini, 240
Watch and Ward, 27
Watch Committee, 123
Waziristan, 98, 106
Welwood, Mr, 260
Whitehall, 16
Whyatt, Sergeant, 124
Wigram, Captain G. F., 209
Wilkins, Major, 248
Wilkinson, R. A., 112
Wilkinson, R. S., 201
Willcocks, Major P. T., 233
Windeatt, Lieutenant-Colonel J. K., 213
Woodley, Bill, 152
Wormwood Scrubs, 126

Yates, Driver, 124